PROTECTION OF PROPERTY RIGHTS WITHIN THE EUROPEAN CONVENTION ON HUMAN RIGHTS

'Mal canın yongasıdır'

Turkish Proverb

(Property is a chip detached from the body)

This book is dedicated to Mr Fahrettin AKIN, my teacher at primary school, whose passion for helping his students and whose respect for his job have always been a source of inspiration for me for all of my life.

Protection of Property Rights within the European Convention on Human Rights

ALI RIZA ÇOBAN
University of Kırıkkale, Turkey

ASHGATE

Published by
Ashgate Publishing Limited
Gower House
Croft Road
Aldershot
Hants GU11 3HR
England

Ashgate Publishing Company
Suite 420
101 Cherry Street
Burlington, VT 05401-4405
USA

Ashgate website: http://www.ashgate.com

British Library Cataloguing in Publication Data
Çoban, Ali Rıza
Protection of property rights within the European
Convention on Human Rights
1. European Convention on Human Rights 2. Right of property – Europe
I. Title
340.9'4'094

Library of Congress Cataloging-in-Publication Data
Çoban, Ali Rıza, 1971-
Protection of property rights within the European convention on human rights / Ali Rıza Çoban.
p. cm.
Includes bibliographical references and index.
ISBN 0-7546-2387-4
1.Right of property--Europe. 2. Human rights--Europe. I. Title.

KJC1261.C63 2003
346.404--dc22

2003058364

ISBN 0 7546 2387 4

Printed and bound by Athenaeum Press, Ltd.,
Gateshead, Tyne & Wear.

Contents

Preface

This book examines the property rights guarantee of the European Convention on Human Rights in Article 1 of Protocol No 1 (P1-1). A number of social, political, and legal developments in Europe, which took place within the last two decades, made P1-1 a significant international human rights instrument for the member states to the Convention. P1-1 makes social and economic policies of the governments in approximately 43 European countries, which affects pecuniary rights of individuals, subject to international supervision of the European Court of Human Rights. Determination of clear boundaries of the guarantee provided by P1-1 is important both for the member states and for the Court. A theoretical framework is necessary in order to clarify how far P1-1 does allow public authorities to interfere with property rights. This book aims to provide such a theoretical framework.

The ideas in this book were developed during my PhD study at the University of Leeds. This book is a slightly modified and updated version of my PhD thesis submitted in 2002. I owe many thanks to my supervisors, Professor Clive Walker, Head of the Department of Law, University of Leeds, and Professor John Bell, Director of the Centre for European Legal Studies, University of Cambridge, for their encouragement, constructive criticism, and invaluable comments and suggestions. They were both severe critics of my work, and they helped me to organise my ideas and to develop a comprehensive theoretical framework. Both Professors have read all drafts, always with a careful interest. They also helped me to make the text readable in English.

I am also grateful to Professor Colin Warbrick of Durham University and Professor Tom Allen for their time, interest, and invaluable comments as examiners of this work as a thesis. Their suggestions made this work more complete. I should also mention Yaman Akdeniz, Kerem Altiparmak, Basem al-Nimer, and Ali Delice, my colleagues and friends, among many others, at Leeds, to whom I owe particular thanks for their criticism, support and friendship. My sponsor, the Turkish Ministry of National Education, deserves special thanks – without their financial support, this work would not be possible. I would also like to thank the editorial team of Ashgate for their understanding, patience and professionalism during the publication process. Last, but not least, I owe special thanks to my wife, Serap, and my daughter, Sena, and my family for their patience and forbearance. I have neglected them during the preparation of this work.

Chapter 1

Introduction

Is the acquisition and possession of property a human right? This is a question which should be contemplated within a moral and legal context. That is to say, whether the right to property is a human right is a moral question to which an answer must be sought within moral theory. Nevertheless, it has been considered as a political question and it has been at the centre of the political discourse in the last two centuries. The focus of the discussion was the role attributed to the right to property within the political structure of society. For some (liberals) it was a keystone right,[1] the guardian of every other right,[2] but for others (communitarians) it was the main enemy of equality and freedom.[3]

Historical experience has vindicated this political approach to some extent. Quite often, the right to property has been used as a political tool. For example, the British Empire was not enthusiastic about providing legal guarantees for property rights in the colonies during the colonial period, but it was quite eager about the inclusion of property right guarantees in the independence constitutions, when former colonies gained their independence, in order to protect the property of white minorities in those countries.[4] The motive for such eagerness was political rather than moral or philosophical. Similarly, it was the right to property on which capitalists depended when exploiting other people's labour. It was sometimes used to justify unjust allocations of property. The political divergence between liberals and communitarians about the right to property was also very deep.

Therefore, it was very difficult to reach a consensus, in a politically divided world, about whether property is a human right during the preparation of human rights documents. So, it is not surprising that the United Nations Covenants did not include a right to property. But the European Convention on Human Rights (ECHR) included a property guarantee in Article 1 of Protocol No.1 (P1-1). Although the application of P1-1 was very limited until the 1980s, a number of political and legal developments during the 1980s and 1990s made P1-1 an

---

[1] Rose, C., "Property as the Keystone Right?" (1996) 71 *Notre Dame Law Review* 329.

[2] Ely, J., *The Guardian of Every Other Right: Constitutional History of Property Rights* (OUP: Oxford, 1992).

[3] Proudhon, J., *What is Property?* (Howard Fertig: New York, 1966).

[4] For a detailed examination of the drafting of the right to property in Commonwealth constitutions see Allen, T., *The Right to Property in Commonwealth Constitutions* (CUP, Cambridge, 2000).

important international human rights instrument for the European countries which are party to the Convention (ECHR).

Firstly, a number of developments have affected the nature of private ownership. During the last two decades, the world has witnessed a movement from a socialist and (or) social (welfare) state towards a market-oriented state. A 'new public management' approach, which was developed in the USA and UK at the beginning of the 1980s and followed by other Western and Eastern (after the collapse of socialism) European countries, led to the privatisation of public services and big industries. This process has affected private ownership in two ways. On the one hand, the scope of private property enlarged enormously within the whole of Europe. On the other hand, private property rights came into conflict with other fundamental rights and they were subjected to more regulations. Moreover, increasing concern about environmental protection led to a new realm of conflict between property rights and environmental regulation. Furthermore, new technological innovations created new interests that could be defined as property such as separate body parts, human genetic materials, information, software, cyber-space, and radio spectrum, etc. These new forms of property have posed new challenges for the definition of property. All these developments require a close look at property rights.

Secondly, the legal structure of the Convention protection system has been changed significantly by the entry into force of the 11th Protocol in 1998. Individual application and the jurisdiction of the Court became compulsory for every member state. Moreover, many Eastern European countries, which have not completed their transition from socialist and centrally planned economy to free market economy, became party to the Convention. When all these developments are taken into account, examination of P1-1 has a great importance, because both the magnitude and variety of cases that come before the Court have greatly increased. In order to deal with such demand the Court needs a consistent theoretical approach to the right to property. Although some monographs[5] have been published on the subject of P1-1, they rarely provide a coherent theoretical analysis of the case-law of the Convention organs.

Moreover, the world has been witnessing a globalisation process for at least two decades. One of the basic tenets of globalisation is the free movement of international capital in the global market. Nevertheless, security of property rights is a significant precondition for an international investor to make an investment in a foreign country. Therefore, international human rights law can function as a tool to guarantee alien property rights.

This book examines the protection of property rights within the European Convention on human rights. It aims to provide a theoretical analysis of P1-1. The main question to which an answer will be sought in this book is 'what is the importance of private property for a dignified life and to what extent can private property be interfered with by public authorities legitimately?' The book comprises

---

[5] Sermet, L., *The European Convention on Human Rights and Property Rights* (Council of Europe Publishing: Strasbourg, 1998) (revised edition); Rook, D., *Property Law and Human Rights* (Blackstone Press: London, 2001).

two parts, one of which looks at the theoretical aspect of property rights and the other an analysis of the application of P1-1. It examines, in the theoretical part, three interrelated questions: What is property? Is property a human right? and What are the limitations of property? This part provides a theoretical background to examine case-law of the Convention organs in the second part. The second part is allocated to the examination of the application of P1-1 by the Convention organs. Mainly, the historical background of P1-1, the theoretical and political strands which affected the formation of P1-1, the scope and nature of the guarantee provided by P1-1, the power of states, allowed by P1-1, to interfere with property rights and limits of it, and the relationship between P1-1 and other articles of the Convention are the subject of scrutiny in the second part. A brief outline of chapters can be summarised as follows.

The theoretical part of the book comprises three chapters. Chapter 2 examines the definition of constitutionally protected property. The definition of constitutional property is quite important because definition itself constitutes a limitation to the protected interests. But the definition of property is not as easy as it seems. Different legal systems define the inclusion of property quite differently. Moreover, some jurisdictions attribute different meanings to private law property and constitutionally protected property. Therefore, in Chapter 2, the private law meaning of property will be examined and then whether there is a difference between private law property and constitutional property will be scrutinised.

Three questions are significant in terms of the definition of property. What kind of rights or entitlements does property give to the right-holder (owner) over the objects of property? What kinds of rights does the owner have against other people through the right to property? and What kind of things can be the object of ownership? In terms of the first two questions, property is understood as relationships: a relation to the things (objects of property) and a relation to others through the things. In the third sense, property is understood as objects. Therefore, in order to grasp the true meaning of property these questions will be examined in some detail in Chapter 2. Property-as-relationship comprises the extent of entitlements afforded to the right-holder by a right to property, and the corresponding duty or duties to the right to property. The questions of whether property is a single right or a bundle of different rights and whether the limitations or duties arising from property should be included in the definition of property are also relevant. Property-as-objects comprises the things (material and ideational) that can be the objects of property. In this respect, the new subject matters of ownership such as human genetic materials, body parts, cyber-space, radio wave frequencies, will be discussed as well as the traditional movable and immovable corporeal things and incorporeal rights.

Constitutional property will be given an expansive meaning to comprise whole patrimonial interests and legitimate expectations arising from private and public law relationships.

Chapter 3 examines the question of whether property is a human right. If human rights are described as moral rights, the question can be reformulated as 'are there valid moral reasons justifying that the right to property should be recognised and protected?' In this book a pluralistic justificatory argument for property rights is suggested. Mainly four different moral arguments – utility and efficiency, labour theory of property, Hegelian personality theory, and political liberty and autonomy – are examined. The key concept in this pluralistic theory is personal autonomy. All four justificatory moral arguments revolve around the concepts of freedom and of autonomy. Therefore, Raz's autonomy-based freedom theory is accepted as the main justificatory base for property rights.

Two versions of utility argument – traditional and economic utility arguments – will be examined. It will be suggested that although utility argument favours existence of property, it attributes only instrumental value to the property rights and autonomy in general for maximisation of utility. Thus, it will be given a secondary role to the utility argument in justification of property. Three other elements of the pluralistic theory – labour, personality, and autonomy – produce sound arguments in favour of private property and attribute intrinsic value to private property for a valuable and dignified life. But these arguments provide only a *prima facie* justification for the existence and recognition of property rights. They do not justify absolute property rights and, therefore, they can be restricted for legitimate moral reasons.

Chapter 4 examines the limitation of property. How far and on what grounds can property be interfered with by government legitimately? Public authorities can interfere with property rights for different aims. According to the aims of public authorities, a triple taxonomy of interferences will be suggested. These are taxation, taking of property by power of eminent domain, and controlling the use of property by police power regulations. The aim of taxation is to finance public services (or to create an autonomy-enhancing society if it is expressed in Raz's terminology) and it can be justified on the equal sharing basis. But the main discussion regarding taxation is whether redistributive taxation can be justified. In this chapter, two mainstream theories of liberal thought about redistributive taxation, Rawls' 'difference principle' and Nozick's 'entitlement theory' will be examined as examples of many different views about the subject. But redistributive taxation will be justified on the grounds of Raz's autonomy principle.

Most of the discussion about constitutional property is spent on takings. The main discussion about takings is when a regulation constitutes takings and the amount of the compensation which must be paid as a recompense for property taken. This chapter examines the conditions of takings in a theoretical point of view. And finally, Chapter 4 examines theoretical aspects of police power regulations.

The second part of the book comprises four chapters. In order to evaluate how the right to property is regulated and protected under international human rights law, the ECHR has been chosen because it has the most developed human rights protection system. And it also has almost fifty years of application and highly developed case-law, so it is more appropriate than any other human rights convention to see how far property rights are protected by international human rights protection mechanisms.

Chapter 5 examines the historical background and drafting process of the property rights guarantee in P1-1 in order to reveal what philosophical and political concerns urged the inclusion of such a guarantee in the European Convention on Human Rights. The published *Travaux Préparatoires* of the ECHR are the main source of information for this chapter. Examination of preparatory works will shed light on the interpretation of this guarantee by the Convention organs.

Chapter 6 looks at the nature of guarantee provided by P1-1. It focuses on two main questions. Firstly, it examines the extent of the concept of 'possessions'. It evaluates the case-law in this regard under the light of the theoretical framework drawn in Chapter 2. Secondly, it examines the nature of responsibility that is imposed by P1-1 on the contracting states. Do contracting states have positive obligations to protect property or do they have only negative obligation not to violate? And it also examines whether the states are responsible for only public authorities' actions or inactions, or can they be held responsible for the actions of private individuals as well?

Chapter 7 concerns the limitations of the right to property which is allowed by P1-1. How far can contracting states interfere with property rights legitimately? The Convention organs have defined three types of interference according to the impact of interference with property. Two of them (deprivation of property and control on use) have been deduced from the letter of P1-1 and the third (interference with substance of property) is merely a judicial construct. However, this classification has a number of difficulties in application. Therefore, Chapter 7 suggests another triple taxonomy which is linked to that defined in Chapter 4 (taxation, takings, and police power regulations). Afterwards it examines the conditions of the legitimate interference with property. Firstly, interference must be legal. It should depend on clear, foreseeable, and accessible legal rules. Secondly, it should have a legitimate aim. And the means used must be appropriate and necessary to pursue the aims. Interference should also strike a fair balance between the interest of the individuals and public interest. And lastly, if the interference constitutes a taking, the loss of the private owner should be compensated. The jurisprudence of the Convention organs will be evaluated in this regard under the light of theoretical approaches developed in Chapter 4.

Chapter 8 looks at the relations between P1-1 and other articles of the Convention. Five different articles (Articles 8, 14, 41, 6, and15) of the Convention and their relations with property rights are scrutinised in this chapter. Four of them provide extra substantive (Articles 8, 14, and 41) and procedural (Article 6) guarantees for property rights or some kind of property rights in addition to P1-1. But Article 15 provides extra limitation powers to the contracting states to derogate from their obligations under P1-1. The interaction between these articles and P1-1 is important in understanding the real picture of property guarantees provided by the Convention.

This book examines the property right guarantee provided by P1-1 under the light of a theoretical framework. And it provides some theoretical tools for the Court to apply in review of the cases before it. It examines property rights within a moral and legal context rather than a political context. It does not attempt to examine, for example, the relations between property rights and democracy. Neither does it endeavour to make a comparative analysis. Only occasionally, some comparisons have been made between the jurisprudence of the European

Court of Human Rights and that of national courts such as the US Supreme Court or German Federal Constitutional Court. A comparative analysis, in different levels (between ECHR and EU law or public international law), might have provided valuable insights for legal consideration. But it is another job for another day.

PART I:
THEORETICAL ASPECTS OF PROPERTY RIGHTS

Chapter 2

What is Property? Definition of Constitutional Property

2.1. Introduction

This chapter looks at different aspects of the concept of 'property' and delineates its indicia for the purpose of constitutional and human rights discourse. As a legal and social institution governing the use of things and allocating the elements of social wealth,[1] property had and has very different forms in different cultures and different legal systems. However, considering the aim of this book (the examination of property under the European Convention on Human Rights), only a definition of constitutional property which is common to all Europe will be aimed at here.

When we talk about property as a social and legal institution governing the use of things and allocating the elements of social wealth,[2] it is not clear what kind of property system we are talking about. Are we talking about common property or state property or group property or private property? All of these systems regulates the use of things and allocate or distribute elements or items of social wealth in some way. However, when we talk about a constitutional right to property, we mean private property. The subject of this book is a right to private property as a human right. Therefore, the meaning of property will be examined here in this sense. Three questions are significant in this respect. What kind of rights or entitlements does a private property give to the right-holder (owner) over the objects of property? What kinds of rights does the owner have against other people through the right to property? and What kind of things can be the object of ownership? In terms of the first two questions, property is understood as relationships: a relation to the things (objects of property) and a relation to others through the things.[3] In the third sense, property is understood as objects. These

---

[1] Harris, J. W., *Property and Justice* [hereinafter *P&J*](Clarendon Press: Oxford, 1996) p.3.

[2] I am using the term 'social wealth' cautiously in the sense of totality of goods or material objects without attributing or implying any communal ownership over them. If the term 'social wealth' were used to imply that totality of the scarce material objects were under the common ownership of society without considering how those goods had been produced, the conclusions we reach about property would be different.

[3] Lametti, D., *The Deon-Telos of Private Property: Ethical Aspects of the Theory and Practice of Private Property* [hereinafter *Deon-Telos*](unpublished D. Phil. thesis: Oxford, 1998).

three questions will be examined here in some detail. A number of recent studies examining different aspects of property made my job relatively easier in this respect.[4]

Under the heading of *property-as-relationship,* different aspects of the concept of property are examined such as the extent of entitlements afforded to the right-holder by a right to property, whether property is a single right or bundle of different rights, whether the duties arising from property should be included in the definition of property, and what are the corresponding duty or duties to the right to property. Under the heading of *property-as-objects,* the things which can be the objects of property will mainly be scrutinised. In this respect, in addition to the traditional movable and immovable corporeal things and incorporeal rights, the new subject matters of ownership such as human genetic materials, body parts, cyber-space, radio wave frequencies, will be discussed as well.

The definition explicated above describes property as a relationship between private individuals and it is silent to some extent about the relationship between property-holder and the state. However, the constitutional protection of property is mainly about a relationship between individual owners and the state (public authorities). The question of to what extent property rights can be interfered with by public authorities under public law is the main theme of constitutional property discourse. Thus, after defining property in a private law sense, it is necessary to discuss whether a distinct definition is needed for constitutional discourse. This chapter proposes that a distinct definition is needed for constitutional property, considering the value protected by constitution or human rights documents. It proposes that constitutional property should be defined in terms of patrimonial rights. That is, the concept of property should be understood as comprising the whole of a person's assets assessable in monetary terms. Moral justification of such a definition can be found in autonomy-based freedom theory which will be offered in this book as the main justificatory theory for property.

2.2. Private Property Rights

Here, it is necessary, first, to clarify the concepts of property, private property and ownership and their relation to each other. Human beings live in a physical environment and need goods to survive. That is, they interact in some way with

[4] See Waldron, J., *The Right to Private Property* [hereafter *RPP*] (Clarendon Press: Oxford, 1988); Munzer, S.R., *A Theory of Property* (Cambridge: Cambridge University Press, 1990); Harris, J. W., *P&J*; Harris, J. W. "Is Property a Human Right?" [hereafter Human Right] in Janet McLean (ed.) *Property and Constitution* (Hart Pub. Oxford, 1999); Penner, J., *The Idea of Property in Law* [hereafter The Idea] (Clarendon Press: Oxford, 1997); Penner, J., "Hohfeldian Use Rights in Property." in Harris, J. W. (ed.) *Property Problems: From Genes To Funds* (Kluwer Law International, 1998); Penner, J., "Bundle of Rights Picture of Property" [hereafter The Bundle] (1996) 43 *UCLA Law Review* 711; Lametti, D., *Deon-Telos*; Lametti, D., "Property and (Perhaps) Justice" (1998) 43 *McGill Law Journal* 633.

their physical environment and some type of property relationship is necessitated between persons and material objects. Nevertheless, items of material resources are in greater demand than supply. Therefore, property relationship will exist not just between individuals and material resources but also among individuals with respect to resources. A polity will thus develop legal and social norms to embody and regulate the facets of this relationship.[5] In the widest sense, an institution or a system of rules governing access to and control of goods or material resources is defined as property.[6] That is, property is an organising idea.[7]

In this approach, property seems to be the most comprehensive concept comprising different sub-conceptions including 'private property'. Other sub-conceptions can be joint, group, corporate, communitarian, common, state, or public property.[8] So, if property is an institution governing the control and allocation of material objects, 'private property' places the ultimate control over scarce resources in the hands of the individual. In a private property system, individuals are granted powers over the control and use of a resource. The most obvious manifestation of vesting control in a single person is characterised as the ability to exclude others from access to or use of that same resource.[9]

The concept of ownership is used as synonymous to private property in civil law. In common law, however, though it is sometimes used as synonymous to private property, the concept of property is wider than ownership and comprises lesser interests (non-ownership proprietary interests)[10] as well. Therefore, the main concept to be examined here will be private property and the concepts of property and ownership will be used in relation to private property.

To find a common definition of private property in Europe, however, is not as easy as it seems. Despite the familiarity and ubiquity of the concept of property in lay discourse, it is surprisingly difficult to define it in legal and political discourse. The sources of the difficulty are various. Firstly, property is understood differently by different disciplines such as economy, law, political theory, and philosophy.[11]

Secondly, different legal systems define the concept of property differently. Continental civil law and common law systems come from different origins and traditions. While the codified civil laws on the Continent have mainly developed from the Roman law sources, the common law, although Roman law affected it to some extent, has developed from the feudal traditions and maintained a different property regime from the Roman tradition.[12] The distinction between

---

[5] Lametti, D., *Deon-Telos* p. 37.

[6] Waldron, J., *RPP* p.31.

[7] Harris, J. W., *P&J* p.63.

[8] *Ibid.* ch. 7.

[9] Lametti, D., *Deon-Telos* p.40.

[10] Harris, J. W., P&J p.55.

[11] Reeve, A., *Property* (Macmillan: London, 1986) p.10.

[12] Samuel, G., "Are Property Rights So Simple in Europe?" [hereafter Property] in P. Jackson and D. C. Wilde (eds.) *Property Law: Current Issues and Debates* (Ashgate: Dartmouth, 1999) p.161; Samuel, G., "The Many Dimensions of Property" [hereafter

law and equity in England resulted in a more multi-dimensional system from Continental laws.

Thirdly, there is an ambiguity in legal and philosophical discourse over the usage of the term 'property'. Sometimes it is used to refer to an institution and sometimes it is synonymous with the term 'ownership'. The importance of this distinction for our purpose is that if property is a human right, then what is its scope? Do human beings have a right that their community introduce or maintain a private property institution or does anyone have a right to own a particular resource?[13] Harris examines more ambivalence and scepticism arising from Hohfeldian influence over legal thinking which we will examine in detail below.

Fourthly, the notion of property is not static. Always new types of property appear, and these new kinds of property contribute new dimensions to the nature of proprietary relationships. These new relationships urge a more expanded analysis of different theoretical concepts of law rather than the classical analysis which focused on the ownership of land and other movable tangible objects.

There are significant differences among the concepts used in different laws to express the institution of property in Europe.[14] These differences comprise both the extent of entitlements included in the concept of property and the extent of objects which can be subject matters of proprietary interests. While the English concept of 'property' and the French *propriété* are very comprehensive, comprising both ownership and lesser interests on resources and a variety of things that could be the object of property rights – land, tangible and intangible movable things such as chattels, debts, money in the bank, shares in company, patent and copyrights – some other laws, (German *Eigentum,* Dutch *eigendom* and Turkish *mülkiyet*) use the concept in a more restrictive sense comprising only ownership rights over only movable and immovable corporal things.[15]

In addition to these conceptual differences among different jurisdictions, a taxonomy of rights and place of property rights in such a classification differs widely between common and civil law systems. In a common law system the discussion has been focused on the dichotomy between *rights in rem* and *rights in personam.*[16] According to this dichotomy, property rights differ from other private

---

Dimensions] in Janet McLean (ed.) *Property and Constitution* (Hart Pub. Oxford, 1999).

[13] Harris, J. W., *Human Right* p.65.

[14] Mincke, W., "Property: Assets or Power? Objects or Relations as Substrata of Property Rights" in J. W. Harris (ed.) *Property Problems: From Genes to Pension Funds* (Kluwer Law International: London, 1998) p. 78.

[15] For example, Turkish Civil Code indicates the things that can be object of immovable property and movable property in articles 632 and 686 respectively. Objects of immovable property are things that cannot be moved from their places. These are land, mines, and rights that can be recorded to register of title deeds separately and permanently. Objects of movable property are the things that can be transferred from one place to another and natural powers that are not immovable and suitable to acquisition.

[16] See Hohfeld, W. N., *Fundamental Legal Conceptions as Applied in Judicial Reasoning* (Yale University Press, 1923); Honoré, A. M. "Rights of Exclusion and

law rights as being *in rem*. *Rights in rem* are rights over things whereas *rights in personam* are rights against persons.

The German, Dutch, Swiss, and Turkish laws are more straightforward in distinguishing property rights from other rights. In order to distinguish property rights from other rights two different dichotomies are utilised; real (*iura in re*)/ personal rights (*iura in personam*) and absolute[17]/relative rights. The first approach makes the distinction between the rights which clearly have an object such as property rights in respect of a corporeal thing and rights the object of which are not so apparent such as obligations. The second approach makes the distinction between absolute rights, which are potentially directed against everybody, and relative rights which are directed against a certain debtor only. This classification evaluates rights in terms of a relationship created between persons, and it focuses on the power that exists when a right is vested to somebody.[18]

Another important distinction made by civil law is between personality rights and patrimonial rights.[19] Personality rights include a right to privacy, a right to bodily integrity, and a right to dignity. Personality rights attach directly to the person and they cannot be alienated.[20] Patrimonial rights include the whole of cashable rights and they can be alienated.[21] So, property rights are defined in civil law system as absolute patrimonial rights. That is, they are distinct from personality rights such as right to privacy or right to bodily integrity because the object of property is distinct from those rights although all of them give the right-holder the power to exclude others. And property rights do not comprise debt since it can be directed only against a single person or definite persons (debtors).[22] But, the distinction between patrimonial and personality rights is not clear in common law. However, it is of great importance for our purposes in order to define the scope of property rights. Therefore, it will be examined in detail below under the

---

Immunities Against Divesting" (1960) 24 *Tulune Law Review* 453; Eleftheriadis, P., "Analysis of Property Rights" (1996) 16 *Oxford Journal of Legal Studies* 31; Kocourek, A., *Jural Relations* (Indianapolis, 1928) 2nd ed. P.201.

17 'Absolute' in this sense is not used in the same way as the English 'absolute title'. It does not mean that the right is not limited by others rights. It means it can be availed against all persons.

18 Mincke, *op.cit.* 6.

19 'The patrimony is a universality representing the whole of a person's assets and liabilities assessable in monetary terms and often described as a 'container' for the congeries of specific real and personal rights and obligations a person can have at a given moment.' Lametti, D., *Deon-Telos* ...p. 33.

20 The issue of separation of personality rights from property rights will be examined in detail below under the heading of property as objects.

21 Samuel, G., Dimensions ... p.59.

22 Constitutional guarantee of property rights in article 14 of the Basic Law of Germany, however, is not limited to Civil Code's definition of property, but it comprises all pecuniary (patrimonial) rights established in domestic law. German Federal Courts interpret constitutional property as more expansive than property in private law. See Alexander, G. S., "Constitutionalising Property: Two Experiences, Two Dilemmas" in J. McLean (ed.) *Property and Constitution* (Hart Pub. Oxford, 1999).

heading of property-as-object. The distinction between *rights in rem* and *rights in personam* is irrelevant for our purpose since patrimonial rights comprise both.

The differences in approach to property in private laws in Europe makes a common definition impossible and necessitates a distinct one for constitutional property.

2.2.1. Property-as-Relationship

Traditionally property is defined both in the common law and in civil law as a right of a person with respect to a thing.[23] That is, it establishes a power relationship between a person and a thing. The title of ownership gives to the title-holder (a person) a right to enjoy, to use, or to dispose of a thing. This relation between a person and a thing, however, is meaningful only in a social environment. That is, such a relation can be called a 'right' only if it is recognised and respected by other people. Therefore, a right to property also refers to a power to exclude others from things. In this second sense, the relationship is to others through resources. Hence, property (as relationship) involves the factual or juridical relationships one has with the objects of property, and by either extension or necessary implication, the relationship one has with others with respect to these objects. It is a relationship both to and through the resources.[24] In this sense, property is a power against others (society) and the state and gives the owner an area of freedom against state.[25] Blackstone[26] defined the right to property as 'that sole and despotic dominion which one man claims and exercises over the external things of the world, in total exclusion of the right of any other individual in the universe'. He said, 'one of the absolute rights inherent in every Englishman, is that of property, which consists in the free use, enjoyment, and disposal of all his acquisitions, without any control or diminution, save only by the laws of the land'.

However, the extent and the nature of the entitlements included in the right to property is a matter of controversy. Whether property is a single right to exclusive use over a thing against all other persons or whether it is a bundle of different rights against others with respect to things is a matter of long debate among Anglo-American jurists.

2.2.1.1. Bundle of rights metaphor Following Hohfeld's[27] analysis of rights as paired jural relations between persons, the idea of rights over things lost its importance to a significant extent in Anglo-American legal reasoning. According

---

[23] Donahue, C., "The Future of the Concept of Property Predicted from Its Past" in J. R. Pennock, and J. W. Chapman (eds.) *NOMOS XXII: Property* (NUP: New York, 1980).

[24] Lametti, D., *Deon-Telos* p.34.

[25] This aspect of property makes it one of the most controversial subjects of the political debate and, therefore, it should be justified.

[26] Blackstone, W., *Commentaries on the Laws of England* (1766) (Dawsons: London, reprinted 1966) (4 vols. II.I.2).

[27] Hohfeld, W. N., *Fundamental Legal Conceptions as Applied in Judicial Reasoning* (Yale University Press, 1923).

to his analysis, a right is one of four different entitlements (claim right, privilege, power, or immunity) against another person or persons with a correlative obligation (duty for claim, no-right for privilege, liability for power, and disability for immunity). He refused the idea of a right over a thing. In his view, physical relations with a thing such as to physically control and use it are not jural relations and they could exist quite apart from the law of organised society. Since the purpose of the law is to regulate the conduct of human beings, all jural relations must be predicated on such human beings.[28] The distinction between *rights in rem* (multital) and the *rights in personam* (paucital), according to Hohfeld, is only numerical. While 'a paucital right, or claim is either a unique right residing in a person (or group of persons) and availing against a single person (or single group of persons); or else it is one of a few fundamentally similar, yet separate, rights respectively against a few definite persons, a multital right, or claim is always one of a large class of fundamentally similar, yet separate, rights, actual and potential, residing in a single person (or single group of persons) but availing respectively against persons constituting a very large and indefinite class of people.'[29]

The effect of this argument over property rights can be summarized in three distinct points. Firstly, it rejects the idea that a property right is a right to a thing.[30] Secondly, it does not account for a single right protecting a single interest and called property right. But, property rights are the aggregation of many separate, single rights, or claims, privileges (liberties), powers and immunities against many separate single persons each of whom owes a single duty, no-right, liability or disability. Thirdly, property rights do not have any intrinsic difference from other private law rights; rather the difference is only extrinsic or numerical. Property rights are a bundle of similar rights against many separate single persons.

Although Hohfeld's argument has been criticised widely,[31] it has had a significant impact on the Anglo-American legal reasoning. By being conjoined with the analysis of ownership offered by Honoré,[32] it encouraged the bundle of

---

[28] *Ibid.* 74.

[29] *Ibid.* 72.

[30] Some writers argue that the Hohfeldian approach does not undermine person-thing relationships. They claim that from a Hohfeldian perspective, an owner's entitlements are held against other persons and are held over a thing or set of things. A complete Hohfeldian explication of property rights includes both of those aspects. See Kramer, M. H., Book review of Harris' *P&J* (1997) 56 *Cambridge Law Journal* 642.

[31] See for criticism of Hohfeldian analysis of property rights, Honoré, A. M. "Rights of Exclusion and Immunities Against Divesting" (1960) 24 *Tulune Law Review* 453; Eleftheriadis, P., "Analysis of Property Rights" (1996) 16 *Oxford Journal of Legal Studies* 31; Penner, J.E., "Hohfeldian Use Rights in Property" in J. W. Harris (ed.) *Property Problems: From Genes to Funds* (Kluwer Law International, London, 1998); Penner, "Bundle of Rights Picture of Property" (1996) 43 *UCLA Law Review* 711; Penner, *The Idea of Property in Law* (OUP: Oxford, 1997).

[32] Honoré, A. M., "Ownership" in A. G. Guest (ed.) *Oxford Essays in Jurisprudence* (Clarendon Press: Oxford, 1961).

rights theory of property which is a mainstream theory.[33] Hohfeld's analysis is merely descriptive. It does not say which entitlements are involved in the concept of property. Honoré's analysis of ownership complements this flaw. He specifies the standard incidents of the liberal concept of full individual ownership common to Western legal systems. He mainly argues that although different legal systems have different approaches to property and its importance and the things capable of being owned, standard incidents of ownership do not vary from system to system and have a tendency to remain constant from place to place and age to age.[34]

He enumerates eleven incidents of ownership which include the right to possess, to use, to manage, to the income of the thing, to capital, to security, the rights of incidents of transmissibility and absence of term, the prohibition of harmful use, liability to execution, and the incidents of residuary character. A system of private property should recognise the standard incidents. But all elements of his list of incidents are not individually necessary conditions for the person of inherence to be designated owner of a particular thing in a given system.[35] Honoré's standard incidents of property comprise not only rights but also some duties as well.[36]

The Hohfeld-Honoré analysis, complementing each other, has led to a 'bundle of rights' theory of property.[37] The bundle of rights picture of property has been regarded as a satisfactory explanation of property rights by both scholarly writers and courts in common law.[38] A similar theory, in civil law, has been suggested by Scandinavian legal realist philosophers. The starting point of discussion there was criticism of the concept of subjective right. Danish philosopher Alf Ross offered a concept of bundles of claims in place of a subjective right. According to this theory, a right is nothing but a loose abstraction of such a bundle of claims. That is, a right is defined by the claims of which it consists. One consequence of this theory is the vanishing of the distinction between *rights in rem* and *rights in personam*. The most spectacular result of the theory emerges in the transfer of a right. There is no longer the need to transfer the right in its entirety. The right can pass gradually, claim by claim.[39] One effect of this theory can be seen in the Swedish Social Democrats' approach to property. They see property as a bundle of rights that is divisible. Accordingly, instead of requiring full transfer of rights from capitalist owners to community, property can be

---

[33] This approach has been applied to definition of property by, e.g., Becker, L.C., *Property Rights: Philosophical Foundations* (Routledge and Kegan Paul: London, 1977); Waldron, J., *RPP*; Munzer, S.R., *A Theory of Property* (Cambridge: Cambridge University Press, 1990).

[34] Honoré, A. M., *op.cit.* 32.

[35] *Ibid.* p.111.

[36] Whether duties or liabilities attached to property should be included in the definition of it will be examined further below. See p. 16.

[37] Penner, J., *The Bundle*... p.713.

[38] See *op. cit.* 33.

[39] Mincke, W., *op.cit.* 14.

subjected to a gradual process of socialisation through a socially controlled market.[40]

Penner, the strongest opponent of the bundle picture, argues that two different versions of bundle of rights thesis arise. The substantial version is that property is a bundle of rights in the sense that property is a naturally complex normative relation that should be regarded as a historically contingent association of various rights. The conceptual version suggests that property is a concept without a definable 'essence' and different combinations of the bundle in different circumstances may all count as property and no particular right or set of rights in the bundle is determinative.[41] In Penner's view, these two versions of bundle of rights thesis are related, and support each other. In short, bundle theory defines property as an aggregate of many different rights, privileges, powers, and immunities.[42]

Penner has raised several objections to the bundle metaphor. He argues, firstly, that the bundle metaphor does not suggest any clear methodology for dealing with the concept of property. It does not offer any criterion to decide whether something is property, or can or should be treated as property. Secondly, he asserts that Hohfeldian schema of rights and correlative duties does not fully conform to property rights.[43] Thirdly, he argues that bundle theory disintegrates the interest protected by property and makes it indefinable. He argues that if property is an aggregative complex, and it is a matter of judgement to decide which particular aggregates of more basic elements constitute property in any given context, then the concept of property is a flexible one, without any necessary defining features. In that case, the criteria employed in applying the concept may be nothing more than the separate elements in the bundle of rights.[44]

Penner's latter criticism is based on his individuation of property law in terms of interest protected by it. According to his approach, every branch of law protects a different interest. The interest protected in contract, for example, is the interest in forming co-operative relationships by making bargain agreements. That is 'agreement for consideration' or bargain.[45] The interest protected in property is the interest in 'exclusively determining the use of things'. Therefore, the unified concept of property law should be the exclusive use of things. In Penner's view, the bundle theory disintegrates the interest in property by defining the property in terms of the 'right' to property. Accordingly, the concept of property is not directly related to any body of law, and in order to show how our interests in property are recognised in law, one must make recourse to rules in many branches of law such

---

[40] Tilton, T., The Political Theory of Swedish Social Democracy: Through the Welfare State to Socialism (Clarendon Press: Oxford, 1990) p. 266.

[41] Penner, J., *The Bundle* pp.722-23.

[42] Munzer, S., *A Theory* p.23.

[43] Penner, J., "Hohfeldian Use Rights in Property." in Harris, J. W. (ed.) *Property Problems: From Genes To Funds*. (Kluwer Law International. 1998).

[44] Penner, J., *The Bundle* p.724.

[45] Penner, J., *The Idea* p.51.

as real and personal property, consumer and commercial law, equity, tort and criminal law.[46]

Penner argues that the bundle metaphor is founded on a mistaken impression of how property protects the use of things. It is assumed that property is a natural composite that can be carved at the joints into freestanding parts. According to Penner, the reason why property is complicated is the natural ability of people to use different kinds of things in different ways.[47]

The relationship to things and relationship to others are intertwined in the bundle of rights theory of property. As indicated above property cannot be defined in terms of only a relationship to a thing or only a relationship to others. Both are intrinsic elements of a property institution.[48] Both Penner's and Harris's definitions of property comprise significant insights into the nature of property rights. Therefore, their definitions will be examined here seriatim.

Penner suggests a unitary definition for property. According to his definition 'the right to property is the right to determine the use or disposition of an alienable thing in so far as that can be achieved or aided by others excluding themselves from it, and includes the right to abandon it, to share it, to license it to others (either exclusively or not) and give it to others in its entirety'.[49]

His definition unifies the right to property as a single right. It is a variant of the view that the right to property is a right to exclude, but it includes some specific features. The concept of 'use' in Penner's definition represents the relationship to things. The relationship to others through things is represented by the concept of exclusion. Object of property is represented by the concept of 'a thing' which will be examined below under the heading of property-as-objects.

Penner's concept of 'use' is a social one. He defines property like a gate, not a wall. The right to property permits one not only to make solitary use of his property *via* the exclusion of others, but also permits one to make a social use of it *via* the selective exclusion of others. The important feature of property is the individual's determination of the disposition of a thing, not any requirement that one uses it on one's own.[50] That is, concept of use includes control powers as well.

He uses the concept of 'use' in a wide sense to include the power to alienate property. In his view, therefore, the right to property comprises the right to transfer as well as to abandon. But, for the sake of distinguishing property from contract, he argues that the right to property does not entail a right to bargain about making a transfer or licensing the use of his property. So, he claims that property entails a right to give, but not sell, because making contract about property is application of general right to contracts.[51] Although this argument is problematic in

---

[46] Penner, J., *The Bundle* p.741.

[47] Ibid. 766.

[48] Snare, F., "The Concept of Property" (1972) 9 *American Philosophical Quarterly* 200; Campbell, K., "On the General Nature of Property Rights" (1992) 3 *The King's College Law Journal* 79.

[49] Penner, J., *The Bundle* p. 742; See also *The Idea* p.152.

[50] *Ibid.* 743.

[51] *Ibid.* 746; *The Idea* p.91.

some ways[52] – for example, money is meaningless without its exchange capacity – I will not attempt to refute it here, because the distinction between contractual and property rights is not relevant for the purposes of this book. In any case, they will be considered as property for constitutional purposes if they are patrimonial in character.

The idea that property is a right of exclusion means that it is correlative of a general duty that all others have to exclude themselves from the property of others and it is not the right physically or by order or otherwise to actually exclude others from one's property. That is, correlative of exclusive use is a general duty of non-interference. Penner defines this duty of non-interference as a duty *in rem.*[53] The duty is directed to things, that is, objects of property. This implies that property does not protect personal rights and rights in personality-rich relationships. The duty to respect property by non-interference should not involve the duty-ower in any personal dealings with the owner in order to respect his ownership. The relation is mediated via the thing the owner owns, not on the basis of their personal interactions. The practice of property protects the ownership relation by instituting a blanket prohibition on the interference with things that others own. This duty illustrates the way in which property rights are *rights in rem.* Unlike the Hohfeld's thesis, all people simply have a duty not to interfere with the property of others. In general, if it is not his and he has no permission from the owner, he has a duty not to interfere with it. He does not need to know who owns it. It is an impersonal duty, correlating with an impersonal right as one can imagine. This duty can prohibit two classes of interference; specific interference with the owner's own use and the unlicensed use of property by a non-owner which to some extent disposes the owner. Both clearly interfere with the owner's determination of how his property is to be used. These interferences can be seen in one of many formats; holding, occupation, consumption, destruction, dispossession, etc. The format of interference might vary according to the nature of property. For instance, land cannot be consumed, while a pencil or copyright cannot be occupied.[54] Penner's concept of a duty *in rem* constitutes a strong challenge to the Hohfeldian approach.

Harris defines property in terms of twin, and mutually irreducible, notions of 'trespassory rules' and 'the ownership spectrum'.[55] Trespassory rules make reference to a relationship with others. He uses the notion of trespassory rules in a

---

[52] Penner, if I understood correctly, confuses the power of owner to make legal transactions over his property and actual contractual transactions. That is, my power to sell my car is involved in my right to property over my car. Therefore, person X cannot sell my car to someone else without my consent but I can. But actual sale contract is subject to contract law. His classification of gifts outside the contract is also not true in civil law. Donation is accepted as a contract in civil law but it imposes an obligation to only one party of the contract.

[53] Lametti, D., *Deon-Telos* p.307.

[54] Penner, J., *The Idea* p. 128; *The Bundle* p. 807.

[55] Harris, J. W., *P&J* pp. 23 ff; *Human Right* p. 67.

very wide sense to encompass 'all rules which, by reference to a thing, impose obligations upon an open-ended range of persons, other than some specifically excepted individual, or group (right-holder), not to make use of a thing without consent of that individual or group'.[56] Such rules may be enforced only by informal social pressure, or by civil or criminal legal sanctions. These sanctions can be negative bans (mostly) or positive requirements to restore. And they are applied not only to material things like land and chattels but also to ideational entities like intellectual property. Harris argues that without trespassory rules we cannot speak of a private property, but only a common property.[57]

The existence of trespassory rules alone is not, however, a sufficient condition for existence of a property right.[58] Another component of property, for Harris, is the ownership spectrum. Basic characteristics of the ownership spectrum are elaborated in three elements. Firstly, they all involve a juridical relation between a person and a thing. Secondly, the juridical relation consists of an open-ended set of privileges and powers. Thirdly, they authorise self-seekingness on the part of the right-holder.[59] In Harris' view ownership interests are not finite bundles of rights, rather they comprise open-ended sets of use privileges, control powers and powers of transmission. For example, if A owns a pen, normally no one can question A's liberty to scratch his head with it, or to use its back to scrape a sticky stain on his desk or do any number of unlistable things with it. Nor can anyone question A's powers to control a similarly open-ended set of uses by others, nor A's powers to sell it or give it away to any of an unlistable class of persons.

The range of ownership spectrum extends from, as Harris calls it, 'mere property' to 'full-blooded ownership'. In Harris' definition, 'mere property' includes no power to transmission and use privileges and control powers included in it might be considerably circumscribed, while still being open-ended. For instance, a statutory tenant of a dwelling cannot do many things with it, but still the things he can do are open-ended. 'A full-blooded ownership is a relationship between a person and a thing which entails, *prima facie,* unlimited privileges of use, or abuse over the thing, and, *prima facie*, unlimited powers of control and transmission, so far as such use or exercise of power does not infringe some property independent prohibition'.[60] However, use privileges, control powers and transmissibility rights may not always exist together in some property institutions. Most of the cashable rights, for example, do not include use privileges and control powers but they can be transmitted, for example rights over bank accounts and rights over business goodwill.[61] Harris defines some concepts according to

---

[56] Harris, J. W., *Human Right* p.67.

[57] *Ibid.*

[58] Harris gives the example of regulatory regimes set up in the UK by the Human Organ Transplant Act 1989 and the Human Fertilization and Embryology Act 1990. See *Human Right* fn.7 and accompanying text. This issue will be examined in this chapter later. But, all personality rights are examples of the right which enjoy trespassory protection but they are not property rights.

[59] Harris, J. W., *Human Right* p.67.

[60] *Ibid.* 68; See also *P&J* p. 30.

[61] Vallentyne, P., Review of *P&J* (1999) 108 *Mind* 581.

existence and combination of use privileges, control powers, and transmissibility powers. If the rights generated by trespassory rules are open-ended but do not authorise self-interested exercise (and instead are constrained by a duty to promote some goal), they are *quasi-ownership property rights* (e.g. rights of trustees and of government officials).[62] If the rights vested in a person over a thing are not open-ended but do authorise self-interested exercise, Harris call them *non-ownership property rights* (e.g. easement, servitude, and mortgages). The key concept here is the *open-endedness* of use privileges and control powers. Nevertheless, as Rainbolt[63] explicated, while a set of use privileges and control powers can be larger or smaller, it is difficult to draw a line that usefully separates open-ended entitlements from not open-ended ones.

Harris' unpacking of components of property reveals that the entitlements over a thing can be narrow or wide but they still constitute property as long as they enjoy some degree of trespassory protection or they are assignable as part of a person's private wealth. That is, even if some entitlements are not accorded trespassory protection, they can still be conceived as property if they can be a subject of transmission as part of a person's private wealth. In some civil law systems, for example, some cashable rights such as business goodwill are not accorded trespassory protection but they can be transferred and come within the scope of expropriation rules.[64]

His approach also refutes a totality approach to property. He argues that full-blooded ownership does not imply, even *prima facie*, any privilege to break property-independent prohibitions. He defines a property-independent prohibition as one which is addressed to all persons irrespective of whether they own anything.[65] For example, stabbing someone with my knife is not included in my ownership of the knife. The prohibition of stabbing someone else is not relevant to my ownership of the knife. He contrasts property-independent prohibitions with three types of rules, namely property limitation rules, expropriation rules, and appropriation rules. According to Harris, contrary to property-independent prohibitions, those rules are related to property institutions because they all presuppose ownership interests.

It is necessary here to consider whether duties or limitation rules should be included in the definition of property. Honoré included in his standard incidents of ownership at least two duties, the prohibition of harmful use and liability to execution.[66] Honoré's incident of prohibition of harmful use comprises Harris' classification of both property-independent prohibitions and property limitation rules, and incident of liability to execution comprises Harris's expropriation rules. Leaving the discussion about the taxonomy of duties or limitations included in property institution to Chapter 4 of this book, it will be examined here whether

---

[62] Harris, J. W., *P&J* p.31.
[63] Rainbolt, G., Review of *P&J* (2000) 111 *Ethics* 173.
[64] Harris, J. W., *Human Right* p.71.
[65] Harris, J. W., *P&J* p.32.
[66] Honoré A. M., *op.cit.* 32.

these duties or limitations should be included in the definition of property. Honoré obviously included these incidents in his definition. But Harris defined, first, *prima facie*, property without taking into account the property limitation, expropriation and appropriation rules, then connected them into property institution within property's minimal structure as a part of justice discussion.[67] That is, they are not intrinsic to a definition of property.

Lametti does not agree with Harris and argues that if justice reasons can justify only a limited institution of property, then property limitation rules must be a conceptually necessary feature of property systems if such systems are going to accord in practice with their justifying reasons.[68] Lametti's objection to Harris is not to his taxonomy of the categories of rules of property institution, and components of the taxonomy, but rather over the status accorded to each type of rules. He argues that private property, resources, and social wealth generally exist to serve a greater good and private property should be defined in terms of and to best serve this purpose.

Harris' approach seems more practical, because the justifying reasons of the property interests and justifications for limitation rules are not the same even if they can be defined in a same unitary moral theory. Although both reasons are moral reasons, as Harris argued, limitation reasons do not independently exist, they presuppose the existence of property rights. But property-justifying reasons can independently justify *prima facie* property rights. In practice, to accept Harris' or Lametti's argument makes a difference only in terms of burden of proof. Harris' argument requires limiting government to prove moral justification of its interference because otherwise the owner has, *prima facie,* property rights, but Lametti's argument imposes the burden of proof on the property owner. He may need to prove that he has a moral right to property and there is no moral justification for interference with his property because limitations are intrinsic to property institution. Apart from this, in practice, whichever of these arguments are accepted the inclusion and limitations of property will not change.

To sum up, the entitlements included in property comprise, *prima facie*, open-ended use privileges, control powers, and transmission powers. Any combination of these entitlements vested in an individual with respect to a thing constitutes property. Although most private laws require a minimum intensity of these entitlements before attributing the epithet of property to them, for constitutional purposes any entitlement with respect to a thing should be regarded, *prima facie,* as property. For example, most private laws do not consider mere use rights over a thing arising from a contract as property, but it is suggested that they should be considered as property in the constitutional context. Whether these entitlements are different appearances of a single right called property or every single entitlement included in the property constitutes a stick in a bundle of rights does not make much difference in terms of constitutional discourse. At the end of the day, every intervention to one or some or all of these entitlements will constitute an interference with property. However, if a constitutional clause makes

---

[67] Harris, J. W. *P&J* ch. 3.
[68] Lametti. D., *Deon-Telos* p.304.

a distinction between different kinds of interferences with property it becomes relevant. The European Convention on Human Rights, indeed, does make such a distinction between deprivation of property and control of use of property. Nevertheless, as will be explained in Chapters 4 and 7 below, such a distinction is not suitable for a number of reasons. There is no moral distinction between depriving someone of some, or all of his wealth over a thing and should be justified equally.

The correlative duty to the right to property is a general right not to interfere with others' property. Such a duty is not related to owner's identity. If something is not mine, I have a duty not to interfere with it unless the owner consents. I do not need to know who owns it to refrain from interfering with it.

Before finishing this section, it is necessary to point out two significant issues regarding the range of entitlements included in property. Firstly, Penner argues, if I understood correctly, that the right to property protects only use of things, not the exchange value of things. This idea emerges from his endeavour to distinguish property from contract. He claims that the fact that an owner captures the market or exchange value of a thing does not merely derive from his having the right to property, but from his having exchange rights, i.e. the right to contract. It is the individual's exploitation of his property rights and contract rights together that will secure him an exchange value for the use of his property.[69]

According to Penner, property protects the value of a thing to the extent that the duty of non-interference protects whatever value an owner can extract from it in a condition of non-interference. This approach is totally unacceptable in terms of constitutional property approach. It is true that the exchange value of a thing is determined by market conditions and a state cannot be held responsible for the fluctuations in the market value of a thing. But this does not mean that public authorities are not responsible for acts or regulations reducing the market value of things.

As Harris indicated, the institution of property serves the dual functions of controlling the use of things and allocation of wealth. The latter function is served by the exchange value of things to a significant extent. Therefore, property is defined not only in terms of use, but also in terms of wealth.[70] Property justification reasons, which will be examined in the next chapter, justify not only use value of property, but also exchange value of property, because exchange value (totality of wealth) is an important factor for an individual to realise his plans (autonomy). Thus, constitutional protection of property should comprise both use value and exchange value of property. If an act or regulation of public authorities affects exchange value of a thing substantively without limiting the use of it, we cannot say that there is no interference with property. In the *Sporrong and*

---

[69] Penner, J., *Use Rights* p.173.

[70] Rudden, B., "Things as Thing and Things as Wealth" in Harris, J. W., (ed.) *Property Problems: From Genes To Funds* (Kluwer Law International, 1998), it also appeared in (1994) 14 *Oxford Journal of Legal Studies* 82; see also Harris, J. W., *P&J* p.140.

Lönnroth[71] case, for example, the European Court of Human Rights ruled that expropriation permits which did not limit the owners to use their property constituted interference with property.

Secondly, Munzer[72] adds a psychological element to the entitlements included in property. He argues that property includes a dimension that makes possible legal expectations[73] with respect to things. Property is a ground for the disposition to predict, *inter alia*, the future use and enjoyment of things together with the attitude of feeling entitled to count on them. This dimension of property plays a significant role in its justification by autonomy-based freedom theory. People can make future plans and engage in creative activities depending on the protection provided by property institution. Therefore, a good legal system should secure these expectations. In analysis of constitutional property, we will suggest that such legal expectations constitute property and public authorities should take account of these expectations when interfering with property rights.[74]

I do not need to take position in a debate over whether property is a single right or a bundle of different rights. No matter which of these theories is accepted, open-ended use privileges, control powers and transmission powers over things – either as being one of the sticks in a bundle (bundle approach), or as being a form of use (single right approach) – constitute *prima facie* property rights, and any interference of public authorities with these interests should be justified. Every single entitlement with respect to a thing constitutes property. These entitlements comprise transmission powers as well. That is, Penner's sharp distinction between contract and property is not acceptable for constitutional discourse. A regulation restricting my power to sell my car constitutes an interference with my property. These entitlements, however, are not absolute. Legislation can define the inclusion of entitlements included in a proprietary right. For example, a right to license constitutes property under the conditions laid down by legislation regulating it. These entitlements constitute, *prima facie*, property right, that is, they can be limited for legitimate purposes that will be examined in Chapter 4.

2.2.2. Property-as-Objects

In the last section, the extent of the entitlements included in property has been examined. But this is not sufficient to define property. To complete the definition it is necessary to look at which things can be the objects of property. In this section, therefore, the subject matter of property will be examined. We have defined property above in terms of dual functions of controlling the use of things and

---

[71] *Sporrong and Lönnroth v. Sweden,* judgement of 23 September 1982 (App. Nos.7151/75 and 7152/75) Series A no. 52.

[72] Munzer, S.R., *A Theory* p. 23.

[73] Munzer defines an expectation as a disposition to predict that a certain event will occur together with an attitude of desiring and feeling entitled to count on its occurrence. It is not simply a hope, prediction or expecting. See *Ibid.* p.28.

[74] See Rose, Carol M., "Property and Expropriation: Themes and Variations in American Law" (2000) *Utah Law Review* 1.

allocation of wealth. Such a definition makes reference to the concepts of 'thing' and 'wealth' as objects of property. Thus, a comprehensive definition of object of property should comprise both a concept of 'thinghood' and a concept of 'wealth'.

To begin with the latter, Harris makes reference to a connection between the concepts of scarcity and wealth in terms of property.[75] He argues that if there is an abundance of resources, that is, more of them available for instant use than all those seeking to exploit may desire, there is no wealth to be allocated. In his view, even if such things contribute to the well-being of individuals, they are not part of social wealth, because there is no need to make distributive choices. In such cases there is neither trespassory protection nor are they assignable to individuals (lack of exclusivity). Therefore, there is no property. Thus, according to Harris, sunlight and air cannot be objects of property as long as the abundance persists. Existence of social regulation regarding such abundant resources (existence of property-independent prohibitions and property limitation rules such as environmental and planning regulations) does not create property over such resources. But if the abundance ceases – for example, fostering of a program for the production of electricity from wind power or sunlight – this may have the effect of creating ownership interests over such resources.

The scarcity is not a very strict requirement for existence of proprietary interests, because many things are naturally scarce, or abundance can easily turn into scarcity. For example, sea sand is abundant at the seashore, but transportation of it to somewhere else can make it scarce. Therefore, we can say that if there is more than one person demanding the same thing (material or ideational), it is to be regarded as scarce (and an element of wealth) and can be an object of property. We do not need to create a concept of scarcity over ideas in order to recognise intellectual property rights or the right to property over information.[76]

However, the degree of scarcity can play a significant role in acquisition and the nature of property. A polity may decide that too scarce things cannot be acquired by first occupancy. For example, a polity can ban acquisition of property rights over radio spectrum by first occupancy and can adopt a licensing system because available radio wave frequencies are very limited.[77] But a relatively less scarce thing, i.e. a domain name on the internet,[78] can be acquired by first occupancy.

---

[75] Harris, J. W., *P&J* p.23.

[76] Nigri, D. F., "Theft of Information and the Concept of Property in the Information Age" in Harris, J. W., (ed.) *Property Problems: From Genes To Funds* (Kluwer Law International, 1998); Harris, J.W., *P&J* p.341.

[77] For discussion of property rights over radio spectrum see; Spiller, P. T., and Cardilli, C., "Towards A Property Rights Approach to Communications Spectrum" (1999) 16 *Yale Journal on Regulation* 53; White, L. J., " 'Propertyzing' the Electromagnetic Spectrum: Why It's Important, and How to Begin" (2000) 9 *Media Law and Policy* 19; Corbett, K., "The Rise of Private Property Rights in The Broadcast Spectrum" (1996) 46 *Duke Law Journal* 611.

[78] See Boyle, J., *Shamans, Software, and Spleens: Law and The Construction of the Information Society* (Harvard University Press: London, 1999).

The degree of scarcity can also be very significant in determination of which things can be objects of private property. A polity may decide that a scarce thing cannot be an object of private ownership, or the extent of proprietary entitlements over such a thing can be more limited than full-blooded ownership. For example, pieces of cultural heritage, forests, seashores, or mines can be prohibited from private ownership. Or a limited proprietary interest can be recognised over such resources. The owners of cultural heritage might be banned from changing it substantively, or can be forced to permit the public to see it. That is, the legislative body can determine the inclusion of a right to property. However, scarcity is not a morally binding reason for such policies. Other considerations may favour different policies. That is, state has a wide margin of appreciation in this regard. But if such a scarce thing is once put under private ownership, any introduction of a chance in law banning private ownership over it, or introducing a restricted form of property, should respect the legitimate expectations of private owners.

As for the 'thinghood', the concept of 'thing' in the legal sense comprises most material objects and contrasts with persons. That is, things, which can be objects of property, are distinct from persons. In most legal systems, a person is not regarded as owning his body, reputation, skill, honour, or dignity.[79] The rights to one's body, reputation, skill, honour, or dignity cannot be objects of property. Such things are not regarded in one's patrimony. They constitute one's identity and they cannot be detached from oneself without damaging one's identity or personality. But the question is how things can be distinguished from personality.

But first, it is necessary to justify why we should differentiate personality or identity from the things that can be objects of property. A possible explanation can be as follows. Personality is related to one's being and protects one's dignity. But property is related to one's autonomy and protects one's autonomous conduct. As indicated in the last section, property includes transmission powers as well. That is property can be transferred to others permanently. However, personality and its components cannot be treated as a commodity in the market.[80] If human dignity is undermined for the sake of autonomy, autonomy loses its own value because autonomy is morally valuable only as an extension of human dignity. If personality and its components are alienated, it is impossible to mention about an individual's human dignity. Therefore, slavery is not legitimate and has been prohibited.

If we return to the problem of distinguishing things from persons, a number of criteria have been suggested. Firstly, it has been offered that it is the best approach to try to classify the things that can be owned without attempting to establish a definition of things. This is Honoré's position. In his view to look at the meaning of the word 'thing' will not tell us which protected interest is conceived in terms of ownership. When the legislature or courts think that an interest should be alienable and transmissible, they will reify it and say that it can be owned, that is,

[79] Honoré, A. M., Ownership p.130.

[80] Munzer, S., "Human Dignity and Property Rights in Human Body Parts" in Harris, J. W., (ed.) *Property Problems: From Genes To Funds* (Kluwer Law International, 1998).

property. They will not say that it can be owned and is *a res* because of a prior conviction that it falls within the appropriate definition of thing.[81]

Traditionally, objects of property are classified as corporeal or tangible things (choses in possession) such as land and chattels and incorporeal or intangible things (choses in action) such as intellectual property and other cashable rights, for example, debts, money in the bank, and shares in a company. For Honoré, the classification of things into material objects and rights in them, claims and collections of objects is more useful than that into corporeal and incorporeal. His list of 'things' is as follows: (1) Material objects and interests in material objects. (2) Claims, and interests in claims. (3) Fixed collections of material objects, claims, or both. (4) Variable collections of material objects, claims, or both. (5) Funds.[82]

However, such a list of objects of property is hardly helpful to find an answer to the rough question of whether body, labour, reputation, separate body parts, human genetic material, human reproductive material, or embryo can be objects of property. Therefore, a criterion or criteria is needed to distinguish things which can be objects of property and those which cannot. He implicitly makes reference to the concept of 'alienability'.[83]

Harris suggests a 'distancing' test. Accordingly, for an entity to be a proprietary subject matter, a human subject must be distanced from it in two ways. It must be something others could be accused of 'taking' and something the subject himself could be seen to control or use as 'owner'.[84] He formulates the distancing test as follows: 'Before any entity, material or ideational, can be subjected to a property institution it must be (1) susceptible of specific trespassory protection; and (2) a potential subject of an ownership or quasi-ownership interest; so that it is (3) reifiable as a person independent resource.'[85] This formulation can also be reduced to an alienability thesis, because the first two elements of the test are also applicable for personality rights. One's rights to bodily integrity or to reputation or to privacy also enjoy trespassory protection and the right-holder has open-ended use privileges over them. For example, my body is protected against outsiders by civil and criminal law. If someone injures or sexually harasses me, he infringes my personality not my property. I can decide to do boxing, to work or to have sexual relationships with others; this does not mean that I own my body. But what makes these rights impossible to conceive as property is that they cannot be owned by others.

Munzer uses the notion of 'transferability' to distinguish between property rights that one has in one's body from other personal rights. He sees one's rights with respect to his body as a bundle of rights and claims that within this bundle some elements or sticks are 'personal rights' and others are 'property

[81] *Ibid.* 131.
[82] *Ibid.* 132.
[83] *Ibid.* 133.
[84] Harris, J. W. *P&J* p.332.
[85] *Ibid.* 334.

rights'. 'Personal rights' are body rights that protect the interests or choices other than the choice to transfer. 'Property rights' are body rights that protect the choice to transfer.[86] Personal rights embrace a wide range of exclusive privileges and liberties from bodily integrity to privacy and freedom of expression. Munzer classifies gratuitous transfers as weak property rights and transfers for value as strong property rights.[87] Although this classification of rights over one's body as personal rights and weak and strong property rights is illuminating, it does not offer any criteria to decide when body rights become transferable that is proprietary.

In a later essay, Munzer examined the property rights in human body parts in terms of human dignity.[88] He examines how selling human body parts can offend human dignity but he does not raise any objection to gratuitous transfers, that is, donation of organs. From a Kantian perspective, he defines human dignity as an unconditioned and incomparable worth that is enjoyed just by virtue of being human. Accordingly, entities with dignity differ sharply from entities that have price on a market. Therefore, treating human beings as a commodity in the market offends human dignity. As a part of the self, the human body, in its togetherness with the self, constitutes the person. The parts of the body that are integral to the normal biological functioning of a person, therefore, cannot be treated as commodities. He also argues that donating body parts is not a market and does not make body parts into commodities.

Considering these points Munzer offers two strategies for propriety of body parts. The 'integration strategy' insists on the unified organisation of various body parts that make up a living human being. The significance of a part for the normal biological functioning of the body determines the seriousness of concerns about body parts as commodities. The concern is less serious for replenishable parts such as hair, nail, blood, and semen, etc. It is more serious for a paired but non-renewable organ such as a kidney. And it is more serious still for single non-renewable organs such as the heart, liver, or spleen.[89]

The second strategy, 'derived-status strategy', determines the degree of concern according to the parts' personal connections with a human being. For example, a kidney's function is not especially personal, so the sale of a kidney raises less concern. But the sale of testicles or sperm raises serious concern because any child conceived through them will have the genetic make-up of the seller rather than the recipient. The ultimate use of the part is also relevant. For example,

---

[86] Munzer, S., *A Theory of Property* (CUP: Cambridge, 1990) p.48.

[87] Munzer exemplifies weak property rights with respect to body as gratuitous donations of organs during life upon death. Strong property rights include power to sell bodily fluids such as blood and semen, or a contract for the future delivery of one's body after death. See *Ibid.* 51.

[88] Munzer, S., "Human Dignity and Property Rights in Human Body Parts" in Harris, J. W., (ed.) *Property Problems: From Genes To Funds* (Kluwer Law International, 1998); see also "Kant and Property Rights in Body Parts" (1993) 6 *Canadian Journal of Law and Jurisprudence* 319; "An Uneasy Case Against Property Rights in Body Parts" (1994) *Social Philosophy and Policy* 259.

[89] *Ibid.* 35.

if a sold skin becomes a graft for a burn victim, the concern is minimal, but if it is used for upholstery, the concern is great. There is also a difference in the degree of concern between the sale of parts of cadaveric flesh and a living person.[90]

Munzer's strategies make reference to the connection between body parts and personality, but still do not offer a clear-cut criterion when body parts can be regarded as proprietary subject matters, that is, commodity. Penner's 'separability' seems to suggest this needed criterion.[91] The separability thesis is useful not only for deciding when body parts can be objects of property, but also for distinguishing any personality right from property.

According to Penner, objects of property rights are things. Property is a right to things; it is not things themselves. He argues that the distinctive character of being a thing is lack of personality. The essential feature distinguishing property is that it consists of a right to a thing that is only contingently connected to any particular person. He argues that there is a significant distinction between the things which lack personality such as objects, space, ideas, and even particular concretely specified relations between people, i.e. debts and things which do have or significantly involve personality. Property refers to a particular human practice, practice of dealing with things, which stands in contrast to our practices of dealing with other people.[92]

Both personality rights and property involve exclusive use. One has the right of exclusive determination of what one will do with one's body as does one in respect of those things that are one's property. The distinction between the two is that an owner is not necessarily connected to, but is separable from, the things he holds as property.[93] Penner asserts that intention, social convention and technology plays a significant role in the separability of things from personality. For example, one's right over one's image is a right of personality. So if someone takes A's picture without his consent, he infringes A's personality right (the right to privacy in some legal systems). Or if a photographic studio displays A's picture on its window without A's consent, still it infringes A's right to personality. But if A decides to be a photo model and poses for some pictures for an agency, those pictures become commodities and objects of property. What makes a personality right property here is A's intention to sell his particular images. Similarly, social convention also affects the extent of the things that are separable from personality. Suppose that in a society one's hair was considered to be essential to one's identity. Cutting a man's hair might be regarded as battery, and selling of hair to make a wig could be prohibited. Technology can also play an important role. If science assures that removal of an organ is absolutely risk-free and the person will remain essentially the same person, such an organ can be regarded as a commodity and becomes an object of property.

---

[90] *Ibid.*

[91] Penner, J., *The Idea* ch. 5; *The Bundle* pp. 802 ff.

[92] Penner, J., *The Idea* p.105.

[93] Penner, J., *The Bundle* p. 805.

In Penner's view, 'thinghood' is a conceptual criterion in respect of what things can be objects of property. The things that are not aspects of ourselves or our ongoing personality-rich relationships to others, that is, contingently related to us, can be regarded as a commodity and subject matter of property. The contingency will change given the surrounding personal, cultural, and technological circumstances.[94] Penner argues that the key for thinghood is not alienability, or transferring the value of thing. For example, performing an employment contract, and exchanging labour for payment, does not make labour our property, because one's labour cannot be separated from the labourer. So, labour should not be conceived as property and part of one's patrimony. Otherwise, in case of bankruptcy, creditors would have the right to compel the bankrupt to work to pay his debts. Similarly, our rights over our image or body also cannot be regarded as property until they are actually separated from our personality. If we accepted that one's kidney is one's property, in case of bankruptcy, creditors would have the right to ask one to sell one's kidney to fulfil one's debts.

Therefore, until something becomes commodity and part of one's patrimony it should not be considered as property. But if a body part is separated from a person, it turns into a commodity and becomes a proprietary object.[95] That is, potential separability is not enough to make something a commodity, rather it should be actually separated. However, the property rights over body parts can be restricted. For example, sale of such organs can be allowed only for medical use, because even if it is separated from the person, some connection to the person still remains. To sum up, the suggested criterion for thinghood in this study is actual separability of a thing from personality.

Completing our study on the definition of private property, we can define it as follows. Property is a *prima facie* right to exclusive and open-ended use, control, and transmission of things (material and ideational) that are separable from persons and legitimate expectations with respect to those things. In this definition the right to property protects both interest (use privileges and transfer powers) and choices (control powers and transfer powers) and, therefore, requires a combination of interest and will theory of rights. However, as indicated above most private laws restrict the indicia of property to only *rights in rem*. They do not include the rights stemming from contract within the right to property. But such a sharp distinction is not functional for constitutional discourse. The totality of someone's wealth, no matter whether its source is contract or ownership, is

---

94 *Ibid.* 807.

95 See Boulier, W., "Sperm, Spleens, and Other Valuables: The Need to Recognise Property Rights in Human Body Parts" (1995) 23 *Hofstra Law Review* 693; Cain, A. S. P., "Property Rights in Human Biological Materials: Studies in Species Reproduction and Biomedical Technology" (2000) 17 *Arizona Journal of International and Comparative Law* 449; Miranda, A., "The Legal Status of the Pre-Embryo: Some Comparative Considerations Prompted by *Davis v. Davis*" in Harris, J. W., (ed.) *Property Problems: From Genes To Funds* (Kluwer Law International, 1998); Beyleveld, D. and Brownsword, R., "Patenting Human Genes: Legality, Morality, and Human Rights" in Harris, J. W., (ed.) *Property Problems: From Genes To Funds* (Kluwer Law International, 1998).

valuable for him to realise his autonomy and should enjoy constitutional protection in the same way. Both the use value and exchange value of the things are to be considered as constitutionally protected property. Therefore, the meaning of constitutional property will be examined next.

2.3. Constitutional Property

Considering the different approaches to the definition of private property in different legal systems, a distinct and common definition for constitutional property can be offered. The differences of the aims pursued by private law and constitutional law can justify such a distinct definition. The aim of private law is to regulate relationships between individuals and the definition of property in private law depends on the different aspects of the legal relations among individuals. But the aim of the Constitutional law is to regulate relations between individuals and state, and to protect individuals against state. Therefore, property should be defined in terms of this aim in constitutional discourse. Autonomy-based freedom theory suggests that property is valuable as a means of realising one's autonomy and plans. So, a constitutional definition of property should take into account this aspect.

In practice, the concept of property in constitutional property protection clauses has been interpreted more broadly than its technical meaning in private law. This expansive interpretation of property rights can be seen in the judgements of the US Supreme Court and German courts, namely the Federal Constitutional Court, Federal Court, and Federal Social Court.

For example, the Fourteenth Amendment to the US Constitution provides: 'nor shall any State deprive any person of life, liberty, or property, without due process of law'. The Supreme Court has, on occasion, ruled that the word 'property' in this provision should be given an expansive interpretation.[96] In the *Goldberg*[97] case, the Supreme Court decided that welfare payments constitute property and termination of welfare receipt without a proper hearing is being denied due process. In another decision the employment expectations of a university teacher who has a tenured post was accepted as property[98] and it was ruled that he is entitled to a hearing before a decision not to renew his appointment. However, it should be noted that these cases are related to the due process clause of the US constitution. The US Supreme Court interprets due process property

---

[96] Harris, J. W., *P&J* p.152.

[97] *Goldberg v. Edwards*, 397 US 254 (1970).

[98] *Perry v. Sinderman*, 408 US 593 (1972).

broader than just compensation property.[99] The Court treats as just compensation property only common law property.[100]

In Germany, although the subjective public rights are not accepted as property rights in private law, they constitute property in the constitutional meaning and benefit from constitutional guarantee.[101] In 1952, the Federal Court of Germany (*Bundesgerichtshof*) decided that to be able to live a free and responsible life as a human being in dignity without being a simple object of the state, a person needs a secure sphere where his property is protected against actions of public authorities. Since public authorities' actions can adversely affect the whole patrimony of individuals, the constitutional guarantee of the property also should include whole patrimony that has economic value.[102] So, if a right has an economic value, regardless of whether it is private or public law right, it should be protected by the constitution. The Federal Constitutional Court also adopted a similar view[103] and expanded the meaning of *Eigentum* to include *rights in personam* (*vertropsposition*) such as debts, money in the bank, shares in companies, etc.[104] Public law claims such as benefits and pension are also under the guarantee of the constitution as long as the claimant contributes to such funds. However, constitutional guarantee protects only existing interests, not expected or possible interests.

The Federal Social Court expanded the meaning of *Eigentum* to a right to open a clinic if the conditions laid down by law are met.[105] Licences necessary to carry out a business also benefit from the constitutional guarantee of the property if they had been issued and began to be used.[106]

There have been some scholarly enterprises to expand the scope of constitutional property clauses. From economic analysis of law[107] to MacPherson's

---

[99] Just compensation property is used here to express the 'takings' clause of the US Constitution included in the Fifth Amendment. See Massey, S.J., "Justice Rehnquist's Theory of Property" (1984) 93 *Yale Law Journal* 541.

[100] *Ibid.* p. 544.

[101] Stücke, A., *Eigentum an Wirtschaftssubventionen* (Berlin, 1991); Leisner, W., *Eigentum Schriften zu Eigentumsrecht und Wirtschaftsverfassung* 1970-1996 (Herausgegeben von Josef Isensee: Berlin, 1996).

[102] Collection of Decisions of the Federal Court in Civil Matters -BGHZ 6, p.270 (278).

[103] See for example Collection of Decisions of the Federal Constitutional Court – BVerfGE 14, 288(299); 22, 241 (253).

[104] Leisner, *op.cit.* 100 p.38.

[105] Collection of Decisions of the Federal Social Court -BSGE 5, 40 (43).

[106] For the constitutional property and jurisprudence of the Federal Constitutional Court in Germany see, Kommers, D. P., *The Constitutional Jurisprudence of the Federal Republic of Germany* (Duke University Press: London, 1997) (Second Edition); Antinori, M. R., "Does Lochner Live in Luxembourg?: An Analysis of The Property Rights Jurisprudence of The European Court of Justice" (1995) 18 *Fordham International Law Journal* 1778.

[107] Demsetz, H.,"The Property Rights Paradigm" (1973) 33 *Journal of Economic History* 16; Calabresi, G. and Mellamed, A. D., "Property Rules, Liability Rules, and Inalienability: One View of the Cathedral" (1972) 85 *Harvard Law Review* 1089: Barzel, Y., *Economic Analysis of Property Rights* (CUP: Cambridge, 1989).

property rhetoric,[108] or to Reich's new property[109] or to Ackerman' s constitutional theory[110] a number of arguments have been offered to expand the scope of property rights to all private law rights without distinguishing whether they are patrimonial or personal rights. As indicated in the last section personality rights should not be considered as property rights. Therefore, such arguments should be rejected. For example, Ackerman proposed that the 'takings' clause of the Fifth Amendment to the US Constitution – 'nor shall private property be taken for public use, without just compensation' – be interpreted expansively to include all regulations restricting the freedom of individuals to use anything. He maintains that ordinary conceptions of property lead to insuperable problems in applying the takings clause. He contends that as a result of the separation of powers all actions of the government should be reviewed by the judiciary. From the point of view of a 'Scientific Policy-Maker' the 'takings' clause can open judges to apply an extraordinarily wide review over the legislative and executive measures. If his approach is accepted the takings clause can turn into a protective blanket over private wealth. But such an approach replaces the concept of human rights with property rights. And property rights lose their context in human rights discourse. The same criticism can also be raised against MacPherson's rhetoric. He claims that all necessities of a fully human life such as income and political rights should be considered as property.

Reich asserted that in modern Western societies most of the wealth is allocated in the form of 'government largesse', for example welfare benefits, government contracts, etc. The discretionary power of government to award, withhold, or terminate this largesse threatens the independence of individuals, therefore the entitlement to this largesse should be considered as property in order to remove the discretionary element. Reich's argument can be accepted as long as those entitlements are understood as cashable rights and constitute elements of one's patrimony. Otherwise, a right to medical care, or a right to free education, etc., cannot be considered as property.

In public international law also, the concept of property is not limited to *rights in rem*. The Permanent Court of International Justice interpreted the concept of property in its widest sense as identical with the concept of vested rights.[111]

---

108 MacPherson, C. B., *Property: Mainstream and Critical Positions* (Blackwell: Oxford, 1978).

109 Reich, C. A., "The New Property" (1964) 73 *Yale Law Journal* 733.

110 Ackerman, B. A., *Private Property and Constitution* (Yale UP, 1977).

111 PCIJ, 12 December 1934, Series A/B No.63 p.88; for a general analysis of property rights in public international law see Norton, P.M., "A Law of the Future or a Law of the Past? Modern Tribunals and The International Law of Expropriation" (1991) 85 *American Journal of International Law* 474; Schachter, "Compensation for Expropriation" (1984) 78 *American Journal of International Law* 121; Jimenez de Arechaga, "State Responsibility for the Nationalization of Foreign Owned Property" (1978) 11 *New York University Journal of International Law and Policy* 179; Dolzer, R., "New Foundations of the Law of Expropriation of Alien Property" (1981) 75 *American Journal of International Law* 553.

For the purposes of this book, property will be defined in terms of patrimonial rights. Since all economic interests of an individual serve to realise his plans and to realise himself as an autonomous person, all the actions of public authorities that adversely affect those interests reduce the possibility of autonomous conduct. Therefore, all the economic interests of individuals should *prima facie* be protected. Any right with regard to a thing should be conceived as property for constitutional purposes. Property protects both use value and exchange value of things. So any act or regulation of a state adversely affecting either the use or exchange value of a thing should be justified. The advantage of the expansive definition is that it gives opportunity to review the legitimacy of the interferences with such economic interests.

2.4. Conclusion

This chapter suggests that constitutional property should be defined independently of a private law definition of property and include all patrimonial rights of a person. Making a distinction between the definition of private law property and constitutional property is not common in legal literature. However, given the differences between aims of private and constitutional laws, such an approach seems appropriate and compatible with the applications of different national high courts such as the American Supreme Court, the German Federal Constitutional Court and the European Court of Human Rights. It is also compatible with the application of public international law.

The patrimony of a person is composed of his entitlements with respect to things. Therefore, the scope of constitutional property is broader than ownership. It includes, *prima facie*, both existing interests in using and exchanging things and legitimate expectations with respect to things. The difference between private property and constitutional property is that the inclusion of constitutional property is much broader than private property. The constitutional property includes both private law contractual rights and some public law rights such as pensions and benefits in addition to private property. However, this definition is a *prima facie* definition. That is, the interests included in property are not absolute. They can be restricted for legitimate purposes.

Constitutional property does not include personality rights. The criterion distinguishing personality rights from patrimonial rights is the actual separability of the things that can be object of the patrimonial rights from personality. In this regard, a significant question about constitutional property is whether one's job is to be considered in one's patrimony and enjoy constitutional protection of property since it is an important element of an individual's wealth in modern societies. Although the American Supreme Court treated one's job position as one's property for the due process clause of the US constitution, it seems difficult to accept one's job as one's property. But patrimonial rights arising from one's job, such as wage or salary, constitute property. For example, if someone loses his job in breach of labour contract, the rights arising from such breach are to be considered as his property within the constitutional context.

Chapter 3

Is Property a Human Right? Moral Justifications for Property Rights

3.1. Introduction

This chapter undertakes a philosophical inquiry about the question of whether property is a human right. Although the concept of human rights is the subject of philosophical controversy,[1] it can be defined as moral rights that all persons have simply by virtue of being human.[2] The basis of human rights is morality. To be able to claim that a right is a human right, one should show that there are sufficiently strong moral reasons that that right should be enjoyed by all human beings. So, the question 'Is property a human right?' can be reformulated as 'Are there valid moral reasons justifying that the right to property should be recognised and protected?' That is, justification of property requires one to put forward a reasonably valid moral argument to the effect that persons should have property rights over things to be upheld, recognised and protected by governments.[3]

Justifications for property, as Becker[4] maintains, can be examined at three different levels: 'general', 'specific', and 'particular' justifications. A general argument for justification of property is always institution-focused.[5] In other words, a general justificatory argument establishes that a system of private property in which everybody can own possessions ought to exist as an institution. On the other hand, specific justificatory arguments give answers to the question of why there ought to be a specific sort of property right (e.g. ownership of land). For example, an argument proposing that copyrights over computer software should be

---

[1]For a general discussion of human rights see for example, Douzinas, C., *The End of Human Rights: Critical Legal Thought at the Turn of the Century* (Hart Publishing: Oxford, 2000); Perry, M. J., *The Idea of Human Rights: Four Inquiries* (OUP: Oxford, 1998); Pennock, J. R. and Chapman, J. W. (eds) *Human Rights* (NOMOS XXIII), (NYUP: New York, 1981); Shestack, J., "The Philosophic Foundations of Human Rights" (1998) 20 *Human Rights Quarterly* 201.

[2] Gewirth, A., "The Basis and Content of Human Rights" in Pennock and Chapman, *op.cit.*1.

[3] Becker, L., *Property Rights: Philosophical Foundations* (Routledge & Kegan Paul: London, 1977) p.22; Becker, "The Moral Basis of Property Rights" [hereinafter Moral] in Pennock, *op.cit.*1.

[4] *Ibid.* p.10.

[5] Harris, J. W., *Property and Justice* [hereinafter *P&J*] (Clarendon Press: Oxford, 1996) p.165.

established is a special justificatory argument. Particular justifications give answers to the question of why a particular person ought to have particular property rights in a particular thing.[6]

However, much of the philosophical and political discourse on justification of property is institution focused. The focus of discussion is whether a system of property is morally required for an autonomous and good life. In this chapter, the inquiry will also revolve around the question of whether existence of a system of private property is necessary for people to live a valuable and dignified life. But, at the same time the arguments put forward to justify a general system of private property also suggest some answers to the questions of what sorts of property rights should exist (specific) and which particular persons should have what particular rights.

Justification of property is an endless job. Since Aristotle, countless arguments have been proposed to justify property. Apparently, many of them include some sound arguments. Nevertheless, none of them has produced a completely satisfactory justification for property rights. Neither will this chapter find the final solution to the question of justification of property. Debate over property rights will probably endure forever. However, this does not mean that property rights cannot be justified. In fact, this chapter suggests that a right to property can be justified and a pluralistic justificatory argument is more responsive to the questions revolving around the institution of private property.

Four different arguments will be examined here: utility and efficiency, labour theory of property, Hegelian personality theory, and political liberty and autonomy. Although they depend on very different moral bases, they are not necessarily separate from each other. As Ryan maintains,[7] they inevitably run into each other. The key concept in this pluralistic theory will be personal autonomy. All four justificatory moral arguments revolve around the concepts of freedom and of autonomy. Three of the elements of pluralistic theory – labour, personality, and autonomy – produce sound arguments in favour of private property and attribute intrinsic value to private property for a valuable and dignified life. Utility argument, on the other hand, also favours the existence of property, but it attributes only instrumental value to the property rights and autonomy in general for maximisation of utility. Thus, it will be given a secondary role to the utility argument in justification of property.

This survey is important in order to understand the philosophy behind the claim that property is one of the human rights, in general, and to understand ideas that underlie the property rights regulation of the First Article of First Protocol (P1-1) to the European Convention on Human Rights, in particular. Although these theories grounded their ideas on different moral bases, they affected the legal documents in different proportion. Examination of these theories provides us with a tool to evaluate why property rights are human rights, what property rights are human rights, and for what purpose and to what extent property rights can be

[6] Becker, *op. cit.* 3 p.23.

[7] Ryan, A. *Property* (Open University Press: Milton Keynes, 1986) p.52.

qualified. So to understand the place of property rights in today's legal and political structure, examination of these theories can be useful.

3.2. Utility Argument for Private Property

One of the justificatory arguments for property rights comes from the utility argument that is one of the most influential theories in Western legal and political thought. The utility argument plays a double role in the regulation of rights, both justificatory and restrictive. Many legal institutions are created for the general interest, and these institutions include some limitation rules grounded on the utility argument.[8] This is so in property rights as well. Property rights can be justified by utilitarian grounds as well as restricted for the sake of general interest or common interest.

Utilitarianism is a moral and political theory that is originated from criticism of natural law theories. Bentham,[9] criticising natural law theory as being unhelpful in offering determinate guidance on moral and political issues, argued that the only proper basis for determining how we should live, what law we should have, and so forth, is the principle of utility. In Bentham's words, 'the greatest happiness of the greatest number' is the main maxim of utilitarianism. There are many different moral and political theories that fall under the general rubric of utilitarianism, but their common feature is that they take the fundamental basis of morality to be the requirement that happiness should be maximised.[10] In essence, utilitarianism is a goal-based argument; its main purpose is to achieve the greatest collective human utility. So, moral and legal rules, according to utilitarianism, are acceptable to the extent that their acceptance and enforcement promotes total or average utility of society.[11] However, what is the utility to be secured is a matter of controversy. A number of definitions offered by distinct utilitarians are pleasure, happiness, welfare, preference satisfaction, and so on.[12]

3.2.1. Justification of Property by Utility

The utilitarian defence of property is the defence of the legal recognition of ownership as an instrument in promoting the greatest happiness. Utilitarians believe that unless individuals have the right to appropriate, use, transfer, and bequeath objects of value or interest, it would be impossible to use the raw materials provided by nature for anything other than the simplest sort of immediate consumption. So, in order to secure the appropriation, use, and transfer of things

---

[8] Simmonds, N.E., *Central Issues in Jurisprudence: Justice, Law, Rights* (Sweet and Maxwell: London, 1996) p.144.

[9] Bentham, J. *An Introduction to the Principles of Morals and Legislation* (OUP: Oxford, 1996).

[10] Simmonds, *op.cit.* 8 p.15.

[11] Ryan, A., *op.cit.* 7 p.53.

[12] Munzer, S.R., *A Theory of Property* (CUP: Cambridge, 1990) p.193.

and, as a result of this, to incite people to work more effectively, the creation of property rights is dictated by utility.[13] There are many variations of the utility argument. But utilitarian justification of property can be examined in two different variants of argument: traditional version and economic version.

The traditional argument defines 'happiness' very broadly, so as to include the whole range of human satisfaction. It maintains that human beings, in order to achieve happiness, which is their ultimate end, need to have private property rights as a rule-governed institution. Utilitarians argue that without securing appropriation, use and disposal of things by a social institution, it is impossible for people to work industriously and as a result, it is impossible to achieve a reasonable degree of happiness. And such a security in possession and use can be provided by a system of property rights. Therefore, a system of property rights is necessary if individuals are to achieve even a reasonable degree of happiness.[14]

This theory is based on the argument that people need to acquire, possess, use and consume things and need a system of property rights to secure these activities to achieve a reasonable degree of happiness. A number of different reasons – security and stability, incentive to productivity, etc. – have been proposed to justify this point.[15] The security argument asserts that to carry out purposeful life human beings need the use of tools and raw materials. A continued availability of the necessary tools and materials is important to predict with greater certainty the success of one's efforts. Since human beings, unlike animals, anticipate the future, they can experience pleasure when their expectations are fulfilled, and experience pain when they are disappointed. If utility is the presence of pleasure and absence of pain, then utility will be promoted by securing persons' expectations with respect to things they possess. Bentham strongly stressed the security principle as the most important subordinate of utility.[16] Some contemporary proponents of utility argument such as Carol Rose[17] also follow the security and stability thesis to justify property rights.

The incentive argument remarks that individual possession of things is more effective than individual use of common possessions to achieve happiness. As Aristotle maintained,[18] individual ownership creates a more thorough and stable community of interests and better promotes efficient, economical, and careful use of things than does common ownership. Without private property institution, a

---

[13] Ryan, A., *op.cit.* 7 p.54.
[14] Becker, *op.cit.* 3 pp.57-58.
[15] Becker, *op.cit.* 3 p.63.
[16] Bentham, J., *The Theory of Legislation* C. K. Odgen (ed.) (Littleton: London: 1987).
[17] Rose, C., *Property and Persuasion: Essays on the History, Theory and Rhetoric of Ownership* (Westview Press: Oxford, 1994); Rose, C., "Property and Expropriation: Themes and Variations in American Law" (2000) *Utah Law Review* 1: Rose, C., "Property as the Keystone Right?" (1996) 71 *Notre Dame Law Review* 329.
[18] Aristotle, *Politics*, Book II, chapter 5 in Richard McKeon, (ed.) *The Basic Works of Aristotle* (Random House: New York, 1941), p.1151.

society could not achieve increases in totality of social wealth because there would be neither incentive to creative work nor market.[19]

Utilitarians argue that a coercive institution with respect to acquisition, possession, use, and consumption of things is a necessary proponent of utility argument because otherwise the selfishness of human beings, their limited generosity and relative scarcity of desirable goods available for acquisition make the stability impossible. If security of possession or use, and control of acquisition require a system of property rights, then property rights are needed to guarantee the stability for as long as one's purposes require. And also, since the people who work to acquire things or who labour to make things more useful or pleasing would not be happy if they were not guaranteed to get their labour's consequences, security of possession and control of acquisition is required.[20]

Therefore, a system of property rights is necessary as a general justification because property satisfies the need for security in possessions, and allows the natural incentive to labour to succeed.[21] The argument produces the conclusion that some property rights in some things are necessary. To decide what sort of property rights people should have, first one has to determine what sort of things people need to acquire, use, and consume in order to achieve a reasonable degree of happiness. Second, one needs to determine what sorts of property rights are necessary to meet human needs. And third, one has to show that denying people what they need or want, in the absence of showing that the denial is necessary for some countervailing good, is unjustifiable.

The economic version of utility argument claims that the traditional arguments are far from guiding to political and legal theory because of the difficulty of measuring human happiness (felicific calculus) and the difficulty of interpersonal comparisons and suggests an economic analysis to make utility arguments more rigorous.[22]

Their main contribution to the theory is a definition of the concept of value. Economic analysis assumes that a human being is a rational maximiser of his satisfaction.[23] What someone wants is, by definition, what he wants to pay for – either money or the deployment of some other resources that he has, such as time and effort. That is, a thing has value for a person when that person values it. How much value a thing has for a given person is said to be measured by the maximum that person would be willing to pay to get it, or alternatively, the minimum the person would be willing to take to give it up. They have made value measurable by money and they assume that this will not be a serious difficulty for a discussion of property rights.[24]

---

[19] Harris, J. W., *P&J*, p.279.
[20] Becker, L., *Moral* p.65.
[21] Ryan, *op.cit.* 7 p.56.
[22] Harris, J. W., *Legal Philosophies* (second edition) (Butterworths: London, 1997) p.46.
[23] See Posner, R., *Economic Analysis of Law* (fifth edition) (Aspen: New York, 1998); Barzel, Y., *Economic Analysis of Property Rights* (CUP: Cambridge, 1989); Demsetz, H., "Toward A Theory of Property Rights" (1967) 57 *American Economic Review* 347.
[24] Becker, *op.cit.* 3 p. 68.

Economists offer two arguments for the general justification of a system of property rights. The first one argues that when the total cost of external disutilities of non-ownership use or enjoyment of a scarce good becomes greater than the costs involved in creating and maintaining a system of ownership rights which minimises such externalities, then that system of property rights is justified by considerations of utility. External disutilities, here, means the sum of the costs of the disutilities – frustration of purpose, lost opportunities – created for each by the actions of others. This argument is sound as long as the dominant guiding principle is one of minimising costs. The second general argument is related to allocative transactions. Since in the case of the non-existence of property rights the transactions related to the resources used for the production of goods would not be safe and easy, such transactions would not maximise the total of individual satisfactions. So to maximise the total of satisfactions, stabilisation of allocative transactions must be provided by property rights.

Economic analysis, in place of Bentham's idea of the greatest happiness of the greatest number, offers a technical concept of 'efficiency' at the level of specific and particular justification in order to avoid interpersonal comparisons of utility.[25]

Economists distinguish the allocation of recourses used for the production of goods from the distribution of goods produced. And a good allocation is typically called efficient, and a good distribution is typically called just and fair. How can the concept of efficiency be applied as a criterion of social choice? Because efficiency invokes individual welfare rather than social welfare across individuals, efficient allocations and just distributions are defined by reference to special concepts of Pareto optimality and Pareto superiority and Kaldor-Hicks efficiency. To decide which policy is efficient, each of these concepts compares proposed systems in terms of the allocation of resources to produce individual welfare. According to this, a system is Pareto superior to the previous one if at least one person increases in welfare and no one decreases in welfare.[26] Pareto superiority is a situation in which, after a change in allocation or distribution, at least one person believes he is better off by it while no one believes that he is worse off.[27] And lastly, a new system is Kaldor-Hicks efficient if those whose welfare increases could fully compensate those whose welfare diminishes, so that at least one individual has an increase in welfare.[28] Since economists assess value subjectively according to people's preferences, definitions of optimality and superiority here depend on that subjective value concept as well. Whether people believe that they will be better off, worse off, or the same under any proposed change is measured by their willingness to pay for the change, or to agree to it only if they are paid for it. According to this, for example, a reallocation is efficient if, after negotiated compensations have been promised by those who stand to gain from the proposal to those who stand to lose by it. Conversely, a reallocation is

---

[25] Harris, *op.cit.* 22 p.47.
[26] Munzer, *op.cit.* 12 p.198.
[27] Becker, *op.cit.* 3 p.70.
[28] Munzer, *op.cit.* 12 p.199.

inefficient if gainers from that change believe that they have to pay more than their gain or if losers believe that they cannot get adequate compensation for their loss. In the same way a redistribution is just when the price gainers are willing to pay is equal to the price losers are willing to accept.[29] As can be seen, each of these criteria of efficiency yields only ordinal, not cardinal or interpersonally comparable rankings. That is they can tell us which situation is better, but not how much better.[30]

Some points need to be indicated about the use of these definitions. First, these definitions are embedded in an 'ideal market model' of economic transactions in which all participants are rational maximisers of their own values, all participants are 'perfect competitors' – that is, no one is able, by unilateral action, or by intentional multilateral action, to influence the price of goods – and in which transaction costs are zero – that is, in which it costs nothing to persuade others to behave rationally and come to know and act upon their own rational self interest.

Second, when these materials have been used at the level of specific justification, they have been applied to a wide range of problems raised by property rights. Liability rules governing the use of property, zoning regulations and the issue of just compensation are examples. Of course, in all legal activities, these matters cannot be evaluated in adequate detail, but these materials can make it possible to make some useful general observations about economic arguments for specific justification. But still the difficulty of measurement survives – who can measure interpersonal welfare changes and how? And when the measurement, if possible, should take place? That is, are the long-term or short-term effects of a system's changes to be considered?

Third, when these materials are used to construct social policies with regard to property rights, most of the justificatory weight must be borne by non-economic or meta-economic principles of a frankly normative sort principle of justice for example. So, these economic analyses alone cannot settle the question of specific justification.[31]

Munzer, as an element of his pluralist theory, proposes a combined principle of utility and efficiency.[32] The combined principle maintains that property rights should be allocated so as to maximise utility regarding the use, possessions, transfer and so on of things and to maximise efficiency regarding the use, possession, transfer and so on of things.

3.2.2. Evaluation of Utility Arguments

Utilitarianism does not distinguish very readily between the need for property and the need for private property.[33] It can justify both public property and private

[29] Becker, *op.cit.* 3 p.70.
[30] Munzer, *op.cit.* 12 p.200.
[31] Becker, *op.cit.* 3 p.71.
[32] Munzer, *op.cit.* 12 pp.191 ff.
[33] Ryan, *op.cit.* 7 p.56.

property. If people prefer some public services to be conducted by public bodies, the principle of utility justifies public ownership of necessary goods to carry out those services. Or if some plausible empirical assumptions are made about people's preferences, such as propositions that people prefer to have intimate articles as a basis for personality, a range of personal goods such as control, privacy, and individuality, and an opportunity to develop such beneficial character traits, it justifies the private ownership of things. But in these cases, to say that people 'should have property rights' is to say that utility and efficiency support making them available to people generally through the operation of an appropriate economic system, not that every person must have such rights or that no person may reject them.[34]

As for the question of whether utility says something about distribution of private property, utilitarianism is not directly concerned with how welfare is distributed; its main concern is with the maximisation of welfare, with how much there is in total.[35] If a utilitarian is faced with a choice between two policies by one of which welfare is equally distributed and by the other of which gross inequalities of welfare exist, he will simply choose that policy by which the sum total of welfare is higher.

However, it is not true to think that because the distribution of welfare does not concern the utilitarian, he is also not concerned with questions of how wealth, resources, and opportunities should be distributed.[36] On the contrary, it can be said that the utilitarian, given some plausible assumptions, favours a moderately equal distribution. One assumption which requires moderate egalitarianism is the diminishing marginal utility of money and other material goods to satisfy preferences. Another one is that wide differences in wealth produce preference-dissatisfaction in those who are least well-off. A third assumption is that, if inequalities of wealth involve unequal ownership of productive resources, and if this unequal ownership spawns alienation, exploitation, severe problems of production, or large differences in economic power, then intense preference-dissatisfaction arises. As a result, if one is building a theory of property, one should include appropriate mechanisms to institute and maintain a moderately equal distribution. Utility argument, however, does not say what mechanisms are required. A combination of taxes and redistributive programs may be an answer.[37]

Given some assumptions, the principle of utility favours some private property institutions, as long as those institutions increase the total sum of wealth and preference-satisfaction. For example, if modern corporation and its relation to public and private ownership are assessed under the utility argument, it can be said that the unique aim of corporation, profit maximisation, can be supported by utility principle insofar as greater productivity yields a greater capacity to satisfy human preferences. Or as an another example, if there are great wealth inequalities in a society, and these inequalities persist because of inadequate taxation of gratuitous

---

[34] Munzer. *op.cit.* 12 pp. 209-212.
[35] Simmonds, *op.cit.* 8 p.31.
[36] *Ibid.* p.32.
[37] Munzer, *op.cit.* 12 p. 214.

transfers, the principle of utility, assuming that these inequalities of wealth cause decline of overall satisfaction, favours heavier taxes on gifts and inheritances. Many other property related issues can be assessed under the light of principle of utility such as land reforms, housing problems and so on.[38] So, principle of utility can shed light on designing institutions which permit private ownership. In the same way, it can also favour some specific rules of private law. For example, assuming that if people are free to act as they wish with respect to their property, they will likely better satisfy their preferences, it furnishes a general reason for making liberty a prominent feature of institution of private property.

3.2.3. Criticisms of Utility Argument

Can utility argument justify property rights as human rights? Defining human rights as the moral rights of each person by virtue of being human, as an autonomous agent, the question can be reformulated as 'Can utilitarianism justify any moral right?'[39] Utilitarians attribute an instrumental value to the rights rather than an intrinsic value. Rules of utilitarian institutions confer rights, not because of each person's own needs of agency, but for utilitarian grounds or reasons, focused on the requirements of maximising utility. So, rules' ascription of rights is derivative and calculative in a way. Since the primary aim of utilitarian rules is to maximise utility overall, the way in which rights get distributed is always worked out with a view not simply to the individual person's needs of agency, but rather to the production of the greatest total or average amount of goods. Thus there is always the possibility that rules as well as actions justified by utilitarian calculus may require removing rather than protecting goods that belong to individuals as a matter of their moral rights when such removal serves to maximise utility overall. The calculus may require using some persons only as means for others, without regard to the former's own rights.[40] In other words, utilitarian arguments are reversible, that is, since all justifications rest on a consideration of consequences, consequences may force a reconsideration of what is being justified.[41] It can be said that only in a certain limited sense can utilitarianism be held to justify any moral rights. It ignores the distinctness of individuals, and defines the rights in terms of goods, as Rawls maintains.[42]

If a distinction is drawn between essential and accidental justifications, utilitarian justifications of moral rights are only accidental, because the aggregative grounds on which they are based do not directly make reference to the moral value of an individual. Even if the utilitarian calculation comes out in such a way as to justify rules or institutions that require that each individual should have a moral right, this is an accidental result. It is not based directly on what each individual

[38] *Ibid.* p. 216.

[39] Gewirth, A., "Can Utilitarianism Justify any Moral Right" in *Human Rights: Essays on Justification and Application* (Chicago: The University of Chicago Press, 1984).

[40] *Ibid.* p.154.

[41] Ryan, *op.cit.* 7 p.59.

[42] Rawls, J. *A Theory of Justice* (Revised edition) (Oxford: Clarendon Press, 1999) p. 95.

must have in order to fulfil his needs of agency.[43] Rights are justified by utilitarianism only insofar as they may be instrumental in fulfilling the duties incumbent on all individuals and on government to promote or maximise utility. So, utilitarianism gives rights a role subordinate to the maximising of total utility. To sum up even if utilitarianism and other aggregative and collectivist theories attribute some rights to individuals, their possession of these objects is rendered much less direct and normatively less sure because it is derivative from and contingent on broader social goods.

As a conclusion, the utilitarian justification of property rights is accidental and derivative. It cannot guarantee for every individual stable property rights, since it ignores the distinctiveness of individuals. Individuals' rights can always be overridden by considerations about the aggregation or maximising of utility. Therefore, utilitarianism standing alone cannot give a satisfactory justification for private property rights as human rights. But it can be considered as a part of a more comprehensive moral theory that justifies and protects private property rights for every individual.

3.3. Natural Right to Property and Labour

The core of the labour theory is the idea that people are entitled to hold property, whatever they produce by their own initiative, intelligence, and industry. This idea was enunciated by John Locke firstly in the context of natural rights theory.[44] Locke's ultimate aim related to property was the protection of private property rights against arbitrary governmental interference. His ideas' basis was that rights of private property are among the rights that men bring with them into political society and for whose protection society is set up.[45] Government and other people should respect property rights of the individual because he gained them by his labour in the state of nature before society is established by social contract. That is, labour is the basis of just property acquisition. Locke's idea found a place for itself in later human rights documents (American and French Declarations). Some other theories, similar to Locke's but slightly modified to meet critics, have been put forwarded to defend private property by later philosophers such as Mill[46] and Nozick.[47] Here mainly Locke's theory will be examined to see to what extent it can justify private property rights. However, Nozick's and Mill's contributions will be evaluated within their context.

---

[43] Gewirth, *op.cit.* 39 p.155.

[44] Becker, *op.cit.* 3 p. 32.

[45] Locke, J., *Two Treatise of Government*, Peter Laslett (ed.) (CUP: Cambridge, 1988) p.138.

[46] Mill, J. S., *Principles of Political Economy: With Some of Their Applications to Social Policy*, in J. M. Robson (ed.) *Collected Works of John Stuart Mill* (Routledge and Kegan Paul: London, 1965).

[47] Nozick, R., *Anarchy, State and Utopia* (Basic Books: New York, 1974).

3.3.1. Natural Right to Property

In order to understand how property rights are natural rights we need to look at what a natural right is. The concept of 'natural rights' precedes the concept of 'human rights'. Here it will be used as a synonym of human rights. According to Hart,[48] a natural right has two important characteristics. First, a natural right 'is one which all men have if they are capable of choice, they have it *qua* men not only if they are members of some society or stand in some special relation to each other'. Second, a natural right 'is not created or conferred by men's voluntary action'. Thus, a natural right is not created by law, or convention, but exists independently of human action. As Dworkin[49] points out, to believe in natural rights is simply to take the protection of certain individual choices as fundamental. Or in Harris' words[50] 'natural rights are such rights as follow from the interaction between the formal and substantive requirements of just treatment and the facts of the world'. These definitions of natural rights are not different from our definition of human rights at the beginning of this chapter. Then, how are property rights natural rights? Can a relationship arise between a person and a thing such that, independently of social convention or positive legal provision, that person ought to be conceded by others' ownership use privileges and control powers over that thing?[51] According to Locke, the answer should be 'yes'. In Locke's idea private property rights are natural rights – not in the sense that men are born with them, but in the sense that, though they are acquired rights, they are acquired as a result of actions and transactions that men undertake on their own initiative and not by virtue of the operation of any civil framework of positive rules vesting those rights in them. The account of how and why these special rights of private property arise out of such actions and transactions is the basis of Locke's account of the moral importance of the duty to respect property holdings.[52]

3.3.2. Appropriation of Property by Labour in the State of Nature

Locke claims that private property rights are possible apart from government and positive law. He maintains that there are principles of natural justice that govern property holdings and these can be deployed critically against any government that threatens to interfere with or redistribute the property of citizens. To this end, he argues that property owning got under way at a time when there was no government, and that the function or end of government is to protect property holdings that it has not itself constituted.

Then what is the principle of natural justice governing property holdings? Locke explains his ideas referring to an assumed state of nature. In Locke's theory,

---

[48] Hart, H. L. A., "Are There Any Natural Rights" in J. Waldron, *Theories of Rights* (OUP: Oxford, 1984) p.77.

[49] Dworkin, R. *Taking Rights Seriously* (Duckworth: London, 1977) p. 177.

[50] Harris, *P&J* p.182.

[51] *Ibid.* p.182.

[52] Waldron, J., *A Right to Private Property* (Clarendon Press: Oxford, 1988) p. 138.

there is a strong theological reasoning. He bases his ideas on Commands of God. Accordingly, the world with all its fruits and benefits is created for the use of humankind. God intends as many of us as possible to survive and requires us to carry out that purpose, and therefore, God has commanded us to labour for our subsistence. Though these are Commands of God, they can be inferred by our instincts and reason, that is, these are natural.[53] In these conditions, what is the meaning of the world being created for all? Is it an original communism in which each individual was conceived to have inseverable, inalienable, and imprescriptible claim-rights in common with the rest of humankind to the use of each and every resource? (If so, it is impossible to develop a private property theory.) Or, is it an original communism in which individuals have alienable claim-rights in common? (If so, a private property theory can be developed only by everybody's consent.) Or, is it an original communism as a system of pure liberties, involving no claim-rights at all? That is, original communism meant an absence of private property rights in resources when they were created.

Locke's conception of original communism is closer to the last one, rather than the second. He does not believe that God's original gift to human beings establishes inalienable and imprescriptible common rights in relation to every use that could be mode of every resource. On the contrary, he believes that it is possible for an individual by his actions to exclude the common rights of other persons.[54] However, he does not believe that original communism should be thought of as a right-vacuum awaiting the acts of acquisition that would establish exclusive rights. Since in his view, each individual has a duty and right to self-preservation, s/he is endowed in common from birth with certain determinate claim rights.

Locke believes that appropriation is necessary for the satisfaction of individual needs because appropriation yields more industriousness.[55] Although the world is created for human beings in common, it cannot remain common forever since God gave it to them for their benefit or use. But how is private property created? What distinguishes the appropriator from the rest of mankind, who originally had common rights in the resources he has appropriated? Which crucial action in the process of appropriation creates moral title for the appropriator over the thing appropriated? Since by the vindication of appropriation everyone's moral position would be altered – the appropriator acquires rights and powers, and everyone else duties that they did not have before – something that has been done must have made a big moral difference.[56]

Sidestepping consent theory that requires a common consent to acquire ownership over a common good, Locke proposes the labour theory as a justificatory reason. According to his argument, the justificatory base of private property is labour – the energetic initiative of man. Locke explains how previously common good becomes the property of someone in particular by labour theory. His

---

[53] Locke, I § 86.
[54] Locke, II§ 27.
[55] Locke, II § 37.
[56] Waldron, *op.cit.* 52 p.172.

theory attempts to connect a man's right to the resources he has appropriated with the rights that he has in relation to himself and his actions. The first labourer gains ownership of a resource and thereafter it is always dealt with as private property. Since the second labourer is not dealing with common goods, he cannot commit an act of appropriation in the same sense. Locke's labour theory of appropriation is not simply a first occupancy argument. Although his theory is more or less coextensive with the first occupancy, with regard to the fruits and animals of earth, the difference is especially important in the case of land. According to Locke, simply marking is not enough to appropriate land. A person must work in order to appropriate it.[57]

3.3.3. Justification of Property by Labour

In literature three different versions of labour theory have been proposed:[58] self-ownership and mixing one's labour with resources, creation-without-wrong, and the labour-desert version. Although it seems difficult to separate elements of labour theory without distorting its inner logic, examination of these elements separately seems easier.

Self-ownership rhetoric is the core of Locke's theory of appropriation and justification of his labour theory. The justification proceeds in two stages. Firstly, Locke expands a theory of self-ownership – a man has exclusive property in his person – to his actions, and his labour. Secondly, there is an account of how the force of this property right is transferred to the appropriated resources – this is Locke's theory of mixing one's labour.[59]

This justification argues that if someone is not a slave, nobody else owns his body but he owns himself. Consequently, the labour of his body and work of his hands are also his property. Whenever someone, by his labour, changes a thing from its natural state to make it more useful or beneficial to him, he has mixed his labour with it, that is, joined to it something that is his own. For this labour being the unquestionable property of the labourer, no one but he can have a right to what that is once joined to. This is so at least where there is enough and as good left in common for others and where what one takes is no more than one can use.[60]

Harris does not accept the last premise in this version. He argues that if mixing one's labour creates property rights, why should it matter that there might

---

[57] Locke, II § 27.

[58] Becker, *op.cit.* 3 pp. 33 ff; Becker, "Acquisition of Property by Labour" 73 *The Journal of Philosophy* (1976); Harris, *P&J* p.189.

[59] 'Though the earth and all inferior creatures be common to all Men, yet every man has a Property in his own person. This is nobody has any right to but himself. The Labour of his body, and the work of his hands, we may say, are properly his. Whatsoever then he removes act of the State that Nature Hath provided, ... he hath mixed Labour with, and joyned to it something that is his own, and thereby makes his Property. It being by him removed from the common state Nature placed it in, hath by this labour something annexed to it, that excludes the common right of other Men.' Locke, II §27.

[60] Becker, *op.cit.* 3 p.33.

not be enough and as good for others or why should the owner be answerable to others if he chooses to spoil what is his?[61] But it seems that Locke inserted these provisos in his theory to strengthen the morality of the theory of acquisition, and to explain why an individual can acquire a common good without consent. But in the end, this version of the theory, with or without these provisos, fails to justify property rights. This formulation can be criticised in three steps excluding sufficiency and spoilation provisos: self-ownership; labour as a commodity; and mixing labour with resources.

Firstly, self-ownership rhetoric is used in two meanings: to express bodily-use freedom principle and to provide a justificatory argument for property institutions.[62] Leaving aside the former, we are going to examine the thoughts of philosophers who propose the latter usage. Beginning with the premise of self-ownership, they move to the conclusion that every individual has a natural right to own the fruits of his or her labour. Besides Locke, Nozick also appeals to the self-ownership argument for natural property as part of his critique of redistributive taxation. Nozick, by running back the steps in the above formulation, reaches the conclusion that if someone's fruits of labour is seized from him this is equivalent to forcing him to work for others, that is it makes him a slave.[63] But since the abolition of slavery, human beings have been removed from the property agenda. Individuals have personality rights, rather than property rights, over their bodies.

Secondly, owning labour, the second step of formulation, is also a controversial issue. Is labour (action) a commodity that can be the subject matter of property rights? As examined in the last chapter labour cannot be separated from personality and, therefore, cannot be accepted as a commodity that can be the subject matter of property.[64] Waldron remarks that self-ownership and the ownership of actions in Locke's theory can be interpreted as a right to personal liberty.[65] Locke connects a man's property in his person with his 'being master of himself'. This interpretation seems plausible. But there is no need for self-ownership rhetoric to vindicate autonomy and freedom.

The third step, mixing one's labour with resources is also very controversial. Locke's theory claims that the labourer, by adding something (labour) which he owns to an object, gains ownership over that object because that object contains something which the labourer owns. So, taking the object out of the labourer's control without his consent is a way of taking his labour from him without his consent; it therefore amounts to violation of the right of the labourer over his labour. Therefore, no one may take the object from the labourer without his consent and the object is his property.

It is questionable how an action (labouring) can be mixed with a material.[66] Even if this objection can be refuted, then as Nozick[67] maintains why

---

61 Harris, *P&J* p. 198.
62 *Ibid.* p.189.
63 Nozick, *op.cit.* 47 p.174.
64 See Chapter 2 above.
65 Waldron, *op.cit.* 52 p.183.
66 *Ibid.* p.190.

should anyone think that mixing one's labour with a thing is a way of making the thing one's own, rather than a way of losing one's labour? And why does the labourer gain ownership of the whole object rather than just the value his labour added? Locke thinks that the proportion of value labour produced is definitely much more than the value nature produced. He goes on to estimate the extent of the difference that labour makes. He argues that the major proportion (9/10 or 99/100) of the goods useful to the life of human beings is the effect of labour.[68] When this argument is evaluated together with sufficiency and spoilation provisos, we can see that Locke wants to justify appropriation of common resources without consent.[69] If he can show that labour makes for the greatest part of the value of things, then anyone complaining about exclusion by an appropriator can be accused of desiring almost nothing but the benefit of another's pain. And if a labourer does not work and produce the value, the good would not occur. So, others lose nothing by appropriation of the resources by labour. This is especially plausible in the case of land because if an appropriator did not cultivate the land it would be a waste ground. But this argument can justify enclosure of goods only in the age of plenty. But still the labour theory of value is historically an important claim, since it influenced the labour theories of value by Adam Smith and Marx, although their theories concern exchange value whereas Locke's theory is a use value.[70]

Some idealist and personality interpretations of Locke's account of property have been proposed in order to avoid the consent problem. But none of them has produced a sound explanation.[71]

To sum up, self-ownership rhetoric and the mixing-labour version of labour theory, in its original position, fail to justify the private acquisition of property. But it can be utilised from its arguments to develop a private property theory. Especially if its self-ownership and labour-ownership premises are interpreted as personal autonomy and freedom and its labour theory of value can be vindicated, by combining these with other premises that are going to be examined next, a justificatory theory for private property can be developed. At the end of this section, such an argument will be suggested.

The second version of labour theory is creation-without-wrong argument. This argument has been formulated by Harris[72] on the basis of sufficiency and spoilation provisos of Locke. These provisos require, first, that property right arises 'at least where there is enough and as good left in common for others'.[73] And secondly, that it applies only to 'as much as any one can make use of to any advantage of life before it spoils'.[74] Harris claims that if the labourer gains

---

[67] Nozick, *op.cit.* 47 p. 175.
[68] Locke II § 40.
[69] Waldron, *op.cit.*52 p.192.
[70] *Ibid.* p.191.
[71] See for example, Olivecrona, K., "Locke's Theory of Appropriation" *Philosophical Quarterly*, 24 (1974); Tully, J., *A Discourse on Property: John Locke and his Adversaries* (CUP: Cambridge, 1980).
[72] Harris, *P&J* p.197.
[73] Locke, II § 27.
[74] *Ibid.* § 31.

ownership of what is created as a result of self-ownership, these limitations are meaningless. So, he argues that a distinct argument is possible. But, in Locke's formulation the separation of the provisos from the self-ownership argument does not seem possible, because Locke needs these provisos to justify the moral appropriation of common goods without consent. However, it is necessary to remember that these provisos are valid only for the situations of appropriation of a thing common to all. That is, this theory mainly considers the original appropriation of land and other natural resources. So, if someone creates without using any natural resources, these provisos are not applicable. For example, if someone composes a song, or paints a picture using some simple materials, there is no need to investigate whether he left enough and as good to others.

How can these Lockean provisos be interpreted? If it is thought that when someone takes resources by labouring on them, he must leave behind enough resources of the same quality for others to appropriate, then nobody may appropriate unless everybody can. Or does Locke mean that once there has ceased to be enough left for everybody, unilateral appropriation is no longer a sufficient bases for exclusive property; it must now be underwritten by consent?[75] The latter approach seems plausible. Locke probably means that, in an age of scarcity, unilateral appropriation of natural resources cannot be justified, whereas it is possible in an age of plenty. For example, as indicated in the last chapter, an abundant resource such as a domain name on the internet can be appropriated without the consent of others (political society). But a scarce thing such as a radio wave frequency cannot be appropriated unilaterally and consent is required (a licence for example).

Locke claims that appropriation of private property is possible without consent on the condition that the products must not be spoiled or wasted. If a labourer does not properly use a resource, it becomes common again. But his concept of use is very broad. It is use to any advantage of life. Then, the meaning of spoilation or waste in Locke's theory is the negligent or deliberate loss of use value of the product without use. This proviso does not generate any quantitative limit to human possessions. The amount a person can appropriate is determined not by this proviso, but by the amount of labour he is capable of expending and by the various modes of use and consumption that are open to him.[76] But with the growth of a money economy, this proviso has lost its quantitative delimiting character, although qualitatively its terms remain the same; appropriate as much as you can with your labour, but do not let anything perish uselessly in your possession. Harris argues that this spoilation proviso serves as a guarantee underpinning the 'enough and as good' limitation.[77]

Mill[78] proposes a labour argument for the appropriation of property without making reference to the self-ownership rhetoric. He proposes his argument for the real world of scarcity rather than for a supposed state of nature. According

---

[75] Waldron, *op.cit.* 52 p.216.
[76] *Ibid.* p. 209.
[77] Harris, *P&J*, p.198.
[78] Mill, *op.cit.* 46 pp.199 ff.

to Mill, the fundamental justification for the institution of private property is the right of producers to what they themselves have produced. This principle is applicable to all kinds of goods other than land.[79] It is inapplicable to the raw material of the earth – land – because no one made the land and appropriation of it by some necessarily left others bereft of what was the original inheritance of the whole species.[80] Mill gives the essential justificatory role of private property to labour and he tries to explain all issues around it. According to him, the current inequalities in property holding are the result of former labour. In fact, he does not defend the inequalities that arise because of inheritance and gifts. For him, the unowned advantage of those who have inherited the savings of others over the industrious whose predecessors have not left them anything should be curtailed, as much as is consistent with justice to those who thought fit to dispose of their savings by giving them to their descendants.

In Mill's view, ownership of land is justifiable as long as labour requires it. It is only valid, in so far as the proprietor is its improver. His main justification for land is that in order to cultivate land, the appropriator labours on it (to clear land, buildings, fences) and the fruits of his industry cannot be reaped in a short period. The labour and outlay are immediate, but the benefit is spread over many years, perhaps over all future time.[81] However, this right is not as strong as ownership of movables.[82] His justification for land ownership can be seen as a kind of economic utilitarian argument.

His argument supposes that once the institution of property is adopted, producers have a natural right to what they produce. His reason is the creation-without-wrong argument. According to Mill, if someone produces something without breaching others' actual rights, he has a natural right to exclude others from using it.

A version of the creation-without-wrong argument can also be found in Nozick.[83] According to his entitlement theory a property holding is just only if it is acquired in conformity with one of the just acquisition, just transfer, or rectification principles. Though he does not attempt to define what is the principle of just acquisition, he contends that Locke's 'enough and as good' proviso can be stated in such a way as to yield the principle of just acquisition. So long as the appropriation did not make other people worse off, all things considered, than they would have been had it not occurred, then the appropriation is just; and making this comparison one may take into account all the familiar incentive and market instrumental advantages of private property institutions.[84] But Nozick's argument is far from providing a justification to any natural right to ownership. He does not give any answer to the question, worse off than what?

---

79 *Ibid.* p.217.
80 *Ibid.* p. 227.
81 *Ibid.* p.227.
82 *Ibid.* pp. 230-31.
83 Nozick, *op.cit.* 47 p.180.
84 *Ibid.* pp.175-82.

To sum up, creation-without-wrong argument can be formulated as follows: if a person (1) creates a new item of social wealth, and (2) wrongs no one in doing so, it follows that he ought to be accorded ownership of that new item.[85]

Harris argues that the scope of the creation-without-wrong argument is drastically reduced by the social character of labour.[86] This criticism is right if the production is confined to goods. But if it is evaluated in a wide sense to include any value demanded in the market, it still has a wide application scope.

Harris proposes another objection to this argument. He claims that this argument suffers from a fatal flaw; it presupposes a unilateral power to create new trespassory rules.[87] He maintains that the labourer can only become an owner if new trespassory rules are brought into existence protecting his ownership interests. Otherwise, he cannot prevent others' use of the new product. Becker puts the same objection in a different way. He says that property confers the rights to the owner and duties to others, so these duties constitute a loss of liberty for others.[88] These objections are nothing more than a reformulation of Proudhon's question 'Who set you the tasks and by what right do you demand payment from us for labour which we did not impose on you?'[89]

These objections are valid only for the acquisition of natural resources which are originally common for all and scarce. But if natural resources are abundant, or the product is produced without using any natural resource, why cannot the producer prevent others from using his product? It is the right of the labourer to ask 'I worked and took pain for it, why should you benefit from it?' Morality exists independently of human contracts. Therefore, a newborn baby does not need to contract with all other individuals to prevent them assaulting him. As soon as he is born, morality requires others not to assault him. It is obvious that the new born baby does not need to ask consent of all other persons before he was born not to suffer interference with his personality and bodily integrity rights. Can it be asked of the baby 'Who called you to come to the world, why should we respect your rights?' Then why should the creator of a thing not prevent others from interfering with it?

One other objection to this argument comes from Becker.[90] He argues that, acquiring property by labour, the industrious gains competitive advantages over the non-industrious. And he supports his idea by referring to the language of work ethic. He maintains that the concept of 'industrious' substitutes the terms 'aggressive', 'intelligent', and 'strong'; and the concept of 'non-industrious' substitutes the terms 'passive', 'unintelligent', and 'weak'. And he asks, 'Why should the aggressive inherit the earth, after all?' This objection can be refuted by arguing that if people inherit some different characteristics by birth, it is not the task of law to remove these differences. For example, some people are genetically

---

85 Harris, *P&J*, p.197.
86 *Ibid.* p.202.
87 *Ibid.* p.202.
88 Becker, *op.cit.* 3 p.44.
89 Proudhon, J., *What is Property?* (Howard Fertig: New York, 1966) p.84.
90 Becker, *op.cit.* 3 p.45.

tall and others short. A tall one has the advantage of playing basketball well. Should the law wipe these differences out to provide equal opportunity? If it is assumed that playing basketball is a good, does justice require tall ones be shortened? This objection presumes that the only good or fundamental good is having property, so it thinks that if people's worth is equal, they should have equal property or income. But this is misleading; for some people the ultimate aim is to lay down and drink beer and watch TV, for others the ultimate good is fame, for some others to travel all over the world, for others to invent something, for others to compose a song and for some others to earn as much money as possible. So why should only the ones who work for money share their goods with others? And lastly, it is not always true that the intelligent, strong, and aggressive people are rich while passive, unintelligent and weak ones are poor.

Harris argues that the creation-without-wrong argument constitutes a justification only for fruits. That is if someone creates something from a thing which is originally his, this argument can justify the ownership of the new item. So, it constitutes a property-specific justice reason internal to the operation of property institution.[91] But since we indicated above the acquisition of property by a producer over the value he produced does not constitute unilateral creation of trespassory rules, it can be said that this argument also constitutes a general justificatory reason, especially for intellectual property rights.

Another version of labour theory is the desert argument. Harris[92] formulates the core of this argument as follows; if a person by his labour confers benefit on others, he deserves to be rewarded with property. This argument is a natural right argument since it focuses on the actions of individuals and produces conclusions about what, in justice, is due to individuals.[93]

Traces of the desert argument can be found in both Locke and Mill. Locke adds to his arguments the observation that 'he who appropriates land to himself by his labour does not lessen but increases the common stock of mankind'.[94] And when Mill proffers a general critique of contemporary property institutions, he makes passing references to the mismatch between meritorious work and reward.[95] But some modern property theorists such as Becker,[96] Munzer[97] and Harris accept the desert principle as the core argument for founding just property claims on labour.

Becker sees the right to property as a reward for a virtuous act. He claims that the case of a person's adding value to the world, in the sense of discovering, inventing, or improving something which helps others, can be the basis for a desert claim. He formulates this idea as follows. A person who, in some morally permissible way, and without being morally required to do so, 'adds value' to

---

[91] Harris, *op.cit.* 22 p. 204.
[92] *Ibid.* p. 204.
[93] Harris, *op.cit.* 22 p.205.
[94] Locke, II § 37.
[95] Mill, *op.cit.* 46 pp.203-9.
[96] Becker, *op.cit.* 3 pp.46-54.
[97] Munzer, *op.cit.* 12 pp.256-87.

others' lives deserves some benefit for it.[98] But his claim is not acceptable because he argues that a labouring work is morally valuable only if it benefits others and deserves rewards. His notion of reward also can be criticised, because property rights to the value produced by labour is a natural entitlement not a reward for labour.

Munzer's argument does not include either the requirement that the product should benefit others or the notion of reward. He examines labour-desert theory in a two-stage inquiry. In the first stage, he constructs labour-desert theory in an imaginary state of nature in which some strong assumptions preside. And then he revises this initial theory to meet the requirements of contemporary social and economic life. His initial theory is not different from Locke's account of the labour theory of property.

According to Munzer's labour-desert argument, if someone works productively and produces something, then he deserves moral property rights in the product in virtue of his labour. This principle rests on a conception of persons as autonomous agents who, by their actions in the world, are responsible for changes in the world and deserve or merit something as a result. In Munzer's theory, the labourer gains ownership of product not as a reward for his product benefitting others, but simply in virtue of labour. Even if an institution of private property is founded on desert by labour best promotes utility, that does not contaminate the initial reason furnished by desert based on labour.[99] But this theory is a labour-desert *prima facie* theory, rather than a labour-desert entitlement theory. To deserve something is a *prima facie* reason to have it. To be entitled to something implies that reasons dictate having it. So, this argument involves relative, rather than absolute desert. The labourer's desert rests on his own actions in relation to the product in question and the argument shows that the labourer is more deserving than others of the product. But it does not indicate that other people fail to deserve property rights in the product. So, the labourer's entitlement is not absolute, because the necessary condition of deserving the rights absolutely is that other persons do not deserve them in any degree.

In a revised version of the labour-desert theory, Munzer suggests that moral duties may require limitation of property rights of the labourer. To replace the Lockean sufficiency proviso he suggests that desert theory should be limited from outside the theory by other moral considerations such as utility and justice. He expands the scope of labour theory from material products to services and from the right to property over a product to a right to wages, since the nature of labour has changed completely in modern society. In contemporary society, workers deserve property rights in their wages rather than end products, and mostly there is no product at all. In fact, in modern society property rights in many things stems from exchange, rather than original acquisition. In all of these cases revised labour theory requires that the recompense received by the labourer be proportional to the work done, though commensurability is difficult to ensure.[100] In mass-production

---

98 Becker, *op.cit.* 3 pp.50-51.
99 Munzer, *op.cit.* 12 p. 266.
100 *Ibid.* p.280.

work-places and service sectors, it is impossible to calculate the value of a labourer's work, so the value of work should be determined by the free market through service contracts.[101]

To sum up, Munzer remarks that under the revised labour theory, desert based on labour is still an anchor of *prima facie* moral property rights. And these rights can still serve, in turn, as a *prima facie* justification for legal property rights. These property rights are qualified by restrictions some of which stem from revised labour theory, others stem from different areas of a full theory of property. Although these restrictions are not part of the revised labour theory, it identifies some of the places where such restrictions are apt to apply. Bearing these restrictions in mind Munzer argues that the revised labour theory is partly a labour desert entitlement theory. Desert plays a fundamental role in it, and desert in it is socially qualified rather than being individualistic. It includes some restrictions from outside the theory. So, it is not a full account of entitlement.[102] But most of the restrictions Munzer inserted into the labour theory are not intrinsic to the theory.

These characteristics of Munzer's theory weaken the human rights character of property rights, because he gives priority to utility and justice arguments which reduce property rights to a social arrangement rather than being a generally applicable individual moral right. But we can utilise from his revised theory taking into account our objections to his theory.

3.3.4. Evaluation of Labour Theory

Considering all these points discussed above, a sound labour argument can be formulated as follows. If a person as an autonomous agent chooses to work and produces a value without breaching any other's actual rights, he has a moral right to property over the value he produced. The background thesis of the argument is that every individual is a separate autonomous agent who is responsible for his actions. Recognition of his agency is fundamental for him to be an end and to live a meaningful life, rather than being simply a means for other ends. So, morality requires that he is responsible for his actions. If he does something wrong, he deserves punishment and if he produces something he is entitled to have his product. So, if someone produces something by his free choice and his labour, not to recognise his entitlement to the results of his actions constitutes ignorance of his free agency. Therefore, morality requires others to respect the labourer's entitlement to his actions' results as long as they do not constitute breach of others' rights. And there is no wrong for the labourer to exclude others from his product, because others lose nothing by being excluded from the product. Since the

---

[101] This proposal includes a jeopardy. What happens if labourer is exploited by employer? It is necessary to take necessary measures to prevent exploitation. Especially, it is quite important to ensure a real perfect competitive market. For example, a minimum wage policy can be legitimate, and utilitarian considerations can be taken into account in the determination of wage policies.

[102] Munzer, *op.cit.* 12 p.285.

exclusion of others does not impose on them a positive duty, the labourer does not need to get others' consent to work and produce and it is not a unilateral creation of duty to others. But if it imposes a positive duty on others then it constitutes a unilateral duty creation and it requires others' consent. (That is why the human rights character of welfare rights is difficult to justify. There can be moral reasons for social solidarity but not rights. Even if they constitute rights they are recipient rights, and their duty bearers are not definite. For example, whose duty is it to look after children, or disabled persons, or the elderly? Is it their parents' or their local community's or their state's or all humanity's responsibility to provide such assistance.) The suggested argument is not incompatible with the principle of equality. The principle of equality suggests that everyone has fundamental rights equally. The labour principle recognises everyone's equal opportunity to productive work. Some may argue that disabled or elderly people do not have an equal opportunity to work. In the next chapter, it will be argued that morality and autonomy principles may require re-distributive taxation to provide equal opportunity.[103]

The only intrinsic limitation to this argument is that the action of the labourer must not violate others' actual rights. If the natural resources are accepted as common for all, this argument cannot justify property rights over scarce natural resources such as land, mines, etc., since nobody produced these things. But this does not mean that these things cannot be the subject matter of private property rights. Rather they can only be acquired by getting others' consent and paying their recompense. (For example paying tax for these resources.) The consent here should not be understood as individual consent, but since we live under a governmentally ruled organised society, it means to get allowance or licence from government. These kinds of property can be justified by other moralities such as utility, but not by labour theory.

There are some extrinsic problems to the acquisition of property by labour. These are not to be considered constituent elements of labour theory. For example parents' moral duty to look after their children may require them to spend some of their money on their children. Their duty does not depend on their getting income by their labour. On the contrary, the duty is general, and so no matter whatever way they get property it survives. So, it is not necessarily intrinsic to any theory of just acquisition of property. Government's power to impose tax, the execution of court judgements, the liability of an owner against penalties, also cannot be considered as intrinsic elements of any property acquisition theory. If welfare rights are accepted as human rights, they are not also intrinsic to any property acquisition theory. They are subject to the limitation of property rights. Therefore, labour theory justifies *prima facie* property rights over the value produced by labour.

The labourer's entitlement can be defined by considering the function of labour in the modern socio-economic context. In modern society, work is not an individual action, but a social activity. It occurs in a social context, it is done either for and with others or in relation to others. And its tie with product is very weak. In

---

[103] See Chapter 4 below.

many situations, there is not even any product at all, but only service. Therefore, labourers gain moral property rights over the produced value commensurate with their efforts. But their entitlement is mostly to get wages rather than to have some part of the product. Here the problem of commensurability occurs. How can a labourer's share in a product or service be calculated? It is impossible to measure one's labour's partake in the value produced exactly. So, the value of labour should be determined by free market through service contracts.

To sum up, if work is done individually, the labourer gains moral property rights over the product, but if it is done for or with others, the labourer gains moral property rights over his wage. This labour theory explains how a property can be acquired justly. But the way of gaining property is not only acquisition. Mostly it is gained by transfer. But in order to be transferred all property should be acquired first. The labour theory shows that just original acquisition of property can be possible by virtue of labour. Examination of whether past acquisitions are just is the subject of discussion of justice in allocation of property.

3.4. Property and Personality

This section looks at the relationships between personality and ownership of property and seeks whether this relationship can justify private property rights or not. If it can be indicated that there is a positive relationship between private property holding and achieving a proper self-development or self-realisation, it can then be said that the respect for human dignity requires the recognition of private property rights. Such an argument can be found in Hegel's *The Philosophy of Right.*[104] Hegel's discussion of property can be described as the personality theory of property.

There are, however, other arguments that put the discussion on the relationship between personality and property in a different context. One such argument comes from Radin.[105] She examines the justification and delineation of property rights in terms of personhood. She produces a personhood dichotomy according to which property rights can be divided into two categories – personal and fungible in terms of their relationship with personhood. In a continuum from fungible to personal, the personhood perspective generates a hierarchy of entitlements for property rights; the more closely connected with personhood, the stronger the entitlement is.[106] Her argument, rather than being a full theory of general justification of property rights, claims that some property rights have a closer relationship with personhood and they should be recognised and protected more strongly. Her argument can supply some useful ideas for us but it is unhelpful in finding a general justificatory base for property. Thus, the main focus of this section will be on Hegel's discussion of property.

---

[104] Hegel, G. W. F., *The Philosophy of Right* (trans. by Knox) (Clarendon Press: Oxford, 1965).
[105] Radin, J. M., "Property and Personhood" (1983) 33 *Stanford Law Review* 957.
[106] *Ibid.* p.986.

3.4.1. Hegel's Account of Property

Hegel's discussion of property has been interpreted variously. Most of the interpretations can be placed under the general rubric of a personality theory of property. The personality theory of property explains property as a relation between persons and things which is essentially determined by the nature of persons and things, specifically by the fact that persons have free will and things do not.[107] There are, however, some commentators who object to this generalisation. While Harris[108] interprets Hegel's theory as a freedom argument rather than a personhood theory,[109] a communitarian interpretation of Hegel's theory can be found in Ryan's *Property.*[110] Ignoring these differences in interpretation of Hegel we will try to give his account of property in general.

The Philosophy of Right is divided into three parts: Abstract Right, Morality and Ethical Life. These parts represent the stages of the development of the absolutely free will. At the first stage – Abstract (or Formal) Right – the will is immediate and its concept is personality. Personality is characterised by the ability to choose freely, to act as an agent capable of originating action.[111] Persons are isolated from their network of specific social, political, economic attributes and roles, and they are equal as abstract persons. The right is negative and formal, and it has priority over goods. The embodiment of will, at this stage, is on immediate external things. Hegel examines property, contract, and civil and criminal wrongs at this stage. At the second stage, Morality, the will is reflected from its external embodiment into itself. At this stage consciousness is no longer mere personality, but regards itself as a subject, an existential being with a determinate history and various needs, interests, desires and projects.[112] The good is appearance of right and characterises what ought to be. At the final stage, Ethical Life, the will is the unity and truth of the first two abstract moments. At this stage, conflicting elements of the first two stages are transcended and reunited in a harmonious way. In Ethical Life right appears as it actually is, in a society in which individual self-determination is the goal of society and society the goal of individual's self-determination.[113] This stage is the largest part of the book and depicts the step-by-step progress of the idea of right, as it becomes fully instantiated in actual human society through the forms of Family, Civil Society, and the State.

Hegel's concern is about the description of 'what is', rather than a description of 'what ought to be', imperative ethics. So, his discussion is

---

[107] Penner, J. E., *The Idea of Property in Law* (Clarendon Press: Oxford, 1997) p.167.

[108] Harris, *op.cit.* 22 p.234.

[109] For a detailed discussion of Harris's interpretation of Hegel, see Lametti, D., *The Deon-Telos of Private Property: Ethical Aspects of the Theory and Practice of Private Property* (unpublished D. Phil. thesis: Oxford, 1998); Lametti, D., "Property and (Perhaps) Justice" (1998) 43 *McGill Law Journal* 633.

[110] Ryan, A., *Property* (Open University Press, 1987). For same interpretation see Ryan, A., *Property and Political Theory* (Basil, Blackwell, 1984).

[111] Hegel, *op.cit.* 104 § 33.

[112] *Ibid.* § 105-106.

[113] Penner, *op.cit.* 107 p.170.

explanatory, rather than being justificatory.[114] As Pottage[115] argued, it is difficult to attribute a right-based argument to Hegel. But his explanation can be helpful to show that there is a relation between property holding and individual autonomy and personality. As indicated above, Hegel explores property in the Abstract Right. Therefore, Hegel's analysis in Abstract Right does not show the final form of private property institution in the actual society. When he considers the major political institutions such as family, civil society, and the state (Ethical Life), he sometimes asserts and other times limits or transforms property according to the qualities of the institutions and the needs of individuals.[116] Hence, anything that is said about the relations between personality and property at the level of abstract right is not to be interpreted as definitive justifications for property institution.[117] Nevertheless, his theory shows that there is a relation between individual personality and property, and he argues that a political system which does not recognise any private property institution violates the right of personality.[118]

Hegel defines right as 'an existent of any sort embodying the free will',[119] or in other words, embodiment of the self-conscious freedom. Thus, for him, the objective of the philosophical inquiry of right is the examination of the way will for itself manifests in actual human relations. 'Right' concerns how persons, who make free choices, can make freedom the goal of those choices. In this view, freedom is not simply an instrumental capacity for achieving some ends, but itself is the end. In order to understand the nature of right, the actual human relations which show the effect of persons making free choices must be examined. In other words, theorising some fundamental concepts of the free will is not enough to understand right; rather looking at actual social relations over the course of history as manifestations of free will is necessary. For Hegel the simplest of those relations are embodied in the law, specifically in property, contract, and civil and criminal wrong.[120]

In Hegel's theory, a person is the subject of the free will, and personality begins with the subject's consciousness of himself as a completely abstract ego in which very concrete restriction and value is negated and without validity.[121] And 'personality essentially involves the capacity for rights and constitutes the concept and the basis of the system of abstract and therefore formal right. Hence the imperative of right is "be a person and respect others as persons"'.[122]

---

[114] Reeve, A., *Property* (London: Macmillan, 1986) p. 141.

[115] Pottage, A., "Property: Re-appropriating Hegel" (1990) 33 *Modern Law Review* 259; Harris, J. W., *Property and Justice* (Oxford, Clarendon Press, 1996) p.232.

[116] Stillman, Peter G., "Property, Contract and Ethical Life in Hegel's Philosophy of Right" in Cornell, Rosenfeld, Carlson (eds.) *Hegel and Legal Theory* (Routledge: London, 1991).

[117] Harris, *P&J*, p.232.

[118] Hegel, *op.cit.* 104 § 46 A, Hegel criticises Plato's Ideal State stating that it violates the right of personality by forbidding the holding of property.

[119] *Ibid.* § 29, 30.

[120] Penner, *op.cit.* 107 p.172.

[121] Hegel, *op.cit.* 104 §35.

[122] *Ibid.* §36.

3.4.1.1. Abstract Right and property Hegel's Abstract Right is a logical construct. At this stage of its immanent development, the free will has the determinate character of immediacy and abstract universality. It takes the form of self-consciousness or personality. Since the person, in Hegel's conception, is merely an abstract unit of free will or autonomy, it has no concrete existence until that will impacts on the external world.[123] For personality, the restriction of being only subjective is a contradiction and nullity. So, personality tries to overcome this restriction and to give itself reality, to actualise itself.[124] Within this struggle of the will, the relation of it to things, to others, and to itself governs the content of Abstract Right.

The will's (personality) relationship with the external world of things constitutes property. Hegel extends his argument to property by asserting that 'a person must translate his freedom into an external sphere in order to exist as Idea'.[125] In Hegel's view, a person has an absolute right of appropriation on external things. He maintains that 'a person has as his substantive end the right of putting his will into any and every thing and thereby making it his, because it has no such end in itself and drives its destiny and soul from his will. This is the absolute right of appropriation which man has over all things'.[126]

The justification of his absolute right is that person has 'will' and things do not.[127] A property is a thing that contains a person's will, embodiment of personality into an external object. Within this perspective an object becomes property only when a legal subject puts his or her will into it by appropriating this object as a means for a subjective end.[128] For Hegel, the importance of appropriation is the actualisation of freedom, rather than the satisfaction of needs.[129] This also explains the principle of first occupancy. Since the first appropriator's will is embodied in the possession of a thing, the second appropriator does not confront a will-less thing.[130]

How then is personality or free will embodied in an object? According to Hegel, property involves the embodiment of one's will in an object. But merely

---

[123] Radin, *op.cit.* 105 p.972.

[124] Here, Hegel's developmental account of the evolution of the human subject can be seen. He sees the subject as dependent upon an ongoing project of socialisation, education and cultural integration. In Hegelian terms, individuals must evolve from an immature condition of being free in themselves, i.e. in principle only, to exercising that form of effective self-determination which makes them free 'in and for themselves', i.e. in concrete social practice. § 10, 24, 41.

[125] *Ibid.* § 41.

[126] *Ibid.* § 44.

[127] This requires that the objects of property must be single external things that are wholly distinct from the internal subjective constituents of personality of individuals. See Hegel, *op.cit.* 104 § 65, 66, 75; Salter, M.G., "Hegel and Social Dynamics of Property Law" in Harris, J. W. (ed.) *Property Problems: From Genes To Funds* (Kluwer Law International, 1998).

[128] Salter, *op.cit.* 127 p.260.

[129] Hegel, *op.cit.* 104 § 45.

[130] Penner, *op.cit.* 107 p. 174.

directing one's will on an object is not sufficient to embody it therein. There has to be some physical relation between a body inhabited by the will in question and the external object in which that will is to be embodied.[131] In his view, taking possession, use and alienation of property are different expressions of the will of the possessor in relation to the thing.[132]

Hegel discusses three ways of taking possession: physically grasping, forming and marking.[133] The first way of taking possession of an object is by directly physically grasping it. Hegel considers this 'the most complete of these modes, because than I am directly present in this possession, and therefore my will is recognisable in it'.[134] He claims that grasping makes will recognisable in the object. But it is subjective, temporary, and restricted in scope. It is unsatisfactory because it is precarious, lasting only as long as possession itself. The second mode of taking possession is the imposition of form. This is superior to the first because the change in the character of taking can be permanent and reflects the appropriator's will even if he is not in physical association with it.[135] The final mode of taking possession is that of marking the object. In this case, the will is not actual but is represented. This is superior to forming because it directly and unambiguously represents the appropriator's will, but it is very indeterminate.[136]

After discussing the various modes of taking possession, Hegel proceeds to analyse the use of the thing. In his view, the way of using something reveals a concrete relation between will and object. He argues that use manifests the will of possessor by displaying how the object is fitted into the pattern of his needs, inclinations, and desires.[137] In use of the object, it acquires a negative character in relation to the externalisation of one's will.

And lastly, Hegel insists that ownership involves the power to alienate resources or to transmit them to another by gift or exchange. Alienation of property follows from the fact that as a willing being, a person can withdraw his or her will from any thing that is separable from him or her.[138] Therefore the goods which are internal to personality or constitute one's own private personality and the universal essence of one's self-consciousness are inalienable and his right to them is imprescriptible.[139]

Hegel's argument, the embodiment of will (or personality) into an external object, is generally interpreted as meaning that appropriation makes the object a part of body.[140] But this straightforward reading seems misleading. When

---

[131] Hegel, *op.cit.* 104 § 51, 52; Waldron, *op.cit.* 52 p.364.
[132] Hegel, *op.cit.* 104 § 53.
[133] *Ibid.* § 54.
[134] *Ibid.* § 55.
[135] *Ibid.* § 56.
[136] Penner, *op.cit.* 107 p.174.
[137] Knowles, D., "Hegel on Property and Personality" (1983) 33 *The Philosophical Quarterly* 45.
[138] Hegel, *op.cit.* 104 § 65.
[139] *Ibid.* § 66.
[140] Knowles, *op.cit.* 137 p. 51.

Hegel says, 'it is only the will existent in an object that can suffer injury',[141] he does not say that my property is a part of my body. But he probably claims that if I feel pain when my property is injured it shows that there is a relation between property and personality.

3.4.1.2. Property and personality In Hegel's theory, a person's will is embodied in an object to the extent that his will has made a difference to the object.[142] What, then, is the ethical importance of property for personality?

As explained above, personality, for Hegel, means self-consciousness or free will. And property is the actualisation of self-consciousness. The relation between property and personality is that property makes personality recognisable. Without embodiment, the will is only a possibility.

According to Waldron, the importance of property to individual will, in the Hegelian approach, is that the actions that an individual performs on or with this object now may constrain or determine the actions that he can perform on or with it later. This is how an object can embody a will – by registering the effects of willing at one point of time and forcing an individual's willing to become consistent and stable over a period. But this effect can be lost if others are also working on the object for purposes of their own in the meantime. That is why private property, as a system which assigns enduring objects to the exclusive control of individuals, is necessary. Otherwise, embodiment and its beneficial effects on willing would not be possible.[143] However, this argument is valid only for personally created property such as intellectual property but not applicable to most of the things produced by a process of mass production and property acquired by transfer.

Another effect of private property on personality is that personality is recognised thanks to property rights by others. Hegel stresses that it is only insofar as my will is embodied in objects that it becomes capable of being recognised by others. The need for mutual recognition of persons can justify private property, because only in a system of private property do 'mine' and 'thine' donate enduring, exclusive, and relatively unlimited rights of use and decisions that persons have in relation to enduring objects. By objectifying his will in the world, Hegel's person not only brings that will into a stronger and more mature relation to itself, but also brings it into a relation with the similarly matured wills of other persons.

This is a crucial point in Hegel's thought. A being may be defined and understood only by contrasting it with something else. If this is applied to the self-definition of a human being, then a human can only define himself by distinguishing himself from something he is not. And the exclusionary character of private property plays an important role in the development of this self-understanding. When a person wants to satisfy his needs in a world where resources are moderately scarce, the norms protecting private property in the face of his temptation are a basis for the distinction of one such need-laden will from

[141] Hegel, *op.cit.* 104 § 96.
[142] Waldron, *op.cit.* 52 p.373.
[143] *Ibid.* p.374.

another. We are not merely the locations of needs and wants. We are also individual wills in a process of growth. That growth, at the point where property is important, is growth at an individual level. So property protects the development of will by erecting normative fences around the objects in which wills have become embodied. But such fences make sense only in a common world of property holders, and this leads to the recognition of underlying identity as between self and other.[144] This aspect of recognition reaches its highest form in contract and exchange.

To sum up, in Hegel's view, property owning is important to individuals since it is only through owning and controlling property that a person can embody his will in external objects and begin to transcend the subjectivity of his immediate existence. In working on an object, using it, and having control over it, an individual confers on his will a stability and maturity that would not otherwise be possible, and enables himself to establish his place as one in a community of such wills.

What conclusion can be inferred from this argument? Is it commanded that everyone must have property, or everyone should have opportunity or liberty to acquire property? Hegel does not argue that everyone must embody his will into an object. And he stresses the factual inequality of men in skills, endowments, and other mental and bodily characteristics, and he argues that individuals have a right that this inequality should be permitted to prevail in economic life. So, we have more reason to think that Hegel's argument promotes the right that everyone should have an opportunity to acquire property. The fact that he recognises a first occupancy theory and never mentions a qualification also support this idea. Waldron argues that if this view is accepted, then, if one never actually has property, since the will is matured and stabilised by its actual exercise on objects, by reflection of itself into itself involved in labour and subsequent use, then one never gets the benefit of the exercise of one's will on objects; one's will never develops in the way that Hegel thinks it is important for one to develop.[145] However, such a reading, as Pottage remarked, seems misleading because it assumes that a person can only become a full ethical person by investing his will in objects. But Hegel's theory of embodiment can be seen as an exercise of personality rather than being constitutive of personality.[146] What is essential to the maintenance of personality, in Hegel's theory, is that one's will, once it has been embodied, should be recognised and respected. In other words, the primary necessity is that each member of society should have the capacity to own concrete possessions.[147]

3.4.1.3. Transcending Abstract Right In Abstract Right, Hegel presents an extensive, comprehensive, and powerful statement of the person's right to property, since it is bound up with freedom, personal equality, and domestication

---

[144] *Ibid.* p.377.
[145] Waldron, *op.cit.* 52 pp.347 ff.
[146] Pottage, *op.cit.* 115 p. 262.
[147] *Ibid.* p.266.

of nature. But Abstract Right is the simplest form of life and its specific contents – property, contract, and civil and criminal wrongs – are inadequate, primitive, thin and insufficient. The model of human being and of social interaction that derives from Abstract Rights alone are one-sided and narrow; for example, from rights alone it is difficult or impossible logically to deduce human love and love-based institutions such as family. But people live in a social context, in a social and political environment with a specific history and specific needs, impulses and inclinations. They interact with other persons. Within this context, in Ethical Life – actual social and political sphere – freedom and necessity are reconciled.[148] Paradigmatic property rights are directly actualised only by the system of needs and the administration of justice. Since individuals are transformed into members of a community, some of their property transforms into community resources.[149]

Indeed, abstract personality, the moment of property, is not isolation from the other moments of the dialectic of freedom. It is only in historical terms that each of these moments – Abstract Right, Morality and Ethical Life – presents itself in isolation. Hegel's theory is a definition of 'what is', his definition is a reconciliation of freedom and necessity. This theme of reconciliation implies that, although the particular will accommodates to the universal, neither is abrogated. That is, universal will – Abstract Right; property – and particular will – Morality; needs, impulses and inclinations – are harmonised in actual social and political life. Property rights exist in a dialectical tension with the 'higher demands' and they can only fully be understood in terms of this relation. Property rights are not absolute rights at all; they are qualified by higher demands of morality or equity.

3.4.2. The Value of Hegel's Theory of Property

Hegel's account of property is neither natural rights-based nor instrumental (utilitarianism). 'The rational aspect of property is to be found not in the satisfaction of needs but in the superseding of mere subjectivity of personality.'[150] Nor do human beings have property by virtue of their interaction with the world and with each other. But acquisition of ownership is inferred from the embodiment of abstract personality in things.[151]

Hegel's discussion of property shows that persons are categorically different from things, by virtue of having personalities. The constitution of personality is the will, and by virtue of that, persons may determine the use of things. Since property, in Hegel's theory, is the actualisation of personality, the recognition or assertion of property implies the recognition of personality. So, the respect for the right of exclusive use derives precisely from the respect for others as autonomous agents.[152]

---

148 *Ibid.* p.263.
149 Stillman, *op.cit.* 116 p.222.
150 Hegel, *op.cit.* 104 § 45.
151 Harris, *op.cit.* 22 p. 235.
152 Penner, *op.cit.* 107 p.173.

This argument plays an important role in the justification of property. It assumes that consciousness, or free will, has an intrinsic value deserving to be respected. And it shows that property is important to exercise free will. If it is accepted that self-realisation is a moral value which should be pursued by a political society, then recognition of private property rights is necessary. However, Hegel's account of property in Abstract Right justifies not an absolute right to property but only a *prima facie* right to property because in actual political society, property will be qualified by other moral considerations. The restricting considerations will be examined in the next chapter.

Hegel's account of property can be conceived as a justificatory reason for property rights as an element of a pluralistic moral theory. Personality argument constitutes a *prima facie* general justification for a private property institution. Other components of pluralistic theory complete the shortcomings of personality theory. For example, personality theory accepts that absolute right to appropriation will be actualised by the system of needs and the administration of justice. But it does not indicate in what conditions the appropriation, use and alienation of property is just. Labour theory discusses the just conditions of appropriation. Utility argument deals with the needs. The autonomy argument defines the legitimate boundaries of government's power of interference with property.

3.5. Political Liberty and Private Property

This section looks at the connections between different conceptions of liberty and property and whether these connections justify private property rights. The abundance of different views on both what freedom is and what the connections between liberty and property are makes this job not easy in any way. To examine the relationship between private property and freedom, it is necessary to look at, first, the connections between rights and liberty briefly. It has been argued that there is a special connection between talk of rights and the value of individual freedom. Cranston argues that freedom constitutes the only appropriate subject matter for human rights. According to his view, talk of rights to material well-being or to certain sorts of services is a distortion of rights except to the extent that those goods can themselves be regarded as involving aspects of individual liberty.[153] Some others maintain that even if there are rights to goods other than liberty, still the underlying point of rights discourse is to maintain a certain pattern or distribution of human freedom. According to Hart, the fundamental general right, presupposed by all other rights discourse, is the equal right of all men to be free.[154] Although such analytic connections between rights and freedom are increasingly unpopular among right-based theorists[155] the securing of an area of

---

[153] Cranston, M., "Human Rights: Real and Supposed" in D. Raphael (ed.), *Political Theory and Rights of Man* (Macmillan: London, 1967) pp.38 ff.

[154] Hart, H. L. A. "Are There Any Natural Rights?" in J. Waldron, *Theories of Rights* (OUP: Oxford, 1984) pp.77-8.

[155] Waldron, *op.cit.* 52 p.291.

moral space within which individuals are free to pursue their own plans and project is, for many theorists, the chief point of thinking in terms of rights.[156]

Why is such importance attributed to freedom in the discourse of rights? Two of the answers that might be given to this question are self-ownership and autonomy.[157] As we have seen above[158] the self-ownership theory is not plausible to justify rights. Most of the liberal philosophers depend their ideas on the concept of autonomy. So, the concept of 'autonomy' will be the main concern of this section.

In terms of the relationships between autonomy and property rights, two different approaches can be observed.[159] The first one is the attempt to derive property rights directly from the thought that individuals are free autonomous agents whose freedom is not to be overridden save to protect the freedom of others. The second argument is that property rights can create options and enhance individual autonomy and are, therefore, constituent elements of autonomous life. The first idea is a proprietary interpretation of natural rights theory under a different label. The concept of liberty underlying this view is the freedom in negative sense. Becker's justification of property by political liberty can be placed within this category.[160] The second approach relies on the justification of rights by autonomy as constituent elements of autonomous life. Raz's autonomy-based freedom theory is in line with this second approach and it will be accepted as the main justificatory argument for property rights in this book. Raz does not give an instrumental value to the rights.[161] Rather, rights have intrinsic value as being constituent elements of an autonomous life in his theory.

3.5.1. Autonomy

The significance of freedom in legal philosophy and in rights discourse is generally grounded upon the concept of autonomy. But different scholars have attributed very diverse meanings to the concepts of both autonomy and freedom. The diversity between positive and negative conceptions of liberty has a great importance in political and legal philosophy. The examination of these concepts is also necessary to determine the place of Raz's autonomy-based freedom theory which is used as the justificatory base of private property in this book. Therefore, here, first, the negative and positive conceptions of freedom or liberty will be examined briefly and then the concept of autonomy will be scrutinised.

The negative conception of liberty can be defined as the absence of external obstacles.[162] Someone is said to be free to the degree to which no man or

---

[156] Jones, P., *Rights* (Macmillan: London, 1994) p.122.
[157] *Ibid.* p.123.
[158] See section 3 above.
[159] Ryan, A., *Property* (Open UP: Milton Keynes, 1987) p.77.
[160] Becker, *op.cit.* 3 p.75.
[161] For a contrary view see Jones, *op.cit.* 156 p. 125.
[162] Taylor, C., "What is Wrong with Negative Liberty?" in A. Ryan, *The Idea of Freedom* (OUP: Oxford, 1979) pp.175-94.

institution interferes with his activity. Political liberty in this sense is simply the area within which a person can act unobstructed by others.[163] If someone is prevented by other people from doing what he could otherwise do, he is to that degree unfree. If this area is contracted by other people beyond a certain minimum, then he can be described as being coerced or enslaved. In the negative theory, 'coercion' implies only the deliberate interference of other human beings within the area in which one could otherwise act. An individual lacks political liberty only if he is prevented from attaining a goal by human beings.[164] In this sense, liberty is distinct from ability. It does not cover the ability to do whatever one wishes. For example, if someone cannot read because of his blindness, it does not mean that he is unfree. Therefore, mere incapacity to attain an end is not lack of political freedom.[165]

Negative liberty depends on moral individualism which requires governments to avoid pursuing any conception of the good life. That is, political institutions should be neutral to the purposes of individuals, any perfectionism or paternalism should be excluded from politics.[166] So, the state does not dictate any purpose since it accepts people as what they actually are. Everyone has a right to determine his purposes freely. It facilitates pluralism in that way. People are free to do whatever they wish. But freedom cannot be unlimited in a social context. Especially liberty of the strong must be restrained. Nevertheless, liberty can be restricted only to prevent harm to others.[167]

The negative conception of liberty has been criticised by the proponents of positive interpretations of the freedom. They argue that absence of external obstacles alone is not enough to be free; it is necessary to free men from their internal and natural fetters as well.[168] The positive criticism of negative conception of liberty focuses on its shortcomings especially in two points. It claims that the absence of external obstacles is not enough to be free; individuals should have some intellectual capacity, and a range of options. Someone is free only to the extent that he has effectively determined himself and the shape of his life. This is an exercise-concept.[169] The idea here is that freedom is something like a moral status to be attained through one's efforts and perhaps with the assistance of others.[170] In this view, someone is free as far as he realised his potential. If he is totally unaware of his potential, or if he is paralysed by fear of breaking with some norms which he has internalised, but which does not authentically reflect him, he cannot be said to be free. So making discrimination among motivations behind acts

---

[163] Berlin, I., "Two Concepts of Liberty" in *Four Essays on Liberty* (OUP: Oxford, 1969) pp.118-72.

[164] *Ibid.* p.122.

[165] *Ibid.* p.122.

[166] Raz, J., *Morality of Freedom*, (Oxford: Clarendon Press, 1986) p.400.

[167] Mill, J. S., *On Liberty* (Penguin Books: London, 1974) pp.141 ff; Hart, "Rawls on Liberty and Its Priority" in Norman Daniels (ed.) *Reading Rawls* (SUP: Stanford, 1989) p.243.

[168] Taylor, *op.cit.* 162 p.182.

[169] *Ibid.* p.153.

[170] Waldron, *op.cit.* 52 p.298.

or purposes is necessary. Being able to do 'what one wants' can no longer be accepted as a sufficient condition of being free. To be accepted as free, according to positive theory, one must be motivated by authentic desires.[171] This view accepts that some internal desires and feelings also constitute obstacles to freedom.

The positive theory depends on the rejection of moral individualism which defends that the ultimate determinant of good or evil is the individual himself. In contrast, perfectionist or paternalistic moralities on which positive liberty depends accept that there are objective criteria of good and evil. Paternalism, however, can lead to authoritarian social doctrines which make liberty virtually identical with authority. All rational constructivist theories derive from such a paternalistic understanding that justify the coercion of some people by others in order to raise them to a 'higher' level of freedom.

The importance of the distinction between positive and negative conceptions of freedom for property discourse is that positive libertarians argue that if someone is too poor to afford something on which there is no legal ban, he is no freer to have it as he would be if it were forbidden him by law. Therefore, they argue that to be free everyone should have at least minimum requirements of a decent life. It is true that poverty prevents individuals buying what they want, but it cannot be said that they have lack of liberty. However, Marxist, socialist and some utilitarian and Christian doctrines identify the cause of poverty and weakness in arrangements made by other peoples, and claim that poverty and weakness are coercion or slavery.[172] According to these political doctrines, the cause of poverty is only unjust social arrangements. If someone lacks material means as a result of his laziness, extravagance, or lack of mental or physical capacity, or natural reasons, then he begins to speak of being deprived of liberty.[173] This issue will be evaluated further below. Now it is time to look at the concept of autonomy.

Many philosophers place much stress on the concept of autonomy of the individual in the justification of rights. The concept finds its roots in Kant's theory of rights.[174] The value of autonomy, according to Kant, arises from human beings' unique status among other creatures in being capable of autonomous conduct. Only human beings possess reason that enables them to decide what they ought to do. The things other than human beings that are characterised by not having will or reason, act according to instinct. Their acts are governed by nature. By contrast, human beings have will, and following their rational will they act autonomously, for they act, not under the sway of an external or natural force, but according to

---

171 Taylor, *op.cit.* 162 p.180.

172 Here the problem is the belief that those who have most material resources exploit those who have not. And it is mostly true. However, this exploitation takes place through the execution of contracts, especially service contracts. The important thing in contract is free and equal consent of parties. If one party is in a hard condition and the other party exploits his situation, justice requires the protection of the weak one. This is not limitation of freedom. On the contrary, it is protection of equal liberty.

173 Berlin, *op.cit.* 163 p.123.

174 See Rosen, A. D., *Kant's Theory of Justice* (Cornell University Press: London, 1993); Murphy, J. G., *Kant: The Philosophy of Right* (Mercer University Press: Georgia, 1994).

their own conception of what they ought to do. So, being possessed of a will is not to be treated as a mere 'thing' which has value only in so far as it serves human purposes. A person, as an autonomous agent, has intrinsic value; he is not to be used merely as the instrument of other's purposes.[175]

All persons are to be regarded as 'ends in themselves' and therefore, each person should be equally respected by other persons. This view is the foundation of Kant's theory of human rights. But the link between Kant's conception of autonomy and the right to freedom is not straightforward. His conception of autonomy is narrow in that he holds that individuals act autonomously only in so far as they follow the dictates of reason, which dictates the same for everyone. If it is accepted that a person is autonomous only when he acts rationally, and that reason dictates everyone the same thing, then a right grounded in autonomy might be to act only as that reason dictates. And freedom that is deemed to issue from our autonomy might therefore be quite immature.[176] Such a conception of autonomy, as Berlin points out, has sometimes been associated with repressive regimes.[177]

Later liberal theorists have widened the concept of autonomy so that it encompasses people's general ability to make choices, to formulate plans and projects and to be the authors of their own aims and aspirations. According to this, autonomy is a distinct human capacity and source of his moral importance. To determine what is the proper treatment to human individuals and particularly what rights they posses, it is necessary to take full account of their nature as autonomous beings. If people are not to be allowed the freedom to develop and to act upon their capacity for autonomous conduct, it constitutes the ignorance of their being human and of being able to live a distinctively human life. On this view, individuals' rights are grounded in their very natures as human persons. The essence of this view is the Kantian ground that the critical determinant of individual's rights is their status as autonomous beings. Individuals have rights to basic freedoms because their nature as autonomous beings must be respected.[178]

Raz's autonomy-based freedom theory also depends upon a Kantian conception of autonomy. For Raz, the autonomous person is the author of his own life. The ideal of personal autonomy is the vision of people controlling, to some degree, their own destiny, fashioning it through successive decisions throughout their lives. In other words, it is that of autonomous life. The capacity for autonomy or conditions of autonomy is a secondary sense of autonomy. These conditions consist of three components: appropriate mental abilities, an adequate range of options, and independence.[179] However, these conditions are not simply

---

[175] Kant, I., *Grandwork of the Metaphysic of Morals*, in H. Paton (ed.) *The Moral Law* (Hutchinson: London, 1945) p.91.
[176] Jones, *op.cit.* 156 p. 128.
[177] Berlin, *op.cit.* 163 p.152.
[178] Jones, *op.cit.* 156 pp. 128- 9.
[179] Raz, *op.cit.* 166 p.372.

instruments for the attainment of autonomous life. They are components of an ideal of autonomy that is intrinsically valuable; therefore, they have intrinsic value.[180]

In Raz's theory, one of the constituent elements of autonomous life is the mental ability of a person. He maintains that since the ideal of autonomy is a life freely chosen, it necessarily requires that the person must have the mental abilities to form intentions of sufficiently complex kind, and plan their execution. These mental abilities include minimum rationality, the ability to comprehend the means required to realise his goals.[181] What Raz emphasises by inserting mental ability as a requirement of autonomous life is that children and mentally ill persons do not have the ability to act autonomously and they can be restricted from free choice since they do not have the ability to choose.

As for the second component of capacity for autonomy, to have an adequate range of options, Raz argues that to be autonomous a person must not only be given a choice but he must be given an adequate range of choices.[182] Autonomy is exercised through choice, and choice requires a variety of options to choose from. These options must include a variety of morally acceptable options. There must be more valuable options than can be chosen and they must be significantly different, to meet the precondition of adequacy of options.[183] This requires also moral pluralism and a culture of tolerance. Respect for personal autonomy may require tolerating bad or repugnant actions as well. Autonomy is blind to the quality of options chosen and it is consistent with the presence of bad options. But his theory does not lead to moral individualism. He defends some kind of perfectionism.[184] He claims that autonomy-based freedom does not extend to the morally bad and repugnant. Since autonomy is valuable only if it is directed at the good, it supplies no reason either to provide or to protect bad options. Bad options contribute nothing to value of autonomy. He leaves the judgement of good and bad to the conventions, changing moral values. He points out that moral values can change from time to time and from culture to culture.[185]

The last requirement of autonomous life, independency – exclusion of coercion and manipulation – is the one which both positive and negative libertarians are agreed on. It is obvious that if someone is prevented from realising his plans he cannot live an autonomous life.

Raz locates the value of freedom in this ideal of personal autonomy. Autonomy-based freedom, understood both as the absence of coercion and manipulation and as the presence of worthwhile options, can be possible only in shared institutions, values and opportunities. Thus, the ideal of autonomy justifies some individual rights and some collective goods. For example, the conditions for autonomy which characterise modern societies include collective goods such as a

---

[180] For discussion of three categories of intrinsically valuable things and their distinction from instrumentally valuable things see Raz, *op.cit.* 166 p.200.

[181] Raz, *op.cit.* 166 p.373.

[182] *Ibid.*

[183] *Ibid.* p. 398.

[184] Jones, *op.cit.* 156 p.132.

[185] Raz, *op.cit.* 166 p.375.

culture of tolerance, a range of career options, pluralistic democracy, and an open society. Personal autonomy depends on the persistence of these collective goods. Therefore, liberal rights have some collective aspects.[186] For example, the justification of the special rights and privileges of the press such as protection against action for libel or breach of privacy, access to information, priority in access to courts or to parliamentary sessions, are in its service to the community at large. So, he argues that rights are not to be understood as inherently independent of collective goods, or as essentially opposed to them. On the contrary, they both depend on and serve collective goods. Hence, there is no general rule giving either rights or collective goods priority in cases of conflict.[187] Though an individual's freedom sometimes conflicts with the interest of others, it also depends on those interests and can be obtained only through collective goods which do not benefit anyone unless they benefit everyone.[188]

Even if a person lives in an autonomy-enhancing society, it does not guarantee that he would live an autonomous life, because capacity for autonomy is distinct from its exercise. Exercise of autonomy depends on the ability of a person to find his place in his environment. So, autonomy is a matter of degree both as a capacity and as an ideal.[189] Then what are the requirements of respect for autonomy?

Raz argues that since autonomy is morally valuable there is reason for everyone to make himself and everyone else autonomous. However, it is the special character of autonomy that one cannot make another person autonomous. One can bring a horse to the water but cannot make it drink. So, respect for autonomy requires only securing the background conditions which enable a person to be autonomous, but not to coerce him to be autonomous.[190]

Raz claims that autonomy-based duties that are aimed at securing autonomy as a capacity go far beyond the negative duties of non-interference. If the duties of non-interference are autonomy-based then the principle of autonomy provides reasons for holding that there are other autonomy-based duties as well. To justify some positive duties he widens the scope of the harm principle. This aspect will be considered in the next chapter where the limitations of property are examined.

Although it has some weak points, Raz's autonomy principle seems capable of explaining the role of freedom and rights in political structure. It is a modest approach that is far from both extremist individualist libertarians and extremist communitarians.

As a result, Raz's theory gives a general character of an autonomy-enhancing society but it does not give a list of rights. His theory aims to establish a free person. However, it allows discrimination between valuable and worthless or even detrimental freedom, according to their contribution to the ideal of personal

186 *Ibid.* p. 253.
187 *Ibid.* p. 255.
188 *Ibid.* p. 250.
189 *Ibid.* p. 391.
190 *Ibid.* p. 407.

autonomy.[191] Therefore, his theory is consistent with the protection of some basic rights by constitution. The ideal of autonomy can determine which rights are basic rights. Raz's theory of autonomy-based liberty seems consistent with the philosophy behind the European Convention on Human Rights.

If this autonomy-based freedom is accepted as the basis of the justification of rights, is it possible to justify property rights? Now the connection between property and autonomy-based freedom will be examined.

3.5.2. Connections Between Property and Autonomy

There are many aspects of connections between property and freedom. In terms of the justification of property, the question is whether private property rights are constituent elements of an autonomous life. In another words, is a system of private property necessary to facilitate an autonomy-enhancing society? Three different lines of argument give an affirmative answer to this question. The first line of argument derives property rights directly from the thought that individuals are free agents whose freedom is not to be overridden except to protect the freedom of others. This idea depends on the negative sense of liberty – not to be interfered with by others. The second line of argument proposes that property rights create opportunities, facilitate options and enhance autonomy.[192] The basis of this argument is positive liberty in its capacity sense. The third line of argument depends on the concept of privacy. These arguments are all related to general justification of property rights. They claim that if liberty is the ultimate value for human being, a free life is only possible in a system of private property.

The first line of argument justifies property rights as a derivative of liberty. If individuals are equally free to do whatever they want without breaching others rights they are free to acquire, things, control them, exclude others from their use, modify them, and use them as wealth. The prohibition of such activities, i.e. elimination of property rights altogether, would require a comprehensive and continuous abridgement of people's liberty to which they are entitled morally. So, the rules regulating acquisition, use and alienation of property are required to preserve liberties to which people are entitled. Therefore, property rights are justifiable.[193] The crucial point in this theory is the claim that private property rights are constituents of freedom and that the prohibition of such rights constitutes the abridgement of liberty. It is suggested that this line of argument can justify private property rights only in conjunction with the labour theory of property.

As for the autonomy argument, it is necessary to look at the relationship between private property rights and the conditions of autonomy. One element of autonomy is the exclusion of coercion and manipulation. The question here is whether private property rights exclude coercion. Marxist and socialist doctrines claim that the presence of private property limits the liberty of non-owners. According to these doctrines a system of private property and market system – i.e.

---

[191] *Ibid.* p 246.
[192] Ryan, *op.cit.* 7 p.77.
[193] *Ibid.* p.75.

capitalism – provides freedom only to those who enjoy the means of production while it enslaves the working class. For example, Cohen criticises the liberals and libertarians for misusing the concept of liberty. He argues that they look only at freedom which is intrinsic to private property, but they do not notice the limitations of freedom of non-owners which necessarily accompanies it.[194] He defines freedom as 'when a man cannot do as he wishes, because others will interfere, he is unfree'.[195] And he concludes that private property always limits liberty. This view is evidently true if it is thought that property in anything means, inter alia, that other persons are not at liberty to use, consume, alter or otherwise deal with whatever it is without the owner's leave.[196] However, if liberty is understood in its pure negative sense, all rights constitute obstacles to freedom. Such an absolute freedom is never possible if there are two persons in a place. The existence of any rule, any system of property limits the liberty. Even the non-existence of any system limits or abolishes freedom, because a 'free for all' would be 'coercive for all'. Any property system will involve a complex distribution of freedoms and unfreedom. In a system of private property, a person is at liberty to make use of the resources assigned to him, but he is not free to use the resources assigned to others in any way, at least not without their permission. In contrast, in a system of common property a person's freedom to make use of any resource is not limited by anybody else, though it is limited by the fact that others are also at liberty to use it and that its use is regulated on the bases of some fair principle.[197]

One may argue that private property offers in fact a greater net amount of liberty for everyone than a system of common property or vice versa. However, to calculate which system of property is more conducive to liberty is not an easy task to be fulfilled. Cohen himself accepts that which form of property is better for liberty, all things considered, is a question that may have no answer in the abstract. Which form is better for liberty may depend on the historical circumstances.[198]

Another point to bear in mind is that this discussion ignores the source of things. It assumes that there are things in a common pot waiting to be appropriated, used, and consumed. But, in reality, most things and values other than natural resources are produced by people. So the question is whether settled property rights with associated legal security for contract, inheritance and other elaborations of ownership rights minimise the coercive element in production and distribution.[199] Of course, the system of property is not the unique element that determines the character of a political system. If a political system allows the property owners to misuse their property, for example, to buy legislature, police power and judge as early American industrial barons did, it is obvious that private property does not minimise coercion. But this does not impugn the thought that a

---

[194] Cohen, G. A., " Capitalism, Freedom and The Proletariat" in A. Ryan, *The Idea of Freedom* (OUP: Oxford, 1979) pp.9-25.
[195] *Ibid.* p.11.
[196] Ryan. *op.cit.* 7 p.78.
[197] Waldron, *op.cit.* 52 p.294.
[198] Cohen, *op.cit.* 194 p.15.
[199] Ryan, *op.cit.* 7 p.80.

secure system of property rights would be minimally coercive. If 'non-coercion' is the dimension of autonomy-based freedom, the attack on the idea that a secure system of private property could be minimally coercive is sociological rather than philosophical. Marx's attack on capitalism relies in part on the fact that capitalism originated in the forcible expropriation of small farmers' lands; they were thrown off the land and offered the non-choice of working as labourers or starving. Their wage contracts were not freely made. And his other attacks depend on the unfairness in service contracts. He argues that labourers receive less than their contribution to the product. These facts can be explained by historical circumstances rather than philosophical reasons.[200]

As for the relationship between private property and the second element of freedom – i.e. expansion of options – the question is whether private property facilitates options. As defined above autonomy is to value an individual always as an end, not means for other's ends.[201] The autonomous person shapes his life through his free decisions. To be able to do so, he should have an adequate range of available options. In a system of common property or planned economy, since everything is planned centrally, individuals would not have opportunity to shape their own lives by their own decisions and plans.

Therefore, one of the more persuasive routes from freedom to ownership is to point to the increased options that the invention of ownership brings about. Without guarantees of future control over the objects of ownership, individuals cannot create novel objects, cannot engage in exploratory economic and productive behaviour. Property allows people to contract with one another for future performance conditional on half-predictable events taking place. Innovation, imagination, creativity are the terms to conjure with.[202] This argument is distinct from utilitarian argument because it cares about the expansion of options rather than caring about satisfying pre-existing desires.

Hayek's defence of private property and the free market can be located within this tradition.[203] He maintains that a system of private property allows people to determine their ends and to find out how to optimise the use of all available resources. He is quite clear that it is not a utilitarian argument because it does not propose a planned society so as to attain predefined ends (maximisation of total happiness) by known means. He argues that openness of human nature and indeterminacy of what is available to satisfy people's desires justifies an emphasis on private ownership.

To sum up, it can be said that only in a secured system of private property rights would people have enough options to create their own lives. So, a system of private property rights is compatible with autonomy-based freedom and it is a constituent of autonomous life.

---

[200] Ryan, *op.cit.* 7 p.81.
[201] Kant, *op.cit.* 175 p.91.
[202] Ryan, *op.cit.* 7 p.85.
[203] Hayek, F. A., *Law, Legislation and Liberty* vol. 1 *Rules and Order* (Routledge & Paul Kegan: London, 1982) p.113.

Another line of justification of property by autonomy can be linked to the concept of privacy.[204] Accordingly, if every resource is publicly controlled or in principle available for use by all on equal terms, the use of material resources by an individual will in every case count as an 'other-regarding' action. Since every action involves the use of some material resources, it would follow that individuals were answerable to others for each and every action they performed. Such complete answerability would be morally exhausting and individually debilitating; therefore, it would be intolerable. It follows that to be able to live an autonomous life a person should have a realm of private freedom where he can make decisions about what to do and how to do it, justifying these decisions, if at all, only to himself. In order to realise these decisions and plans he needs to have control of a certain material environment from the use of which the interest and concerns of others and of society generally could be taken to be excluded. So, a system of private property that involves the exclusion of others from individual property is necessary.[205]

Lastly, it is necessary to discuss the situation of a person who is faced with abject and long-term material deprivation. A person in such a situation would be preoccupied with his most impelling needs and would have neither the opportunity nor the psychological space to consider in general how he wants his life to go. His behaviour would be composed almost entirely of actions impelled by the elementary need to find subsistence. Immersed in his basic needs, he never has the opportunity to attain the autonomy and control of his desires that we value in human freedom. This implies that being an autonomous person positively requires some degree of material security. However, this cannot be evaluated independently of other requirements of autonomous life, being morally, politically, and economically independent. When all these requirements are evaluated together it can be said that the ideal of autonomy generates a very strong argument for an ideal of property-owning democracy in which it is the moral duty of governments to provide a guaranteed material security to all on the basis of resources or sources of income that they own.[206]

To sum up, if Raz's autonomy-based freedom is accepted as the justificatory base for human rights, it can be said that a secured system of private property rights is constituent of an autonomous life, because only in a system of private property rights will people have adequate options to create their own life. Therefore, people have a fundamental right to private property. This justification includes two stages: first, it justifies the existence of a system of private property rights. And secondly, as a consequence of autonomous choice, if one chooses to work and produce something or earn some money without breaching others' rights, the respect for autonomy requires respect for the fruits of autonomous choice.

---

[204]Harris, *op.cit.* 22 p.224; Clark, L., "Privacy, Property, Freedom and the Family" in R. Bronaugh (ed.) *Philosophical Law* (Greenwood Press: London, 1978).

[205] Waldron, *op.cit.* 52 p.295.

[206] *Ibid.* p.307.

3.6. Conclusion

The main conclusion of the chapter is that property rights can be justified by more than one moral theory. If Raz's autonomy-based freedom is accepted as the ground of human rights, different arguments can be proposed for private property rights. According to autonomy-based theory, the justificatory base of human rights is the capacity of human beings to autonomous conduct. An autonomous life requires the minimisation of coercion and manipulation and the availability of an adequate range of options. This autonomy argument promotes justification of private property rights in all levels, i.e. general, special and particular justificatory levels. That is, the respect for autonomy requires, first, the existence of a system of private property (general justification) and secondly, in a system of private property if one, as an autonomous agent, chooses to labour and produce a value without breaching others' rights, it requires recognition of consequences of autonomous conduct (special and particular justification).

For general justification of a system of private property rights by autonomy-based freedom, different arguments can be put forward. Firstly, a system of property rights is option-facilitating, it provides enough options for individuals to plan and shape their lives (Autonomy argument). Secondly, a system of private property promotes individuality and privacy by providing a right to exclusive use of things (Privacy argument). Thirdly, such a system provides an opportunity for individuals for self-realization and recognition by appropriating, using, and alienating things (Personality argument).

Special and particular justification of property rights by the ideal of autonomy depends on the labour theory. The term 'labour', here, is understood widely including any physical, mental, or entrepreneurial initiative. Respect for autonomy requires respect for the fruits of peaceful autonomous conduct. If an autonomous agent produces or gains something by working, thinking, contracting without breaching others' rights, he is entitled to the fruit of his action. Denial of his entitlement means denial of his autonomy. (Although the right to contract is distinct from property, a system of private property cannot be imagined without a right to free contract, and it [right to contract] can also be justified by the ideal of autonomy.)

The utility argument and its efficiency principle can play a secondary role in justification of a system of private property. Since autonomous life is possible only in an autonomy-supporting society, material well-being can be accepted as an aspect of autonomy-enhancing society and indirectly of autonomous life. The efficiency principle of economic analysis can help to determine how natural resources should be owned and operated so as to increase the well-being of society. It can be argued that private property rights can increase human well-being because it constitutes an incentive for labour and creative activity. For example, it can be argued that if natural resources are owned privately and operated privately, they can be more productive and more beneficial to human beings. But since the utility argument has only a secondary role it should not account for existing property rights appropriated justly. Even if, as a result of utilitarian calculus, public interest requires the expropriation of privately owned property, priority of property rights requires compensation to be paid in return.

However, property rights are not absolute or limitless. Since the moral reasons set out in this chapter justify only *prima facie* property rights, other moral reasons, which will be examined in the following chapter, can justify limitation of these rights. If appropriation, use, or alienation of property injures others' rights, it must be restrained. And since autonomy is possible only in an autonomy-supporting environment, governments may restrict property rights in order to establish and maintain and even to develop such a society. But there must be a fair balance between individual's interests and public interest. The measures taken by government should be proportional to the aimed ends. These limitations will be examined in the next chapter.

To sum up, this chapter suggests that the right to property can be justified as a *prima facie* human right. The moral arguments proposed here justify that there should be a system of private property and a free market system which provide individuals with the opportunity to have private property and which guarantees that property against interferences. But they do not guarantee that every individual will have private property. The conclusions attained in this chapter will guide us to understand the nature of the regulation of P1-1 and to evaluate the Convention organs' related jurisprudence in terms of moral theory in the following chapters.

Chapter 4

Limitation of Property Rights

4.1. Introduction

In Chapter 2, constitutionally protected property was defined as comprising all vested pecuniary rights and legitimate expectations relating to patrimonial rights. It was also remarked that property rights embrace open-ended use rights, control powers, and transaction powers with respect to things. And the previous chapter showed that those rights could be justified as *prima facie* human rights on the grounds of at least four sound moral arguments revolving around the concepts of autonomy and freedom. Therefore, Raz's autonomy-based freedom theory was accepted as the main justificatory base for property rights. Since property rights can be justified as *prima facie* human rights, it was argued that they could be restricted for legitimate moral reasons. This chapter looks at those moral reasons on the grounds of which property rights can be restricted or interfered with by government. In other words, the subject of this chapter is the question of how far and on what grounds can property be interfered with by government legitimately? Determination of the justificatory basis of governmental interference is necessary to establish the limits of just interference. In order to decide whether actions of governmental bodies violated the property rights of individuals we should have the criteria of legitimate intervention. As the moral justification of property rights depends on autonomy-based freedom theory, moral justification of interferences with property may also be found in this theory. Every interference with property should aim to establish, to continue or to advance an autonomy-enhancing society.

According to the aims of public authorities, three different kinds of interferences can be distinguished. These are taxation, taking of property by power of eminent domain, and controlling the use of property by police power regulations. A number of other taxonomies can also be proposed. For example, Harris puts forward a classification which comprises four categories of limitation rules: property-independent prohibitions, property-limitation rules, expropriation rules, and appropriation rules.[1] The European Convention on Human Rights includes a triple taxonomy according to the effect of interference over property: interference with the essence of property, deprivation, and control of the use of property.[2] Nevertheless, in terms of determination of the legitimacy of interferences the above taxonomy seems to be the best approach because moral justification of interferences depends on the aims of public authorities.

---

[1] Harris, J. W., *Property and Justice* (Clarendon Press: Oxford, 1996) p.32.

[2] For a detailed discussion of this taxonomy see Chapter 7 below.

Firstly, relying on its taxation power, government can take some of the property of individuals in order to provide public services. There is no objection to financing public services through taxation on the basis of equal sharing of public burdens. However, there is no common sense about which services should be considered as public services. The main question is whether welfare services should be provided by public funds or, in other words, whether morality or justice considerations require the government to interfere with the allocation of resources through redistributive taxation. Moral legitimacy of redistributive taxation is a matter of philosophical controversy. There are many different arguments from utilitarianism to various egalitarian theories about how the allocations of resources are just. However, to see whether a sound moral argument can be proposed to limit the power of redistributive taxation of government in this chapter, only two of them, Rawls' 'difference principle' and Nozick's 'entitlement theory', will be examined because they represent two mainstreams of liberal thought. A slightly modified form of Raz's argument, on the basis of harm principle, will be adopted as the main justificatory base of redistributive taxation. The European Convention on Human Rights does not include any limitation over the taxation power of the state. Thus, contracting parties have a wide margin of discretion to determine their own social policies.

Secondly, governmental interference may occur in the form of expropriation of existing property of individuals when public interest requires. The moral basis and conditions of expropriation will be the subjects of scrutiny. In this context, the concept of 'public interest' as a justificatory base of expropriations, the requirement of compensation and the principle of proportionality will be the main themes of inquiry.

The third form of governmental interference is control of the use of property by police power regulations. Control of the use of property is a very wide concept. It includes various aspects of conflict of rights and balancing these conflicting interests. Many different criteria have been suggested to reconcile conflicts of rights. The Convention sets the notion of 'general interest' as the acceptable cause of control of use of property. This notion seems to be derived from the utility argument, but there are other arguments that can shed light on the limitation of property rights. The social function theory of property was a prominent approach when the Convention was drafted. In this chapter, along with the social function theory of property, Rawls' first principle of justice (priority of liberty) – liberty can be restrained only for sake of liberty – and the harm principle will be examined. In this book, the harm principle will be considered as the main justificatory basis of police power regulations.

During the examination of basic arguments, in this chapter, Raz's theory of autonomy-based freedom will always be considered as the overarching principle to determine basic standards of limitation of property rights.

4.2. Taxation

In order to provide basic public services such as national defence and security, and the administration of justice, government needs monetary resources. Taxation has long been accepted as a legitimate power of a sovereign authority as a means of financing public expenses. Taxation has been justified on the basis of equal sharing of public burdens. Article 13 of the French Declaration of Rights, 1789 states that 'for the upkeep of a police force and for the expenses of the administration, common taxation is indispensable. This should be shared equally among all citizens, according to their means'.

There is no controversy about whether government should have the power of taxation. But the problem is what is the limit of this power? Does government have an unlimited power to impose taxes on citizens or is there a limit to this power? A possible answer to this question comes from utilitarian theories. Utilitarianism suggests that excessive taxation is a disincentive to fruitful work and investment and reduces the total utility. Public choice theorists also argue that there should be constitutional limits to public expenses and taxation.[3] But it is difficult to set a clear legal limit on the power of taxation. The only concrete legal limit on the power of taxation is prohibition of discrimination. Discriminatory taxation is not acceptable. This issue will be examined in Chapter 8.

The main discussion in political philosophy about taxation is whether redistributive taxation is legitimate. Distribution of property has always been one of the most controversial themes in political philosophy. Does justice require any governmental interference in the social distribution of goods? If so, on what grounds should the goods be distributed? The problem is that if it is supposed that autonomy includes freedom to accumulate resources without limit, then the rich will, in the outcome, have the ability to pursue life-plans which are denied to the poor, so where is equality? On the other hand, if it is insisted that resources should be equally (or on another basis) divided, how can anyone pursue an autonomous life?[4]

Two rival approaches can be observed to the question of what justice is. Some theorists give the central role to commutative or corrective justice. Justice for them is primarily a matter of property rights, keeping of contracts and correcting of injuries. In this view, the question of distributive justice arises only when the owner of some property wishes to distribute it. A rival approach gives the upper hand to redistributive justice. Here the basic question of justice concerns how the benefits and burdens of social life should be distributed. Once a just distribution is achieved, any upset in the *status quo* must be rectified in order to

---

[3] Buchanan, J. and Brennan, G., "Towards a Tax Constitution for Leviathan" in Buchanan J. and Tollison, R. (eds.) *The Theory of Public Choice II* (University of Michigan Press: Michigan, 1984).

[4] Harris, J., *Legal Theories* [hereafter *Legal*] (Butterworths: London, 1997) (Revised Edition) pp.282-3.

restore the distributively just situation. This is the role of corrective justice.[5] Two major divisions of liberal thought, egalitarian liberalism and libertarian liberalism, represent these rival approaches that turn on the implications of autonomy for resource distribution. For instance, whereas Rawls adopts the latter approach, Nozick is a good example of the former.

Of course, there are many other arguments about how resources should be allocated. For example, Munzer argues that the principle of equality and justice requires that everyone should be guaranteed a minimum amount of property necessary for a decent life, and that inequalities of wealth which are wide enough to disrupt fully human life should be narrowed by government intervention (by taxation and welfare distribution).[6] However, putting the needs as basis of rights includes theoretical and practical difficulties. Which needs do yield rights? The importance of needs changes from one person to another, from one society to another and from time to time. Moreover, what is the measure of minimum?[7] Leaving aside the other arguments, Nozick's and Rawls' theories will be examined here.

4.2.1. Nozick's Entitlement Theory of Distributive Justice

Nozick's approach to the distributive justice arguments is shaped by the concepts of basic (natural) rights and the minimal state.[8] He starts from the position that individuals have certain basic rights and duties, in particular the rights not to be harmed in life, health, and liberty. On this ground a minimal state can arise without violation of individual rights, but extensions of state activity beyond enforcing the law against harms and threatened harms to life, health and liberty are not legitimate.[9] The state may not use its coercive apparatus for the purpose of getting some citizens to aid others, or in order to prohibit the activities of people for their own good or protection. So, in his view, the most extensive state, which can be justified, is the minimal state. Any extension of power of the state by considerations of distributive justice violates the people's rights.

Nozick claims that putting the problem as 'how the goods of a society should be justly distributed' is not neutral. It presupposes that resources exist in a big social pot waiting to be justly allocated by some central authority. But there is no pot, only people and associations of people, the natural world and what people produce. There is no central distribution; no person or group entitled to control all the resources, jointly deciding how they are to be doled out.[10] The alternative term he proposes instead of 'distribution' is 'holdings'. A principle of justice in holdings describes what justice requires about holdings. Nozick proposes an entitlement

---

[5] Simmonds, N. E., *Central Issues in Jurisprudence: Justice, Law and Rights* (Sweet & Maxwell: London, 1986) pp.72-3.

[6] Munzer, S., *A Theory of Property* (CUP: Cambridge, 1991) pp.241 ff.

[7] Penner, J., *The Idea of Property in Law* (Clarendon Press: Oxford, 1997) pp.210 ff.

[8] Nozick, R., *Anarchy, State and Utopia* (Blackwell: Oxford, 1974) ch. 7.

[9] *Ibid.* p.149.

[10] *Ibid.*

theory to explain how property rights can be appropriated justly and how justice in holdings could be ensured.

Nozick criticises all redistributive theories for violating liberty.[11] He classifies theories of justice so that whole ranges of theories can be levelled with one objection. According to Nozick's classification, theories of distributive justice can be divided in two ways. They can be patterned or unpatterned, and they can be historical or unhistorical.[12] Historical theories of distributive justice make the justice of a distribution depend on how it came about. It will follow from a historical principle of justice that past circumstances or actions of people can create differential entitlements or differential deserts to things.[13] When a distribution is patterned there is some dimension such that each individual's ranking on that dimension corresponds to the ranking of his share of resources. The most celebrated patterned principles of distributive justice include 'to each according to his merit', 'to each according to his need', and 'to each according to his contribution'.

Principles of distribution that are neither historical, nor patterned specify the structure or profile of just distributions, but do not assign particular individuals to particular positions within these distributions. Nozick calls such principles 'current time-slice principles' or 'end-result principles'.[14] Utilitarian or egalitarian theories are examples of end-state principles. While end-state principles usually do not determine the size of individual's shares, patterned principles do. But both are principles for determining the (relative) size of shares.

Nozick's theory of just distribution, the entitlement theory, is neither an end-state nor a patterned theory. It is unpatterned and historical. It specifies just distribution not by giving a rule for the size of individual shares, nor by stating a mandatory profile or range of profiles for the pattern made by the sizes of individual shares, but by listing procedures by which individuals may justly acquire title to particular resources. According to entitlement theory, though the size of just holdings is always determinate, it does not determine the holdings' justice. Justice of holdings depends solely on the methods by which an individual acquires holdings. Since past circumstances or actions of people can create differential entitlements, Nozick calls the entitlement theory a historical principle of justice.[15] A distinctive feature of entitlement theory is that it connects individuals with particular holdings acquired by particular procedures.[16]

Nozick makes the entitlement theory the beginning and end of distributive justice.[17] He argues that all patterned and end-state principles are wrong because

---

[11] Wolff, J., *Robert Nozick: Property, Justice and The Minimal State*, (Stanford University Press, Stanford 1991) p.75.

[12] O'Neill, O., "Nozick's Entitlements" in J. Paul (ed.) *Reading Nozick: Essays on Anarchy, State and Utopia*, (Blackwell: Oxford, 1982) p.307.

[13] Nozick, *op.cit.* 8 p.155.

[14] *Ibid.* p.154.

[15] *Ibid.* p.155.

[16] O'Neill, *op.cit.* 12 p.308.

[17] Scanlon, T., "Nozick on Rights, Liberty and Property" in J. Paul (ed.) *Reading Nozick: Essays on Anarchy, State and Utopia*, (Blackwell: Oxford, 1982) p.109.

they require continuous interference to the liberty of people to restore disturbed patterns or end-states by voluntary transfers. He explains how liberty upsets patterns by his famous Chamberlain example. Suppose in a society a favoured patterned or end-state distribution is realised, (D1). This distribution can be changed into another distribution (D2) by any one of a variety of means, by gifts, by a successful business or as Nozick suggests by all one million basketball fans willingly paying Wilt Chamberlain 25 pence for each match for the privilege of watching him playing basketball. (D2) does not fit the favoured pattern, so to maintain (D1) a government either would have to restrict these activities or would have to restore (D2) by taxation and redistributive payments. Such continuous interference is obviously unacceptable for an autonomous life. So, the patterned conception of justice cannot be correct.[18] Nozick, to make such measures seem more alarming, ties them to more extreme forms of intervention. He argues that 'taxation of earnings from labour is on a par with forced labour'.[19]

He bases his theory on the basis of separateness of individuals and claims that the coercion of one person to aid another violates the former's rights. However, he ignores that if this principle is taken as absolute, no one can live because every child needs to be taken care of by his/her parents to live and grow up. Nozick should consider that all systems of law coerce parents to take care of their children and, if his claim is right, breach their rights. Moreover, some disadvantaged groups of society such as disabled or elderly people require the help of others to survive. Therefore, some form of moral paternalism is indispensable. Raz's autonomy-based theory offers a better approach to redistributive taxation. But a detailed criticism of Nozick's theory will be left to the end of the examination of his entitlement theory.

4.2.1.1. Entitlement theory According to Nozick's entitlement theory, the subject of justice in holdings consists of three major topics, original acquisition of holdings – the appropriation of unheld things – the transfer of holdings from one person to another, and rectification of previous injustice.

Historical entitlement theories explain the justice or injustice of the distribution of resources, not in terms of structural features of the distributive outcomes in question (such as whether the holdings are equal, or proportionate to the distribution of something else, like need or moral desert), but rather in terms of the procedures by which the distribution was arrived at. It is a system of pure procedural justice. If procedures that are followed by individuals to acquire control over resources are just, then the acquisition is also just. There are two basic processes, according to Nozick, by which people may come to be entitled property.

> 1) A person who acquires a holding in accordance with the principle of justice in acquisition is entitled to that holding.
> 2) A person who acquires a holding in accordance with the principle of justice in transfer from someone else entitled to the holding is entitled to the holding.

---

[18] Nozick, op. cit. 8 p.163.
[19] *Ibid.* p.169.

3) No one is entitled to a holding except by (repeated) applications of 1 and 2.[20]

That is, property may either be justly acquired from those who already justly hold it, or, in certain circumstances, it can be appropriated from nature if it is unowned. Thus, Nozick supplies principles of 'justice in transfer' and 'justice in acquisition' to tell us which methods or procedures must be followed if possession is to be construed as legitimate ownership. The third principle of justice in rectification, to remedy any past injustices, completes Nozick's entitlement theory of justice. This theory provides the background to the claim that individuals have absolute private property rights that are just as strong as their body rights.[21]

What, then, makes acquisition procedure just? Nozick does not himself embark on the task of specifying which procedures for acquiring control over resources from their natural state are just and which unjust. One possibility is that he intends a creation-without-wrong theory of acquisition.[22] We already discussed whether such an argument could justify property rights in the previous chapter. There is no need to repeat those discussions here.

Nozick puts great stress on the principle of justice in transfer since holdings in a society are shaped thorough the transfers. Nozick's principle of just transfer includes three different claims.[23] In his view, a transfer is just if and only if it is voluntary. Firstly, he claims that voluntary transfers can upset any pattern, transforming it into a new distribution. Secondly, if a distribution (D1) is just and people voluntarily moved from it to a new one (D2), surely D2 is just too. And lastly enforcing a pattern requires an unacceptable violation of people's liberty.

The main claim of Nozick is that whatever arises from a just situation by just steps it is just. To make this claim valid Nozick needs to argue that if a transaction is voluntary, then it is just. That is, voluntariness is sufficient for justice.[24] He also implies that voluntariness is necessary for justice, a transaction is just only if it is voluntary. The first problem with this claim is to determine when a transaction is voluntary. For example, if a worker is faced with the choice of working or starving, is the choice to work made voluntarily? It is so, in Nozick's view, provided all those whose actions affect the conditions of choice have acted without violating rights.[25] Contract laws include detailed variations of such situations. Here is not the place to discuss these situations in detail.

But what happens if everyone concerned has acted in a voluntary fashion? Can third parties object to a new distribution that has not affected their shares? One possible response is that the situation of third parties can be adversely affected as a result of accumulation of resources in one hand.[26] For example, a

---

[20] Nozick, *op.cit.*8 p.151.
[21] Wolff, *op.cit.* 11 p.10.
[22] Waldron, J., *A Right to Private Property* (Clarendon Press: Oxford, 1988) p.262.
[23] Wolff, *op.cit.* 11 p. 80.
[24] *Ibid.* p.83.
[25] Nozick, *op.cit.* 8 p.262.
[26] Cohen, G. A., "Robert Nozick and Wilt Chamberlain: How Patterns Preserve Liberty", *Erkenntis,* 11(1977) p.15.

class of people will emerge who can raise house prices through speculative buying, and lower wages by forming cartels. And especially if it is considered that these accumulations and inequalities increased through bequest over generations, it can be said that voluntary transfer can lead to substantial unfairness. Thus on this ground, modern laws actually restricted some transactions even if they are voluntary. Competition laws, anti-trust and cartel laws, and consumer protection laws include some restrictions on voluntary transactions. Similarly, allocation of resources in one hand can also lead to the restriction of others liberties through the exploitation of the political system.[27] Therefore, restrictions on voluntary transactions may be required. These restrictions can be justified on the ground that if such transactions are allowed they cause the exploitation of weak people by economically strong ones. And this exploitation destroys the autonomy of individuals.

As for Nozick's claim that to enforce a pattern requires continuous and unacceptable intrusions into people's lives, only a few egalitarian writers have ever advocated a pattern as rigid as Nozick suggests. Many opponents of redistribution defend a weak or loose pattern, which does not constitute a serious restriction to liberty as Nozick exaggerated.[28] It may be defensible to sacrifice some liberty to support other goals, especially to preserve the autonomy of people.[29] Most theorists claim that some public services such as education and health care should be provided by taxation to maintain an autonomy enhancing society.

However, Nozick claims that taxation involves grave infringement of liberty. In his view, income taxation is on a par with forced labour.[30] His idea is that taxation is a way of forcing people to work for others. The only legitimate forms of taxation are to fund defence, the police and the administration of justice. Here, there is a problem in Nozick's theory. What happens if some of the people cannot afford the protection services? For example what happens in a minimal state if some people cannot afford to pay tax for police protection? Would they be protected against crime? If so, how can he justify the fact that some of the people must be made to pay for the protection services supplied to those who cannot afford them? So, it can be said that redistributive taxation can be justified and tolerated to some extent in order to maintain an autonomy-enhancing society, though it requires unequal sharing of public burdens.

The third principle of entitlement theory is that of justice in rectification. The problem of rectification in Nozick's theory is more complex than it seems. Especially if it is considered that his other two principles are vague and undefined and all state transfers are illegitimate according to his theory. How can these past

---

[27] Baker, C. E., "Disaggregating the Concept of Property in Constitutional Law" in Mercuro, N. and Samuels, W. J., (eds.) *Fundamental Interrelationships Between Government and Property* (Jai Press Inc: Stamford, 1999); Robertson, M., "Liberal, Democratic, and Socialist Approaches to the Public Dimensions of Private Property" in McLean, J., (ed.) *Property and Constitution* (Hart Publishing,: Oxford, 1999).
[28] Wolff, *op.cit.* 11 p.91.
[29] Raz, J., *Morality of Freedom* (Clarendon Press: Oxford, 1986).
[30] Nozick, *op.cit.* 8 p.162.

injustices be corrected? How far in the past should violations of principles of justice in acquisition and in transfer be corrected?

As a result, it can be said that although Nozick's theory of entitlements seems simple and attractive, it includes some practical and theoretical problems. It is far from justifying absolute right to property and capitalist freedoms. But its flaws are not more than any other political theory. So, it can be said that in principle the entitlement theory is *prima facie* a sound and attractive theory and preferable to any other patterned theory of distributive justice in terms of autonomy-based freedom. It can be argued that existing holdings of property are just as long as they have been acquired in conformity with the just appropriation rules. But a different conclusion can be reached from Nozick on the basis of entitlement theory. There are other moral reasons that justify redistributive taxation. Raz's justification of taxation on the basis of autonomy-based freedom is one example. And it can be fused with Nozick's basic entitlement theory.

4.2.2. Rawls' Theory of Justice

Rawls' *A Theory of Justice*[31] is one of the most influential works of the last three decades in its subject. For Rawls the primary subject of justice is the basic structure of society, or more exactly, 'the way in which the major social institutions – such as political constitution, principal economic and social arrangements – distribute fundamental rights and duties and determine the division of advantages from social cooperation'.[32] He proposes a contractarian theory according to which the object of the social contract is to determine the principles of justice for the basic structure of society. Principles of justice, in Rawls' view, are ones that free and rational persons concerned to further their own interests would accept in an initial position of equality as defining the fundamental terms of their association.[33] Rawls calls this way of regarding the principles of justice 'justice as fairness'. Rawls explains his objective for justice as fairness as to give theoretical grounds for constitutional democracy and to provide a reasonably systematic alternative to utilitarianism because, in his view, utilitarianism includes weaknesses as a basis for the constitutional democracy. In particular, it is far from providing a satisfactory account of basic rights and liberties of citizens as free and equal persons, a requirement of absolutely first importance for an account of democratic institutions. So, he uses social contract both for the justification of rights and for the explanation of the features of a well-ordered society. But as Dworkin stated, only right-based theories are compatible with the contract model.[34] The right lying at the heart of Rawls' deep theory is the right of each individual to equal concern and respect. This right is not the product of the contract but a presupposition of Rawls' use of contract. The role of contract is to decide which of

---

[31] Rawls, J., *A Theory of Justice* (Revised Edition) (OUP: Oxford, 1999).
[32] *Ibid.* p.6.
[33] *Ibid.* p.10.
[34] Dworkin, R., " The Original Position" in N. Daniels (ed.) *Reading Rawls* (Blackwell: Oxford, 1975).

several ways of implementing such equal respect and concern is to be preferred. He presupposes a general egalitarian right rather than particular liberties like Locke and Mill did.

Under the veil of ignorance in original position, according to Rawls, the rational individuals will choose two principles of justice:

> 1. Each person is to have an equal right to the most extensive total system of equal basic liberties compatible with a similar system of liberty for all.
> 2. Social and economic inequalities are to be arranged so that they are both:
> a) to the greatest benefit of the least advantaged, consistent with the just savings principle, and
> b) attached to offices and positions open to all under conditions of fair equality of opportunity.[35]

According to Rawls, formulation of two principles of justice presupposes that, for the purposes of a theory of justice, the social structure has two distinct parts, the first principle applying to the one and the second principle to the other. So, he makes a distinction between the aspects of the social system that defines and secures the equal basic liberties and the aspects that specify and establish social and economic inequalities.

According to the first principle – 'Liberty Principle' – all persons should share the basic liberties equally. Political liberty, and freedom of speech and assembly; freedom of thought and liberty of conscience; freedom of person; the right to hold personal property and freedom from arbitrary arrest and seizure are important among these basic liberties. These liberties are to be equal by the first principle. Thus, basic liberties can be limited only for the sake of liberty. This principle has priority over the second principle. That is, there can be no justified reduction of people's basic liberty for the sake of greater economic well-being.[36] The first principle is going to be examined under section 3 of this chapter which is related to the control of use of property.

4.2.2.1. The difference principle The second principle of justice, 'the difference principle', which is related to the distributive shares, holds that social and economic inequalities are only fair so far as they work to the advantage of the least advantaged people in society. This principle will be our primary concern here. The difference principle applies to the distribution of income and wealth and to the design of organisations that make use of differences in authority and responsibility. While the distribution of wealth and income need not be equal, it should be to the advantage of the least favoured group in society. And positions of authority and responsibility should be open to all.

The second principle includes two rules: the difference principle and fair equality of opportunity. The difference principle requires that inequalities in the distribution of resources must be justified by reference to the interests of the least

---

[35] Rawls, *op.cit.* 31 p.266; Rawls gives different formulations of his principles of justice. The quoted one is his final version. See for other versions p.53 and p.66.

[36] Wolff, *op.cit.* 11 p.119.

well-off. In Rawls' view, in the original position rational persons will choose the difference principle according to maximin rule. The maximin rule holds that alternative options should be ranked in terms of their worst outcomes.[37] For example, in the choice of one of A, B, and C options, suppose that A provides a range of resource distributions from zero to 1000 in the society, B from 10 to 20, and C from 5 to 50, the best one is B because the best worst outcome is 10. In the original position, since people are deprived of the knowledge of their own status in society and they would base their choice on very conservative and cautious criteria of rational decision, they will choose the difference principle as a basic principle of justice to regulate their society because the best worst outcome is offered by the difference principle. If, when the veil of ignorance is lifted, I discover that I am one of the least advantaged persons, I can rest assured that everyone will be labouring for my benefit, since the difference principle will permit other people to improve their material welfare only if, in doing so, they also benefit me.

Rawls' theory differs from the utilitarianism in the sense that although the utilitarians allow the differential earnings and incentives in order to increase the general or overall welfare, Rawls allows such inequalities only when they are necessary to increase the welfare of the least advantaged.[38]

The conception of equal opportunity seeks to ensure that people's prospects are determined by the accident of their natural talents and the amount of effort they put in to using those talents; their prospects should not be determined by the accident of social class and fortune. Rawls claims that natural talents and abilities are irrelevant from the point of view of justice. 'We no more deserve our talents and abilities than we deserve our parents' fortune.'[39] So, talents and abilities are regarded as common assets that must be exploited for the benefit of everyone.[40] So, Rawls' theory of justice ignores the principle of desert.[41] One of the most criticised aspects of Rawls' theory of justice is his idea that talents and abilities are to be regarded as common resources to be exploited for the benefit of everyone. Nozick criticises this idea since it ignores the separateness of individuals.[42] He asks why should the same argument not be applied to bodily organs. Some people have two healthy kidneys and two eyes and others not. This difference is also arbitrary from a moral point of view.

Nozick's main criticism of Rawls' theory of justice focuses on the fundamental philosophical grounds supporting the difference principle.[43] In Rawls' view, the issue of justice arises by viewing society as a 'cooperative venture for mutual advantage'.[44] The basic structure is a public system of rules defining a

---

[37] Rawls, *op.cit.* 31 pp.132 ff.
[38] Michelman, F., "Constitutional Welfare Rights and A Theory of Justice" in Daniels, N. (ed.) *Reading Rawls* (Blackwell: Oxford, 1975).
[39] *Ibid.* p.63.
[40] Simmonds, *op.cit.* 5 p.44.
[41] Rawls, *op.cit.* 31 pp.273-4.
[42] Nozick, *op.cit.* 8 pp.227 ff.
[43] *Ibid.* pp.183 ff.
[44] Rawls, *op.cit.* 31 p.4.

scheme of activities that leads men to act together so as to produce a greater sum of benefits and assigns to each certain recognised claims to a share in the proceeds.[45] Social co-operation makes possible a better life for all than any would have if each were to live solely by his own efforts. When people co-operate, they create new benefits, producing more than would have been possible without co-operation, but they also undertake new duties. As a result of co-operation a surplus value occurs. So, for Rawls, the issue of distributive justice is the question of the fair division of this social product, and the burdens that produce it.[46] And according to Rawls, the difference principle captures the fair terms of co-operation. Difference principle ensures that inequalities are justified only if they improve the condition of the worst-off group as much as possible. Other members of society can increase their shares only if the shares of the least well-off rise as well.

How then does Rawls justify the others' sacrifice for the benefit of the worst-off? One of Rawls' answers is that natural obligations of individuals require the best-off to sacrifice for the benefit of the worst-off, because the most important natural duty is to support and to further just institutions.[47] Another possible answer depends on the idea that those who are able to do better are those who are better endowed with social assets such as advantageous family and class background, or natural assets, such as strength, charm, skill, intelligence, which are arbitrary from a moral point of view, so they are not morally entitled to benefits of those social and natural assets.[48]

However, Rawls' idea attracts many criticisms. First of all, this idea puts Rawls himself in the same position with the utilitarians he strongly criticises: ignorance of the separateness of individuals.[49] Secondly, if natural abilities are common assets of society, then why do parties choose the difference principle rather than absolute equality? The option of absolute equality would be the most guaranteed choice for self- or group-interested rational persons. Rawls' reply is that the general rule is equality; inequality is the exceptional one that is justifiable only if it works out better for everyone.

Another related objection is that if desert claims on the basis of personal labour are discounted on the basis of Rawls' argument, then the negative desert claim that criminals deserve punishment should also be denied.[50] Rawls' reply to this objection is that criminal punishment and the distribution of economic and social advantages are completely different issues. These arrangements are not the converse; the function of unequal distributive shares is to cover the cost of training and education to attract individuals to places and associations where they are most needed from a social point of view.[51] So, according to Rawls, in a reasonably well-

---

45 *Ibid.* p.74.

46 Wolff, *op.cit.* 11 p.119.

47 Rawls, *op.cit.* 31 p.293.

48 *Ibid.* p.63.

49 Flew, A., "Social Justice Isn't Any Kind of Justice" (1997) 2 *Liberal Dusunce*, 5 pp.55-65.

50 Sandel, M., *Liberalism and the Limits of Justice* (CUP: Cambridge, 1982) pp.89 ff.

51 Rawls, *op.cit.* 31 p.277.

ordered society those who are punished for violating just laws have normally done something wrong.

The second rule of the second principle of justice is the fair equality of opportunity. Rawls claims that the equality of opportunity does not lead to a meritocratic society, and it does not mean careers open to talents. Rather it tries to provide equality for all to produce the best social outcome for all.[52] Since this rule is not related to the subject of this book directly, it will not be considered further.

So, what does the difference principle offer for the question of welfare rights and redistributive taxation? To what extent can a government levy taxes on individuals to finance public services such as education, health care, and transfers such as disability allowances? To answer these questions we should look at the application of the difference principle.

How can the principles of justice be realised in a society? According to Rawls, the application of the principles of justice will be realised in a four-stage sequence.[53] After the principles are determined in the original position behind the veil of ignorance, it is necessary, in the second stage, to prepare a constitution in accordance with the chosen principles of justice to design a system for the constitutional powers of government and the basic rights of citizens. The difference principle comes into play at the third, legislative stage. It dictates that social and economic policies be aimed at maximising the long-term expectations of the least advantaged under conditions of fair equality of opportunity, subject to equal liberties being maintained. At this point, the full range of general economic and social facts is taken into account. This second part of the basic structure contains the distinctions and hierarchies of political, economic, and social form which are necessary for efficient and mutually beneficial social co-operation. Thus, the priority of the first principle of justice to the second is reflected in the priority of the constitutional convention to the legislative stage.

The last stage is that of the application of rules to particular cases by judges and administrators, and the following of rules by citizens generally.

The difference principle will be applied to the distribution of primary social goods. And since other social goods will be closely correlated with income and wealth, the main subject of difference principle is inequalities in the distribution of income and wealth and accordingly the creation of new jobs and positions to which special economic rewards are attached or an increase in the income associated with an existing job.[54] However, its application is not limited to jobs or offices in the narrow sense, as it includes all the most general features of the basic structure of a society that give rise to unequal shares of primary social goods. In the case of economic goods these will include the system of money and credit, the laws of contract, the system of property rights and the laws governing

---

[52] *Ibid.* p.73.

[53] Rawls, *op.cit.* 31 pp.271 ff.

[54] Scanlon, T. M., "Rawls' Theory of Justice" in N. Daniels (ed.) *Reading Rawls* (Blackwell: Oxford, 1975) pp.192 ff.

the exchange and inheritance of property, the system of taxation, and the institutions for the provision of public goods.[55]

So, in all these laws the advantage of worst-off should be taken into account. Rawls does not discuss how the difference principle is compatible with the right to have personal property, which is one of the constitutional rights. Neither does he discuss what the right to have personal property includes. Since the right to property is a basic liberty, it has priority over the difference principle. That is, to interfere with the right to property for the sake of the difference principle is not legitimate. However, to be able to apply difference principle it will inevitably interfere with property rights in the classical meaning. In order to avoid such an inconsistency he should either explain the inclusion of the right to property or should justify the interferences with property for the sake of the difference principle.

The most important difficulty in the application of the difference principle is to determine the worst-off group and to calculate the possible effects of a proposed policy. It is difficult to find objective criteria to calculate the possible effects of a proposed social or economic scheme.

Rawls is mainly concerned with an ideal theory – the principles of justice in a well-ordered society. However, his difference principle does not determine a set of welfare rights, neither does it suggest a definite minimum for every individual in society which should be provided by a public authority through redistributive taxation.[56] Therefore, the difference principle does not seem helpful for us to determine criteria for the legitimate interference with property rights.

Raz justifies taxation on the basis of the harm principle.[57] According to his theory, since autonomous life is possible only in an autonomy-enhancing society, it is the moral duty of government to establish such a political environment. So, the government can impose taxes justly to establish autonomy-supporting institutions. These taxes can be justified by people's duty to respect autonomy. Since the autonomous life is a morally desirable end, it is the moral duty of individuals to help others' autonomy. This is a perfectionist interpretation of harm principle and relies on a positive liberty approach. It justifies compulsory taxation on the basis of autonomy-based duties.

However, it seems possible to draw a distinction between negative and positive duties. An individual's primary duty to others is a negative duty; not to interfere. The positive duty is a secondary duty; it is contingent to the others' situation. If everyone can afford the conditions of autonomy by oneself, no body has any positive duty to others, because everyone is primarily responsible for their own life. Positive duties do not always recognise claim rights to their recipients, because positive duty limits the duty bearer's autonomy to some degree. The positive duty of individuals to help others' autonomy is also a matter of degree. Their primary responsibility is to themselves and their families, then to their local community, afterwards to their country, and lastly to all humanity. Only members

[55] *Ibid.* p.193.
[56] Michelman, *op.cit.* 38 p.325.
[57] Raz, *op.cit.* 29 p.417.

of a family have claim-rights to get positive help from each other. In other cases, it is the power of legislator to determine who will get help when and how. Although there seems a contradiction in this argument, it is consistent with the European Convention on Human Rights' regulation. The Convention recognises the power of states to collect tax for welfare services, but it does not recognise the rights of individuals to claim welfare. This approach seems to be much more acceptable to many member states whose constitutions include provisions making reference to 'social state'.

To sum up, Raz's autonomy-based liberty theory provides a better justification for redistributive taxation on the basis of the duty of individuals to respect for autonomy. Since the government has a duty to create an autonomy-enhancing society, it is legitimate to levy taxes on individuals to pursue this aim. Raz's interpretation of harm principle will be examined further below in the section concerning the harm principle. The difference between taxation and takings will also be examined in the following section.

4.3. Takings

The second form of authority of government is the power of 'eminent domain'. The eminent domain power can be defined as the state's prerogative to seize private property, dispose of its ownership, and assume full legal right and title to it in the name of some ostensible public good.[58] To be able to fulfil its duties and functions the government needs some material goods. If the eminent domain power is not recognised, the government has to get such goods through purchasing from the free market. Free market transactions, however, are not always suitable and efficient to realise large projects such as building highways, railways and so on which may require the specific property of several individuals for their realisation. Therefore, eminent domain power has long been recognised as a legitimate authority of state even by natural law doctrines.[59] However, the power of eminent domain has been restrained by the 'public interest' and 'compensation' requirements to prevent the abuse of such a strong power. The 'public interest' requirement serves to prevent arbitrary government and arbitrary confiscation of private property. The compensation requirement serves to equalise the sharing of public burdens. These basic requirements can be seen in the writings of Hugo

[58] Rubenfeld, J. "Usings" (1993) 102 *Yale Law Journal* 1077.

[59] For example Hugo Grotius writes '... But we must also observe this, that a King may two ways deprive his subjects of their right, either by way of punishment, or by virtue of his Sovereign Power. But if he do it the last way, it must be for some publick advantage, and then the subject ought to receive, if possible, a just satisfaction for the loss he suffers, out of the common stock...' *The Rights of War and Peace* (London, 1725) B. II Ch. XIV para. VII. (Translation of *De Jure Belli Ac Pacis*, 1625).

Grotius.[60] The great continental theorist of eminent domain asserted that compensation was a natural or necessary corollary of power itself.[61]

However, in the US, before the compensation clause was included in the US Constitution by the Fifth Amendment,[62] republican ideology prevented payment of compensation for government 'takings'.[63] Republican thought, which includes a belief in common good and a conception of society as an organic whole, sees the state's role as to foster the virtue of making the individual unselfishly devote himself to the common good. As Wood asserted, the essence of republicanism was the sacrifice of individual interests to the greater good of the whole.[64] When this communitarian belief was united with the faith in legislatures to perceive the common good, the individual rights played no more than a secondary role in republican thought. Then the individual has an option no more than to trust legislature to protect his rights. As Thomas Paine asserted 'all property is safe under their protection'.[65] Today's compensation laws can be seen as a struggle between these two ideologies (individualist natural law and republican communitarianism).[66]

One of the main problems concerning takings is the difficulty of distinguishing it from police power regulations. There is a rich American literature and Supreme Court jurisdiction about regulatory takings. So, examination of American experience may be illuminating. However, it is necessary, at the beginning, to make clear the conceptual differences between continental Europe and American constitutional understanding of takings. Although the Americans use the concept of 'taking' in a broad meaning in order to comprise any adverse effect on private property caused by government action and requiring payment of compensation, most of the European constitutions use the term 'expropriation' in a narrow and technical meaning of conveyance of title to an immovable property from individual owner to a public authority by an administrative decision. Other terms used to express the conveyance of title to private property are 'nationalisation' for companies and 'confiscation' for movables and chattels. While French lawyers mention 'deprival of property',[67] English lawyers call it

---

[60] *The Rights of War and Peace (De Jure Belli Ac Pacis)* B II Ch. XIV para. VII (London, 1725) (1625) (Translated by several people for the Prince of Wales) see *op. cit.* 2 for the text.

[61] Rubenfeld, *op. cit.* 58 p.1114.

[62] The Fifth Amendment to the US constitution rules that '… nor be deprived of …or property, without due process of law; nor shall private property be taken for public use, without just compensation'.

[63] Trenor, William M., "The Origins and Original Significance of the Just Compensation Clause of the Fifth Amendment" (1985) 94 *Yale Law Journal* 694.

[64] Wood, G., *The Creation of the American Republic 1776-1787* (New York, 1969) p.53.

[65] Thomas Paine quoted by Trenor *op. cit.* 63 p.701.

[66] Malloy, Robin P., " A Classical Liberal Critique of Takings Law: A Struggle Between Individualist and Communitarian Norms" in Nicholas Mercuro (ed.) *Taking Property and Just Compensation* (Kluwer AP: London, 1992).

[67] Bell, John S. *French Constitutional Law* (Clarendon Press: Oxford, 1992) p. 182.

'compulsory purchase' and Australians 'resumption'.[68] Finally, the Convention uses the term 'deprivation'[69] which comprises all expropriations, nationalisations, confiscations and maybe more. So the terms 'taking' or 'deprivation' will be preferred here to 'expropriation' since they are more inclusive.

Here first, the difference between taxation and takings will be examined and then the conditions of takings will be scrutinised.

4.3.1. Takings and Taxation

A 'taking' is defined as an adverse effect, which should be compensated, on private property caused by government action.[70] However, this definition is far from being explicit, because it leaves vague what the adverse effect is. Almost all actions of government cause some advantages for some people while causing some disadvantages for others in a private property economy. So it is necessary to determine which adverse effects constitute taking.

One of the questions to be examined is how can takings be distinguished from taxes? Munzer argues that the difference between taking and taxing can be clarified by the distinction between fixed and unfixed distributions of property. In his view, a distribution is unfixed if it is vulnerable to legitimate tax on income or wealth and fixed if it is not thus vulnerable. According to this distinction, moral and political problems of takings arise only insofar as a distribution is fixed, because there is no private property in a full sense to be taken insofar as legitimate taxes have been paid. The standard background for takings presupposes that legitimate taxation is not in the picture anymore. This theory suggests that legitimate taxes are not takings.[71] However, this idea is not helpful in solving the problem since it does not clarify which taxes are legitimate. Sometimes an excessive taxation may amount to taking. Epstein[72] argues that though taxes are not different from takings in nature – the common purpose of all taxes and takings is to raise the revenues necessary to support various state activities – and taxation is *prima facie* a taking of private property, there are justifications available for taxation. Nevertheless, this argument is also unhelpful in making the distinction clear because the justificatory bases of both the takings and taxations are broadly the same; to finance public policy in order to enhance the public interest.

The difference between takings and taxes can be found in the distinction between the burdens they impose. While taxing imposes an equal burden on all members of the society in the same position, taking imposes a specific burden on

---

[68] Garner, J.F. (ed) "Compensation for the Compulsory Acquisition of Land" in *Compensation for Compulsory Purchase* (London, 1975) (Published by The UK National Committee of Comparative Law) p.4.

[69] Art. 1 of the First Protocol to the Convention states in the first paragraph that '... No one shall be deprived of his possessions except in the public interest...'

[70] Munzer, *op. cit.* 6 p.420.

[71] *Ibid.* p.421.

[72] Epstein, R., *Takings: Private Property and The Power of Eminent Domain* (Harvard University Press: Cambridge, 1985) p.100.

only some members of society.[73] For example, if a law requires everyone who purchases a car to pay a definite amount of money to the government, it is a tax law. But if a city council decides to expropriate a plot of land which is owned by person A to build a school, it amounts to taking because the burden of the policy is imposed only on A. Although a governmental act is not immunised against the question of takings merely because it has been labelled a tax, most taxes are not takings because they spread the cost of operating the governmental apparatus throughout the society rather than imposing it upon some small segment of it. What makes taking individual property without compensation unacceptable is that it imposes an excessive burden on some individuals to finance public interests. Thus once the cost of the governmental act diffuses broadly, though perhaps not to every member of the society or to each in identical amounts, it would seem that the essential problem of taking would be overcome. Still in some hard cases, especially if the so-called tax burden is imposed on only a small group of people, it can be difficult to decide whether the regulation is taxation or takings. In such cases the question of equality before the public burdens arises.[74]

4.3.2. Public Interest

The sovereign power of the state does not give it the authority to take any individual's property without cause. Grotius writes that 'But we shall only observe, that there are some of the civil laws that are plainly unjust, as those by which all ship-wreck's goods are confiscated. For to take away any man's property without a cause, is manifest injustice'.[75] According to his opinion, a state (King) can deprive his subjects of their rights only 'for some publick advantage'.[76] To justify the state's interference with private property many constitutions and human rights documents require it to be in the public interest.[77] The aim of this requirement is to protect the individual against arbitrary confiscation of his property. The state can use its eminent domain power only for the public good. Then what is the public interest and how does it overcome the individual's human rights?

Although there are many different theories of the public interest, these theories, according to Held,[78] can be analysed in three different general categories:

---

[73] Sax, J., "Takings and Police Power" (1964) 74 *Yale Law Journal* 36-76.

[74] For example, the German Federal Constitutional Court found some tax laws unconstitutional recently on the grounds that they violated the principle of general equality. See the *Coal Penny* case (91 BverfGE 186 [1994]) and the *Interest Tax* case (84 BverfGE 239 [1991]) quoted by Kommers, Donald P., *The Constitutional Jurisprudence of the Federal Republic of Germany* (Duke University Press: London, 1997) (Second Edition) p.246.

[75] Grotius, B.II Ch. VII para.I.

[76] *Ibid.*

[77] For example the French Declaration of The Rights of Man and of The Citizen, 1789, states, in Article 17, that '... No one can be deprived of it (property), except when public necessity ... requires it...' the German Constitution, 1946, states, in Article 14, that 'property may be taken by expropriation only in the public weal...'

[78] Held, D., *Public Interest And Individual Interests* (Basic Books: New York, 1970).

preponderance or aggregative theories, unitary theories and common interest theories. This classification depends on the relationship posited between the public interest and the interests of the individual members of the society and the conception of interest which itself is in use.[79]

According to aggregative theories, 'interest' is defined by individuals subjectively and public interest is no more than the aggregation of individual interests. It has no independent content. This theory is closely linked to utilitarianism. So it attracts all the criticism directed towards utilitarianism. One is that there is no practicable mechanism for determining what is in the interest of a preponderance of individuals. Given finite resources, it is logically impossible to maximise the satisfaction of disparate individual interests in any straightforward sense. Some interests should be sacrificed for the sake of the greater satisfaction of others. However it is technically impossible to calculate what is the greatest possible amount of interest satisfaction since there is no objective means of measuring the value of different interest to different people. The only possible result that will be reached by voting is dominance of majority over minority interests in any conflict. Thus, it is morally unacceptable under the autonomy-based freedom theory.[80]

Unitary theories assume that there is an overriding public interest that transcends and reconciles apparently conflicting individual or sectional interests. According to unitary theories, individual interests can objectively be determined consistent with a theory about what they ideally ought to want or what is good for them. In order to transcend apparent conflicts between individual or sectional interests they must either conceive the existence of alternative policies which will please everyone or remove some interests from the calculation by defining them *a priori* as illegitimate within an overriding scheme of moral values.[81] This second option comprises the danger of paternalism. Moreover, it assumes that it is possible to develop an internally consistent unitary moral theory. Nevertheless, since the conflicts of interests are inescapable, in practice, politically strong groups may identify their own interests as public interests.[82]

In Held's classification, the third category of public interest theories is common interest theories. Common interest theories distinguish public interest from individual interests. In these theories public interest refers to interests that all members of the public have in common. According to Barry,[83] interests include both subjective and objective features. For him, actions are in people's interests if they increase their opportunities to get what they want for themselves. While specification of goals remains a subjective question for individuals, how best to

---

[79] McHarg, A., "Reconciling Human Rights and the Public Interest: Conceptual Problems and Doctrinal Uncertainty in the Jurisprudence of the European Court of Human Rights" (1999) 62 *The Modern Law Review* 671-96.

[80] Lyons, D., "Utility and Rights" in J. Waldron (ed.) *Theories of Rights* (OUP: Oxford, 1984).

[81] McHarg, *op. cit.* 79 p.675.

[82] *Ibid.* p.676.

[83] Barry, N., *Political Argument* (Harvester Wheatsheaf: London, 1990) chs 10-14.

achieve them is in principle objectively determinable. Accordingly, though individuals can have different interests in respect of the same situation since they occupy different roles in society, a collective agreement can be found in the same situation. Then public interest is any action that is conducive to the fulfilment of goals that the public wants for itself as a whole.

However public interests are not simply interests that individuals coincidentally happen to share, but they are discovered by asking 'what sort of society do we wish to live in?' and 'how best can we achieve those goals?' So public interests necessarily imply universality. That is, individuals have an interest in it simply because they are members of society, not because they occupy a special role in the society.[84] To express the same idea Barry[85] and Bell[86] use different language. They make a distinction between common interests and public interests and use the term 'common interests' to express group interests. For example, doctors or nurses have special interests in opening of a new hospital in a city since they will have new job opportunities. Although doctors and nurses have common interests in this situation, their common interests are not the public interests of being a doctor or nurse. However, at the same time, they have interests, as being members of society because they themselves or their families will have better conditions to access health care. These interests are public interests. So a policy aiming to open a new hospital is in the public interest if it aims to improve health services for all residents in the city. But if such a policy mainly aims to create new job opportunities for doctors and nurses, it is not in the public interest. So the public interest does not comprise all potential public policy goals, only those concerning the promotion of collective welfare broadly defined. The public may choose to sacrifice collective welfare to the promotion of particular individual or group interests or in pursuit of other ideals that are valued as ends in themselves regardless of their instrumental benefits.[87] For example, if we look at the example above, the city residents may approve building a new hospital only to provide new job opportunities for health sector workers, although the city does not need a new hospital to improve health services. They may aim, in this case, to keep more doctors and nurses available in the city in case of need, and so there is public interest.

Since in this approach the public interest is determined by people's preferences, it can be expressed within the context of particular political systems. So its content may vary in different societies and over time. One objection to common interest theory is that it is unlikely that people always agree about the social goals or means of achieving them. However, because it is difficult to identify group interests, the decisions of a democratic majority about public goals can be treated *prima facie* as valid, as long as they constitute genuinely universalisable interests. If everyone benefits somehow from policies even if they

---

[84] McHarg, *op. cit.* 79 p.677.
[85] Barry, *op. cit.* 83 p.190-206.
[86] Bell, J., "Public Interest: Policy or Principle?" in Roger Brownsword (ed.) *Law and The Public Interest* (Franz Steiner Verlag: Stuttgart, 1993).
[87] *Ibid.*

do not personally share the goals in question, those policies can be said to be in the public interest. In such cases, even if some will lose and some will gain as a result of policy, it can be justified as in the public interest if it provides some contribution to the fundamental structure of the community as a whole.[88]

Whichever of these theories is accepted, the main determinant of the public interest will be the democratic government or legislator. Whenever a conflict arises between individual and public interests, they should be weighed against one another and whichever is the stronger should prevail. In the context of judicially protected human rights, however, it is doubtful whether courts may legitimately carry out such a balancing exercise. In preponderance theories the role of judge in cases of conflict is very limited because the majority's preference always prevails.

In the common interest conception the public interest is determined by the public and once it is determined, it is, in principle, an objective question whether particular actions contribute towards public goals. Whenever public interest defences are invoked, then the role of judge is limited to the technical task of checking that the actions complained of really do contribute to one of the objectives sanctioned by the rights document. The judge should consider how the rights of individuals are affected by governmental actions rather than whether the decisions are in principle right. So the judges may engage in a rational balancing process, and hence give stronger protection to rights via the concept of proportionality.[89] Applying this test, a court would ask not merely whether impugned acts serve legitimate collective aims, but whether it is necessary to encroach on rights to such a degree in order to achieve those goals. If not, the intervention is not proportional and the defence fails.

This analysis, however, according to McHarg, attracts two criticisms. Firstly it makes the protection given to rights highly context-dependent.[90] That is, it makes the protection vulnerable to change and in relation to supra-national rights documents subject to varying interpretations in different member states. Secondly, counter to the common interest theorists' claim, this approach gives greater weight to public interests than individual rights.

In the unitary version of public interests, both public goals and individual rights are derived from the same moral theory. So choices between individual rights and collective goals are not made by weighing mutually valid principles in each case. Rather, courts must define the respective scope of rights and collective goals in order to remove conflicts between them. Courts may induce a set of clear rules and a list of clear exceptions by making reference to some pre-existing moral theory or overarching moral principle to guide and justify decision-making. However, these theories are abstract in nature and they can themselves be controversial, on the one hand, and they are unlikely to bear sufficient relation to the text of the rights documents to be plausible as theories of interpretation on the

---

88 Bell, *op. cit.* 86 p.30.

89 Alexy, R., "Individual Rights and Collective Goods" in C. Nino (ed.) *Rights* (Aldershot: Dartmouth, 1992).

90 McHarg, *op. cit.* 79 p.679.

other hand. Therefore it is unrealistic to expect judges to develop their own unifying theories.

McHarg proposes a more practicable version of unitary theory.[91] In his approach each right should be taken separately considering the purposes it is intended to serve and the nature of the protection it ought to confer. If in any given case an alleged interference strikes at the heart of the right, making the right meaningless, then the right must prevail, notwithstanding that this hampers the achievement of some desirable collective goal. This approach is similar to the doctrine of an indefeasible core of right, which requires making a distinction between the core of the right which cannot be interfered with, and its periphery, in which it may legitimately be restricted.[92]

This approach seems more advantageous than the common interest approach: firstly, by giving a more active role to judges in setting and defending common human rights standards; secondly, by offering a greater certainty as to the scope of rights than *ad hoc* weighing the individual and common interests; thirdly, giving judges a defence against accusations of political decision-making and usurpation of the democratic function. However, it also has some weaknesses. First, it is unlikely to provide consensus on the purposes of rights. So, the classical debates about interpretation of laws (historical or purposive interpretation or contextual interpretation) arise in the context of supra-national human rights documents as well. Second, while definitional approach protects the core of rights strongly, it gives no authority to judges to assess whether public policy is justified outside the core of rights.[93]

In practice, the European Court of Human Rights seems to be approaching the issue of public interest in the area of property rights as parallel to the common interest theory. Although the Court examines whether an alleged policy is in the public interest, it recognises a wide margin of appreciation to the states to determine what is in the public interest.[94] Its judicial review is limited to the proportionality test.[95]

---

[91] *Ibid.* p.681.

[92] Örücü, E., "The Core of Human Rights and Freedoms: The Limit of Limits" in T. Campbell et al (eds.) *Human Rights* (Basil Blackwell: Oxford, 1986).

[93] McHarg, *op. cit.* 79 p.683.

[94] The court made clear its place in public interest examination in the *James* Judgement stating that 'because of their direct knowledge of their society and its needs, the national authorities are in principle better placed than the international judge to appreciate what is in public interest'. And it defined the scope of its review asserting that 'The court ... will respect the national legislature's judgement as to what is in the public interest unless that judgement is manifestly without reasonable foundation' (para.46) *James and Others v UK* Judgement of 21 February 1986, Series A No. 98.

[95] In the *Katikaridis v Greece* and *Tsomtos and Others v Greece* cases the Court found the law prescribing a method for valuation of expropriated property was unreasonable. *Katikaridis v Greece* and *Tsomtos and Others v Greece* Judgements of 15 November 1996, Collection of Judgements and Decisions 1996-V Nos. 20 and 21; See Sermet, Laurent, *The European Convention on Human Rights and Property Rights*, (Council of Europe Publishing: Strasbourg, 1998) pp.33 ff.

The US Supreme Court's standard of public use necessity is even looser than the European Court.[96] The Supreme Court displays a tolerant attitude towards legislative identifications of the public interest and legislative determinations of how that interest will be served.[97] The Supreme Court traditionally applies to public interest necessity a minimal rationality standard.[98] The French Constitutional Council has also adopted a similar approach. In the *Nationalisation*[99] case the Council decided that it had the right to review the assessment of public interest requirement. However, it would only intervene where there had been a manifest error in evaluation.[100]

Although the public interest requirement is inserted into the takings clauses of legal documents to prevent arbitrary interference of state with private property, ironically determination of what the public interest is is left to the legislatures by courts. And this requirement is almost dysfunctional in practice. The only commonly articulated restriction on the power of legislatures in this regard is the ban on compulsory transfers of private property to individuals for purposes of purely private gain.

Leaving aside discussion of the European Court's jurisdiction until Chapter 7, here a two-step test can be suggested to decide whether a public policy interfering with the private property rights is legitimate, that is in the public interest. In the first step Raz's autonomy-based freedom theory, as a unitary overarching principle, can guide in deciding whether a proposed policy is serving the public interest. Accordingly, a judge who examines whether a policy violated individual human rights will look at whether the aim of governmental policy is serving to establish an autonomy-enhancing social and economic environment. In such assessment the judge should look behind the expressed aim considering all conditions, especially if an alleged policy is benefiting some individuals or groups. For example, if a legislative or administrative act, despite its general terms, aims to benefit only some individuals, it should be found illegitimate. In any case it is possible to raise reasonable causes to justify expropriation for public interest. Even the condemnation of one business in favour of another big and strong company may raise reasonable causes such as creating new jobs, increasing the tax revenues and so on.[101] However, the concept of public interest should not be broadened so as

---

96 Curtis, Jerome J. Jr., "Comparison of Regulatory Takings Under the United States Constitution and the European Convention on Human Rights" (1989) 14 *European Law Review* 67.

97 The Supreme Court ruled that '... the legislature, not the judiciary, is the main guardian of the public needs to be served by social legislation ...' *Berman v. Parker*, 348 U.S 26, 32 (1954).

98 Curtis, *op. cit.* 96.

99 CC decision no. 81-132 DC of 16 January 1982, Nationalizations, Rec.18; GD, no.33; SB 67 quoted by Bell, J., *French Constitutional Law* (Clarendon Press: Oxford, 1992) pp. 338 ff.

100 *Ibid.* p.178.

101 To see how the American authorities use the eminent domain power in favour of strong companies see Timmons, D. and Womack, L. "Eminent Domain or Domination?" (2000) 24 *Real Estate Issues* 44.

to comprise such cases. This approach brings a radical challenge to most of the European laws, because it offers a specific content for public interest whereas in many European jurisdictions, public interest is accepted as merely a framework – the outcome of a process. However, the content of public interest – advancing autonomy-enhancing society – is open to a broad interpretation.

In the second step, the judge should look at whether the applied policy is proportionate. That is, the means employed are necessary and suitable to pursue aimed objectives. If the policy is appropriate to pursue the legitimate aim, then the judge should decide that the applied policy is in the public interest. Then it should be assessed whether compensation is required.

If the policy fails to satisfy the legitimacy test – it is not in the public interest – it is null and void. For example, suppose that land is expropriated by a city council to transfer to a private company. The sole reason is that the manager of the company donated a lot money to the governing party during the election campaign. No matter what excuses are stated, such an expropriation should be nullified. Even if some compensation is paid, such a policy should not be approved by the judge.

4.3.3. Moral Theory of Compensation for Takings

The first question to be raised here is why government should compensate when public interest prevails over individual right. And the second is when, and how generously, the government should compensate. Two extreme positions are that government should never compensate, on the one hand, and that it should always compensate, on the other hand. Both positions are unacceptable. A rule offering no compensation would undermine the stability of private holdings. On the other hand, a rule offering total compensation is simply inapplicable, since almost all actions of the government affect the value of possessions or economic interests. So, when should government compensate the losses?

4.3.3.1. Public payment for public goods The basic principle requiring compensation is the equal sharing of public burdens. The unfairness in taking is the state's seizing the wealth of some for the benefit of all. Three hundred years ago Pufendorf wrote,

> Natural equity is observed, if, when some contribution must be made to preserve common thing by such as participate in its benefits, each of them contributes only his own share, and no one bears a greater burden than another.[102]

This logic of natural law theorists found a place itself in later constitutions and human rights documents. The French Declaration of Rights, 1789, justifies the taxation on equal sharing basis. Article 13 states that 'For the upkeep of a police force and for the expenses of the administration, common taxation is indispensable.

[102]Pufendorf, Samuel, *De Jure Naturae et Gentium*, Libri Octo 1285 (1688) quoted by Rubenfeld, op.cit. 58 p.1136 footnote 265.

This should be shared equally among all citizens, according to their means'. And Article 17 subjected the taking of private property for public necessity to just and prior indemnity. The US Supreme Court has expressed this view on numerous occasions. In *First English Evangelical Lutheran Church* it ruled 'It is axiomatic that the Fifth Amendment's just compensation provision is "designed to bar Government from forcing some people alone to bear public burdens which, in all fairness and justice, should be borne by the public as a whole"'.[103]

However, if this principle is applied strictly, it conflicts with the redistributive justice considerations. To make a distinction between uncompensable redistributive taxation and compensable takings some differences have been proposed. For example, in the case of taxation, it may be said that even progressive taxes still produce benefits for the taxpayers, creating reciprocity. But when an individual's house is condemned to build a park for his neighbours, there is no such reciprocity. Or it can be said that taxes do not single persons out, as do exercises of eminent domain, but rather spread the relevant burden throughout the entire class of persons satisfying designated criteria of wealth or income.[104] It is difficult, however, to construct a consistent takings theory upon them. The reciprocity principle may especially pose serious difficulty in finding reciprocal benefits in each progressive taxation. For example, do rent-control laws produce benefits for landlords sufficient to offset their effects on rent receipts? Reciprocal benefit argument can be utilised in determination of the amount of compensation, but it cannot be adopted as a criterion to determine whether a taking has occurred. For example the height restrictions on buildings imposed by the planning laws without compensation can be justified on the grounds that such laws benefit all owners.

As for the singling out argument, it seems sounder than reciprocal benefit theory. It may assist to apply the equal protection principle. However, some difficulty still arises in determining when singling out does occur. For example, say to apply a development plan a government exercised eminent domain over a large area, dispossessing thousands of owners to build a big dam. Should the compensation rights of these owners be nullified since the state acted against a great many? The answer should be 'no', because there is still unjustified singling out here. Although there are many other owners, only their lands were expropriated. Once the duty to bear public burdens is justified, then the examination should focus on whether such burdens are equally shared. Unequal burden can be justified only by redistributive justice considerations and such burden should also be shared equally by those who are in the same position.

4.3.3.2. Efficiency justifications (economic analysis) Utilitarian theories try to justify compensation requirement in terms of economic efficiency. The most

---

[103] *First English Evangelical Lutheran Church v. County of Los Angeles*, 482 U.S. 304, 318-19 (1987) (quoting *Armstrong v. United States*, 364 U.S. 40, 49 (1961)).
[104] Rubenfeld, *op. cit.* 58 p.1137.

famous utilitarian explanation belongs to Michelman.[105] He uses the utilitarian approach to answer the question of when governmental action is legitimate and when government should compensate. To pursue the utilitarian ideal – maximize net gains and minimize net losses – he defines three special terms: 'demoralization costs', 'settlement costs' and 'efficiency gains'. 'Demoralization costs' are the disutilities to uncompensated losers and their sympathisers and the lost future production from impaired incentives or social unrest that would arise if no compensation for government action were paid.[106] 'Settlement costs' are the total value of the time, effort and resources that would be required in order to reach compensation settlements to avoid demoralization costs. And 'efficiency gains' are the excess of the gains produced by a government action over the losses inflicted by it, not including demoralisation and settlement costs. It includes interpersonal comparison of gains and losses.[107]

According to Michelman, any time a government action is proposed, it is necessary to assess the costs and benefits of the governmental action itself and the costs and benefits of paying compensation to demoralised persons. The first assessment determines whether the action is justifiable. If the costs of demoralisation and of settlement both exceed the efficiency gains of the proposed public policy, then the action is unjustifiable. Such a policy should not be undertaken since the gains of the measure will not be worth its costs. The second assessment gives an answer to the question of whether government should compensate for taking. If government action is justifiable then the utilitarian approach is to pay the lower of the demoralisation and settlement costs. That is, if demoralisation costs are higher than settlement costs, then the government should compensate. On the other hand, government should not compensate if settlement costs exceed the demoralisation costs.[108]

Munzer advances Michelman's theory of taking as a part of his three principles of theory of property.[109] He revises the first assessment of Michelman by proposing a partial compensation. That is, if demoralisation and settlement costs are modified (by offering partial compensation) and efficiency gains exceed modified costs, then government action can be justified. Secondly, he replaces Michelman's terminology with new ones. He substitutes 'noncompensation costs' for demoralisation costs, 'compensation costs' for settlement costs and 'utility and efficiency gains' for efficiency gains. These new terms are more inclusive than Michelman's terms. For example 'noncompensation costs' includes all costs of risk

---

105 Michelman, F., "Property, Utility and Fairness: Comments on the Ethical Foundations of 'Just Compensation' Law" (1967) 80 *Harvard Law Review* 1165-1258.

106 *Ibid.* p1214.

107 Munzer, *op. cit.* 6 p.426.

108 For a detailed criticism of Michelman's theory see Fischel, William A., *Regulatory Takings: Law, Economics and Politics* (Harvard University Press: Cambridge, 1995) ch 4.

109 Munzer, *op. cit.* 6 chs 14-15.

aversion in addition to inclusion of demoralisation costs. Munzer's[110] utility and efficiency principle of takings clarifies some concepts used in Michelman's theory. For example, in Munzer's theory maximisation of utility means maximisation of preference satisfaction, especially those preferences that involve rational and institutionally legitimate expectations concerning material things.

These moral theories of takings obviously need to be detailed in many ways. And they are not flawless. They all presuppose that utilitarianism is the best moral theory to reconcile public policies and individual rights. So they attract all criticisms which can be directed towards utilitarianism. Therefore, they can hardly help in solving the legal problem of takings fully. However, Munzer's analysis distinguishing the just existing property allocation from partly just allocations can be utilised to determine when and how much compensation should be paid. For example a law aiming at the correction of past wrongdoings, say to correct the effect of colonialism, should be treated differently from a law restraining the rights of legitimate owners.

While in the former situation failure to pay full compensation can be tolerated provided that their legitimate expectations are respected, in the latter full compensation is required.

4.3.3.3. Instrumentalism Rubenfeld proposes a different approach to the taking issue redefining the aims of constitutional rights.[111] According to his opinion, the main aim of the rights is to ensure that individuals are political ends not means. So they should be treated as the state's authors not tools. If a law takes over individuals' rights, it both commits an injustice to the individual, who ought to be recognised and treated as a political end, and threatens the political liberty of the people, who are supposed to be the state's authors not its tools. The rights have both intrinsic and purposive values. These twin aspects of rights are two sides of a single coin: in violating each of these rights, the state fails to respect its citizens. In this theoretical framework, the point of compensation law is to protect owners against instrumentalisation for state's policy. The right of compensation guards individuals against state instrumentalisation in the form of a conscription of their property.[112] It offers that if the state wants to use property, it should make it (property) first its own property, paying the market value as compensation.

He defines property, in a Hegelian way, as the embodiment of human will and subjectivity. A person's property, in his view, precisely by being marked off legally and conventionally as his, stands as the repository, the emerging reflection, of what ought to be his politically independent will. Therefore, when the state takes a thing marked off as belonging to a private person and puts it to use, it

---

[110] Carol Rose argues that Munzer's theory is not morally pluralistic and other principles can be inserted into the principle of utility and efficiency (maximisation of preference satisfaction). See Rose, Carol M., " 'Takings' and The Practices of Property: Property as Wealth, Property as 'Propriety'" in *Property and Persuasion: Essays on The History, Theory and Rhetoric of Ownership* (Westview Press: Oxford, 1994) 49-70.

[111] Rubenfeld, *op. cit.* 58 p.1142.

[112] *Ibid.*

compromises the independence of his will; it impresses this embodiment of his independent subjectivity into state service, and to that degree the owner is instrumentalised as well. This theory necessarily gives more importance to thing-like property than money, because he accepts that abstract property's capability of being used by state is less than thing-like property. Even, in his view, (which is unacceptable in terms of autonomy-based theory) money, being a highly abstract right masquerading as a thing, is unusable. He tries to justify the difference between taxes and takings on this ground.[113]

On this background, he offers a 'using' theory for takings. Following the words of the US Constitution,[114] he argues that a taking occurs only if a property is taken for public use. That is, if property is not affirmatively conscripted into service for a state-dictated use, if it is merely proscribed a use to the owner, or restricted to be exercised a use of his own choosing, there is not a taking. He shifted the takings analysis from the concept of 'taking away' the property to the concept of 'taking over' property. By doing so, he leaves the protection of property against arbitrary destruction or taking away without putting into any use to the other clauses of the US Constitution. Especially Due Process and Equal Protection clauses guarantee the property against arbitrary governmental interference. However, this is nothing more than a technicality, the owner is not being compensated for taking clause but for infringement of due process or equal protection clauses.

Rubenfeld's 'Usings Theory' and its instrumentalisation theory, despite its valuable contribution to the takings argument, is not free from some crucial flaws. Firstly, his definition of property is not the only sound argument explaining the right to property. His theory attributes more value to thing-like property and use-value than abstract property and exchange-value. However, this theory cannot be acceptable from the point of view of the autonomy-based freedom argument because respect for autonomy of individuals largely consists in securing for them adequate options, that is, opportunities and the ability to use them. Both the use-value and exchange-value of property represents opportunities for their owner and denying of any of these values diminishes his opportunities.[115] Most of the welfare of the contemporary individual consists of monetary advantages such as share rights, entitlement rights from government, pension rights rather than things. So leaving these legal monetary interests vulnerable against governmental interference injures the autonomy of persons as much as taking over their 'things' does.

Secondly, it is not always easy to determine when governmental interference constitutes mere proscription and when conscription to the state-mandated use. For example, he defines the banning of coal mining that harms the houses and roads on the surface as conscription of subject coal into the state service as a support foundation for other people's buildings, city streets and so on

---

[113] *Ibid.* p1147.

[114] The Fifth Amendment to the US Constitution states that '... nor shall private property be taken for public use, without just compensation'.

[115] Raz, Joseph "Autonomy, Toleration and the Harm Principle" in Ruth Gavison (ed.) *Issues in Contemporary Legal Philosophy* (Clarendon Press: Oxford, 1987).

in *Pennsylvania Coal Co.*[116] However, he accepts the cutting down of cedar trees to preserve the health of nearby apple orchards as mere proscription in *Miller.*[117]

And lastly in some cases mere proscription might be so injurious to the owner that not paying compensation for his losses may harm the sense of justice and fairness. Especially if as a consequence of change in situations a legal activity becomes conceived harmful and is prohibited, the principle of legal security may require some compensation since people's legitimate expectations have been exhausted. Or recognition of a transitional period in order to leave time for people to prepare themselves for a new situation can be an appropriate remedy.

Next, following the examination of justifications of police power regulations, the difference between takings and police power regulations will be explored.

4.4. Control on Use of Property by Police Power Regulations

The third power of the state is its authority to pass regulations governing the use of private property rights. This power of state is sometimes called 'the police power'.[118] At the beginning, it is necessary to distinguish two types of regulations concerning property. The first type of regulations defines the inclusion of property. For example, a statute regulating the conditions of a licence, or a statute limiting the duration of copyrights, defines the nature and inclusion of property. Such regulations are not the subject of this section. Such regulations can be disputed only if they change the inclusion of a right by violating legitimate expectations of the owners. The second type of regulations restricts the use of property and they are the subject of this section.

The main justification for this power is the state's mediator role in the resolution of conflicts between individual rights. Government can restrict the use of property to protect health, safety, and morals of the community. However, inclusion of this power depends on the role attributed to the state. In a communitarian state, this power comprises all kinds of regulation promoting the public good. But in a night watchman liberal state, the inclusion of police power is restricted to the prevention of harm to others. Modern liberal democratic states stand somewhere between these two kinds of states. The European Convention on Human Rights holds the aim of regulating the use of property as to advance 'general interest'.[119] However, there is no definition of 'general interest' either in the *travaux préparatoires* or in the case-law of the Convention organs. In the

---

[116] *Pennsylvania Coal Co. v. Mahon*, 260 U.S. 393, 417 (1922).

[117] *Miller v. Schoene*, 276 U.S. 272 (1928).

[118] Especially in American legal literature it is called police power. See Sax, Joseph L., "Takings and Police Power" (1964) 74 *Yale Law Journal* 36 footnote 6.

[119] Art.1 of the First Protocol states '... The preceding provisions shall not, however, in any way impair the right of a state to enforce such laws as it deems necessary to control the use of property in accordance with the general interest or to secure the payment of taxes or other contributions or penalties'.

Convention organs' jurisprudence the concept of general interest has not been treated as distinct from the concept of public interest.[120] Therefore, the difference in the text of the Convention can hardly help us to make a distinction in terms of aim between deprival of property and control on use of property.

The main difference between use of eminent domain power and regulation (police) power is that the former requires that the losses it caused should be compensated – though the text of the Convention does not mention such a requirement explicitly – while the latter does not. However, the form of the act of state – whether it is formal expropriation or regulation – is not sufficient to determine when payment of compensation is required. Neither is the distinction between deprival of property and control on use of property helpful to decide when the losses should be compensated. Thus, some substantial criteria are necessary to determine in what circumstances, and how generously, the state should compensate those who suffer loss as a result of legitimate policy choices that affect the value of their possessions or economic interests.[121] American courts and scholars[122] have debated the issue of regulatory takings for more than a century. American experience can be utilised in order to distinguish takings from police power regulations.

But first, it is necessary to look at the moral justifications for police power regulations. As indicated above the extent of police power regulations may differ according to adopted political ideology. The communitarian theories expand the scope of police power regulations enormously. According to these theories, property is a social construct and it serves social functions. The social function theory of property has been defended on many different grounds from Christian social theory[123] to socialism. Duguit's social function theory of property – a theory that was highly prominent when Article 1 of Protocol 1 (P1-1) was drafted –

---

[120] Anderson, D., "Compensation for Interference with Property" (1999) 6 *European Human Rights Law Review* 543; Peukert, W., "Protection of Ownership Under Article 1 of the First Protocol to The European Convention On Human Rights" (1981) 2 *Human Rights Law Journal* 37 p.62.

[121] *Ibid.*

[122] See for some important literature Michelman, Franc I., "Property, Utility, and Fairness: Comments on the Ethical Foundations of 'Just Compensation' Law" (1967) 80 *Harvard Law Review* 1165-1258; Sax, J., "Takings and Police Power" (1964) 74 *Yale Law Journal* 36; Sax, "Takings, Private Property and Public Rights" (1971) 81 *Yale Law Journal* 149; Epstein, R., *Takings: Private Property and The Power of Eminent Domain* (Harvard University Press: Cambridge, 1985); Mercuro, N., (ed.) *Taking Property and Just Compensation* (Kluwer AP: London, 1992); Fischel, W. A., *Regulatory Takings: Law, Economics and Politics* (Harvard University Press: Cambridge, 1995); Douglas, W. Kmiec, "The Original Understanding of the Taking Clause is Neither Weak nor Obtuse" 88 *Columbia Law Review* (1988); Oswald, Lynda J., "Property Rights Legislation and The Police Power" (2000) 37 *American Business Law Journal* 529; Rubenfeld, J., "Usings" (1993) 102 *The Yale Law Journal* 1077

[123] Hervada, J., "The Principles of the Social Doctrine of the Church" at http://www.columbia.edu/cu/augustine/arch/social.html.

widens the scope of the police power of a state enormously.[124] Leon Duguit, a French constitutional theorist, wrote at the outset of the twentieth century that:

> the individualistic system of property is breaking down because it tends to protect individual uses alone which are considered as sufficient in themselves ... Today there is a very clear sense abroad that the individual is not the end but the means; that the individual is only a wheel of a huge mechanism, the body social ... Every individual is under an obligation to perform a certain function in the community, determined directly by the station which he occupies in it... For social reasons he is under a duty, therefore, to perform this work and society will protect his acts only if he accomplishes it and in the measure in which he accomplishes it. Property is no longer a subjective right of the owner; it is the social function of the possessor of wealth...[125]

In this communitarian theory, a state is merely a body of men issuing orders. The authority of a state is justified by the function it performs, and according to Duguit, that function was to provide for certain social needs.[126] Private property is justifiable to the extent that it served and is limited by this social mission. According to this theory, private ownership implies a degree of obligation or serves a social function.[127] However, this theory does not specify what are the obligations arising from property ownership. It gives a blank cheque to public authorities to interfere with property rights. This theory argues that property is a social construct whereby society creates and maintains property rights in the first place. And for this reason inherent in the state's creation of property is its ability to limit the extent of property interests for broader social purposes.[128] Nevertheless, most of the proponents of this theory have raised nothing more than a harm principle as public dimension of property. Accordingly, if use of property inflicts harm to the public, such use can be restricted. Of course, the concept of harm should be determined according to evolving social conditions. The social function theory of property has not produced a sensible moral reason to restrict property

---

[124] The effect of this theory on the drafting of P1-1 can be seen in the second paragraph of the article. It hardly restricts the power of the state to regulate the use of property rights. Convention organs have developed some restrictions gradually such as proportionality.

[125] Quoted from Leon Duguit, *Les Transformations Generales Du Droit Prive* (1918) by Schneiderman, D., "Constitutional Approaches to Privatisation: An Inquiry into the Magnitude of Neo-liberal Constitutionalism" (2000) 63 *Law and Contemporary Problems* 83.

[126] Duguit, L., "The Law and the State" (1917) 31 *Harvard Law Review* 1.

[127] Juergensmeyer, J. C., "Florida's Private Property Rights Protection Act: Does it Inordinately Burden the Public Interest?" (1996) 48 *Florida Law Review* 695.

[128] Cordes, M. W., "The Public/Private Balance in The Land Use Regulation" (1998) *Michigan Law Review* 1; Gray, K., "Equitable Property" (1994) 47 (2) *Current Legal Problems* 157; See also Gray, K. and Gray, S., " Civil Rights, Civil Wrongs and Quasi-Public Space" (1999) *European Human Rights Law Review* 46; Gray, K., "Property in Thin Air" (1991) 50 Cambridge Law Journal 252.

apart from harm principle, therefore, it will not be considered as a separate moral justification for police power regulations.

Relating to the legitimate limitation of rights basically two liberal doctrines are distinctive: Mill's 'harm principle' and Rawls' 'liberty principle'. Both theories can be utilised to justify the laws restricting the use of property. Firstly the harm principle will be examined here; especially Raz's[129] interpretation of harm principle as justification of positive duties will be considered. Then Rawls' 'liberty principle' and how it can be applied to limitation of property rights will be reviewed.

4.4.1.Harm Principle

One of the famous justifications for restriction of rights is Mill's harm principle. Mill states that:

> ...the sole end for which mankind is warranted, individually or collectively, in interfering with the liberty of action of any of their number, is self protection. The only purpose for which power can be rightfully exercised over any member of a civilised community, against his will, is to prevent harm to others. His own good, either physical or moral, is not sufficient warrant.[130]

According to Mill, the only justification for the use of law against citizens is prevention of harm to other citizens. The law is limited in its function to the action which is threatening society in some way. This principle also offers that the law should be limited to protecting people against others, not against themselves. The first point prevents the enforcement of moral norms. And the second one is an argument against paternalism or the interference in a person's freedom of action, when it is ostensibly for that person's own good.[131] Mill's principle has been criticised by both legal moralists and paternalist theorists.[132] Especially relating to the decriminalisation of obscene and homosexual acts the harm principle was a subject of controversy. Hart[133] has contributed some insights in to the harm principle. Distinguishing between moralism and paternalism, he did not support coercion for the sake of enforcing society's moral norms while approved the coercion of laws preventing its members from harming themselves.

Related to the property rights the question of whether the harm principle prevents redistributive taxation or provision of public goods out of public funds arises. If the harm principle is understood in Mill's or Hart's sense, it is difficult to justify redistributive taxation or public interest interventions as long as the concept of harm is not redefined. Raz, adopting the harm principle as the sole criterion for coercive interference with the rights of individuals, reaches a different conclusion. According to his autonomy-based freedom theory, respect for autonomy of others

---

[129] Raz, *op. cit.* 29 p. 412.
[130] Mill, J.S., *On Liberty* (Everyman: London, 1972) [First Published 1859] p.78.
[131] Tebbit, Mark, *Philosophy of Law: An Introduction* (Routledge: London, 2000) p.115.
[132] For example see Devlin, P., *Enforcement of Morals* (OUP: Oxford, 1965).
[133] Hart, H.L.A., *Law, Liberty and Morality* (OUP: London, 1963).

requires securing adequate options for others. Depriving a person of opportunities causes him harm. In his view, to harm a person is to diminish his prospects, to affect his possibilities adversely. He makes a distinction between narrow and open-ended broad harm principle.[134] Narrow harm principle allows coercion only for the prevention of harm in the strict sense of the word. However, open-ended broad harm principle allows coercion for the prevention of pain, offence and perhaps some other injuries to a person as well.

Raz argues that the judgement that causing harm is *prima facie* wrong is a moral concept. So if preventing harm is the enforcement of morality, he asks, why stop with the prevention of harm, why not enforce the rest of morality? Would not acknowledgement of such an argument constitute rejection of the harm principle? He says 'no', because he suggests that harm principle is derivable from a morality which assigns high value to individual autonomy and regards the principle of autonomy, which imposes duties on people to secure for all the conditions of autonomy, as one of the most important moral principles. In his view, autonomy-based morality imposes on government not only the prevention of loss of autonomy but also positive duties to provide the conditions of autonomy to people who lack them. So, if the government has a duty to promote the autonomy of people, the harm principle allows it to use coercion both in order to stop people from actions that would diminish people's autonomy and in order to force them to take actions that are required to improve people's options and opportunities.[135] It follows that a government whose responsibility is to promote the autonomy of its citizens is entitled to redistribute resources, to provide public goods and engage in the provision of other services on a compulsory basis, provided its laws merely reflect and concretise autonomy-based duties of its citizens.

This argument justifies taxation and maybe to some extent progressive taxation as well. It may also justify the regulations controlling the use of property as long as they serve to advance an autonomy-enhancing social and economic environment. However, justification of positive duties by the harm principle may especially pose the danger of non-compensation even in the case of exercise of eminent domain power. For example if a piece of land is needed to complete a railroad that would maximise the options of people, then any use of the land other than to complete the railroad is in fact harmful to the public. And it does not require payment of compensation.[136]

If denying the use-value or exchange-value of the property of individuals diminishes their options and injures their autonomy, then how are autonomy-based duties and autonomy-based rights compatible? Raz's suggestion is similar to Rawls' liberty principle. He argues that a moral theory that values autonomy highly can justify restricting the autonomy of one person for the sake of the greater autonomy of others or even of himself in the future.[137] This aggregative suggestion

---

[134] Raz, *op. cit.* 29 p.327.
[135] *Ibid.* p.329.
[136] Rubenfeld, *op. cit.* 58 p.1106.
[137] Raz, *op. cit.* 29 p.331.

may turn the whole theory into utilitarianism. Sacrifice of one person's autonomy for the sake of others does not seem an autonomy-based theory.[138]

Raz's wide harm principle can be utilised as a criterion to determine whether the state is acting in the public interest. However, it cannot be taken as a criterion to determine whether the governmental action is a taking or a police power. Only in the narrow meaning can the harm principle be a justification of police power regulation. That is, regulations restricting the use of property without compensation can be considered as legitimate only if they aim to prevent harm to others. However, it is for the legislator to decide what use is harmful considering the evolving social conditions. For example, a use which was considered harmless ten years ago may be deemed as harmful today because of the changing conditions. But in such cases the regulations restricting the use of property should respect the legitimate expectations of owners. In the next section, the distinction between police power and takings will be examined in detail.

4.4.2. The Principle of Liberty

According to Rawls' theory of justice, basic liberties have priority over the good and they can be restricted only for the sake of liberty.[139] When Rawls first published the *Theory,* he formulated the first principle of justice as follows:

> Each person has an equal right to the most extensive total system of equal basic liberties compatible with a similar system of liberty for all.[140]

This formulation was criticised by Hart as being not explicit and in some way aggregative.[141] He argued that the concept of 'the greater liberty' is unhelpful for a judge or legislature to determine how the different conflicting rights can be reconciled. Giving the example of the right to property as a simple conflict between rights, he asked how the Rawls' formulation could help in the case of conflict between the right of exclusion of the owner over his land and basic liberty of others to free movement. If justice is indeterminate in this minor case of conflicting liberties, then the only choice will be to trust the majority vote of legislators operating under a just constitution and a fair procedure. And the principle of justice does not provide a substantive criterion for limitation of liberties.

Later Rawls changed the formulation of the first principle of justice so as to satisfy Hart's criticism as follows:

---

[138] Ten, C. L., "Comment on Autonomy, Toleration, The Harm Principle" in Ruth Gavison (ed.) *Issues In Contemporary Legal Philosophy* (Clarendon Press: Oxford, 1987).

[139] Rawls, J., *A Theory of Justice* (Revised Edition) (OUP: Oxford, 1999).

[140] *Ibid.* p.266.

[141] Hart, H.L.A., "Rawls on Liberty and Its Priority" in *Essays in Jurisprudence and Philosophy* (Clarendon Press: Oxford, 1983).

> Each person has an equal right to fully adequate scheme of equal basic liberties which is compatible with a similar scheme of liberties for all.[142]

The change is that the words 'a fully adequate scheme' replace the words 'the most extensive total system'. What difference does this change make? Rawls argues that a scheme of liberties is not drawn up so as to maximise anything, and, in particular, not the development and exercise of the moral powers. Rather these liberties and their priority are to guarantee equally for all citizens the social conditions essential for the adequate development and the full and informed exercise of moral powers.

According to Rawls since basic liberties are subject to constitutional regulation, the constitution should guarantee the liberties and their priority and leave the other regulations to the legislative activity. Since basic liberties have priority over the second principle, the right to liberty cannot be limited for the sake of any concept of good. Since Rawls' principles of justice are related to the basic structure of society, they can hardly help to determine specific limitations of rights. So his principles of justice fail to provide us with the legitimate limits of right to property.

However, in cases of conflict between property rights and other basic liberties a balancing test can be applied. For example, if we turn back to the example of Hart, the conflicts between the right to exclude others from property and others' freedom of movement can be solved by a balancing test. If denial of freedom of movement prevents the right-holder from living an autonomous life, and diminishes his options seriously, the right to exclusion of an owner can be restricted to some extent, provided that this restriction does not prevent him living an autonomous life. For example, exclusion of some people from entering a privately owned shopping mall may reduce the opportunities of banned people. On the other hand forcing a private owner to allow such people to enter into the mall does not diminish his opportunities drastically.[143] In that case the owner may be forced to let others enter the privately owned shopping centre. Similarly, property rights cannot be used to infringe other basic rights. The right to exclude others, for example, cannot be used on the basis of racial discrimination. Such uses can be restricted and no compensation is required.

4.4.3. Takings and Police Power Regulations

The next question to be examined is how takings can be distinguished from police power regulations. If there is a formal or *de facto* expropriation or nationalisation, it is obvious that there is a taking. However, it is not always easy to determine which government actions constitute takings. Difficulties arise especially when the government regulations adversely affect private property rights. The US Supreme Court has developed several tests to make this distinction. Some scholarly theories

---

[142] Rawls, J., *Political Liberalism* (Columbia University Press: New York, 1993) p.291.

[143] Gray, K. and Gray S., "Civil Rights, Civil Wrongs and Quasi-Public Space" (1999) *European Human Rights Law Review* 46.

have been offered as well. Yet none is able to solve all takings disputes if offered as a sole test.

One of the oldest theories of taking applied by the US Supreme Court is the physical invasion theory. In this test, first established in the *Pumpley*[144] case, the Court ruled that permanent flooding of property as a result of dam construction constitutes taking although there is no formal expropriation. Invasion theory offers that taking occurs only if the government physically invades private property, and compensation must be paid. Occupations, acquisition of title, and very low government airplane flights directly over private property[145] are examples of physical invasion. In *Loretto*[146] the Court reiterated the invasion theory deciding that a New York statute requiring landlords to permit cable-TV companies to install their equipment in rental apartment buildings constituted an uncompensated taking. Unfortunately, acceptance of the invasion theory as a sole guide provides the government with the necessary tool to use the power of regulation to exploit private owners, for example, where government tries to depreciate the value or inhibit the development of property through zoning so that it has much reduced market value when the government gets around to buying it.[147] Thus the government gets most of the value of the property without any formal taking.[148] Therefore, this theory is incapable of providing necessary protection for private property in the modern world.

One other theory developed by the Court is the noxious use test. The classical case of noxious use test is the *Mugler*[149] case where the Court found that legislation prohibiting the manufacture or sale of alcohol did not constitute taking although the law destroyed the beneficial use of the factory since its aim was solely to prevent individuals from acting in a manner deemed harmful. This test says that, in general, established economic interests cannot be diminished merely because of a resulting public benefit. However, this rule does not apply where the individual whose interests are to be diminished himself created the need for public regulation by his conduct. This test has some appeal. For instance, the imposition of safety regulations without compensation can be justified on the ground that the property owners created the hazard. Nevertheless, the noxious use test is insufficient to explain a great number of other very important cases. For example, a typical nuisance situation is one in which a perfectly lawful industrial enterprise located on the outskirts of the city suddenly finds itself in the centre of a new and unforeseen residential development. In such a situation it can hardly be said that the industrial

---

[144] *Pumpley v. Green Bay Co.* 80 U.S. 166 (1871).

[145] *United States v. Causby*, 328 U.S. 256 (1946).

[146] *Loretto v. Telepromter Manhattan CATV Corp.* 458 U.S. 419 (1982).

[147] A classic example is found in *Miller v. City of Beaver Falls*, 368 Pa.189, 82 A2d 34 (1951). There the city council included plaintiff's undeveloped land in a plot of future parks and passed an ordinance saying that no compensation would be paid for any improvement put upon plotted land within three years following the adoption of the ordinance. In clear effect, the city took an interest in the land in the form of a three-year option to purchase at current value. The Court found it unconstitutional.

[148] Sax, J., "Takings and The Police Power" (1964) 74 *Yale Law Journal* 36-76.

[149] *Mugler v. Kansas*, 123 U.S. 623 (1887).

user created this evil which is now sought to be remedied. The fact is that the evil was created by the unfortunate juxtaposition of two lawful activities. The problem here is inconsistency between perfectly innocent and independently desirable uses rather than a noxious or harm creating activity at all.[150] In such cases the 'legitimate expectations' test can be suggested.

A later employed test is the economic impact or diminution of value. In the *Pennsylvania Coal Co*[151] case the Court for the first time struck down a regulation as an uncompensated taking. The invalidated law was the Kohler Act, under which Pennsylvania had prohibited coal mining that would cause subsidence damage to surface structures, streets, utility lines and so on. The test holds that if government action excessively diminishes the value of property, then there is a taking and compensation must be paid and, if it does not, then no taking has occurred and no compensation need be paid.[152] Sax[153] argues that this theory appears to express two interrelated ideas: (1) that all legally acquired existing economic values are property and (2) that while such values may be diminished somewhat without compensation, they may not be excessively diminished.

The meaning of 'excessive' is necessarily vague, and it does not offer any criteria to determine when a government action constitutes taking. Utilitarian approaches such as Michelman or Munzer's theories may be utilised to determine when the diminished value is excessive. That is, demoralisation or noncompensation costs are likely to be high if the value is greatly diminished. Nevertheless, such an approach scarcely helps the lawyer in determining whether a taking will be judged to have occurred. A judge will not have a clear and definite guidance if he accepts this approach. This approach is similar to the balancing test applied by the European Court of Human Rights. The balancing test simply says that there should be a fair balance between the burden imposed on an individual and the public benefits secured by government action. Since there is not any clear guidance, the judge should assess himself in every single case.

The Supreme Court later, in *Penn Central,*[154] developed an economic viability test according to which regulations may amount to takings only if the size of the economic burden imposed on the property owner by the regulation leaves him with no reasonable economic use. The Court, in this assessment, also took into account the investment-backed expectations of the property owner. The Court decided that the New York City Landmarks Preservation regulation which effectively prohibited the construction of a new high-rise office building above the Grand Central Station Terminal did not amount to a taking because the regulation did not impair the use of the building as a railway station and the expectations of the owner were based on such using. Accordingly, economic viability test suggests that if a regulation destroys all economical use of the property, a taking will be

---

[150] Sax, *op. cit.* 148 p.48.

[151] *Pennsylvania Coal Co. v. Mahon*, 260 U.S. 393 (1922).

[152] Munzer, *op. cit.* 6 p.445.

[153] Sax, *op. cit.* 148 p.53.

[154] *Penn Central Transportation Co. v. New York City* 438 U.S. 104 (1978); see also *Lucas v. South Carolina Coastal Council* 505 U.S. 1003 (1992).

found.[155] Although this approach has brought some significant insights into the regulatory takings jurisprudence such as investment-backed expectations, it is still far from being a solution to the regulatory takings question.

So, none of these tests is sufficient to handle the takings problem individually applied. And, therefore, US courts do not have a single overarching principle to apply in all the cases. And they evaluate every single case separately. Since traditional tests fail in this way, many scholars attempted to produce clear guidance for the takings problems. Among the plentiful academic writings, it is worth mentioning some well-known theoretical approaches here.

Sax has offered two different theories.[156] His first theory defines property as economic values described by a process of competition. So, the essence of property, according to Sax, is not fixity but rather fluidity. Since property is defined as a continuing process, the problem of takings turns on what kinds of competition existing economic values may be exposed to and from what kinds they should be protected. To answer this question Sax, in his first theory, proposes to make a distinction between two kinds of economic loss resulting from government activity and two respective roles played by government in the process of competition from which these losses arise. This analysis rests upon the distinction between the role of government as participant and the government as the mediator in the process of competition among economic claims. The losses to individual property owners arising from government activity of the first type result in a benefit to a government enterprise. But losses arising from the second type of activity are the result of government mediating conflicts between competing private economic claims and produce no benefit to any government enterprise.

So, Sax proposes the rule that when economic loss is incurred as a result of government enhancement of its resource position in its enterprise capacity, then the result should be characterised as a taking, and compensation should be paid. But losses, however severe, incurred as a consequence of government acting merely in its arbitral capacity are to be viewed as a noncompensable exercise of police power. Sax supports his theory with two subordinate arguments. First he claims that the purpose of constitutional protection of property is to guarantee property against arbitrary or unfair government action. Second, when government acts as entrepreneur, there are risks of discrimination, excessive zeal, and unlimited exposure to loss.[157] However, if the entrepreneurial act of state provides a reciprocal benefit or incidental benefit, then in both cases compensation does not need to be paid.

---

[155] Stanley, J. A., "Keeping Big Brother out of Our Backyard: Regulatory Takings as Defined in International Law and Compared to American Fifth Amendment Jurisprudence" (2001) 15 *Emory International Law Review* 349.

[156] The theories appeared in two distinct articles published in a seven-year period. See "Takings and Police Power" [hereinafter Police Power] (1964) 74 *The Yale Law Journal* 36-76; "Takings, Private Property and Public Rights"[hereinafter Public Rights] (1971) 81 *The Yale Law Journal* 149-186.

[157] Sax, Police Power, pp.64-6.

Munzer criticises this theory on the grounds that the distinction between entrepreneur and arbiter is often hard to apply and sometimes the distinction is mainly a matter of form.[158] For example, in the case of historical landscape preservation, is the regulatory act banning changes in historical buildings arbiter or entrepreneurial activity?

The increasing concern for environmental protection incited Sax to offer a more radical theory.[159] He revised the definition of property. While still defining property as involving competition, he emphasises that property is an independent network of competing uses. He claims that property cannot be understood as isolated parcels; rather, the use of any given parcel of property is frequently a use of or demand upon property beyond the border of the parcel. The effects of using property may spill very broadly onto many others. The economic values also can be diffusely held claims. Sax calls these claims public rights. They are entitled to equal consideration with traditional property rights in legislative or judicial resolution of competing uses. Therefore, the problem of takings cannot be solved ignoring the spillover effect. Sax defines three types of spillover effect. The first category includes the cases where use of one person's land physically restricts the uses of other land, as where strip-mining causes drainage problems for lower-lying land. The second category is the uses that interfere (by polluting) with a common good (air, water, visual prospect) to which other people have an equal right. The third category is the uses that affect the wealth or well-being of another. In these cases governments do not have to pay compensation for limitations. Compensation is required only when the government acts in its enterprise capacity and devalues the property that has no spillover effect on a spillover use or government treats differently one of several parcels of property in the same situation.

Sax's revised theory of takings extremely restricts the payment of compensation. Nevertheless, this theory is nothing more than expanding the scope of noxious use. The revised theory is also vulnerable to more criticism.[160] However there is no need, here, to go further.

Oswald[161] proposes to get the takings issue moved out from the fundamental rights discussion and make it a matter of policy. She argues that Government's power to regulate for the common good should remain even if the regulation has a negative impact upon a specific owner. Government should have the power to make regulations in order to adopt the changing social and economic circumstances. And she claims that compensation should not be paid as a matter of rights, rather it should be taken as a matter of policy. So, if the legislature sees it is necessary to pay compensation to make application of policies easy, it can decide to pay compensation. But such an approach can never be a solution, from the point of view of autonomy principle.

---

[158] Munzer, *op. cit.* 6 p.449.

[159] Sax, Public Rights, pp.149-86.

[160] For more criticism of the theory, see Munzer, *op. cit.* 6 pp. 452-5.

[161] Oswald, Lynda J., "Property Rights Legislation and Police Power" (2000) 37 *American Business Law Journal* 529.

The European Convention also does not offer clear criteria to determine when compensation is required and when it is not. The distinction between deprivation and control on use does not seem acceptable in terms of autonomy theory. Since the concept of property comprises both use and exchange values, there isn't a significant moral difference between partial and complete losses to determine when private losses should be compensated. It poses a problem of parcelling.

This survey has shown that both judicial and scholarly proposals fail to provide a satisfactory test applicable for all takings problems. Takings situations differ so greatly that it is almost impossible to construct a test that grapples adequately with the variety and also affords clear and definite guidance to judge. Consequently, maybe the best strategy is to set out a variety of tests and to employ the most appropriate one fitting the conditions of the case in hand. In order to distinguish compensable takings from noncompensable police power regulations, a series of tests can be offered. Firstly, if there is a formal expropriation or nationalisation, full market value should be compensated. Physical invasion normally constitutes taking. However, if there is a reciprocal benefit, for example fitting a police camera over the wall of the house, or if physical invasion does not prevent the owner using his property as a whole, for example fitting a plate to the car, or if it is a requirement to open the commercial use, for example, forcing to permit the installation of cable-TV equipment, compensation may not be required. If property is conscripted to the state-mandated use, it constitutes taking.

If the regulation only forbids the harmful use, it constitutes use of the police power and does not require payment of compensation. The harm principle is accepted in the narrow sense, preventing harm to autonomy. For example, environmental protection laws do not require compensation, provided that property is not conscripted to the public use. But if such laws allocate private property to the state-dictated service, then compensation is required. For example, if a wetland law forbids the owner to use his property and allocates it as a preservation area, it constitutes taking.

However, if a legitimate use is forbidden as a consequence of change in situation, not paying compensation may injure the sense of justice. An autonomous life can be possible only if an individual can make plans and apply them. However, an unstable political and legal environment prevents the application of plans. So in the case of policy changes it is necessary to take into account legitimate expectations. In every single case it is necessary to look at whether an individual is subjected to bare unequal public burden and, if so, his losses should be compensated.

4.5. Conclusion

According to the aims of public authority, three different kinds of interferences can be distinguished. These are taxation, taking of property by power of eminent domain, and controlling the use of property by police power regulations. These powers of government can be justified by the principle of autonomy-based freedom. The duty of public authorities is to create an autonomy-enhancing society in which every individual can realise his or her potential freely. To create such a society, public authorities can interfere with private property.

The first type of interference is taxation. The aim of taxation can be financing public services (providing security, administration of justice and so on) and redistribution. Taxation can be justified on the grounds of equal sharing of public expenses. So, relating to the power of taxation, the most important principle to be observed by the government is the principle of equality in imposing public burdens. Equality principle requires that every individual in the same position should be treated equally in terms of bearing public burdens, otherwise those who are placed under unequal burdens are instrumentalised – they are treated as the means of public policies rather than being the end of them – which infringes autonomy. However, redistributive taxation necessarily ignores this principle because its aim is simply to take from the rich and to give to the poor. Such taxation can be justified by Raz's autonomy-based duty theory. Some unequal taxation can be justified on the grounds of reciprocal benefit or correction of past injustices or redistributive justice.

A general criterion which can be employed to distinguish between takings and taxation is the singling out feature of takings. That is, takings impose the burden of public policies on only some individuals, while taxation places everyone in the same position to bear the burden of public policies on the equal sharing ground. But it is sometimes difficult to apply this criterion when tax laws impose special taxes on only some classes of people.

The takings problem can be analysed in several steps. The first step is the examination of legitimacy of the governmental action. The legitimacy test protects autonomy of individuals against arbitrary interferences of governmental bodies. The objective of interference with property should be to secure public interest. Public interest can be defined in terms of autonomy-based theory. That is, if the aim of the interference is to enhance opportunities for people to realise their plans, then the aim is in the public interest. The second step of legitimacy test is to examine whether the applied policies are necessary and appropriate to pursue aims. This proportionality test also protects individuals against arbitrary interferences.

If the legitimacy test is satisfied, the next step is to determine whether compensation is required. In this stage, it should be observed whether limitation is applied to everyone in the same position equally. Infringement of equality before public burdens makes the individual subject to instrumentalisation. So in order to protect the individual against instrumentalisation it is necessary to equalise burdens among the people. The compensation provides the equalisation. If limitation is applied to everyone in the same position equally, there is no need to pay compensation. (Taxation, planning rules, agricultural policy, etc. – these can also be justified by the principle of reciprocal benefit.) But if the limitation is applied unequally, it is necessary to apply a new test to determine whether compensation is required.

In the third step the aim of interference should be examined. If the aim of limitation is to prevent harmful use of property, there is no need to pay compensation because there is a moral duty binding every individual not to harm others. Therefore, public authorities should prevent harmful use of property (police power regulation). But if the aim of the limitation is to advance public goods, then compensation is required because there is no obligation to bear unequal burden of public goods (takings rule). It is for the democratic legislator to decide which use is harmful. This dynamic aspect of harmful use principle may endanger stability of property. Therefore, in such cases legitimate expectations of the owners should be respected.

Throughout these tests, the principle of proportionality should always be observed as an overarching principle to prevent arbitrary actions of public authorities.

This approach is a realistic one and it will contribute to property discourse both practically and philosophically. In theory, most of the radical liberal approaches are practically impossible to apply in today's modern states. For example, it is unrealistic to expect Nozick's minimalist state to be adopted today. On the other hand, the social function theory of property claims that ownership of property comprises some social responsibilities. Property holding includes some deontological and teleological duties. But they do not specify what those duties are and practically give a blank cheque to the governments to interfere with property. The suggested approach specifies what are the duties arising from ownership.

PART II:
PROPERTY RIGHTS UNDER THE EUROPEAN CONVENTION ON HUMAN RIGHTS

Chapter 5

Background to the Right to Property under the ECHR

5.1. Introduction

In order to evaluate how the right to property is regulated and protected under international human rights law, the ECHR has been chosen because it has the most developed human rights protection system. And it also has almost fifty years of application and highly developed case-law, so it is more appropriate than any other human rights convention to see how far property rights are protected by international human rights protection mechanisms.

To see the application of the theoretical issues discussed in past chapters in practice, regulation of property rights under the ECHR and related case-law will be examined in subsequent chapters. In order to reveal what philosophical and political concerns urged the occurrence of property rights regulation of the Convention mainly preparatory works will be utilised. Examination of preparatory works will shed light on the interpretation of this guarantee by the Convention organs which will be examined in the next chapters. To see how the right of property and the states' power to limit it have been interpreted and how this interpretation evolved the case-law of the Convention organs will be examined.

To be able to understand the development of jurisprudence of the Convention organs regarding Article 1 of the First Protocol to the ECHR (P1-1), it is necessary to be aware of contracting parties' prevailing political and philosophical concerns besides the canons of interpretation. There is a political aspect to the development of jurisprudence of the Convention organs. They are aware that there are limits as to what they can force contracting states to do and change must be gradual.[1] If Convention organs try to force certain values, which are not accepted by all contracting parties strictly, states can leave the Convention, and the Convention fails to pursue its aim. So only by a process of gradual acceptance can the Convention be effective. Although such a pragmatic approach is questionable in terms of moral values and attention should be focused on the legal principles, this political aspect should be borne in mind in appreciating the development of the jurisprudence of the Convention organs.[2] Examination of

---

[1] Van den Broek, P., "The Protection of Property Rights under the European Convention on Human Rights" (1986) *Legal Issues of European Integration* 1986/1, 52-90.

[2] Morrison, C. C., *The Dynamics of Development in the European Human Rights Convention System* (Martin Nijhoff: The Hague, 1981).

preparatory works in detail can illuminate this aspect of jurisprudence regarding the P1-1.

In this section, in order to look at the historical background and drafting process of P1-1, published *travaux préparatoires* of the ECHR will mainly be utilised. However, published *travaux préparatoires* include only debates of the Consultative Assembly, but debates of the Legal Committee, the Committee of Ministers and the Committee of Experts are not included; only proposals and reports of these bodies have been published. Although a large part of the detailed drafting work was undertaken by the Committee of Experts, detailed discussions of these drafts have not been published, and it is a limitation of this chapter in failing to have access to those documents. But discussions which took place before the Consultative Assembly give a general picture of the ideas expressed during the drafting process.

It was not easy to reach an agreement on a formulation of the right to property when the ECHR was being drafted. The right to property proved to be one of the most controversial issues to confront the drafters of the Convention. It took a long time to formulate an article guaranteeing the right to property; that is why it was included in P1-1 rather than in the Convention itself. The following questions were raised during the drafting process.

- Should any right to property be included in the Convention?
- Should the protection protect only personal belongings, or must it be extended to all the rights that a person may acquire with respect to any kind of property?
- Should member states be allowed to take property? If yes, what conditions should be complied with in the exercise of this power?
- When private property is taken, should the owners be afforded compensation and if so, to what extent should payment of compensation be guaranteed?
- If compensation for taking of property is guaranteed, will this guarantee be the same for nationals and foreigners?
- To what extent should member states be afforded a right to impose limitations on the use of property?[3]

Therefore, the heavily controversial issues linked to the right to property gave rise to numerous problems that prevented the drafters from reaching an expeditious agreement on the content of a guarantee of right to property to be included in the ECHR.[4] And the final text included in P1-1 is a result of compromise among different philosophical and political concerns regarding the above-mentioned

---

[3] Aronovitz, A.M., "Individual Patrimonial Rights Under the European Human Rights System: Some Reflections on the Concepts of Possession and Dispossession of Property" (1997) 25 *International Journal of Legal Information* 87-104.

[4] Weil, L. G., *The European Convention on Human Rights: Background, Development and Prospects* (A.W. Sythoff: Leyden, 1963).

controversies rather than being an expression of a single philosophical approach.[5] This feature of P1-1 makes its interpretation more difficult.

In this chapter, first, the appearance of property rights in human rights documents previous to the ECHR will be summarised and then the drafting process of the ECHR and the First Protocol will be examined. Examination of preparatory works of P1-1 will reveal the political and philosophical strands prevailing over the text of the article and will give guidance to interpretation of it. Preparatory works are not only significant as secondary sources of interpretation, but they also guide us to see the changing political, historical and philosophical circumstances which give rise to a teleological approach in interpretation. If a judge knows the historical conditions under which the provision came into existence, he can appreciate the changing conditions fairly while he is giving a meaning to the letter of the provision.

5.2. Property Rights in Human Rights Documents before the ECHR

To understand the philosophical stance of the P1-1, it is useful to examine the regulation of property rights under previous documents. Property rights initially appeared in early bills of rights of the eighteenth century that were introduced as a means to curtail governmental powers. Those early bills of rights reflected the philosophical expositions of natural rights theories that were current at the time.[6] Although these documents were prepared following the American and French revolutions that were fed by republican ideals, they include quite individualistic provisions about the right to property.

The first document that includes the right to property was the Virginian *Declaration of Rights* adopted on 27 May, 1776. It included amongst the 'inherent rights' listed in Art. 1 thereof, 'the means of acquiring and possessing property'. The US Constitution provides a special guarantee to property rights in the Fifth Amendment (1791). It rules that ' ... nor be deprived of ... property, without due process of law; nor shall private property be taken for public use, without just compensation'.[7]

The French Declaration of the Rights of Man and of the Citizens, 1789, proclaimed rights to 'liberty, property security and resistance to oppression' to be 'natural and imprescriptible rights of man'.[8] It regulated right to property as 'property, being an inviolable and sacred right, none can be deprived of it, except

[5] See speech of M. Bastid (France) in Second Session of the Consultative Assembly, Sixteenth Sitting (25 August 1950) in Collected Edition of the "*Travaux Preparatoires*" of the European Convention on Human Rights (hereafter *Travaux*) (M. Nijhoff: Dordrecht,1985) p.114.

[6] Van der Vyver, J. D., "Property In International Human Rights Law" in *Ius Commune*-Book Series- 1996, No:18 International Colloquium pp.451-486.

[7] See http://www.cs.indiana.edu/statecraft/constitution.html.

[8] Art. 2. See Bell, J., *French Constitutional Law* (Clarendon Press: Oxford, 1992).

when public necessity, legally ascertained, evidently requires it, and on condition of a just and prior indemnity'.[9]

Following the rise of positivism and social solidarity argument, the inviolable natural right understanding of right to property lost its influence, and property rights were subject to more limitations.

In the first international human rights document – the Universal Declaration of Human Rights, 1948 – the property rights clause was included in Article 17 as follows:

> 1. Everyone has the right to own property alone as well as in association with others.
> 2. No one shall be arbitrarily deprived of his property.

There was a great deal of debate about this clause, which was adopted only after a series of different drafts and amendments.[10] At an early stage in the preparatory work, the United Kingdom and Australian delegates proposed to delete the clause because, they claimed, the right to property is subject to such extensive national controls that an international norm might become meaningless.[11] In the first draft, only 'personal property' was proposed to be protected, while a later draft would only protect such property as 'meets the essential needs of decent living, that helps to maintain the dignity of the individual and of home'.[12] The final text was prepared by a working group of the Commission on Human Rights consisting of the representatives of France, the Soviet Union, the United Kingdom and the United States. The Article was adopted by the Third Committee of the General Assembly by 39 votes to zero, with one abstention, and by the General Assembly without a vote.

This provision has been interpreted as suggesting a general capacity to own property, or in other words, not to be ruled out of the class of people who may own property,[13] rather than a right to actually obtain property.[14] The reference to the capacity to own property 'in association with others' was inserted to cover collective forms of property, on the proposal of the Soviet Union.

The guarantee against arbitrary deprivation of property, worded in paragraph 2 of Article 17, is not an explicit and strong provision. But it can be interpreted, as a general rule, as prohibiting the taking of property without compensation.[15] However, considering the difficulties emanating from the ideological differences within the international community and other obstacles to the promotion of property rights through the international organisations, an international legal guarantee to the property right cannot escape being of extreme

---

9 Art. 17. See *op.cit.* 8.

10 Rosas, A., "Property Rights" in Alan Rosas et al (eds.) *The Strength of Diversity: Human Rights and Pluralist Democracy* (M. Nijhoff: The Hague, 1992) pp.132-157.

11 UN doc. E/CN. 4/AC.1/SR.8, p.12.

12 UN docs. E/CN.4/21, Annex F, pp.76-77; E/CN.4/95, p.8.

13 Waldron, J., *The Right to Private Property* (Clarendon Press: Oxford, 1990).

14 Rosas, *op.cit.* 10 p.137.

15 *Ibid.*

generality. Article 17 of the Universal Declaration does not constitute an exception to this generality, either.

5.3. The Origins and History of P1-1

During the drafting process of the ECHR the question of whether the right to property should be included in the Convention was discussed in detail. So the history of P1-1 is not distinct from the history of the ECHR. The venture of the Convention begins with the Congress of Europe, held at The Hague in May 1948, convened by the International Committee of unofficial Movements for European Unity. In the Message to Europeans adopted at the end of the Congress, a desire to adopt a Charter of Human Rights and establish a Court of Justice with adequate sanctions for the implementation of the Charter was proclaimed. To realise this desire, in early 1949 the International Juridical Section of the European Movement[16] was formed and appointed to prepare a draft Convention. When the draft was finished, it was submitted, in July 1949, to the Committee of Ministers of the Council of Europe, with a recommendation that it be considered at the first session of the Consultative Assembly.[17]

At the same time, following the adoption of the Universal Declaration of Human Rights by the United Nations, the General Assembly instructed the Commission on Human Rights to prepare a draft Covenant containing binding obligations for states and appropriate measures for its implementation. However, the drafting process took a long time. In 1952 the General Assembly decided that there should be two separate Covenants, to be concluded simultaneously, relating to economic, social and cultural rights, on the one hand, and to civil and political rights on the other. So, when the Council of Europe took up the preparation of a Convention in 1949 it was able to refer to the statement of rights contained in the Universal Declaration and in the first draft of the projected UN Covenant.[18]

Following some hesitation about creating a Convention in Europe distinct from the UN Covenant, preparatory works on the European Convention were commenced by the Council of Europe in 1949. On 12 July 1949 the European

---

[16] The Section was established under the chairmanship of M. Pierre-Henri Teitgen, a former French Minister of Justice, with Sir David Maxwell Fyfe and Professor Fernand Dehausse of Belgium as joint reporters.

[17] For a detailed history of the Convention see Robertson, A. H. and Merills, J.G., *Human Rights in Europe: A Study of the European Convention on Human Rights*. (Third Edition) (Manchester U. Press: Manchester, 1993) (First Published in 1963); Robertson, A.H., "The Political Background and Historical Development of the European Convention on Human Rights" in *European Convention on Human Rights* published by The British Institute of International and Comparative Law, Supplementary Publication No. 11 (Stevens and Sons Ltd: London, 1965); Weil, G.L., *The European Convention on Human Rights: Background, Development and Prospect* (A.W. Sythoff: Leyden, 1963).

[18] Robertson, *op.cit.* 17.

Movement[19] submitted to the Committee of Ministers of the Council of Europe a draft convention that contained a list of political and civil rights including the right to property. Within the list of protected rights in Article 1 the following paragraph was included.

> *k)* Freedom from arbitrary deprivation of property[20]

On 16 August 1949 the Committee of Ministers approved the request that the Consultative Assembly should formulate a Convention only requiring member states to protect those rights and freedoms already assured in their national constitutions. The Committee also requested the Assembly to consider definitions for the various rights to be protected.[21]

The Consultative Assembly began consideration of a European Convention on Human Rights on 19 August 1949. After a general debate on the subject, the issue was referred to the Committee on Legal and Administrative Questions. The Committee's discussions resulted in the Teitgen report of September 1949, which was considered in depth by the Assembly in the same month, and was adopted by the Assembly as Recommendation 38 on 8 September. The Committee took as the basis of its work the Universal Declaration of Human Rights and listed twelve rights which should be protected under the proposed system. These rights contained the right to property.

The Committee first considered the question of what should be the scope of the rights to be protected. Should they be limited to the civil and political rights and freedoms set out in the historic texts such as the American Bill of Rights and the French Declaration of 1789? Or should they extend to cover the rights of an economic and social character which had been incorporated into several of the new constitutions such as the Irish constitution of 1937, the French constitution of 1946, the Italian constitution of 1947 and the Federal German constitution of 1949? The Committee preferred to include only civil and political rights which are accepted after long usage and experience in all the democratic countries.[22] Notwithstanding the Ministers' recommendation, the Committee did not attempt to define the rights in detail. The rights to be guaranteed listed only referenced the corresponding articles of the Universal Declaration. The right to property in paragraph 12 of Article 2 reads as follows:

---

[19] The International Committee of Movements for European Unity was an unofficial organisation whose members were some famous politicians and academics from different countries of Europe. The Movement held the Congress of Europe in The Hague on May 1948.

[20] Draft European Convention on Human Rights prepared by the European Movement see *Travaux,* Vol. I Appendix p.296.

[21] First Session, Fifth Sitting of Committee of Ministers (13 August1949) *Travaux*, Vol. I p.102.

[22] *Travaux*, Vol. I p.218 (Doc. A 290).

12) The right to own property, in accordance with Article 17 of the United Nations Declaration.[23]

However, inclusion of this paragraph of the resolution was problematic. The right to property was not included in the original proposal of the Rapporteur Teitgen.[24] It was proposed by Mr. Bastid's motion and adopted by 10 votes to 8.[25] The extension of the guarantee to cover the right to own property was criticised by some members of the Committee on two different grounds. Certain members of the Committee thought that the right to own property was a social and economic right and there was no reason to differentiate between the right to own property and the other social and economic rights, so it should be excluded from the guarantee, since in principle the social and economic rights were not intended to be covered. Some members of the Committee's objections were tactical. They were of the opinion that it would not be possible at that time to confer on any international organisation the protection of the right to own property, because it would not be possible to make such an organisation responsible for evaluating the legitimacy of the charges and restrictions of various kinds which, according to the economic or social conditions of a country, might be imposed on private property, on account of its social function or general utility.[26] However, the majority of the Committee considered that having regard to the important part played by the right to own property in the independence of the individual and of the family, it should be included in the list of guaranteed rights.[27]

The Consultative Assembly debated each Article of the proposed Convention. During the debates about inclusion of the right to property into the Convention a number of amendments were proposed such as inclusion of a limited guarantee to own property for the owner's personal use,[28] or a guarantee against arbitrary deprivation of property[29] or complete omission of the right to property from the Convention[30] and inclusion of the rights of work, rest, leisure, and an adequate standard of living.[31] These proposals were discussed together in the Assembly since they overlapped.

After a long debate the Consultative Assembly decided, by a vote of 43 to 40, to refer paragraph 12 (the right to own property) together with paragraph 11

---

[23] *Ibid.* p.230.

[24] *Ibid.* p.166 (Doc. A 166).

[25] *Ibid.* p.182 (Doc. A 199).

[26] *Ibid.* p.198 (Doc. A 290).

[27] *Ibid.* p.200.

[28] *Travaux*, Vol. I p.246 (Doc.86); this proposal was cancelled as inappropriate. See Doc. No. 77, Report; Nos. 80 to 85, amendments and official report no.18.

[29] *Travaux*, Vol. I p.254 (Doc. 92); cancelled as inappropriate. See Doc. No. 77, Report; Nos. 80 to 86, 88 to 91, amendments and official report no.18.

[30] *Travaux*, Vol. I p.254 (Doc.93); withdrawn regarding para. 10; Adopted regarding paras. 11 and 12 see Doc. No 77.

[31] *Travaux*, Vol. I p.256 (Doc. 95); cancelled as inappropriate. See. Doc. No. 77, Report; Nos. 80 to 86, 88 to 94 amendments and official report no.18.

(the prior right of parents to chose the kind of education to be given to their children) back to the Legal Committee for further consideration.[32]

Before the Consultative Assembly was the subject matter of the discussion of whether the right to property should be included in the proposed Convention. The differences of opinions that had appeared in the Legal Affairs Committee were also reflected in the discussion on the draft recommendation in the Assembly.[33] The ideas raised in the Assembly can be examined in three groups. The first group defended the inclusion of a guarantee to the right to property. Such ideas came mainly from the Catholic members of the Assembly. They argued that the right to own property is one of the fundamental, natural rights of men and should be included in the Convention. They were of the opinion that the right to own property comes from a natural and eternal law, and therefore, it must be proclaimed that no positive law of civilised and democratic state may violate it.[34] Property is the guarantee of the independence of the individual and family. They pointed out that many totalitarian regimes confiscate the property of individuals in order to suppress the freedom of individuals.

The second group endorsed the inclusion of a limited guarantee for property rights into the Convention. Such approaches arose from a variety of perspectives. Several members made reference to Hegelian personality understanding of property.[35] They claimed that property is an extension or projection of personality and belongings are tied to their owner's being. So they proposed an amendment to change the paragraph to 'The right to own property for the owner's personal use' to indicate that property is a projection of the owner's personality, and therefore commercial property is not a fundamental right and should be excluded from the collective guarantee of the Convention.[36] Apart from this philosophical argument, some pragmatic considerations also gave a result to defence of a limited guarantee against arbitrary expropriation. Considering the difficulty of reaching an agreement on the definition of property to be included in the Convention, some members proposed to provide a guarantee only against arbitrary confiscation of property.[37] They argued that this fundamental minimum of the right to property is the protection against arbitrary acts of totalitarian governments. However, it was argued that the meaning of the notion 'arbitrary' was not explicit and might bring laws adopted by democratically elected legislators before the international authority. Some members argued that an arbitrary action is administrative not legislative.[38]

The third group, in particular the United Kingdom and Swedish members, opposed the inclusion of any guarantee of property rights into the Convention.

---

[32] *Travaux*, Vol. II p.132.

[33] Peukert, W., "Protection of Ownership under Article 1 of the First Protocol to the European Convention on Human Rights" (1981) 2 *Human Rights Law Journal* 37-78.

[34] *Travaux*, Vol. II p.100 (M. Boggiano-Pico, I).

[35] *Ibid.* p. 72 (M. Philip, F); p.98 (M. Dominedo, I).

[36] *Ibid.* p.72 (M. Philip, F).

[37] *Ibid.* p.84 (M. Pernot, F); p.70 (M. Sundt, N).

[38] *Ibid.* p.128 (M. Dominedo, I).

They mainly raised two different objections. One of the objections depended on the tactical grounds. Lord Layton claimed that the proposed convention did not intend to cover a complete or inclusive list of human rights. The aim of the Convention was to define and guarantee the political basis of association of European nations that was the maintenance of certain democratic rights. Therefore, he proposed, two considerations should govern the selection of rights to be included in the Convention: the conclusion of the Convention was urgent and anything that might delay it should be avoided. Secondly, it should be limited to the minimum items needed for immediate purpose. So he pointed out that it is difficult to reach an agreement on the right to property since it was subjected to many kinds of limitations by domestic laws and should not be included in the Convention.[39] Similar considerations were raised by some other members of the Assembly arguing that, depending on a country's economic policy, political opinions varied with regard to the boundaries of the right of ownership. It therefore seemed impossible to arrive at a generally acceptable definition of property.[40]

The second objection to inclusion of the right to property in the Convention came from socialist members of the Assembly. They were of the opinion that the right to property is a social and economic right. They understood the right to property as a positive right to obtain actual property, such as a right to have a house for example, rather than freedom to acquire and possess property.[41] Several speakers argued that it would be unsatisfactory and make a lack of balance if the right to the protection of property were included in the proposed Convention but not social rights such as the rights to work, to leisure, to rest and to a reasonable standard of living.[42]

None of the members who defended the inclusion of the right to own property wanted to include a provision making the right to property an absolute and unquestionable right. Rather, they accepted that use of property should be subjected to limitations for general utility.

A majority was in favour of the inclusion of a provision relating to ownership, but the proposed reference to Article 17 of the Universal Declaration was not felt to be a satisfactory solution. M. Teitgen (France), the Rapporteur of the Legal Committee, indicated that this provision leaves many points vague, such as what the right to property includes, what powers are vested to the state regarding the right to property, what is arbitrary interference?[43] As a result, the right to own property was referred back to the Legal Committee for further consideration.

The part of the draft Recommendation which was not referred back to the Committee was adopted by the Consultative Assembly on 8 September 1949.[44] This draft formed the basis of the works of experts on human rights set up by the

---

[39] *Travaux*, Vol. II p.50.
[40] *Ibid.* pp.60-86 (M. Ungoed-Thomas, UK; M.Edberg, S).
[41] *Ibid.* p.78 (M. Nally, UK).
[42] *Ibid.* p.56 (Lord Layton, UK); p.62 (M. Ungoed-Thomas, UK); p.80 (M. Elmgreen, S); p.98 (M. Callias, UK).
[43] *Ibid.* p.126.
[44] *Ibid.* p.126.

Committee of Ministers. In their report of 16 March 1950 to the Committee of Ministers, the experts recommended the inclusion in the Convention of a provision relating to ownership. They called the attention of the Committee of Ministers to the importance of the right to property, referencing that totalitarian regimes had a tendency to interfere with the right to own property as a means of legitimate pressure.[45]

When the Legal Committee met to reconsider the rights referred back, they established a sub-committee with the task of preparing a definition of property rights.[46] The Committee unanimously approved the following text and submitted it to the Consultative Assembly on 8 August 1950:

> All individuals and corporate bodies are entitled to respect for their property. Such property shall not be liable to arbitrary confiscation. This shall not, however, in any way prejudice the right of the different States to enact such laws as may be necessary to ensure the use of this property for the public good.[47]

It appears in this text that the Legal Committee tried to clear some worries about whether the power of states to control the use of property for the public interest is restricted by property rights guarantee. M. Azara (Italy) explained the theoretical basis of this text as follows:

> …There is clearly established …the fundamental principle that any person, natural or corporate, has the right to respect for his goods and chattels which may not be the object of arbitrary confiscation.
> But, on the other hand, the use which an owner makes of his goods and chattels may not be arbitrary. It is not admissible, however, that the said usage should be contrary to the general interest that such property would end up by being considered, not as a projection of the individual's personality into his effects, according to the elementary rules of law and morality, but as a means of distorting these rules, as a process of emulation, as it were … and there would result from it a species of aberration in the exercise of the right.
> No one today contests the social function of property. This function provides that the utilisation of property, in accordance with the general interest, can be sanctioned by law, only in order to avoid that *cives ad arma veniant*, and each state may decide, through its legislative power, in what form and to what extent the right of the individual should be conformable to the general interest.[48]

The Chairman of the Committee explained the spirit of the proposed text to the Assembly as 'holding divergent political views, to reconcile the social conception of property with the prohibition of arbitrary confiscation'.[49]

During the discussion in the Assembly some members raised their worries about whether the proposed text could bring the nationalisation laws before the

---

[45] *Travaux*, Vol. III p. 262.
[46] *Travaux*, Vol. V p.26.
[47] *Ibid.* p.208.
[48] *Ibid.* pp. 244-46.
[49] *Travaux*, Vol. VI p.76 (Sir David Maxwell-Fyfe, UK).

Court or the Commission. For example, Miss Bacon (UK) asked the Chairman of the Legal Committee (Sir David Maxwell-Fyfe, UK) to give an assurance that 'this article safeguards the right of any state to undertake schemes of nationalisation and for the taxation of wealth necessary to carry out its social policy'.[50] Most of the proponents of the text argued that the proposed Article could never be used to bring the nationalisation or taxation laws before the Court. They recognised that property is a social function and 'the proprietor is put in charge of his property with the sole object of ensuring the maximum return in the general interest'.[51] According to M. Bastid (France) the proposed Article 'reaffirmed that property is an extension of personality; that it should be protected from arbitrary confiscation, that is to say, from those high-handed administrative or private measures of which all the totalitarian regimes furnished such sinister examples'. However, it 'expressly reserved to each state the right to safeguard the social purpose of the property by appropriate legislative enactments'.[52]

Regarding the objection that the right to own property is a social and economic right and that it has no place in the Convention that was meant to deal with personal rights, M. Bastid (France) argued that property had more than an economic significance: it was bound up with the development of the human being. Property is an extension of the man, and man cannot feel safe if he is exposed to arbitrary dispossession.[53] He emphasised that the right to property is an ancient and firmly established right, recognised by all civilised nations and protected against arbitrary confiscation. He claimed that ordinary men who went to battle think that they are defending their right to possession of soil which is 'the fruit of their labour and their lifelong savings, the extension of their individuality and guarantee of their independence'.[54]

On 17 August 1950, the Consultative Assembly, making some amendments, approved the above text and forwarded it to the Committee of Ministers with an urgent request that it should be inserted in the Convention.[55]

However, for reasons which are not known, the Committee of Ministers did not follow the Recommendation and signed the Convention without including a clause guaranteeing ownership. Instead it referred the matter to the Committee of Experts for further consideration and the preparation of a protocol.[56]

In addition to the Assembly's text, two other draft Articles were proposed by the British and Belgian Governments for consideration by the Committee of

[50] *Ibid.* p.138.
[51] *Ibid.* p.116 (M. Bastid, F).
[52] *Ibid.*
[53] *Ibid.* p.118.
[54] *Ibid.* p.122.
[55] *Travaux*, Vol. VI p. 6; the proposed text reads as follows: 'Every natural or legal person is entitled to the peaceful enjoyment of his possessions. Such possessions cannot be subjected to arbitrary confiscation. The present measures may not, however, be considered as infringing, in any way, the right of a state to pass necessary legislation to ensure that the said possessions are utilised in accordance with the general interest.'
[56] Peukart, *op.cit.* 33 p.40.

Experts. The Committee worked on those three texts. The British text proposed that:

> Every natural or legal person is entitled to the peaceful enjoyment of his possessions. This provision, however, shall not be considered as infringing in any way the right of a state to enforce such laws as it deems necessary either to serve the ends of justice or to secure the payment of monies due whether by way of taxes or to ensure the acquisition or use of property in accordance with the general interest.[57]

This text seems to be designed to guarantee the rights of a state to interfere with private property, rather than to protect the right to property against the state. However, the Belgian text was more individualistic and included some guarantees for arbitrary confiscation and compensation for taking of property for public use. The proposed text reads as follows:

> Every natural or legal person is entitled to the peaceful enjoyment of his possessions. No-one shall be deprived of his possessions except in the public interest, in such cases and by such procedure as may be established by law and subject to fair compensation which shall be fixed in advance. The penalty of total confiscation of property shall not be permitted.
>
> The present measures shall not however infringe in any way the right possessed by States to pass legislation to control the use of property in accordance with the general interest or to impose taxes or other contributions.[58]

In their first meeting in Paris on 21-24 February 1951 the Committee of Experts examined these three texts. According to the Committee's report the following formula was accepted as the first sentence of the proposed provision: 'Every natural or legal person is entitled to the peaceful enjoyment of his possessions'.[59] However, opinions were varied about whether the principle of duty to pay compensation for taking of private property for public use should be adopted. While the majority of the delegations were of the opinion that the principle of compensation should be expressly laid down in the protocol in such a way as to make it clear that this principle is binding on national laws, the British delegation opposed the affirmation of this principle for the reasons given below. The British Government thought it could not be worded in such a way as to cover all possible situations and it was inadmissible that international bodies should review the decisions of the competent national authorities on the question of compensation. The French delegation articulated the view that in principle a duty to compensate followed conclusively from the text proposed by the Consultative Assembly, 'such possessions cannot be subjected to arbitrary confiscation' and that it would be difficult to find a more precise formula to cover the special conditions to which the principle of compensation was subject in the laws of all the member countries.[60]

---

57 *Travaux*, Vol. VII p.186.
58 *Ibid*. p.192.
59 *Ibid*. p.206.
60 *Ibid*. pp.206-208.

The French delegation accepted the text proposed by the British delegation on the condition that the above sentence should be inserted after the first sentence of the British text.

After the second meeting of the Committee the following text was submitted to the Committee of Ministers:

> Every natural or legal person is entitled to the peaceful enjoyment of his possessions. No one shall be deprived of his possessions except in the public interest, in such cases and by such procedure as are established by law and subject to such compensation as shall be determined in accordance with the conditions provided for by law.
>
> The present measures shall not however infringe, in any way, the right of a state to pass legislation to control the use of property in accordance with the general interest or to impose taxes or other contributions.[61]

The delegations of France, the Saar and the United Kingdom voted against this text, mainly because they could not accept a definition of the right to property comprising in all cases the principle of compensation in the event of private property being acquired by the state. The Turkish and Swedish delegations abstained.[62]

In further examination delegations agreed upon the following text:

> Every natural or legal person is entitled to the peaceful enjoyment of his possessions. No one shall be deprived of his possessions except in the public interest, and subject to the conditions provided for by law and by the general principles of international law.
>
> The preceding provisions shall not, however, in any way impair the right of a State to enforce such laws as it deems necessary to control the use of property in accordance with the general interest or to secure the payment of taxes or other contributions or penalties.[63]

The grounds of the amendments were explained in the Commentary of the Secretariat-General on the Draft Protocol[64] as follows:

> a) The phrase "arbitrary confiscation" was thought to be too imprecise in a legal text as it is capable of very varying interpretations. Therefore, it was replaced by the phrase "subject to the conditions provided for by law". It was believed to be more precise and to cover adequately the object in mind.
>
> b) There was much discussion as to whether or not it should be stipulated that "no one should be deprived of his property except …subject to compensation". Although the majority of the governments were at one time in favour of a provision to this effect, other Governments felt unable to accept it, as they did not think it possible to express this principle in terms which would be appropriate to all the various types of cases which might arise, and they could not admit that decisions taken on this matter by competent national authorities should be subject

61 *Ibid.* p.230.
62 *Ibid.* p.234.
63 *Ibid.* p.304.
64 *Travaux*, Vol. VIII p.8 (Doc. AS/JA (3) 13; A.S 904 dated 18 September 1951).

> to review by international organs. Nevertheless, the phrase "subject to the conditions provided by law" would normally require the payment of compensation, since it is normally provided for in legislation on the nationalisation or expropriation of property. Further, the phrase "subject to the conditions provided for ...by the general principles of international law" would guarantee compensation to foreigners even if it were not paid to nationals.
> c) The second paragraph was expanded somewhat to make it clear that this article does not prevent the state from collecting taxes, or applying other regulatory measures to the whole of property of individuals in question.[65]

There were no further significant amendments. However, in a letter of 10 July 1951 the Government of the Federal Republic of Germany informed the Secretary General of the Council of Europe that they were prepared to agree to the protocol if it were entered on the records of a sitting of experts or advisors of the Committee of Ministers that the words 'general principles of international law' in the proposed new text were intended to refer to the duty to pay compensation in the case of expropriation.[66] Nevertheless, in a report of the Committee of Experts of 18 July 1951 it was merely stated that the German delegation had drawn attention to the fact that 'the general principles of international law' include the obligation to pay compensation to foreigners in the case of expropriation. It was also noted that, on an indication of the Swedish delegation, 'general principles of international law', to which Article 1 of the Protocol adverts, only applies to the relations between a state and aliens.[67]

As a result the above text was included as Article 1 of the First Protocol to the Convention for The Protection of Human Rights and Fundamental Freedoms signed in Paris on 20 March 1952.[68] Following the ratification of 10 member states, the Protocol entered into force on 18 May 1954.[69] Currently the Protocol is in force in 42 member states.[70] Two member states signed but have not ratified it yet.[71] Among the member states of the Council of Europe only Andorra has not signed the Protocol yet.

To sum up, throughout the preparatory works the discussion was mainly revolved around two rival approaches. On the one hand, the conservative members

---

[65] *Ibid.* p.10.

[66] *Travaux,* Vol. VII p.312.

[67] *Ibid.* pp.316-18.

[68] *Travaux,* Vol. VIII p.212.

[69] The first country that ratified the protocol was the UK the other countries were Denmark, Saar, Greece, Iceland, Ireland, Luxembourg, Norway, Sweden and Turkey. The Netherlands and Germany followed the first ten states. France did not ratify the Protocol until 3 May 1974.

[70] Albania, Armenia, Austria, Azerbaijan, Belgium, Bosnia and Herzegovina, Bulgaria, Croatia, Cyprus, Czech Republic, Denmark, Estonia, Finland, France, Georgia, Germany, Greece, Hungary, Iceland, Ireland, Italy, Latvia, Liechtenstein, Lithuania, Luxembourg, Malta, Moldova, The Netherlands, Norway, Poland, Portugal, Romania, Russia, San Marino, Slovakia, Slovenia, Spain, Sweden, the former Yugoslav Republic of Macedonia, Turkey, Ukraine, United Kingdom.

[71] Switzerland (19 May 1976) and Serbia and Montenegro (03 April 2003)

argued that the right to property is a fundamental right and it should be included into a proposed convention aiming to guarantee a democratic Europe. Their justification of property as a fundamental right was based on several philosophical arguments ranging from natural rights theory to a personality theory and political liberty theory. Although these theories were not discussed explicitly in the committees, the effects of these theories can be seen in the arguments proposed by different members of the committees. For example, some members maintained that property is a natural right sanctioned by divine law, some others claimed that it is a natural extension of personal freedom, others claimed that property is a guarantee of personal freedom and privacy, others asserted that property is an extension of personality. They argued, therefore, that it should be protected against arbitrary confiscation by totalitarian regimes. Although it did not appear explicitly in the *travaux préparatoires,* the discriminatory confiscation of Jewish property by Nazis, or Russian confiscation of foreign property without compensation might be taken into account as fresh memories by those who defended the inclusion of a property guarantee into the proposed convention.

On the other hand, the socialist members claimed that the right to property (as a positive right to have property) is a social and economic right and it should not be included in a document aiming to protect only fundamental rights. Their main worry was that the inclusion of a guarantee for property rights might condemn the social policies and nationalisation programmes they wanted to pursue. The final text can be seen as a compromise between these two rival philosophical and political stances.

5.4. Philosophical Stance of P1-1

The text of P1-1 comprises two philosophical strands relating to the right to property. On the one hand, the first sentence assures that the right to property is a fundamental right. This represents the individual or personal function of the right to property. On the other hand, the second sentence of the first paragraph and the second paragraph recognises states' power to interfere with property for public or general interest. These provisions make reference to the social or public function of property, to serve public interest. This conception suggests that the basic reason why the institution of property is recognised is to advance the collective good of the society.[72] This stance of P1-1, recognising the dual functions of property, is not strange to the European constitutional approach to property. For example, the German Basic Law clearly remarks these double functions of the right to property. Article 14 provides:

> 1) Property and the right of inheritance are guaranteed. Their content and limits are determined by statute. 2) Property imposes duties. Its use should also serve the public weal. 3) The taking of property is only permissible in the public weal. It

---

[72] Alexander, G. S., "Constitutionalising Property: Two Experiences, Two Dilemmas" in J. McLean (ed.) *Property and Constitution* (Hart Publishing: Oxford, 1999).

> may be imposed only by or pursuant to a statute regulating the nature and extent of compensation. Such compensation has to be determined by establishing an equitable balance between the public interest and the interests of those affected. Regarding disputes about the amount of compensation, recourse to the courts of ordinary jurisdiction is available.[73]

Philosophically there is no great difference between P1-1 and this provision of the German constitution apart from the latter's clear compensation guarantee for the taking of property for public weal. So, examination of the German constitutional approach to the right to property may shed light on the philosophical stance of P1-1. There is a strong republican or civic influence in the German approach to property. The aim of recognising the right to property is not to instantiate a neo-classical vision of the minimalist 'night watchman' state and to block legislative or regulatory redistributive measures.[74] Rather it is to protect the right to property as a fundamental moral right within a human society. That is, for a dignified life and self-realisation, recognition of a right to property is indispensable. The individual owner's freedom from external interference with his property is valued just because that is a precondition for him to act in a way that is necessary to realisation of the self. That is, the point of protecting individual ownership is not to create a zone of security from a powerful and threatening state but to make it possible for individuals to realise their own human potential.[75] The civic dimension in the German approach is that property is the material basis for realising a pre-existing understanding of the proper social order. Unlike individual liberalism, individual human dignity exists in a social and economic context and individuals have obligations to create such a society. This approach fuses the traditions of Kantian liberalism and civic republicanism.[76] Although the German interpretation of human dignity and self-realisation is mainly Hegelian, effects of Rousseau's republicanism can also be seen in the political theory of European constitutionalism.[77] Accordingly, individual rights are possible only in a well-ordered society. And individuals' obligations to create such a well-ordered society extend beyond the mere negative duties and include some positive duties. However, it is not clear what these positive duties are. It is more like justification of the social regulation power of the states. This idea can be seen both in the text of P1-1 and in Article 14 of the German Constitution.

Although the text of P1-1 reflects a strong republican approach, it can be interpreted from the point of view of Raz's autonomy principle. The communitarian and paternalistic aspect of Raz's autonomy principle is not far from the German approach. But it gives a definable content to political theory,

---

[73] See http://www.uni-wuerzburg.de/law/gm00000_.html.

[74] Alexander, *op.cit* 72 p.95.

[75] *Ibid.* p.101.

[76] Kommers, D., *The Constitutional Jurisprudence of the Federal Republic of Germany* (Duke UP: London, 1997) p.250.

[77] Antinori, M., "Does Lochner Live in Luxemburg?: An Analysis of the Property Rights Jurisprudence of the European Court of Justice" (1995) 18 *Fordham International Law Journal* 1778.

enhancement of autonomy of the individual. So, it can prevent the undermining of individual autonomy for the sake of autonomy-enhancing society. For example, even if a purpose of advancing an autonomy-enhancing society justifies some public policies, it cannot justify imposing the burden of such a policy only on some individuals.

5.5. Reservations to P1-1

Some reservations were made with regard to P1-1. Luxembourg reserved the applications of Law of 26 April 1951 concerning the liquidation of certain ex-enemy property, rights and interests subject to measures of sequestration.[78] Austria made a reservation in order to avoid any uncertainty concerning the application of P1-1 in connection with some provisions[79] of the State Treaty of 15 May 1955 for the Restoration of an Independent and Democratic Austria.[80]

The Portuguese Government expressed a reservation relating to Article 82 of the Constitution of the Portuguese Republic which provides that expropriations of large landowners, large property owners and entrepreneurs or shareholders may be subject to no compensation under the conditions to be laid down by law.[81] Regarding this reservation of Portugal, the United Kingdom, French and German Governments stated that this reservation did not affect the general principles of international law that require the payment of prompt, adequate and effective compensation in respect of the expropriation of foreign property. Portugal withdrew this reservation in 1987.[82]

San Marino[83] and Bulgaria[84] made reservations to P1-1 regarding the regulations in force concerning the real estate of foreign citizens and regarding the prohibition of foreigners' acquisition of land respectively.

The Spanish Government also, in order to avoid any uncertainty as to the application of P1-1, made a reservation[85] regarding Article 33 of the Spanish Constitution that stipulates the following:

---

[78] Reservation made at the time of deposit of the instrument of ratification, on 3 September 1953.

[79] Reserved provisions of the State Treaty are Part IV 'Claims Arising out of the War' and Part V 'Property, Rights and Interests'.

[80] Reservation contained in the instrument of ratification, deposited on 3 September 1958.

[81] Reservation contained in the letter from the Permanent Representative of Portugal, dated 8 November 1978, handed to the Secretary General at the time of deposit of the instrument of ratification, on 9 November 1978.

[82] Reservation was withdrawn by letter from the Permanent Representative of Portugal, registered at the Secretariat-General on 11 May 1987.

[83] Reservation contained in the instrument of ratification, deposited on 22 March 1989.

[84] Reservation contained in the instrument of ratification, deposited on 7 September 1992.

[85] Reservation contained in the instrument of ratification deposited on 27 November 1990.

> 1. The right to private property and inheritance is recognised.
> 2. The social function of these rights shall determine their scope, as provided by law.
> 3. No person shall be deprived of their property or their rights except for a cause recognised as being in the public interest or in the interest of society and in exchange for fitting compensation as provided by law.

Finally, the Estonian[86] and Latvian[87] Governments declared that the provisions of P1-1 should not apply to the laws on property reform which regulate the restoration or compensation to the former owners or their legal heirs of property nationalised, confiscated, collectivised or otherwise unlawfully expropriated during the Soviet annexation; and privatisation of collectivised agricultural enterprises, collective fisheries and of state and local self government owned property.

5.6. Conclusion

It can be said that the only concrete guarantee of this provision is the reaffirmation of the right to compensation of non-nationals in cases of deprivation of property. The failure to insert a compensation clause for nationals for taking of their property for public use left the guarantee of the Convention for property rights very vulnerable.[88] Reference to national laws provides a procedural guarantee for the process of expropriation, but inability of the Convention organs to review the application of domestic laws by domestic courts weakens this guarantee. The wording of the provision does not provide any further protection which is not included in the domestic laws of the member states. However, it is a success to have the inclusion of the right to property in the Convention since it implies that the right to property is not merely a social and economic right, rather a fundamental right. And it gives the Convention organs the opportunity to improve the guarantee of the Convention for property rights.

P1-1 protects only existing property. It does not guarantee a right to acquire property. So, if someone is left out of the class of people who can own property, he cannot depend on P1-1. For example, if a national law prohibits foreigners' acquisition of property, they cannot bring a case before the Court relying on P1-1.[89] P1-1 clearly defines legal persons as subjects of human rights. Although whether legal persons can be subjects of human rights is controversial philosophically, it meets a practical necessity. Corporate bodies own most of the goods in free market society and leaving their property unprotected is not right. It

---

[86] Reservation contained in the instrument of ratification, deposited on 16 April 1996.

[87] Reservation contained in a Note Verbale from the Minister of Foreign Affairs of Latvia, dated 25 June 1997, handed over to the Secretary General at the time of deposit of the instrument of ratification, on 27 June 1997.

[88] Such a compensation guarantee is established by case-law. See *Lithgow and Others v. UK*, Judgement of 8 July 1986, Series A no. 102.

[89] But such a claim can be based on Article 14 in connection with P1-1.

can be said that legal persons are composed of real persons and protection of legal persons' property is protection of real persons' property indirectly.

Convention organs should consider the effect of the social function-understanding of property which was current at the time when the Convention was drafted, and should take into account the change in that doctrine when they are interpreting the property rights guarantee of the Convention. When the Protocol was drafted the historical factors pushing the drafters was completely different from current concerns. From the 1950s to the year 2000 modern society evolved into late modern society, national states evolved into members of a united Europe. A bi-polar Cold War world order left its place to globalisation and a highly effective market economy. Big public enterprises were privatised both in West European and East European countries. World Trade Organization regulations and European Union Law deeply affected the structure of economies. Following the collapse of the Eastern Bloc, socialist economies changed to the market economy and most of the Central and Eastern European countries became members of the Council of Europe. The Court in its interpretation of P1-1 should consider these broad changes. These changes remark that some of the objections to inclusion of the right to property into the Convention, which affected the structure of the article deeply, have lost their importance today and these changes should be taken into account in interpretation of P1-1. For example, one of the worries about the inclusion of a property guarantee into the Convention was the possibility of condemning nationalisation programmes. Because of that worry, compensation guarantee was not included in the text of P1-1. But today, there is no contracting party to the Convention who aims to apply large nationalisation programmes.

The interpretation methods applied by the European Court of Human Rights are suitable for development of protection for property rights in order to comprise new developments in the social, economic and political structure of Europe.[90] Dynamic, autonomous and effective protection methods give to the

---

[90] For a detailed discussion of interpretation methods applied by the Court see Matscher, F., "Methods of Interpretation of the Convention" in Macdonald, Matscher and Petzold (eds.) *The European System for the Protection of Human Rights* (London, 1993); Harris, O'Boyle and Warbrick, *Law of the European Convention on Human Rights* (Butterworths: London, 1995); Bernhardt, R., "Thoughts on the Interpretation of Human Rights Treaties" in Matscher and Petzold (eds.) *Protecting Human Rights: The European Dimension* (Berlin, 1988); Ost, F., "The Original Canons of Interpretation of the European Court of Human Rights" in Delmas-Marthy (ed.) *The European Convention For The Protection of Human Rights: International Protection versus National Restriction* (M. Nijhoff: London, 1992); Yılmaz, M., *Avrupa İnsan Hakları Mahkemesi Yargısı* (Alfa: İstanbul, 1998); Petzold, H., "The Convention and the Principle of Subsidiarity" in Petzold et al (eds.)*The European System for the Protection of Human Rights* (M. Nijhoff: Dordrecht, 1993); Macdonald, R., "The Margin of Appreciation" in Macdonald et al (eds.) *The European System For The Protection of Human Rights* (M. Nijhoff: Dordrecht, 1993); Eissen, M.-A., "The Principle of Proportionality in the Case-law of the European Court of Human Rights" in Macdonald et al (eds.) *The European System for the Protection of Human Rights* (M. Nijhoff: Dordrecht, 1993); McBride, J., "Proportionality and the European Convention on

Court the tools it needs to establish European standards for property rights. Even if the pragmatic and political aspect of the jurisdiction of the Court (the reluctance of the Court to establish European standards in areas of economic, social and political controversy) is taken into account, new developments still require the improvement of standards for protection of property rights. The Court cannot continue to ignore changes in approach to private property in the laws of the Eastern European countries.

The fear of an enormous increase in the burden of work cannot justify leaving property rights unprotected to a significant extent. The dependence on the fragile consent of contracting states is not a valid excuse for keeping European human rights standards low any more. The significant change in the protection machinery proves that the past fifty years of application of the Convention established a trust of the Convention machinery among the contracting states. This means that a gradual establishment policy was successful, but expired its time. However, this does not mean that the margin of appreciation doctrine should go to the dustbin, but the Court should not use it as an excuse to escape from reviewing property rights disputes. It should define the property rights in abstract first, and then review every single case in its context and assess whether private conditions of the case justify the intervention.

Human Rights" in E. Ellis (ed.) *The Principle of Proportionality in the Laws of Europe* (Hart Publishing: Oxford, 1999).

Chapter 6

Property Rights under the ECHR

6.1. Introduction

In this chapter the first sentence of P1-1, 'Every natural or legal person is entitled to the peaceful enjoyment of his possessions', will be examined. Two distinct questions arise from this sentence. Firstly, what is the extent of the concept 'possessions'? And secondly, what is the responsibility of the contracting states arising from this right? So, the aim of this chapter can be said to delineate the borders of the concept of property rights and to determine the sphere of the responsibility of the state for interferences with property rights.

Although the national constitutions and international human rights documents comprise provisions protecting property rights, they do not define what are property rights. The European Convention on Human Rights does not constitute an exception to this tradition. Consequently, the task of defining what rights constitute property rights is on the shoulders of the judges. The significance of this task is that that definition itself constitutes a limitation over those guarantees provided by the national constitutions and international human rights documents because it determines which rights will benefit from the constitutional and international guarantees and which rights will be left outside the scope of them.[1] So, it is significant to determine criteria defining constitutionally protected property rights.

Theoretical aspects of this question were examined in Chapter 2 in detail. There, the constitutionally protected property was defined as a wider concept than the private law concept of property. It was argued that the aims of constitutional law and private law are quite different. While the aim of the constitutional law is to protect individuals' autonomy against state interference, the aim of the private law is to regulate legal relationships between private individuals. Therefore, the extent of constitutionally protected property can be construed widely to include any vested pecuniary or patrimonial rights that constitute opportunities for an autonomous life. Accordingly, the concept of property in constitutional law comprises the interest included in the private law concept of property as well as other pecuniary interests arising from both private law relationships and public law relationships. It was remarked that such an approach is compatible with both some

---

[1] Allen, T., "Limitations on Constitutional Property Rights" in Jackson, P. and Wilde, D. (eds.) *Property Law: Current Issues and Debates* (Ashgate: Aldershot, 1999).

national constitutional law jurisprudence[2] and public international law applications.[3]

In this chapter, the case-law of the Strasbourg organs regarding the concept of 'possessions' will be evaluated under the light of theoretical conclusions reached in Chapter 2. This chapter will look at whether the case-law of the Convention organs provide us with clear criteria to determine which rights constitute property rights under P1-1. It will also be evaluated whether the Convention's concept of 'property' or 'possessions' are compatible with the approach adopted in Chapter 2.

The second issue that will be examined in this chapter is determination of the sphere of the responsibility of the state for interferences with property rights under the ECHR. This will include the examination of the nature of the responsibility of the state, whether the state has only negative duties – abstaining from interference – or whether it also has positive duties to protect property rights. In this context it will also be examined whether a state is responsible for only public authorities' actions or inactions or if its liability comprises private bodies' actions as well.

6.2. The Concept of Property under The ECHR

The wording of P1-1 does not mention a right to property in the first paragraph, rather it uses the phrase 'peaceful enjoyment of possessions'. It employs the concept of 'property' only in the second paragraph – 'use of property'. In the French version also both 'propriété' and 'biens' terms are used. However, the Court pointed out that the various expressions in P1-1 all, in substance, guarantee the right of property.[4] The Court made reference to *travaux préparatoires* to confirm its interpretation in the *Marckx* case; 'the drafters continually spoke of "right of property" or "right to property" to describe the subject matter of ...Article 1'.

Having established that the protected right under P1-1 is a right of property, the first important question that arises is what does constitute 'property'

[2] The German Constitutional Court and the US Supreme Court attribute a wider meaning to the concept of property for the purpose of constitutional property clauses. See Chapter 2 above.

[3] PCIJ, 12 December 1934, Series A/B No.63 p.88; for a general analysis of property rights in public international law see Norton, P.M., "A Law of the Future or a Law of the Past? Modern Tribunals and The International Law of Expropriation" (1991) 85 *American Journal of International Law* 474; Schachter, O., "Compensation for Expropriation" (1984) 78 *American Journal of International Law* 121; Arechaga, J., "State Responsibility for the Nationalization of Foreign Owned Property" (1978) 11 *New York University Journal of International Law and Policy* 179; Dolzer, R., "New Foundations of the Law of Expropriation of Alien Property" (1981) 75 *American Journal of International Law* 553.

[4] *Handyside v. UK*, Judgement of 7 December 1976, Series A no.24 § 62; *Marckx v. Belgium*, Judgement of 13 June 1979, Series A no.31 §63.

or 'possessions'. The significance of this question is that the definition of property or possessions itself will constitute a limitation over the guarantee provided by P1-1. As examined in Chapter 2 there is no common European concept of property from which the Convention organs infer the meaning of the concept of 'possessions'. The concept of property is defined variously in different European private law jurisdictions.[5] Moreover, in some European jurisdictions private law property is defined differently from constitutional law property.[6] Therefore, the Convention organs needed to define the concept of possessions autonomously. The question was whether this definition would be limited to the traditional concept of property, namely *rights in rem*, or would they adopt a broad definition used in public international law or some national constitutional laws, in which property is equated with vested or acquired rights?

Both the Commission and the Court have preferred the second approach. Here the related case-law will be examined in detail. First the traditional concept of property and possible problems will be highlighted and then the expansive definition will be examined.

6.2.1. Rights in Rem

There is no doubt that *rights in rem* in movable and immovable corporeal things constitute property. The Commission rejected the argument that only movable property could be recognised as possessions.[7] The concept of possession comprises not only ownership rights over corporeal and incorporeal things, but also other *rights in rem*. For example, the Commission recognised that a right limited to the benefit of a restrictive covenant and receipt of an annual rent was a possession.[8] The Court in the *Gasus Dosier*[9] case ruled that '...the notion "possession"...has an autonomous meaning which is certainly not limited to ownership of physical goods: certain other rights and interests constituting assets can also be regarded as "property rights" ...In the present context it is therefore immaterial whether Gasus's right to the concrete mixer is to be considered as a right of ownership or as a security *right in rem*'. In any event it constitutes a 'possession'. The origin of a *right in rem*, whether it is of contractual or statutory origin, is irrelevant to a right

---

5 Samuel, G., "Are Property Rights So Simple in Europe?" in P. Jackson and D. C. Wilde (eds.) *Property Law: Current Issues and Debates* (Ashgate: Dartmouth, 1999) p.161.

6 Stücke, A., *Eigentum an Wirtschaftssubventionen* (Berlin, 1991); Leisner, W., *Eigentum Schriften zu Eigentumsrecht und Wirtschaftsverfassung* 1970-1996 (Herausgegeben von Josef Isensee: Berlin, 1996).

7 *Wiggins v. UK*, App. No. 7456/76, DR 13, pp 40ff.

8 *S. v. UK*, App. No. 10741/84, DR 41, pp. 226 ff.

9 *Gasus Dosier- und Födertechnik GmbH v. the Nedherlands*, Judgement of 23 February 1995, Series A no.306-B, § 46.

being termed as possession.[10] While in *Gasus* the origin of the right to security was contract, the origin of the leasehold in *James*[11] was a statute.

The Court and the Commission established that P1-1 protects only existing property. The Article does not guarantee a right to acquire property whether on intestacy or through voluntary disposition. Therefore in the *Marckx* case the Court decided that expectation of inheritance did not constitute a possession.[12] However, the Court decided, surprisingly, that a right to inheritance or succession came within the sphere of right to family life (Article 8) though it did not guarantee a definite share. And it found that making a distinction between legitimate and illegitimate children in respect of the right to inheritance constituted violation of Article 14.[13] Later in the *Inze* case the Court distinguished its decision in the *Marckx* case and held that when the person providing the inheritance has died, heirs gain the ownership of the estate jointly and it constitutes possession even though the distribution has not yet taken place.[14]

In the above-mentioned *Marckx* case, the Court also ruled that 'the right to dispose of one's property constitutes a traditional and fundamental aspect of the right of property'.[15] Accordingly, this right entitles the owner to enter into a legal relationship with another person, regardless of the form which this relationship takes: sale, rental, usufruct or bequest. The right to dispose of a possession constitutes an asset.[16] However, the Commission did not evaluate different use rights which emerged from ownership separately. It decided in the *Mellacher* application that 'the applicants' contractual rights to rent are ... not a separate property and cannot be considered in isolation. The measures complained of must be examined as to their effect on the real property'.[17] It can be inferred from this decision that the Commission did not treat different use rights as independent property, but as a form of using property. Therefore, property is a single right which gives owners different use rights, rather than a bundle of rights.

In another case the Commission, making reference to the *Van der Mussele*[18] judgment where it was ruled that P1-1 guarantees only existing property, decided that P1-1 did not grant any right of construction of buildings on a piece of land which is owned by an individual.[19] The Commission evaluated the right to

---

[10] Sermet, L., *The European Convention on Human Rights and Property Rights* (Council of Europe Publishing: Strasbourg, 1998) (revised edition) p.11.

[11] *James and Others v. UK*, Judgement of 21 February 1986, Series A no. 98.

[12] *Marckx* case, para 50.

[13] *Ibid.* §. 52, 53, 54; for criticism of this decision see dissenting opinion of Judge O'Donoghue.

[14] *Inze v. Austria*, Judgement of 28 October 1987, Series A no.126.

[15] *Marckx case* § 63.

[16] Sermet, *op.cit.* 10 p.19.

[17] *Mellacher and Others v. Austria*, App. No. 10522/83, 11011/84, 11070/84 Op. Com Publ. Court A, 169.

[18] *Van der Mussele v. Belgium*, Judgement of 23 November 1983, Series A no. 70.

[19] App. No. 11225/84, 7 October 1985 (unpublished); 11628/85, 9 May 1986, DR 47 p.271- In this application the applicant wished to improve his existing sanitary amenities

construction of a building as a separate right, rather than a way of using land. However, in the *Fredin*[20] case, though the right to exploit gravel was not in itself seen as a property right by the Court, it was considered possible that the revocation could be a deprivation of property if it made the property in question valueless. The Commission in the *Pine Valley* application found that 'economic interests connected with outline planning permission constitute "possessions" for the purposes of P1-1'.[21] However, the Court did not consider a right to land development to constitute a separate right from using property.[22] The Court's opinion in this respect established that different use rights do not constitute separate property rights. This view was confirmed by the judgement of *Chassagnou and Others v. France*[23] where the Court held that compulsory transfer of hunting rights over the applicants' land did not constitute deprivation of their rights. Similarly in another case the Court, while finding that exclusive fishing rights constitute possession, decided that an amendment in Finnish law which resulted in depriving the owners of their previous exclusive right to sell fishing licences to their water areas, and thus to control the amount of fishing activities in their area did not constitute deprivation of possession, since they still retained the title to it, but rather constituted a control of use of property within the meaning of the second paragraph of P1-1.[24] Although the Court evaluated these single use rights within the concept of possession, it did not consider these rights separately as property. The reason for this is probably the taxonomy of interferences with property adopted by the Convention organs, because had the Court considered these single use rights as property separately, it would have had to accept any interference with these rights as deprivation of property.[25]

Since the concept of possession has an autonomous meaning,[26] whether a right exists in domestic law is not a question that the Court will decide. So, in the *Matos e Silva* case the Court did not accept the government's argument that the legal position of the applicant as an owner in domestic law is debatable. It ruled that the 'applicants' unchallenged rights over the disputed land for almost a century and the revenue they derive from working it may qualify as "possessions" for the purposes of P1-1'.[27] In *Papamichalopoulos v. Greece*[28] the applicants' ownership had not been formally established, since the property claimed was regarded in law

---

by installing a new and modern water closet. The Commission decided that this could not be regarded as simple maintenance of the existing property.

[20] *Fredin v. Sweden*, Judgement of 18 February 1991, Series A no. 192.

[21] *Pine Valley Developments Ltd and Others v. Ireland*, Op. Com. Publ. Court A, 222.

[22] *Pine Valley Developments Ltd and Others v. Ireland*, Judgement of 29 Nov. 1991, Series A no. 222.

[23] *Chassagnou and Others v. France*, Judgement of 29 April 1999, *Reports*, 1999-III.

[24] *Lena Aschan and Others v. Finland*, Admissibility Decision of the Court, 15 February 2001, App. No. 37858/97.

[25] For a detailed discussion of the taxonomy of interferences see Chapter 7 below.

[26] *Gasus Dosier* case, Judgement of 23 February 1995, Series A no. 306-B p.46, §53.

[27] *Matos e Silva, Lda., and Others v. Portugal*, Judgement of 27 August 1996, (R 1996-IV) § 75.

[28] *Papamichalopoulos v. Greece*, Judgement of 24 June 1993, Series A no.260-B.

as military property. On the basis of certain indications, such as offers of compensation made to all the applicants, the Court decided that 'for the purposes of the present dispute, the applicants must therefore be regarded as the owner of the land in issue'.[29] This decision of the Court has been criticised as exceeding the borders of autonomous interpretation and attempting to define title to ownership and weakening the Convention guarantee making the concept of property fluid.[30] However, the expansive definition is desirable since it gives the Convention organs the opportunity to review interferences with human rights.

In *The Former King of Greece*[31] case also the Court did not accept the Government's argument that royal property had a *sui generis* and quasi-public nature, therefore does not constitute possession under the meaning of P1-1.[32] The Court held that although the royal property in many ways enjoyed a special status, the Greek state had repeatedly treated it as private property and had not produced a general set of rules governing its status as being of a *sui generis* and quasi-public character, therefore the relevant properties were owned by the applicants as private persons rather than in their capacity as members of the royal family; accordingly they constituted a possession for the purposes of P1-1.

Similarly in the *Beyeler*[33] case the Court did not accept the Government's argument that the applicant had not lawfully acquired a *right in rem* of any kind over a Van Gogh painting since the contract on which he had based his claims was automatically null and void. The Court pointed out that 'the concept of "possession" in P1-1 has an autonomous meaning which is not limited to ownership of physical goods and is independent from formal classification in domestic law: certain other rights and interests constituting assets can also be regarded as "property rights", and thus as "possession" for the purposes of P1-1';[34] it decided that 'the issue that needs to be examined is whether circumstances of the case, considered as a whole, conferred on the applicant title to a substantive interest protected by P1-1'. The Court found that the circumstances of this case conferred to the applicant a substantive interest over the painting which can constitute 'possession' for the purpose of P1-1, thus P1-1 was applicable.[35]

To sum up, the Court interprets the concept of possessions independently from the national laws and therefore even if a right or interest is not considered as property or even a right in domestic law it can be considered as possession in the meaning of P1-1. This approach of the Court is consistent with the outcome of

---

[29] *Ibid.* §39.

[30] Sermet, *op.cit.* 10 p.17.

[31] *The Former King of Greece and Others v. Greece*, Judgement 23 November 2000, § 60-66.

[32] The Government argued that the contested estate was inextricably linked to the institution of the Head of State, most of them gained as gifts to the head of state, and enjoyed some tax exemptions, therefore they have a *sui generis* and quasi-public character and did not fall under the notion of possessions protected by P1-1.

[33] *Beyeler v. Italy*, Judgement of 5 January 2000.

[34] *Ibid.* § 100.

[35] *Ibid.* § 105.

Chapter 2 which suggests that any pecuniary interest or legitimate expectation should be considered as property in the constitutional law.

6.2.2. Intellectual Property

There is no doubt that intellectual property rights constitute possessions within the meaning of P1-1. Intellectual property rights comprise copyrights, patents, publishers' rights, trademarks and other protective rights such as industrial design.[36] The established case-law confirmed that these rights are under the guarantee of P1-1.[37] However, it is domestic law and domestic authorities' jurisdiction to decide whether a patent or copyright is established as a right. Although the Commission has examined a number of cases, the Court has not examined the issue of intellectual property rights in detail yet. For example, whether copyright protects only economic interests in artistic productions or does it also protect artistic integrity of the product has not been examined properly yet.[38]

Although intellectual property rights protect both economic and personality rights in products,[39] it is contentious whether P1-1 guarantees the personal aspects of intellectual property rights considering the 'economic value' criterion used by the Convention organs to determine 'possessions' within the meaning of P1-1. In determining the ambiguous subject matter of intellectual property rights such as software and computer programs the Court can utilise other international and national jurisdictions by applying a comparative interpretation.[40] It can be suggested that the separability thesis, which was examined in Chapter 2, can guide to determine whether P1-1 protects the artistic integrity of an art product. Accordingly, since the artistic value of an art product cannot be separated from the artist's personality it cannot be construed within the concept of possessions. For example, if a movie manager or producer sells his rights over the product to a TV

---

[36] Peukert, W., "Protection of Ownership under Article 1 of the First Protocol to the European Convention on Human Rights" (1981) 2 *Human Rights Law Journal* 37-78 p. 50.

[37] For patents see for example *Smith Kline and French Laboratories Ltd v. Netherlands*, App. No. 12633/87 decision. of 4 October 1990, DR 14, p.200; *Lenzing AG v. UK*, App. No. 38817/97, decision of 9 September 1998; *British-American Tobacco Company Ltd v. The Netherlands*, Judgement of 20 October 1995, Series A no.331. In this case although the Court did not examine the applicability of P1-1 it ruled that the right to patent constitutes a civil right; for copyrights see *Aral, Tekin and Aral v. Turkey* App.No24563/94 decision of 14 January 1998.

[38] For examination of this problem see Graber, C. B. and Teubner, G., "Art and Money: Constitutional Rights in the Private Sphere?" (1998) 18 *Oxford Journal of Legal Studies* 61.

[39] Hirş, E. "Eser Sahipligi: Fikri ve Sinai Haklarin Mahiyeti Hakkinda Yeni bir Gorus" (1944) 1 *Ankara Universitesi Hukuk Fakultesi Dergisi* 330.

[40] For a similar approach relating to the interpretation of copyrights under TRIPs (The Agreement on Trade-related Aspects of Intellectual Property Rights) see Helfer, L. R., "A Human Rights Analogy in Adjudicating Copyrights Claims under TRIPs" (1999) 21 *European Intellectual Property Review* 8.

company, he transfers his property rights to the buyer. If the buyer distorts the artistic integrity of the movie by commercial breaks, the dispute is a personality rights dispute rather than a property dispute.

As for the new subject matters for intellectual property rights such as patentability of material of human origin, such matters also have not been examined by the Convention organs yet.[41] In addition to the comparative interpretation, the separability criterion of Penner can be utilised here as well.[42] For example, if new technologies provide that some human material can be separated from the body without damaging the health and morals of the individual and such material creates pecuniary interests, there is no reason not to protect such interests as property. For example, blood, hair, or a kidney can easily be separated from the body without damaging the health of the person and property rights can be established over such materials.

6.2.3. Rights in Personam

As examined in Chapter 2, in some of the contracting states' civil laws *rights in personam* are not accepted as property. However, they are regarded as property in the constitutional meaning. The Convention organs from the beginning consistently have recognised that P1-1 covers *rights in personam*. Not only claim rights arising from a relationship between private individuals, but also claims stemming from public law relationships also constitute possession within the meaning of P1-1.[43] It will be better to examine private law claims and public law claims separately.

6.2.3.1. Private law claims The case-law established that private law assets such as monetary claims based on contract, tort or unjust enrichment are clearly included in the concept of possession as well as shares in companies.[44] The essential characteristic is the acquired economic value of the individual interest.[45] Pure expectations do not have the degree of concreteness to bring them within the

---

[41]There are some works under the Council of Europe in order to prepare a Protocol, concerning the problems relating to human genetics, to the Convention for the protection of human rights and dignity of human being with regard to the application of biology and medicine. See deputies' decision 623/10.2 (March 1998) <www.cm.coe.int/dec/1998/623/102.htm>; Charter of Fundamental Rights of the European Union, (2000/C 364/1) includes a provision requiring 'the prohibition on making the human body and its parts as such a source of financial gain' (Article 3/2). This charter is binding only on Union organs and it has not been entered into force.

[42] Penner, J., *The Idea of Property in Law* (OUP: Oxford, 1997) ch. 5.

[43] Aronovitz, A. M., "Individual Patrimonial Rights Under the European Human Rights System; Some Reflections on the Concept of Possession and Dispossession of Property" (1997) 25 *International Journal of Legal Information* 87.

[44] Gomien, D., Harris, D. and Zwaak, L., *Law and Practice of the European Convention on Human Rights and the European Social Charter* (Council of Europe Publishing: Strasbourg, 1996) (reprinted in 1999) p.313.

[45] Harris, D., O'Boyle, M. and Warbrick, C., *Law of the European Convention on Human Rights* (Butterworths: London, 1995) p.517.

concept of 'possessions'.[46] Therefore, the Commission decided that the claim of a notary to payment for his services does not find protection in P1-1 until it is an actual claim based on services rendered; his expectation that the applicable provisions about notarial fees were not going to be modified does not find protection in P1-1.[47] In very early applications the Commission decided that debts constituted possession.[48] However, the applicant must prove that he is entitled to enjoy assets in question through a document, or judicial decision, etc.[49] The identification of an interest as a right is initially for the national legal system. However, the mere fact that the national law does not acknowledge as a legal right a particular interest does not conclusively determine that the interest is not a 'possession' for the purposes of P1-1.

In *Stran Greek Refineries and Stratis Andreadis*[50] the applicant brought claims against the Government for costs they had incurred and security bonds they had lodged during the life of a contract negotiated between them and the Greek military government in power during the early 1970s. The contract was later terminated on the restoration of democracy in Greece. The applicants and the government agreed to enter into arbitration to settle the claims. An award was made in the applicants' favour, the validity of the award and the amount of the debt owned to them later being confirmed in judicial proceedings. However, the national legislator, passing a law, declared the arbitration clause in the original contract was void and annulled the arbitration award. The government argued that there was no possession within the meaning of P1-1. The Commission and the Court did not agree with the government and ruled that the arbitration award constituted a possession. Similarly, in the *Van Marle*[51] case the Court, though the government argued that there was no right called 'goodwill' in Dutch law, decided that clientele of an accountant, as goodwill of its enterprises constituted possession within the meaning of P1-1.

In another application, the Commission decided that although the applicant had a formal entitlement to a trust's property both as a party to contract and as a trustee, this ownership could not be considered as his own personal right, since the trust was established in the exclusive interest of the children who were the true subject of the trust's property.[52]

---

[46] *Batelaan and Huiges. Netherlands*, App. No. 10438/83 DR 41 p.170.

[47] *X. v. Germany*, App. No. 8410/78, (1980) DR 18; See also *Pudas v. Sweden*, App. No. 10426/83, (1985) DR 40; *Storksen v. Norway*, App. No. 19819/92, (1994) DR 78-A: expectations for future earnings can only be considered to constitute a possession if the income had already been earned or where an enforceable claim exists.

[48] Admissibility Decision of the Commission App. No. 3039/67, Yearbook X, pp516; 5479/72, 10 July 1973 Coll. 44 p.53.

[49] Admissibility Decision of the Commission App. No. 8579/79, 7 May 1980 (unpublished).

[50] *Stran Greek Refineries and Stratis Andreadis v. Greece,* Judgement of 9 December 1994, Series A no. 301-B p.97.

[51] *Van Marle and Others v. Netherlands*, Judgement of 3 June 1986, Series A no. 101.

[52] Admissibility Decision of the Commission App. No. 8387/78, 4 March 1980 DR 19 p.233.

In *O. N. v Bulgaria,* the Commission decided that restitution claims arising from unjust enrichment constituted possession.[53]

As for shares, the Commission decided that 'a company share is a complex thing: certifying that the holder possesses a share in the company together with the corresponding rights (especially voting rights), it also constitutes as it were, an indirect claim on company assets. In the present case there is no doubt that the NK shares had an economic value. The commission is therefore of the opinion that with respect to P1-1, the NK shares held by the applicants were indeed possessions giving rise to a right of ownership'.[54] The Commission abstained to decide whether the power or influence a shareholder may acquire over a company is a possession within the meaning of P1-1.[55] The Court confirmed the Commission's judgement in *Lithgow and Others*[56] where the subjects of application were shares in nationalised companies. In a recent case the Court also treated the right to share in a public company as possession within the meaning of P1-1.[57]

To sum up, economic interests of every kind resulting from relations between individuals constitute 'possession' for the purposes of P1-1. However, the guarantee of P1-1 covers only existing rights; mere expectations without any legitimate base fall outside the ambit of the protection of P1-1.[58] The rights connected with the exercise of an occupation such as employment and business rights will be examined here separately.

6.2.3.1.1. Business and employment rights Although the rights connected with exercise of an occupation are also private law *rights in personam*, they deserve to be examined separately because they generally appear as legitimate expectations. Here basically employment rights and business goodwill will be examined. In spite of the fact that licences required for the pursuit of an economic activity are closely related to the running and goodwill of a business, because a licence claim is a claim against public authority they will be examined under the heading of public law rights.

The Commission ruled, in *X v. Italy,*[59] that 'the examination of whether he was rightly dismissed is not justifiable by the Commission because the Convention

[53] *O.N v. Bulgaria*, App. No. 35221/97, 6 April 2000 ; *M. N. v. Bulgaria*, App. No. 29785/96, 4 April 1996.

[54] Admissibility Decision of the Commission App. No. 8588/79, 12 October 1982 DR 29 p.64; 10000/82, 4 July 1983 DR 33 p.247; 11949/86, 1 December 1986 DR 51 p.195; 12462/86, 13 July 1987 DR 53 p.234; 11425/85, 5 October 1987 DR 53 p. 76.

[55] Admissibility Decision of the Commission App. No. 11189/84, 11 December 1986 DR 50 p.121.

[56] *Lithgow and Others v. UK*, Judgement of 8 July 1986, Series A no.102.

[57] Admissibility Decision of the Court, App. No. 35730/97, 16 January 2001.

[58] For example the Commission in the *G. D. & M. v. Germany* application decided that since the applicants did not show that any right they have exist through court decisions, P1-1 was not applicable to the case. Adm. Dec. of the Com. App. No. 29818/ 96. 20 May 1998.

[59] *X v. Italy*, App. No. 7459/76, 11 DR 114.

does not guarantee the right to employment in public service'. According to the Court's settled case-law, disputes relating to the recruitment, careers and termination of service of civil servants do not as a general rule constitute 'civil right' for the purpose of Article 6 (1).[60] However, that provision is applicable where the claim in issue relates to a 'purely economic' right such as payment of salary[61] or pensions[62] or an essentially economic[63] one. This approach is applicable also for P1-1. That is, contractual rights of employees that have economic character such as wages constitute 'possession'. According to Van den Broek[64] rights arising under a contract of employment such as a right to fixed term, protection against dismissal and levels of benefits are private in character and of economic value. Although these rights are contingent upon the performance of obligations, they are existing rights and should be protected.

However, P1-1 protects only existing or acquired rights, its guarantee does not comprise the acquisition of property, so pure expectations fall outside the scope of P1-1. In *X v. Germany*[65] the Commission decided that notaries' expectations in respect of fees which had been statutorily reduced did not constitute a possession. In that case, the legislation regulating the drawing-up of deeds for universities, churches and other non-profit-making organisations had reduced notaries' fees by between 50 per cent and 80 per cent. The Commission held that their mere expectations that the regulations on fees would not change could not be considered a possession, although a possession would have existed if the claim had been based on services rendered by the notary and on the existing regulations. But the application concerned only potential claims.

The Commission reiterated this approach in the *Casotti and Others*[66] application where the applicants claimed that the law reducing the scope of competence of labour consultants, and extending the competence to represent tax payers before tax courts to other category of persons violated their peaceful enjoyment of possessions as labour consultants. The Commission considered that the profession of labour consultant was a liberal one with no fixed income and no guaranteed turnover. It was naturally subject to the hazards of economic life. And it recalled the previous case-law to the extent that future income constituted a 'possession' within the meaning of P1-1 only if the income had been earned or where an enforceable claim to it existed. However the Commission abstained to decide whether P1-1 is applicable and decided that even if it was applicable, the

---

[60] *Niegel v. France*, Judgement of 17 March 1997, Reports 1997-II p.410.

[61] *De Santa v. Italy*, Judgement of 2 September 1997, Reports 1997-V, p.1663; *Lapalorcia v. Italy*, Judgement of 2 September 1997, Reports 1997-V, p.1677; *Abenavoli v. Italy, Judgement* of 2 September 1997, Reports 1997-V p.1690.

[62] *Francesco Lombardo v. Italy*, Judgement of 26 November 1992, Series A no. 249-B; *Massa v. Italy,* Judgement of 24 August 1993, Series A no. 265-B.

[63] *Nicodemo v. Italy*, Judgement of 2 September 1997, Reports 1997-V, p.1703; *Le Calvez v. France*, Judgement of 29 July 1998, Reports 1998-II.

[64] Van Den Broek, P., "The Protection of Property Rights under the European Convention on Human Rights" (1986) 1986-1*Issues of European Integration* 52.

[65] *X v. Germany*, App. No. 8410/78, 13 December 1979, 18 DR 216.

[66] *Casotti and Others v. Italy*, App. No.24877/94, 16 October 1996.

legislation complained of were designed to promote general interest so the application was inadmissible.

In the *Van der Mussele*[67] case the issue was the absence of remuneration for representation and non-reimbursement of expenses made by the lawyer out of his own pocket under Belgian legal aid legislation. The Court decided that neither payment due for representation nor expenses incurred were possessions. It stated that 'no assessment of fees could be made, because of [the client's] lack of means ...It follows that debt in favour of the applicant never arose'.[68] Regarding the expenses the Court said that 'these expenses were relatively small and resulted from the obligation to perform work compatible with Article 4 of the Convention'.[69] The fact that the applicant was a trainee advocate and that representing people who needed legal aid was part of his education affected the Court's assessment. However, it is doubtful that a debt did not arise because of the client's lack of means, since the legal relationship had already been established and work had been done. Moreover, the refusal to regard expenses as possessions, because they were very small, is hardly convincing.[70]

An owner of a business acquires goodwill and invests capital in fixed costs through running a business whether as a liberal profession or some more entrepreneurial lines. Thus he has many different economic interests and rights. How far such interests fall within the ambit of P1-1 is an issue which is discussed by the Convention organs.

The Commission in *Van Marle,*[71] though it did not find that the freedom to use the title 'accountant' was a right of property, did find that goodwill was a right of property. The Court adopted the Commission's view and decided that 'the right relied upon by the applicants may be likened to the right of property embodied in Article 1: by dint of their own work, the applicants had built up clientele: this had in many respects the nature of a private right and constituted an asset and, hence, a possession within the meaning of Article 1(P1-1)'[72] Accordingly it ruled that 'the refusal to register the applicants as certified accountants radically affected the conditions of their professional activities and the scope of those activities was reduced. Their income fell, as did the value of their clientele and, more generally, their business. Consequently, there was interference with their right to peaceful enjoyment of their possessions'.[73]

---

[67] *Van der Mussele v. Belgium*, Judgement of 23 November 1983, Series A no.70.

[68] *Ibid.* § 48.

[69] *Ibid.* § 49.

[70] Sermet, *op.cit.* 10 fn.38.

[71] *Van Marle and Others v. Netherlands*, App. No. 8543/79, 8674/79, 8685/79, Op. Com. 8 May 1984, Series A no.101.

[72] *Van Marle and Others v. Netherlands*, Judgement of 26 June 1986, Series A no.101, § 41.

[73] *Ibid.* § 42. The Court found in this case that the interference was aimed to promote the general interest and proportionality maintained, thus there was no breach of P1-1.

The Court similarly, in *H v. Belgium,*[74] found that the chambers and clientele of an advocate constitute property interests and as such come within the ambit of the right of property.

However, in a number of cases the Commission found that measures reducing the profitability of some professions did not interfere with property rights. In *Husmann*[75] it decided that the government interference reduced the Barrister's profitability, but not his goodwill. Similarly in an application regarding the Greek customs officers' loss of income due to the abolition of customs barriers within the European Union the Commission noted that, in Greece, the occupation of customs officer is a liberal profession, with no fixed income and no guaranteed turnover, but which is subject to the hazards of economic life. The customs officers could not claim to be entitled to a guaranteed volume of business which could have qualified as a possession.[76]

In a number of cases the Court found that the right to conduct a private medical practice is a civil right for the purposes of Article 6(1).[77] Van den Broek argues rightly that the right to practice a profession or to conduct any other business activity is a social right but not property. It is distinct from a licence or the goodwill of a professional practice which are property.[78]

The Court in an admissibility decision decided that nobility titles which are recognised by Spanish law did not constitute property. It also rejected the claim that such titles confer a social advantage and had a pecuniary value since peerages were used for commercial purposes such as trademarks in the wine and spirit sector. The Court ruled that applicants could not claim any legitimate expectation concerning the commercial exploitation of nobiliary titles, thus applications were incompatible with P1-1 *ratione materiae.*[79]

To sum up, the goodwill of a business or profession amounts to possession, but mere expectations about the income or profitability of a business does not constitute property. Similarly, economic interests arising from an employment contract constitute property but not the contract itself. Now it is time to look at the claims arising from public law relationships.

6.2.3.2. Public law claims Although public law claims do not constitute property under most of the contracting states' civil laws, the Convention organs, in

---

[74] *H v. Belgium*, Judgement of 30 November 1987, Seies A no. 127-B.

[75] *Husmann v. Germany*, App. No. 4653/70, 46 CD 22.

[76] *Greek Federation of Customs Officers, Galouris, Christopoulos and 3333 other customs officers v. Greece*, App. No. 24581/94, (1995) 81-B DR 123; see also *Casotti, Florio and Italian National Council of Labour Consultants v. Italy,* App. No. 24877/94, 16 October 1996.

[77] *König v. Germany*, Judgement of 28 June 1978, Series A no. 27.

[78] Van den Broek, *op.cit.* 64 p.72.

[79] *De La Cierva Osorio De Moscoso, Fernandez De Cordoba, Roca Y Fernandez Miranda And O'Neill Castrillo v. Spain,* App. No. 41127/98, 41503/98, 41717/98, 45726/99, 28 October 1999.

accordance with public international law,[80] interpreted the concept of possessions autonomously and established that all public law claims that have pecuniary value constitute 'possessions' within the meaning of P1-1. In this regard three kinds of claims can be examined separately, namely all kinds of monetary compensation claims against public authorities, pension and benefit claims, and licence claims.

6.2.3.2.1. Pecuniary claims against public authorities Any kind of compensation or restitution claims that have pecuniary value have been regarded as possessions under P1-1. In this regard there are plenty of cases examined by the Commission and the Court. Compensation claims for interference with property are examples of this kind.[81] Statutory claims based on some perceived individual effort or losses suffered because of government action are regarded as possessions.[82] Statutes providing for payment to doctors, lawyers, etc., for work done in public service, rewards for information in a criminal trial or for removal of pets are some of the examples. When these rights are granted in national laws, they are considered as property. However, the right or interest must be sufficiently established and the applicant must show that a right or at least a legitimate expectation which can be realised exists.

The Court in the *Pressos Campania Naviera and Others v. Belgium*[83] case, where the national legislator passing a law with retrospective effect extinguished the liability of private and public operators of pilot services for sea-going vessels and deprived the applicants of compensation claims, did not consider the fact that domestic law did not recognise a right to compensation but considered the law in effect when damage occurred and decided that a possession was at issue. In the *National and Provincial Building Society, Leeds Permanent Building Society and Yorkshire Building Society v. UK*[84] case, where the applicants claimed a restitution of tax (transitional period tax) they had been obliged to pay according to a law which was *ultra vires* because of technical deficiencies, although the applicants did not establish a right before the domestic courts, the Court decided that there was a possession. It stated, 'while expressing no concluded view as to whether any of the claims asserted by the applicant societies could properly be considered to constitute possessions, the Court ... is prepared to proceed on the working assumption that in the light of the *Woolwich 2* ruling the applicant

---

[80] In modern international law there is a tendency to include whole kinds of individual rights in the protection of ownership. See Peukert, *op. cit.* 36 p.45.

[81] See for example, claims for additional compensation for expropriated property, *Akkus v. Turkey*, Judgement of 24 June 1997, Reports 1997-IV; *Aka v. Turkey* , Judgement of 23 Sept. 1998, Reports 1998-VI, *Aktas and Others v. Turkey*, Judgement of 30 January 2001.

[82] Van den Broek, *op.cit.* 64.

[83] *Pressos Campania Naviera SA and Others v. Belgium*, Judgement of 20 November 1995, Series A no.332.

[84] The *National and Provincial Building Society, Leeds Permanent Building Society and Yorkshire Building Society v. UK*, Judgement of 23 October 1997, Reports 1997-VII; see also *S. A. Dangeville v. France*, Judgement of 16 April 2002 (App. No. 36677/97).

societies did have possessions in the form of vested right to restitution which they sought to exercise in direct and indirect ways in the various legal proceedings'.[85]

Sermet argues that the Court, through these judgements, expanded the scope of P1-1 to include a new type of property – property resulting from rights to restitution – and he criticises the Court as defining title to property which does not exist in domestic law. However, he ignores that in all these cases, although the applicants gained a right to compensation under the law in effect, their rights were extinguished by the laws that have retrospective effect. Therefore, there is no extrication from the case-law here, rather there is an effective interpretation of the Convention to provide an effective protection of rights. Otherwise, human rights would have been left unprotected against retrospective laws.

In a recent case the Court also found that although there was no judgement awarding legal costs regarding pending cases, since pending legal proceedings were extinguished by a law, the lawyer, who had a no-win no-fee contract with her clients, had a claim for fees for the acts she did before the law was issued, therefore had a 'possession' within the meaning of P1-1.[86] It also reiterated that future income constituted a 'possession' within the meaning of P1-1 only if it had been earned or where an enforceable claim to it existed.

The Commission established that international treaties between states, which include such provisions as that the 'federal republic shall ensure that the former owners of property seized pursuant to measures ...', do not create individual rights to compensation on the part of the persons concerned.[87]

6.2.3.2.2. Pensions and benefits Pension and benefit claims are among the most debated public law claims before the Convention organs. Whether the pensions and benefit claims constitute property rights protected by P1-1 for claimants is an issue that involves theoretical difficulties. It was argued that 'the new property' comprises all kinds of governmentally allocated wealth such as welfare benefits, government jobs, occupational licences, state franchises, contracts, and subsidies, and access to state-owned resources and to governmental services.[88] Furthermore, it was claimed that equality and justice requires that every person should be provided with a minimum private property necessary for a decent life.[89] However, the Convention organs made clear, from the beginning, that P1-1 does not protect a right to acquire property, but protects only existing property. The right protected by P1-1 does not create a positive duty for government to supply a minimum level of income or property. Rather it protects the freedom of individuals to acquire, enjoy and use property. Thus, the problem of whether pension and welfare benefit claims

---

[85] *Ibid.* § 70.

[86] *Ambruosi v. Italy*, Judgement of 19 October 2000 (App. No.31227/96).

[87] Admissibility Decision of the Commission App. No. 7694/76, 14 October 1977 DR 12 p.131; 9095/80, 5 May 1981.

[88] See Reich, C. A., "The New Property" (1964) 73 *Yale Law Journal* 733.

[89] See Munzer, S., *A Theory of Property* (CUP: Cambridge, 1991); Scheffler, S., "Natural Rights, Equality and the Minimal State" (1976) 6 *Canadian Journal of Philosophy* 59.

fall within the protection of P1-1 was resolved under the light of this approach. Accordingly the Commission in an early case held that 'the making of compulsory contributions to a pension fund may, in certain circumstances, create a property right in a portion of such fund'.[90] However, a substantial difficulty arose to classify which entitlements stemming from pension and social security schemes constitute possession in the sense of P1-1. Although the Court did not hesitate to accept that pension and benefit rights constitute 'civil rights' for the purpose of Article 6,[91] the Commission made a distinction between different social security systems according to their nature.[92] If a social security system is organised on the social solidarity basis and individual contribution is not necessary to be entitled to a pension right or there is not a relation between contributions and ultimate benefits, in such a system no identifiable private rights arise and pension rights fall outside the ambit of P1-1.[93] But if a social security system is organised on a contributory basis and benefits are funded by the participants, such contributions create an individual right over the fund and it should be protected by P1-1.[94] For example, the Commission decided that although the right to unemployment benefit could not in itself constitute 'possession' since no one held an identifiable and claimable share in joint capital, a contribution to the National Social Security Office which finances the body responsible for paying unemployment benefit may create a

---

[90] *X. v. Netherlands*, App. No. 4130/69, Decision of 20 July 1971, Coll. 38, p. 9; similarly the commission ruled in another Application that 'the duty to contribute to a security scheme may, in certain circumstances, give rise to a property right'. App. No. 5849/72.

[91] *Francesco Lombardo v. Italy*, Judgement of 26 November 1992, Series A no. 249-B pp. 26-2 7, paras.14-17; *Giancarlo Lombardo v. Italy,* Judgement of 26 November 1992, Series A. no. 249-C p. 42, paras. 13-16; *Massa v. Italy,* Judgement of 24 August 1993, Series A no. 265-B, p. 20, para. 26; *Pauger v. Austria*, Judgement of 28 May 1997.

[92] Treating, here, pension rights differently for purposes of Article 6 and P1-1 seems similar to the US Supreme Court's distinction between due process property and just compensation property. However, this distinction should be criticised because the coherence of the Convention as a whole demands that the concept of possession in P1-1 be no less a category than the concept of civil rights in Article 6(1). The essence of protected interest measured by its nature and importance to an individual in both articles is the same. While Article 6 (1) provides formal protection, P1-1 protects its substance. Providing more formal protection for an interest than its substance loosens the logic of protection. For a similar approach see Harris et al *Law of the European Convention on Human Rights* (Butterwoths: London, 1995) p.518.

[93] On many occasions the Commission held that the right to an old age pension is not included as such among the rights and freedoms guaranteed by the Convention. See Admissibility Decision of the Commission App. No. 2116/64, 17 December 1966, Yearbook XXIII, p.9; *G. v. Austria*, App. No. 10094/82, 14 May 1984, 38 DR 84.

[94] There are many cases illustrating this opinion. For example see the admissibility decision in following applications App. No. 4130/69, 20 July 1971, Yearbook XIV p.224; App. No. 8247/78, 4 July 1979 (unpublished); App. No. 10443/83, 5 July 1988, 56 DR 20.

property right protected by P1-1, provided that domestic legal requirements governing the aforementioned right are satisfied.[95]

However, in the *Müller*[96] case the Commission decided that even if private rights are created by a pension scheme, the right could not be a guarantee of a particular amount. The Commission considered that 'the operation of a social security system is essentially different from management of a private life insurance company. Because of its public importance, the social security system must take account of political considerations, in particular those of financial policy'. Although it accepted that a substantial reduction in the entitlement could be regarded as affecting the substance of the right created, in that case it did not find such a substantial reduction and so no interference with property rights.[97] According to the Commission's opinion the national authorities have a margin of appreciation in fixing the amount of pensions or benefits. But to be entitled to pension rights, individuals should satisfy the fixed terms of the scheme. That is, the terms of the scheme is binding for individuals, but not for the state. This approach should be criticised, because if payment of compulsory or voluntary contributions to a pension scheme creates a private property, it seems strange to recognise the state's power to reduce the amount of that property as part of its economic policy.[98] So once a private right is established, it should come into the ambit of the protection of P1-1. And the Convention organs should review whether an interference with such a right is legitimate.

Whether the Court would follow the distinction between contributory and non-contributory pension schemes in terms of protection of P1-1 has not been cleared yet. In the *Gaygusuz*[99] case, though the applicant claimed that the right to emergency assistance was connected with the contributions he made to unemployment insurance, the Court ruled, without making reference to that contribution, that 'the right to emergency assistance – in so far as provided for in the applicable legislation – is a pecuniary right for the purposes of Article 1 of Protocol No. 1 (P1-1). That provision (P1-1) is therefore applicable *without it being necessary* (emphasis added) to rely solely on the link between entitlement to emergency assistance and the obligation to pay "taxes or other contributions"'.[100] It

---

[95] Admissibility Decision App. No. 11285/84, 7 December 1987, 54 DR 88.

[96] *Müller v. Austria*, App. No. 5849/72, (1975) 3 DR 25.

[97] *Ibid.* The Commission reiterated this approach on many occasions, for example see following admissibility decisions: App. No.7047/75, 6 December 1977 (unpublished); App. No. 7459/76, 5 October 1977, 11 DR 114; App. No.7624/76, 6 July 1977 (unpublished); App. No. 7633/76, 7 October 1977 (unpublished); 8466/79, 4 July 1979 (unpublished); 9956/82, 3 October 1983 (unpublished); 12264/86, 13 July 1988, 57 DR 131.

[98] See for a similar line of criticism, Van Den Broek, *op.cit.* 64; Harris et al, *op. cit.* 92 p.519.

[99] *Gaygusuz v. Austria*, Judgement of 16 Sept. 1996, Reports1996-IV.

[100] *Ibid.* para. 41. The Court found a violation of Article 14 in connection with P1-1, as the scheme distinguished between nationals and non-nationals, a distinction that lacked an objective and reasonable justification. See also the case *Van Raalte v. Netherlands*, Judgement of 21 February 1997, Reports 1997-I. In this case the Court also found a

is worth, here, considering that the Court indicated that there is no need for a pecuniary right to be linked to the contributions in order to benefit from the guarantee laid down in P1-1.

In a very different context – in calculation of pecuniary damage as a result of violation of Article 8 – the Court considered that the loss associated with the termination of the applicants' participation in the non-contributory service pension scheme constituted future loss and applicants could claim compensation for this loss.[101] In these cases the applicants had been accrued terminal grand and pensions for their services, but they claimed that unlawful termination of their jobs caused future loss in terms of pensions. Although these judgements are not related directly with P1-1, they can be regarded as a clue to the Court's approach to the pension claims. It can be suggested that even if P1-1 does not give rise to demand benefit or pensions funded by a non-contributory basis, had a state already granted such a right, it creates legitimate expectations for recipients of such schemes and any interference with such rights should meet the standards created by P1-1.

6.2.3.2.3. Licences Another area of dispute regarding public law claims is whether a licence to conduct certain economic activities could give the licence holder a right which is protected by P1-1. According to the Commission the answer depends *inter alia* on the question of whether the licence can be considered to create in a licence holder a reasonable and legitimate expectation as to the lasting nature of the licence and as to the possibility of continuing to draw benefits from the licence activity.[102] In the Commission's view a licence holder cannot be considered to have a reasonable and legitimate expectation to continue his activities, if the conditions attached to the licence are no longer fulfilled or if the licence is withdrawn in accordance with the provisions of the law which was in force when the licence was issued.[103] The Commission found that withdrawal of a licence to dispense medicine in accordance with the applicable law did not affect the rights protected under P1-1, although the licence was granted for an indefinite period.[104] In another application the Commission found that the revocation of a licence to operate interurban route traffic in accordance with the applicable legal rules did not constitute interference with the right to property.[105] Similarly the

---

violation of Article 14 in connection with P1-1 since the statute made discrimination, in terms of obligation to contribute to child benefit fund, between single men and women who did not have children and are over 50.

[101] See *Lustig-Prean and Beckett v. UK*, Judgement of 25 July 2000 (Art. 41); *Smith and Grady v. UK*, Judgement of 25 July 2000 (Art. 41). In both cases the Court previously found violation of Article 8 on the grounds that the applicants were discharged from the Royal Navy because of homosexuality.

[102] Admissibility Decision App. No. 10438/83, 3 Oct. 1984, 41 DR 170.

[103] *Ibid. Størksen v. Norway*, App. No. 19819/92, (1994) 78-A DR 88.

[104] *Ibid.*

[105] *Pudas v. Sweden*, App. No. 10426/83, 5 December 1984, 40 DR 203; *Zacher v. Germany*, App. No. 27026/95, 04 September 1996.

Commission found in another application that 'the position of the holder of a driver's licence does not amount to a property right'.[106]

The Court in the *Benthem*[107] case found a licence to exploit an installation for delivering liquid petroleum gas to be property and therefore a civil right for the purposes of Article 6 (1). The Court stated that 'a licence of this kind has a proprietary character, as its shown, *inter alia,* by the fact that it can be assigned to third parties'. But the leading case in this area is the *Tre Traktörer*[108] case where the Court found that a licence to serve beer, wine and other alcoholic beverages constituted 'possession' within the meaning of P1-1. The Court held that 'the economic interests connected with the running of *Le Cardinal* (a restaurant) were "possessions" for the purposes of Article 1 of the Protocol (P1-1). Indeed, the Court has already found that the maintenance of the licence was one of the principal conditions for the carrying on of the applicant company's business, and that its withdrawal had adverse effects on the goodwill and value of the restaurant. Such withdrawal thus constitutes, in the circumstances of the case, an interference with TTA's (the applicant) right to the "peaceful enjoyment of [its] possessions"'.[109]

To sum up, a licence can constitute possession in the meaning of P1-1 as long as the licence holder gets economic interest from it. However, such licences can be withdrawn, complying with the conditions laid down in the relevant domestic law. Such withdrawal does not constitute interference with property. But public authorities should respect the legitimate expectations of the licence holder when applying such a withdrawal.

6.2.4. Conclusion

The European Convention on Human Rights guarantees a right to property in P1-1. But since it does not define what rights constitute property, it is the Convention organs' duty to define what rights constitute property. There is no common concept of property in Europe which the Convention organs could rely on to determine the scope of protection provided in P1-1. Therefore, there has been a need to interpret the concept of property autonomously, so the Court and the Commission have interpreted the concept of possession autonomously and they have adopted an expansive definition which is not confined to traditional concept- *rights in rem*, but comprises all vested or acquired pecuniary interests arising from both private and public law relations. The Strasbourg organs' approach could be inspired by public

---

[106] *X v. Germany,* App. No.9177/80, 26 DR 255.

[107] *Benthem v. Netherlands*, Judgement of 1985, Series A no. 97.

[108] *Tre Traktörer Aktiebolag v. Sweden,* Judgement of 7 July 1989, Series A no.159.

[109] *Ibid.* § 53. The Court considered in this case the revocation of a licence to serve alcoholic beverages as control of the use of property rather than deprivation of possessions. And it concluded that withdrawal of a licence in accordance with the domestic law did not fail the proportionality which must be struck between the demands of the general interest of the community and economic interests of the applicant company.

international law or German Constitutional law tradition and it is consistent with the Convention's effective interpretation. Since the public authorities' interference comprises all pecuniary rights of individuals, the guarantee of the right to property also should include all pecuniary rights which are important for individuals to realise their plans and to live an autonomous life. Otherwise, the individuals would turn into simple means of the state's aims. Therefore, the Convention organs' interpretation of the concept of possessions is favourable from the point of view of the autonomy principle.

The autonomous concept of property includes all *rights in rem* in tangible and intangible things, and *rights in personam* arising from both public and private law relationships. That is, all vested rights which have pecuniary value constitute possession for the purposes of P1-1. The concept of possession also comprises legitimate expectations which create exercisable claims in domestic laws. However, P1-1 protects only existing property rights and not rights to acquire property, so pure expectations cannot fall into the scope of the guarantee laid down in P1-1. Whether a right is established in domestic law is not an issue which can be decided by the Convention organs. However, the domestic authorities' assessment also cannot be accepted as the sole criterion to decide whether an interest, which comes into the ambit of the P1-1, has arisen. In every single case the Court should evaluate whether the circumstances of the case gave rise to such an interest.

It is suggested that the Court should apply its interpretation of the Convention as a living instrument to interpretation of the concept of possession as well, and expand the concept in order to embrace new subject matters of property rights such as new kinds of intellectual property, body parts and radio spectrum.

The established case-law suggests that right to property is a single right which gives different use rights. The right of disposal also should be understood as a way of use. Each use right does not constitute a distinct property right, so interference with such use does not constitute deprival of property. It can be inferred that the Strasbourg jurisprudence does not accept the idea of a bundle of rights theory of property. This conclusion is important for the distinction between deprivation of property and the control on use of property. This distinction is a key element for the jurisprudence on P1-1.

The scope of this section up to here has been the concept of 'possession' in the first sentence of P1-1. In order to complete this examination, the focus of the next section will be the sphere of the responsibility of state.

6.3. The Sphere of the Responsibility of State

This section looks at the question of what kind of duty the right of property imposes on the contracting states as duty-bearer. That is, do the state parties have only negative duty, not to interfere with property rights, or do they also have positive obligations to ensure every individual enjoys such rights? One other and connected issue which will be examined in this context is whether the state is responsible for only public authorities' interferences or will it be responsible for the private agents' interferences as well. In another words, what is the horizontal effect, or third-party applicability of P1-1? Obviously these two questions are closely related to each other. The second question, indeed, is related to a special form of positive obligation, namely to take necessary legislative and executive actions to protect rights against third-party interferences.

6.3.1. The Nature of Obligations Arising from P1-1

These problems are another appearance of the question of the characteristics of human rights. Are fundamental rights liberty rights or claim rights in the Hohfeldian[110] schema of rights? The classical liberal understanding of fundamental rights as pure negative (liberty) rights has not determined the Convention organs' interpretation of the Convention rights. Article 1 of the Convention requires the contracting parties to secure the rights and freedoms included in it. Together with the text of other articles dealing with particular rights, this wording in Article 1 has been interpreted as imposing both negative and positive obligations upon states.[111] The positive obligations require a state to take action to secure human rights. They are generally associated with economic social and cultural rights and commonly have financial implications.[112] However, civil and political rights also may require positive actions. A number of rights regulated in the Convention such as obligations to protect the right to life by law (Article 2(1)), to provide prison conditions that are not inhuman (Article 3), to provide courts, legal aid and translators in connection with the right to fair trial (Article 6) and to hold free elections (P1-3) expressly imposed positive obligations in their texts.

The Court interpreted some other rights as also imposing positive obligations. Among these are the right to respect for family life (Article 8),[113] the right not to join trade unions (Article 11),[114] and the right to education (P1-2).[115] In some of these cases, the state's positive obligations were in the state's relations with individuals, to grant them legal status, rights and privileges to ensure that their Convention rights are secured. But some other positive obligations were related to the relations between private bodies. State's responsibility resulted from failure to protect the Convention rights against interference by other private persons.

---

[110] Hohfeld, W. N., *Fundamental Legal Conceptions as Applied in Judicial Reasoning* (Yale University Press, 1923).
[111] Harris et al. *op.cit.* 92 p.19.
[112] *Ibid.*
[113] *Marckx v. Belgium*, Judgement of 13 June 1979, Series A no.31. The court ruled that, in addition to primary negative undertaking, there may be positive obligations inherent in an effective respect for family life and found infringement of that obligation because Belgian family law did not recognise a child born out of wedlock as a member of the mother's family, thus not allowing the mother and child to lead a normal family life. See also *Airey v. Ireland*, Judgement of 9 October1979, Series A no.32; *Powell and Rayner v. UK* (1990) Series A no. 106.
[114] *Young, James and Webster v. UK*, Judgement of 13 August 1981, Series A no.44.
[115] *Costello-Roberts v. UK*, Admissibility Decision of 13 December 1990, (App. No. 13134/87).

As for the positive obligations with regard to P1-1, the economic character of property rights is of particular interest. In the context of property rights positive obligation does not mean that a state need ensure the existence of a certain distribution of property rights or ensure a certain level of wages or social security to allow individuals to keep or maintain their property. This aspect of property rights distinguishes them from social and economic rights. Other social and economic rights, which have been regulated under the European Social Charter, vest the right-holder with a claim right against public authorities. However, the right to property vests a liberty right with a corresponding negative obligation.

As indicated above the Court and the Commission established from the beginning that a right to property did not guarantee a right to acquire property.[116] Therefore, positive obligations in this context can be understood as the responsibility of a state to preserve a system of private ownership. It must provide a legal system so that property rights can be enforced.[117] The case-law of the Strasbourg organs has not produced too many examples in this regard. For example, in *Immobiliare Saffi v. Italy*[118] and *A. O. v. Italy*[119] the Court found that lack of police assistance for the execution of a judicial decision (the eviction of a tenant) constituted a breach of the applicant's right to property. It implied that the state has a positive duty to provide police assistance to evict the tenant from the applicant's apartment. The Court repeated this judgement in a number of similar cases.[120] However, it did not mention 'positive obligations' expressly. In the case of *Cyprus v. Turkey* the Court did not find violation of P1-1 in respect of alleged failure to protect property from interferences by private persons due to lack of evidence that there was an administrative practice of denying individuals access to a court to vindicate their civil rights.[121] It can be inferred from this decision that states have a positive obligation to protect property against wrongful acts of private individuals, because the Court dismissed the allegations of the applicant government for the reason of lack of enough evidence.

An issue that can be raised in the context of positive obligations of a state under P1-1 is whether a state can be held responsible for lack of action to restore past injustices. This question is particularly significant for former socialist states party to the Convention. The question is whether the confiscations of private property during the socialist era without compensation can be brought before the Court. It is obvious under the Convention system that contracting parties cannot be held responsible for the acts committed before the date the Convention became applicable for them. Such claims will be out of the jurisdiction of the Court *ratione temporis*. But if it is accepted that contracting states are under the obligation of

---

[116] *Marckx* case.

[117] Van den Broek, *op.cit.* 64 p.78.

[118] *Immobiliare Saffi v. Italy*, Judgement of 28 July 1999.

[119] *A.O. v. Italy*, Judgement of 30 May 2000. See also *G.L. v. Italy*, Judgement of 3 August 2000; *Edoardo Palumbo v. Italy*, Judgement of 30 November 2000.

[120] See for a recent case *Ghidotti v. Italy*, Judgement of 21 February 2002, (App. No. 28272/95).

[121] *Cyprus v. Turkey*, Judgement of 10 May 2001, § 271.

correcting the past injustices under P1-1, then it can be argued that a contracting party can be held responsible for not returning the properties confiscated without compensation. In this regard, the case-law can offer two possible lines of argument. Firstly, the concept of 'continuing violation', which was used in the *Cyprus*[122] and *Loizidou* cases, can come to the fore. Accordingly it can be said that confiscations which took place during the socialist era constitute a continuing violation of property rights and the concerned state can be held responsible for the period after the Convention became applicable for it. But the Court sees the expropriation of property as an instantaneous act and does not accept the concept of continuing violation for such transmissions of property. The Court has used the continuing violation doctrine only in the *Cyprus* and *Loizidou* cases. If the Court follows the approach it adopted in these cases, it is expected to find continuing violation in cases of unlawful or *de facto* expropriations. But it has not followed this approach in similar cases. Furthermore, it is highly unlikely that the Court will adopt this approach because of the possible increase in the workload if it does so. The second possible approach is to await a new act of public authorities regarding the properties formerly confiscated without compensation. In a number of Romanian cases, the Court applied this approach.[123] The applicants brought repossession proceedings before the domestic courts to recover properties which were nationalised in 1950. The First Instance Courts allowed the claims and upheld the applicants' right of ownership. But the Supreme Court of Justice quashed the judgement of the Court of First Instance and dismissed the application for confirmation of title on the grounds that the courts did not have jurisdiction to review lawfulness of confiscations. The European Court in all these cases found the violation of P1-1 depending on the decisions of the First Instance Courts. To sum up, the Court found sufficient the existence of a new act of public authorities (the court decision in these particular cases) to apply P1-1 for past unjust interferences with property.

6.3.2. Horizontal Applicability of P1-1

A state's responsibility resulting from the failure to protect the Convention rights against interference by other private persons is called the horizontal effect of the fundamental rights.[124] The case-law has produced a number of examples regarding the horizontal effect of P1-1.

---

[122] *Ibid.*

[123] *Brumerascu v. Romania*, Judgement of 28 October 1999 (App. No. 28342/95); see also *Vasiliu v. Romania*, Judgement of 21 May 2002, (App. No. 29407/95); *Hodos and Others v. Romania*, Judgement of 21 May 2002, (App. No.29968/96); *Surpaceanu v. Romania*, Judgement of 21 May 2002, (App. No.32260/96).

[124] For literature about horizontal effect of the Convention see Drzemczewski, A., "The European Convention on Human Rights and Relations between Private Parties" (1979) 26 *Netherlands International Law Review* 163; Alkema, E. A., "The Third-Party Applicability or 'Drittwirkung' of the European Convention on Human Rights" in Matscher and Petzold (eds) *Protecting Human Rights: The European Dimension* (1988); Clapham, A., *Human Rights in Private Sphere* (Oxford: Clarendon Press, 1993);

Firstly, it is necessary to look at the theoretical aspect of the horizontal effect of the Convention. The concept of 'horizontal effect' *(drittwirkung)*[125] means that the provisions concerning human rights also apply in legal relations between private parties, and not only in legal relations between an individual and the public authorities.[126] If this is understood as the responsibility of individuals for interferences with the Convention rights, it is obvious that there will be no horizontal application of the Convention at the international level because the Convention is a treaty that imposes obligations only upon states.[127] Therefore, a complaint directed against an individual is inadmissible by reason of incompatibility with the Convention *ratione personae*. Direct horizontal application of the Convention at the international level is impossible. However, indirect horizontal application can be possible. That is, an individual can bring up an alleged violation of his fundamental rights and freedoms by other individuals in Strasbourg indirectly, *viz.* when a contracting state can be held responsible for the violation in one way or another.[128]

Regarding the horizontal applicability of fundamental rights, different systems are applied in different national constitutional jurisdictions. Some jurisdictions apply the constitutional rights only in public relations (direct verticality–US). They require a state action in order to apply constitutional provisions. In some jurisdictions fundamental rights are applicable in both private and public relations (direct horizontality–Ireland). Some other jurisdictions apply indirect horizontality. Individuals cannot raise constitutional provisions against other individuals, but courts should interpret law under the light of constitutional values (Canada, Germany). Hunt,[129] regarding the Human Rights Act, suggests a position between indirect and direct horizontal effect, 'application to all law' according to which constitutional rights do not involve private relations but if in any way law involves such relations, the law should be compatible with the Convention rights. For example, if an all-male golf club does not allow women guests into its bar, the Convention rights will not confer a new course of action on

---

Clapham, A., "The 'Drittwirkung' of the Convention" in Macdonald et al (eds) *The European System for the Protection of Human Rights* (M. Nijhoff: Dordrecht, 1993); Harris et al, *Law of the European Convention on Human Rights* (Butterworths: London, 1995) pp.19-23; Van Dijk and Van Hoof, *Theory and Practice of the European Convention on Human Rights* (Kluwer Law Int: London, 1998) (third edition) pp. 22-26; Hunt, M., "The 'Horizontal Effect' of the Human Rights Act" (1998) *Public Law* 423.

[125] *Drittwirkung* means in German law that an individual may rely upon a national bill of rights to bring a claim against a private person who has violated his rights under that instrument.

[126] Van Dijk and Van Hoof, *op.cit.* 124 p.23.

[127] Harris et al, *op.cit.* 92 p.21.

[128] Van Dijk and Van Hoof, *op.cit.* 124 p.23. See, for example, *Plattform 'Arzte für das Leben' v. Austria*, Judgement of 1988, Series A no.139. The Court held that a state must take reasonable and appropriate measures to protect demonstrators from interference by other private persons intent upon disrupting their demonstration in breach of the right to freedom of assembly protected by Article 11.

[129] Hunt, *op.cit.* 124 p.434.

women who want to complain about such arrangements. But if a woman who is physically ejected from the premises sues for assault, she may argue that the common law of trespass cannot be interpreted and applied in such a way as to provide the club with a defence of lawful ejection to the assault claim, because for the Court to accede to the availability of such a defence would itself be in breach of the Convention.[130] It is suggested that this approach is applicable at international level as well. That is, if in any way law is involved in a case it should create the responsibility of state, because the state is behind all law including that regulating private relationships. This does not mean that a state has an objective responsibility for the acts and omissions of its nationals or of individuals under its jurisdiction,[131] but it is responsible for its all actions and inactions, legislative, executive and judicial.

As for the case-law of the Convention organs in this regard, a state may be responsible, according to the case-law, in certain specific circumstances, under P1-1 for interferences with property rights resulting from transactions between private individuals.[132] However, if the facts complained of are not resulting from an exercise of governmental authority but concern exclusively relationships of a contractual nature between individuals, there is no state interference.[133] Therefore, it is not the state's obligation under P1-1 to maintain the purchasing power of sums deposited with financial institutions by way of a systematic indexation of savings.[134]

When a state exercises its legislative or executive powers in connection with civil law relations between private persons, the Strasbourg organs do not hesitate to find the responsibility of the state. In *James and Others*[135] the British Leasehold Reform legislation interfered with the relations between landlords and tenants. The Commission found in a number of applications that governmental authority was involved in complained interferences. For example, the Commission, in *Hiipakka and Others v. Finland*[136] where deprivation did not transfer property from the applicant to the state but it resulted from a plan adopted by the Forestry Board, decided that regardless of the fact that a private road was at issue, the deprivation incurred state responsibility.

However, the case-law is not illuminating about whether governmental authority is involved in the interference if merely a judicial authority is exercised in a case. The Commission, in an application complaining of church contributions

---

130 *Ibid.* p.442.

131 As a rule a state is not internationally responsible for the acts and omissions of its nationals or of individuals within its jurisdiction. See Van Dijk and Van Hoof, *op.cit.* 124 p.120.

132 *MN v. Bulgaria,* (App. No. 29785/96) Decision 4 September 1996.

133 *Gustafsson v. Sweden,* Judgement of 25 April 1996, § 60.

134 App. no: 8724/79, Decision 6 March 1980; DR 20 p.226; App. no: 25045/94, 12 April 1996; *Burrows v. UK,* App. No. 227558/95, 27 November 1996.

135 *James and Others v. UK,* Judgement of 21 February 1986, Seriea A no. 98.

136 *Hiipakka and Others v. Finland,* App. No. 29069/95, 15 May 1996; See also *L v. Finland,* App. No. 18595/91, 5 April 1995; *H v. Finland,* App. No. 18507/91, 5 April 1995.

in Austria, decided that 'the contributions are not levied by the state. Their collection is an autonomous activity of the churches, and the state's activity in this field is limited to the exercise of a power of control. The individual's duty to pay these contributions is considered as an obligation of civil law which the church in question may enforce against the individual concerned by an action in the civil courts. The mere fact that the state courts are available to the church as to any other physical or legal person who wishes to enforce a civil claim does not, in the Commission's view, amount to an interference by the state with the individual's property rights'.[137] The Commission took the same position in a number of cases.

Similarly, in a number of cases the Commission ruled that P1-1 was not concerned with judgements and execution of judgements relating to civil claims or obligations between private individuals.[138] The Commission found that the mere fact that a judicial authority provided a forum for the determination of such a private law dispute did not give rise to interference by the state with property rights under P1-1.[139] It did not accept the applicants' argument that a state was subject to positive obligations under P1-1 to protect the property rights of an individual in the context of a dispute with another private individual to the extent necessary to ensure that in the determination of that dispute all relevant arguments will be fully considered by the courts. However, had the Commission applied the above suggested approach, it would have found the state responsible. That is, if the courts exercise a judicial authority in a case and interfere with property rights, no matter who are the parties to the dispute, the outcome of the exercise of judicial authority should be compatible with the guarantees provided by the Convention.

The Court accepts the responsibility of a state for court decisions regarding the relations between private persons only if such judgements are not compatible with requirements of the right to fair trial regulated in Article 6 of the Convention. For example, in *Estima Jorge v. Portugal*[140] the Court ruled that procedural delays, in breach of Article 6, regarding the execution of a notarial deed providing security for a specific debt between private individuals caused responsibility of the state for the losses caused by that delay. However, if a state does not fail in its responsibilities regarding Article 6, according to the Court, it cannot be held responsible for the results of courts' decisions regarding civil disputes between individuals. In *O.N. v. Bulgaria*[141] the Court found inadmissible the complaints that domestic courts had not taken the effect of inflation into account when deciding on the restitution claim for unjust enrichment. The applicant complained, *inter alia*, that the Bulgarian courts had delivered unjust decisions when they refused to take into account inflation and awarded him sums

---

[137] Admissibility Decision App. No. 9781/82, 14 May 1983, 37 DR 42.

[138] Admissibility Decision App. Nos. 1420/ 62, 1477/62, 1478/62, Yearbook VI, 590; App. No. 8906/80, 7 December 1982 (unpublished).

[139] App. No. 10000/82, Decision. 4 July 1983, D.R. 33 p. 247; App. No. 11949/86, Decision 1 December 1986, *Ruiz Mateos v. UK,* App. No. 13021/87, 8 September 1988, 57 DR 268.

[140] *Estima Jorge v. Portugal*, Judgement of 21 April 1998 (Reports 1998-II, p.762).

[141] *O.N. v. Bulgaria* (App. No. 35221/97) Decision 6 April 2000.

many times less than the real value of what he had given to the other party under the 1975 contract. The substance of the applicant's claim was that the responsibility of the state under P1-1 was engaged, in that domestic legislation and judicial practice did not allow recovery of the real value of his claim. He argued that the applicable domestic law and case-law disregarded inflation to such an extent that they caused a *de facto* deprivation of property in that he – a creditor whose claim had been fully recognised – was only entitled to recover 'one thousandth' of its value.[142]

The Court ruled that P1-1 'does not give rise to any positive obligation for the state to maintain the value not only of deposits, but also of claims or any other asset. It does not require from states to apply "an inflation-rate-compatible" default interest rate to private claims. The convention cannot be seen as imposing on states obligations concerning their economic policy in dealing with the effects of inflation and other economic phenomena'.[143] The Court admitted that this judgement left the applicant to bear disproportionally the consequences of inflation to the benefit of the other party, which seemed contrary to requirements of justice. However, it noted, 'imposing on the State the positive obligation to remedy such situations through legislation or judicial decision would be no less than imposing an obligation to guarantee the value of possessions despite inflation or other economic phenomena'. In this case the Court abstained examining whether the substance of the judgement was compatible with the applicant's property rights protected by P1-1. If it had applied the suggested horizontality principle, it would have found the state responsible for the applicant's losses incurred by the failure of domestic courts to take into account the effect of inflation in the restitution claim.[144]

The Court's correlation between imposing a positive obligation on a state to remedy the effect of inflation in civil proceedings and imposing an obligation to guarantee the value of possessions seems unfounded. Basic fairness requires that public authorities and judicial bodies should not force some individuals to bear a loss in favour of other individuals. Justice may require a state to take some positive actions to exercise fairness. The domestic law's involvement in outcome injustice cannot be denied. Therefore, the state should have been held responsible. Indeed the Commission previously held that it must make sure that in determining the effects on property of legal relations between individuals the law did not create such an inequality that one person could be arbitrarily and unjustly deprived of property in favour of another.[145] But the Court did not consider this authority of the Commission.

---

[142] *Ibid.*

[143] *Ibid.*

[144] To see the attitude of British courts in this regard see Whale, S., "Pawnbrokers and Parishes: The Protection of Property under the Human Rights Act" (2002) *European Human Rights Law Review* 67.

[145] *Bramelid and Malmstrom v. Sweden*, App. Nos. 8588/79, 8589/79, 29 DR 64; app. No. 12462/86, 13 July 1987, 53 DR 234.

6.4. Conclusion

This chapter suggests that the first sentence of P1-1 enunciates a general right to property. This provision, however, protects only existing possessions but it does not guarantee a right to acquire property. That is to say, it is a liberty right, not a claim right in the Hohfeldian schema of rights. So, it does not give an individual a right to claim welfare benefits. But the concept of property or possessions is interpreted expansively so as to include all individual patrimonial rights or all pecuniary rights arising from private and public law relationships and legitimate expectations. Both natural and legal persons' property enjoy the protection of the guarantee enunciated in P1-1.

Since P1-1 protects a negative right to property (a liberty right), the main responsibility of states arising from this provision is a negative obligation not to interfere with property. It does not impose on contracting parties a positive duty to provide property to the individuals. But the contracting parties have a positive obligation to provide effective protection of the property rights. A state should take necessary measures to protect property rights against third-party interferences.

Contracting states are not normally responsible for the relationships between private individuals. But if public authorities are involved in someway in such a relationship, such involvement may bring the responsibility of a state to the fore. This involvement can be administrative, legislative, or judicial. For example, if because of a law in force, an individual's property rights are affected adversely in a relationship between private individuals, a state should be held responsible, because there is the state's authority in all laws including that regulating private relationships.

Chapter 7

Interference with Property Rights under the ECHR

7.1. Introduction

In the last chapter, the first sentence of P1-1 was examined. It was indicated that the first sentence of the article enunciates a general right to property. This provision, however, protects only existing possessions and it does not guarantee a right to acquire property. So, it does not give an individual a right to claim welfare benefits. But the concept of property or possessions is interpreted expansively so as to include all individual patrimonial rights or all pecuniary rights. That is, every natural or legal person has *prima facie* a right to peaceful enjoyment of his/her possessions. However, this right is not an absolute one, and it is subjected to interferences of public authorities. The rest of the article regulates these interferences.

This chapter looks at the second sentence of the first paragraph and second paragraph of P1-1:

> No one shall be deprived of his possessions except in the public interest and subject to the conditions provided for by law and by the general principles of international law.
>
> The preceding provisions shall not, however, in any way impair the right of a state to enforce such laws as it deems necessary to control the use of property in accordance with the general interest or to secure the payment of taxes or other contributions or penalties.

The question to which an answer is sought here is how far a state can interfere with property rights without violating them. This includes examination of types of interferences that are allowed by the Convention, conditions of legitimate interferences and when the actions of public authorities constitute violation of property rights.

In this chapter, first the types of interference with property rights that are defined by the Convention organs will be examined. The Convention organs have defined three types of interference, two of which (deprivation of property and control on use) have been deduced from the letter of P1-1 and the third one (interference with substance of property) is merely a judicial construct. However, this classification that depends on the effect of interference on property is not above criticism. It has a number of difficulties in application. It is far from giving us clear guidance to determine when compensation is required. The Court seems to adopt the rule that in cases of deprivation compensation is required. However, its basis seems unfounded because firstly there is no moral difference between partial or full deprivation of property, and secondly the magnitude of economic loss resulting from use restrictions can be as serious as that of deprivation.[1] On the other hand, some of the deprivations are regarded as controls on use in order to refrain from compensation requirement. Moreover, the Court's criteria for each of the types seem to becoming less and less clear. The Court has a tendency to apply directly a balancing test[2] that makes the distinction among different types of interference less important. However, this represents a threat to the effectiveness and security of the European protection system.

In Chapter 4 where theoretical aspects of limitation of property were examined, another classification based on the purpose of the state's action was suggested. This classification makes reference to states' three different powers corresponding to three different types of interference. These are taking of property by power of eminent domain, taxation and controlling the use of property by police power regulations. Only the case of taking of property for public interest requires payment of compensation. The moral basis of the compensation requirement can be found in different doctrines, namely utilitarianism,[3] and the autonomy of the individual. Autonomy requires an individual to be treated as end of policy, not a means. On this ground the burden of public policies can be imposed on individuals on an equal sharing basis only. In cases of taxation and police power regulation, compensation does not need to be paid.

Although it is possible that some difficulty arises in distinguishing when interference constitutes taking of property and when taxation or police power regulation, some criteria can be offered. A general criterion which can be employed to distinguish between takings and taxation is that takings single out some people to bear the burden of public policies.[4] That is, takings impose the burden of public policies only on some individuals, while taxation imposes on everyone in the same position to bear the burden of public policies on the equal sharing ground. But it is sometimes difficult to apply this criterion when tax laws impose special taxes only on some class of people. Unequal taxation can be justified on different grounds such as reciprocal benefit and redistributive justice. Although many different arguments have been posed in favour of and against

---

[1] Allen, T., "Limitations on Constitutional Property Rights" in Paul Jackson and David C. Wilde (eds.) *Property Law: Current Issues and Debates* (Ashgate: Dartmouth, 1999).
[2] Gomien, D., Harris, D., and Zwaak, L., *Law and Practice of the European Convention on Human Rights and the European Social Charter*, (Council of Europe Publishing: Strasbourg, 1996).
[3] Michelman, Franc I., "Property, Utility, and Fairness: Comments on the Ethical Foundations of 'Just Compensation' Law" (1967) 80 *Harvard Law Review* 1165-1258; Rose, Carol M., "Property and Expropriation: Themes and Variations in American Law" (2000) *Utah Law Review* 1; Allen, T., *The Right to Property in Commonwealth Constitutions* (CUP, Cambridge, 2000).
[4] Munzer, S., *A Theory of Property* (CUP: Cambridge, 1991) p.421.

redistributive taxation in theory,[5] P1-1 has not brought any limitation over the contracting states' power of taxation. The only limitation the ECHR brings over the power of taxation of the states is discrimination prohibition in Article 14.

The main distinction between takings and police power regulations is that the aim of police power regulations is to prevent use of property harmful to the rights of other people.[6] The extent of police power regulations may differ according to adopted political ideology. The communitarian theories expand the scope of police power regulations enormously. According to these theories property is a social construct and it serves social functions. The social function theory of property has been defended on many different grounds.[7] In Chapter 4 the police powers of the state were grounded on the harm principle and Rawls' 'liberty principle'. Raz's autonomy-based freedom principle can be utilised as a compromise between the harm principle and the social function theory of property. It can also be taken as the ground of a balancing test applied by the Court and can guide the Court when it applies a balancing test. The scope of police power regulations is very wide. It comprises a range of regulations from environmental protection to city planning, from historical and cultural heritage preservation to neighbourhood obligations.

This classification can be adapted easily to P1-1. So in this chapter, following the examination of classification of types of legitimate interference with property rights employed by the Convention organs, it will be suggested that the classification depending on the purpose of the state's action can better guide the Court in an examination of whether an act of state has violated property rights.

Having examined the taxonomy of the types of legitimate interference with property, in the following section, the conditions of legitimate interference with property rights will be examined. Lawfulness and legitimacy (being in the public interest) of the interference are general requirements for all types of interference. Compensation and compliance with general principles of international law requirements are applicable only for takings. Although the letter of P1-1 does not explicitly guarantee payment of compensation the Convention organs have established that compensation is an inherent feature of the right to property for taking of private property by power of eminent domain. According to the case-law, however, a reasonable compensation will be sufficient, and full compensation is not required. However, the basis and limits of the discretionary power of public authorities, in this area, should be clearly established. For example, reciprocal benefit or correction of past injustice – for instance, land reform laws aiming to correct unjust allocation of land in a colonial past – may justify payment of a compensation less than market value. Proportionality or balancing individual and common interests of society is a requirement developed by the Convention organs and applicable for all types of interferences.

---

[5] Two different liberal arguments – one in favour of (Rawls' difference principle) and one against (Nozick's entitlement theory of property) redistributive taxation – were examined in Chapter 4.

[6] Sax, J., "Takings and Police Power" (1964) 74 *Yale Law Journal* 36-76.

[7] See Chapter 4 for a detailed discussion of the social function theory of property.

Failure of a state in any of these requirements results in violation of property rights protected by the European Convention. It is important to know the grounds on which the public authorities have failed because the nature of the remedy in a case of violation differs depending upon the nature of the failure. If a state's act fails to comply with lawfulness or public interest requirements or proportionality in one of them, the result should be the annulment of the action and the remedy should be restitution of property. But if violation arises as a result of failure in complying with the compensation requirement, the result should not be annulment of state's action but additional compensation should be awarded. A failure in the compensation requirement may occur either by valuing insufficient compensation or non-payment of compensation in the cases of *de facto* expropriation or regulatory takings. However, in cases of *de facto* expropriation, generally the lawfulness requirement will also be violated.

7.2. Types of Legitimate Interference with Property

According to the classical formulation of the Court, which it repeats in almost all property rights cases, P1-1 comprises three distinct rules.[8] The first rule, which is set out in the first sentence of the first paragraph, contains a general guarantee of the right to property. The second rule, which appears in the second sentence of the first paragraph, covers deprivation of possessions and subjects it to certain conditions. The third rule, which is contained in the second paragraph, recognises that the contracting states are entitled, among other things, to control the use of property in accordance with the general interest. As the Court and the Commission have stated in many cases, these rules are not entirely separate or unconnected. On the contrary, the second and third rules, which are concerned with particular instances of interference with the right to peaceful enjoyment of possessions, are to be construed in the light of the general principle laid down in the first rule.[9]

According to the Court the first sentence of the first paragraph of P1-1 is not only a general statement of the right to property, but it also provides a separate basis for regulating interferences with the property rights that do not qualify as a deprivation or control on use.[10] The Court is of the opinion that if an interference cannot be classified as deprivation or control on use it should be regarded as an

[8] See, for example, *Sporrong and Lönnroth v. Sweden,* Judgement of 23 September 1982 (App. Nos.7151/75 and 7152/75) Series A no. 52, § 61; *James and Others v UK* Judgement of 21 February 1986(App. No 8793/*79)* Series A no. 98 para. 37 and *Lithgow and Others v. UK* Judgement of 8 July 1986, Series A no. 102 § 106; *Iatridis v. Greece,* Judgement of 25 March 1999 Reports 1999-II, § 55; *Carbonara And Ventura v. Italy,* Judgement of 30 May 2000 (App. No. 24638/94).

[9] See for example *Holy Monasteries v. Greece,* Judgement of 9 December 1994, Series A no. 301-A § 56; *James and Others v. The UK,* Judgement of 21 February 1986, Series A no. 98 p. 30 *Pialopoulos and Others v. Greece*, Judgement of 15 February 2001(App. No. 37095/97); *Beyeler v. Italy*, Judgement of 5 January 2000 (App. No.33202/96) § 98.

[10] Harris, D., O'Boyle, M. and Warbrick, C., *Law of the European Convention on Human Rights* (Butterworths: London, 1995) p.521.

interference with the substance of property rights and should be assessed as to whether it complies with the balancing test.[11] The Court has been using this approach more and more in recent cases, but this approach will be criticised below because other forms of interference also affect the substance of property rights. Indeed the problem here is the same as the problem described as regulatory takings in the US.

7.2.1. Deprivation of Property

The second sentence of P1-1 is worded as follows:

> No one shall be deprived of his possessions except in the public interest and subject to the conditions provided for by law and by the general principles of international law.

Here only the concept of deprivation and its difference from other forms of interferences will be examined. The conditions it is subjected to will be examined in the next section. A distinction between deprivation and other types of interference is meaningful only if one assumes that there is a duty to pay compensation on deprivation.[12] Otherwise the distinction will be meaningless because the conditions which the deprivation and control on use are subjected to are the same. They are expressed only in different words but the substance is identical. For example, there is no difference between public interest (in deprivation) and general interest (in control on use). Nor is there any real difference between the phrases 'conditions provided for by law' (in deprivation) and 'laws as it deems necessary' (in control on use).

Deprivation can be defined as dispossession of the subject of property; if all the rights of the owner are extinguished by operation of law or by the exercise of a legal power to the same effect, there will be a deprivation of property.[13] Deprivation, in principle, includes a transfer of property or destruction of it. However, it is not unproblematic to decide when an interference constitutes deprivation. The first difficulty arises from the definition of property rights. If property is defined as a bundle of rights as most common law jurisdictions do,[14] then when will the owner be accepted as deprived of his property? As indicated in Chapter 6 the Court does not accept the bundle of rights theory of property. Accordingly it does not accept different rights arising from property as different

---

[11] *Sporrong and Lönnroth v. Sweden,* Judgement of 23 September 1982 Series A no. 52, § 69.

[12] Peukert, W., "Protection of Ownership under Article 1 of the First Protocol to the European Convention on Human Rights" (1981) 2 *Human Rights Law Journal* 37.

[13] Sermet, L., *The European Convention on Human Rights and Property Rights* (Council of Europe Publishing: Strasbourg, 1998) (revised edition) p. 23; Harris et al, *op.cit.* 10 p.527.

[14] Honoré, A.M., "Ownership" in A. G. Guest (ed.) *Oxford Essays in Jurisprudence* (Oxford UP: Oxford, 1961).

property rights but use of property. So, in the *Tre Traktörer Aktiebolag*[15] case the Court decided, though a licence constitutes property in the meaning of P1-1, that withdrawal of the licence to sell alcoholic beverages did not fall within the ambit of the second sentence of the first paragraph. So it did not constitute a deprivation of property, rather control of the use of property because the applicant company kept some economic interests represented by the leasing of the premises and the property assets contained therein.[16] Similarly, in the *Fredin*[17] case the Court did not find deprivation in the revocation of a permit to exploit gravel in one plot of the applicant's property. However, the Court, in this case, examined whether the seriousness of the effects of revocation constitute *de facto* expropriation. But it refused to examine the effect of revocation on only one plot of land in isolation and considered other surrounding parcels as well when evaluating the effect of interference.

In the *Mellacher*[18] case the Court did not consider the right to get income (rent) from one's property as an independent property right and ruled that restrictions on rent contracts reducing the amount of rents did not amount either to a formal or to a *de facto* expropriation, because there was no transfer of the applicants' property nor were they deprived of their right to use, let or sell it.[19] In the *Iatridis*[20] case the Court did not consider the administrative eviction of a leaseholder of a cinema as deprivation nor control on use but as interference with substance of property. But in *James and Others*[21] the Commission and the Court found that legislation authorising tenants under existing leases to acquire the landlords' rights in the property deprived the landlords of their possessions.

To sum up, the Court accepts deprivation occurs only where the owner has lost title to property formally or *de facto*. According to the Court, deprivation of one or some of the distinct use or disposal rights does not amount to deprivation in the meaning of the second sentence of the first paragraph of P1-1 unless the interference took away all meaningful use of the property in question.

There is no doubt that measures aiming at direct dispossession of the owner such as expropriation[22] or nationalisation[23] constitute deprivation of property. However, in some cases, although there is no formal expropriation or nationalisation, measures applied by public authorities may result in the owners losing title to their property. The Court has not confined the meaning of deprivation to formal takings of property. According to established case-law, in order to determine whether there is a deprivation of property within the meaning of

---

[15] *Tre Traktörer Aktiebolag v. Sweden*, Judgement of 7 July 1989, Series A, No. 159.
[16] *Ibid*, § 55.
[17] *Fredin v. Sweden*, Judgement of 18 February 1991, Series A no. 192.
[18] *Mellacher v. Austria*, Judgement of 19 December 1989, Series A, No. 169.
[19] *Ibid.* § 44.
[20] *Iatridis v. Greece*, Judgement of 25 March 1999, Reports 1999-II, § 55.
[21] *James and Others v. UK*, Judgement of 21 February 1986, Series A no. 98.
[22] *Papachelas v. Greece*, Judgement of 25 March 1999, Reports 1999-II, § 45; *Katikaridis and Others v. Greece*, Judgement of 15 November 1996, Reports 1996-V; *Tsomtsos and Others v. Greece*, Judgement of 15 November 1996, Reports 1996-V.
[23] *Lithgow and Others v. UK*, Judgement of 8 July 1986, Series A no.102.

P1-1, the Court should look behind the appearances and investigate the realities of the situation complained of. Since the Convention is intended to provide 'practical and effective' guarantee of rights, the Court should investigate whether the situation complained of constitutes a *de facto* expropriation.[24]

In the *Holy Monasteries*[25] case, the Court ruled that the creation of a presumption in favour of state ownership of disputed land effectively vested an unchallengeable title in the state because the monasteries were not in a position to prove their own superior title, relying as they did on ancient, adverse possession. So even if the law had not yet been implemented, the presumption created by law constituted a deprivation of property.[26] Similarly the exemption of the state and other organisers of pilot services from their liability for negligent acts by a law retrospectively, deprived the rights deriving from claims for damages which could have been asserted in domestic law up to that point.[27] However, retroactive deprivation of restitution claims for alleged double taxation constituted control of the use of property because the measures were related to the payment of taxation.[28] In another case the Court interestingly ruled that retroactive annulment of arbitration rewards amounted to neither an expropriation nor a measure to control the use of property rather it fell to be dealt with under the first sentence of the first paragraph.[29]

Sometimes property may not be transferred to a public authority, but an action of public authorities may force the owner to transfer his property to other private persons. According to the established case-law there is still deprivation of property. For example, in the *Hakansson and Sturesson*[30] case the applicant had bought farming land at auction, but had been forced to resell it, since the authorities refused to grant him the permit needed to retain it. But in *Bramelid*[31] the Commission said that the deprivation rule applies only to seizures by the state or by one to whom it gives the right to seize, of a specific asset to be used for the realisation of a goal in the public interest. It found regulations that allow a majority

---

[24] *Sporrong and Lönnroth v. Sweden*, Judgement of 23 September 1982, Series A, No. 52; *Carbonara and Ventura v. Italy*, Judgement of 30 May 2000 (App. No.24638/94) § 60; *Belvedere Alberghiera v. Italy*, Judgement of 30 May 2000 (App. No. 31524/96) § 53.

[25] *Holy Monasteries v. Greece*, Judgement of 9 December 1994, Series A, No.301-A; see also *Former King of Greece and Others v. Greece*, Judgement of 23 November 2000 (App. No. 25701/94) § 78.

[26] *Ibid.* § 66.

[27] *Pressos Compania Naviera S.A. and Others v. Belgium*, Judgement of 20 November 1995, Series A, No.332.

[28] *National and Provincial Building Society, Leeds Permanent Building Society and Yorkshire Building Society v. UK*, Judgement of 23 October 1997, Reports 1997-VII, §79.

[29] *Stran Greek Refineries and Stratis Andreadis v. Greece*, Judgement of 9 December 1994, Series A, No.301-A.

[30] *Hakansson and Sturesson v. Sweden*, Judgement of 21 February 1990, Series A, No. 171-A.

[31] *Bramelid and Malmstrom v. Sweden*, (1982) 5 EHRR 249.

shareholder to buy out a minority shareholder in certain circumstances to concern above all the relations of shareholders *inter se* and to have nothing to do with the notion of 'public interest' as commonly understood in the field of expropriations. The Commission's reasoning here seems contrary to systematic of P1-1 because P1-1 classifies interferences according to their effect on the right to property. But the state here uses its regulatory power in order to prevent misuse of minority shareholders' rights against majority shareholders. So it should be considered under the police power regulations. However, the state should play its mediator role in a just way and should compromise the rights of parties.

In cases of temporary transfer of property, the Court considered the interference as an interference with the substance of property rather than deprival of property.[32]

According to the Court, the loss of the applicant resulted from the difference between statutory interest rate applied to his additional compensation claim for expropriation and inflation constituted deprivation of property.[33] The Commission, in a similar case, considered that the applicant's loss resulted from public authorities delay in payment of additional compensation and this in tandem with high inflation amounted to interference with the first sentence of P1-1 whereas the Court did not discuss the issue.[34] But in another case the Court ruled that public authorities' delay in payment of compensation for expropriation could not be equated to a deprivation, but constituted interference with the substance of right to property.[35]

In a number of cases concerning Italy's constructive-expropriation legislation the Court found that physical possession of property by public authorities without formal expropriation amounted to deprivation of property.[36]

In a number of other cases the Court found a *de facto* expropriation. For example, in *Papamichalopoulos,*[37] though the applicants' land was never formally expropriated by the Greek authorities and the applicants remained owner of the

---

[32] *Poiss v. Austria*, Judgement of 23 April 1987, Series A, No. 117; *Prötsch v. Austria,* Judgement of 15 November 1996.

[33] *Aka v. Turkey*, Judgement of 23 September 1998, Reports 1998-VI, para.43; *Gaganus and Others v. Turkey*, Judgement of 5 June 2001 (App. No. 39335/98).

[34] *Akkus v. Turkey*, Judgement of 9 July 1997, Reports 1997-IV; *Yasar and Others v. Turkey*, Judgement of 14 November 2000 (App. No.27697/95); *Hamdi Celebi v. Turkey*, Judgement of 30 January 2001(and 23 other decisions on the same date) (App. Nos. 19264- 19288/92); *Ismihan Ozel and Others v. Turkey*, Judgement of 27 February 2001 (App. No. 31963/96); *Ali Ozturk v. Turkey,* Judgement of 10 April 2001 (and 24 other decisions on the same date) (App. Nos. 19289- 19312/92); *Gulnahar Calkan v. Turkey*, Judgement of 5 June 2001(and 19 other decisions on the same date) (App. Nos.19661-19683/92).

[35] *Almeida Garrett, Mascarenhas Falcao and Others v. Portugal*, Judgement of 11 January 2000 (App. Nos. 29813/96 and 30229/96) § 48.

[36] *Carbonara and Ventura v. Italy*, Judgement of 30 May 2000 (App. No.24638/94 § 60; *Belvedere Alberghiera v. Italy*, Judgement of 30 May 2000 (App. No. 31524/96) § 53.

[37] *Papamichalopoulos and Others v. Greece,* Judgement of 24 June 1993, Series A, No.260-B.

land concerned formally, the Court held that the transfer of the land to the Navy by the Greek dictatorial government and the fact that the Navy exercised full *de facto* control over it for a long time (28 years) constituted a *de facto* expropriation because the applicants were unable either to make use of their property or to sell, bequeath, make a gift of it, and were even forbidden to access it, nor were they provided any form of redress. Similarly in *Vasilescu*[38] the Court ruled that unlawful seizure of valuables in 1966 and the loss of all ability to dispose of the property in issue, taken together with the failure of the attempts for remedy by the national authorities and courts, amounted to a *de facto* confiscation incompatible with P1-1. Although the Court did not name expressly a *de facto* expropriation, it found in the *Brumerascu*[39] case that as a result of the judgement of the Supreme Court of Justice the applicant was deprived of his possessions, though the civil courts, in a decision of 1993 that became enforceable, confirmed that the applicant's heirs' property was confiscated unlawfully in 1950.

In another case the Court held that exercise of the right of pre-emption by tax authorities deprived the owner of her property.[40] The applicant argued, in that case, that pre-emption of her property amounted to a *de facto* expropriation but the Court did not name it *de facto* expropriation because the respondent government did not contest the argument.

In cases of *de facto* expropriation there is a transfer of property to public authorities. The Court has not ruled destruction of property as *de facto* expropriation. In a number of cases concerning the allegations that Turkish security forces were involved in the burning and destruction of houses and their contents in the south-east part of the country where political tension was rife, though no proof of the security forces' participation had been produced, the Turkish Government's failure to produce evidence to the contrary led the Court to find grave violations of both Article 8 of the Convention and P1-1.[41]

In two cases against Turkey[42] the Court decided that since the Turkish Republic of Northern Cyprus (TRNC) was not recognised by the international

---

[38] *Vasilescu v. Romania*, Judgement of 22 May 1998, Reports 1998-III, § 55; see also Djajic, S., "The Right to Property and the Vasilescu v. Romania Case" (2000) 27 *Syracuse Journal of International Law and Commerce* 363.
[39] *Brumerascu v. Romania*, Judgement of 28 October 1999 (App. No. 28342/95); see also *Anghelescu v. Romania,* Judgement of 9 April 2002, (App. No. 29411/95; *Vasiliu v. Romania*, Judgement of 21 May 2002, (App. No. 29407/95); *Hodos and Others v. Romania*, Judgement of 21 May 2002, (App. No.29968/96); *Surpaceanu v. Romania*, Judgement of 21 May 2002, (App. No.32260/96).
[40] *Hentrich v. France*, Judgement of 22 September 1994, Series A, No. 296-A.
[41] See for example *Akdivar and Others v. Turkey*, Judgement of 16 September 1996, Reports 1996-IV; *Mentes and Others v. Turkey*, Judgement of 28 November 1997, Reports 1997-VIII; *Selcuk and Asker v. Turkey*, Judgement of 24 April 1998, Reports 1998-II; *Aksoy v. Turkey*, Judgement of 18 December 1996, Reports 1996-VI; *Dulas v. Turkey*, Judgement of 30 January 2001(App. No. 25801/94); *Bilgin v. Turkey*, Judgement of 26 November 2000, (App. No. 23819/94).
[42] *Loizidou v. Turkey*, Judgement of 18 December 1996, Reports 1996-VI; *Cyprus v. Turkey*, Judgement of 10 May 2001 (App. No. 25781/94) §187.

community, its legislation could not be regarded as valid. Therefore, expropriation made according to the TRNC Constitution was also not valid. Accordingly the Court ruled that displaced Greek Cypriots did not lose their title to their property in Northern Cyprus. As a result it found that the fact that displaced persons were forbidden access to their property and lost all control over them due to the division of the island constituted continuing interference with property. However, this interference did not amount to a deprivation of property, rather interference with the general rule in the first sentence of first paragraph of P1-1.

Lastly, although some interferences result in owners losing their title to their property, they are not considered as deprivation of property, rather they amount to control of the use of property. These mainly include execution of court judgements, execution of fines and penalties, payment of taxes and other contributions, temporary or permanent confiscation, seizure or forfeiture of property for legal proceedings.[43]

7.2.2. Control of the Use of Property

The second paragraph of P1-1 allows the contracting states an almost unlimited power to impose restrictions on the use of property in accordance with the general interest.[44] It reads as follows;

> The preceding provisions shall not, however, in any way impair the right of a State to enforce such laws as it deems necessary to control the use of property in accordance with the general interest or to secure the payment of taxes or other contributions or penalties.

Here only the concept of 'control of the use of property' will be examined. The conditions it is subjected to will be examined in the next section. The scope of the control of use rule is very wide; it comprises all measures taken by public authorities to regulate use or disposal of property that do not fall within the ambit of deprivation rule. P1-1 enumerates two different objectives that may be aimed at by public authorities in enforcing restrictive laws on property; to serve the general interest and to secure the payment of taxes or other contributions or penalties. Mediating different property interests among private persons and the execution of court judgements should also be added to this list.[45]

7.2.2.1. Control of the use of property in the general interest The concept of 'general interest' is so wide that it comprises almost any aim expressed by public authorities. Drafters of the Article refused to restrict the power of contracting states in any way in this respect. Such reluctance of the drafters resulted from both

---

[43] Van Den Broek, P., "The Protection of Property Rights under the European Convention on Human Rights" (1986) 1986-1 *Issues of European Integration* 52.
[44] Van Dijk and Van Hoof, *Theory and Practice of the European Convention on Human Rights* (Kluwer Law Int: London, 1998) (third edition).
[45] Rose, Carol M., "Property and Expropriation: Themes and Variations in American Law" (2000) *Utah Law Review* 1.

practical political and philosophical concerns. The political concern was their reluctance to make economic and social policies of states questionable before international institutions (the Commission and the Court). Such a possibility might have made more difficult the ratification of the Convention.[46] The philosophical reserve was the effect of the social function theory of property. According to this theory individual property rights are justifiable only as long as they serve the public good and are limited by this aim.[47] So the drafters aimed only to prevent arbitrary confiscation of property by this article. The protection in this area has been developed gradually by the Convention organs through the adoption of the proportionality principle.

Public authorities may effect their power to control the use of property by requiring positive action by individuals or by imposing restrictions on activities of the owner. For example, an obligation to fix a plate on one's car, or an obligation on a landowner to plant trees in the interest of environmental protection,[48] or an obligation to take some security measures in order to open a building into a business, and the statutory regulation of shop opening hours[49] all constitute control of the use of property. The examples of imposing restrictions are restrictions arising from town planning, environmental protection, housing policy, rent control, import and export laws, economic regulation of professions,[50] inheritance laws, the seizure of property for legal proceedings,[51] or demolition of a dilapidated house to prevent danger to the public.[52]

As indicated above the planning measures which do not deprive the title of owner to property amount to control of the use of property.[53] For example, a prohibition on living in caravans on the applicant's own land without permission and contrary to planning regulations constitutes control of the use of property.[54] However, not every interference short of deprivation will be an act controlling the

---

46 Collected Edition of the "*Travaux Préparatoires*" of the European Convention on Human Rights (M. Nijhoff: Dordrecht, 1985). Vol. VI; See also Chapter 5 above.

47 See Chapter 4 above.

48 *Denev v. Sweden*, Decision of the Commission (App. No. 12570/86) DR no. 59 p. 127(1989).

49 Admissibility Decision of the Commission CD 9, p.53.

50 *Van Marle and Others v. Netherlands*, Judgement of 3 June 1986, Series A no. 101.

51 Harris, at al, *op.cit.* 10 p.521.

52 Admissibility Decision of the Commission App. No.7965/77.

53 *Fredin v. Sweden*, Judgement of 18 February 1991, Series A, No. 192, where the Court ruled that a revocation of permit to exploit gravel in one plot of land did not amount to deprivation considering the effect of revocation on the whole of the property including surrounding plots; *Pine Valley Developments Ltd. and Others v. Ireland*, Judgement of 29 November 1991, Series A, No 222, where the Court found that the failure to re-validate a planning permission nullified by the courts, resulting in very substantial reduction in the value of land, was not a *de facto* expropriation but a control of use.

54 *Chapman v. UK*, Judgement of 18 January 2001 (App. No.27238/95) para. 120; *Beard v. UK*, Judgement of 18 January 2001(App. No.24882/94); *Coster v. UK*, Judgement of 18 January 2001(App. No.24876/94); *Lee v. UK*, Judgement of 18 January 2001(App. No.25298/94); *Jane Smith v. UK*, Judgement of 18 January 2001(App. No.25154/94).

use of property. Some of the measures constitute interference with the substance of property rights. Nevertheless, the criteria applied by the Convention organs to distinguish when an act constitutes control of use and when interference with substance of property are not clear. The Court in *Sporrong and Lönnroth*[55] decided that prohibitions on construction amounted to a control of use. But expropriation permits, it added, were not intended to limit or control use, neither did they fall within the ambit of deprivation rule because they were the initial step in a procedure leading to deprivation of possession. So they constituted interference with the general rule set out in the first sentence of the first paragraph.[56]

Although the text of P1-1 mentions only control of the use of property, it concerns, in practice, the right to dispose of property as well.[57] The Court, in a number of rent control cases, held that reduction in the amount of the rent by laws amounted to control of the use of property.[58] Restrictions on time, renewal and dissolution of residential rents are also considered as the control of the use of property.[59]

Both transfer of hunting rights over the applicants' land by a law to members of an Association[60] and the abolition of exclusive fishing rights of the owners of water areas[61] amount to control of the use of property in the meaning of the second paragraph of P1-1.

7.2.2.2. Control of the use of property to secure payment of taxes and other contributions or penalties In the area of taxation contracting states enjoy a wide margin of appreciation. The Convention does not impose any limitation on the contracting states' power to levy taxes apart from the non-discrimination rule in Article 14.[62] Levying tax is one of the features of state sovereignty. However any

---

[55] *Sporrong and Lönnroth v. Sweden,* Judgement of 23 September 1982 Series A no. 52.
[56] *Ibid.* § 65.
[57] Sermet, *op.cit.* 13 p.25.
[58] *Mellacher and Others v. Austria*, Judgement of 19 December 1989, Series A, No. 169.
[59] *Scollo v. Italy*, Judgement of 28 September 1995, Series A, No.315-C; *Spadea and Scalabrino v. Italy*, Judgement of 28 September 1995, Series A, NO.315-B; *Immobiliare Saffi v. Italy*, Judgement of 28 July 1999; *A.O. v. Italy*, Judgement of 30 May 2000; *Edoardo Palumbo v. Italy*, Judgement of 30 November 2000, (App. no. 15919/89); *Velosa Barreto v. Portugal*, Judgement of 21 November 1995 (App. No.18072/91).
[60] *Chassagnou and Others v. France*, Judgement of 29 April 1999, Reports 1999-III.
[61] *Aschan and Others v. Finland*, Judgement of 12 February 2001 (App. No. 37858/97).
[62] Article 14 bans discrimination in enjoyment of the Convention rights on the grounds of sex, race, colour, language, religion, political or other opinion, national or social origin, association with a national minority, property, birth or other status. The prohibition of discrimination on the ground of property may cause trouble regarding progressive taxation because progressive tax statutes levy more tax on those who have more property. However, in the *WASA Ömsesidigt and Others v. Sweden* application the issue of discrimination in taxation on the ground of capital assets of insurance companies was raised, but the Commission found the application inadmissible making reference to the wide margin of appreciation left to states in the area of taxation. (*WASA Ömsesidigt and Others v. Sweden,* App. No.13013/87, 14 December 1988) This issue

imposition of tax significantly affects the taxpayer's property rights. Therefore, the Court should review whether the imposition of taxes unjustifiably interferes with property rights.

The phrase 'laws ...to secure the payment of taxes or other contribution or penalties' in P1-1 which allows interference with property when imposing tax, seems only to refer to enforcement measures and not the imposition itself.[63] However, the case-law does not make a distinction between enforcement measures and imposition of tax itself, thus the provision justifies both enforcement measures and imposition of taxes.[64] The Convention organs, though they respect the wide margin of appreciation of national authorities in the area of taxation, can investigate whether the measures are lawful,[65] or arbitrary, abusive, discriminatory or disproportionate.[66] However, in its older case-law the Commission seemed to read P1-1 as not placing any particular limit on national measures in this area. In its report in the *Greek Case* with regard to this provision the Commission held that it does not prescribe any limitation, either of form or of size.[67] Under this approach the power of national authorities to levy taxes, to impose penalties, to make social security contributions compulsory and to impose other levies was left intact as long as they were lawful and did not breach other rights protected by the Convention.

The Court and the Commission, however, have gradually developed a fair balance and proportionality test for this area as well. The Commission in the *WASA Ömsesidigt and Others v. Sweden* application ruled that the fact that national authorities enjoy a wide margin of appreciation in the field of taxation does not bring the issue wholly outside the Commission's control since the correct application of P1-1 is subject to supervision by the Convention organs. And it stated that 'the financial liability arising out of the raising of tax or contributions may adversely affect the guarantee secured under this provision if it places an excessive burden on the person or the entity concerned or fundamentally interferes with his or its financial position'.[68]

However, in examination of the applicable rule the Commission said that 'any legislation which introduces some sort of fiscal obligation will as such deprive the involved of a possession, namely the amount of money which must be paid. However, the second sentence (as in its original ARC) of Article 1 of Protocol No. 1 (P1-1) to the Convention expressly secures to the States, parties to the Convention, the right to enforce such laws as they deem necessary to secure the payment of taxes or other contributions. Accordingly, the Commission will first consider whether the interference with the applicants' right under Article 1 of

---

may become more problematic if the Twelfth Protocol to the Convention, which prohibits any kind of discrimination, enters into force.

63 Van Den Broek, *op.cit.* 43.

64 *Darby v. Sweden*, Judgement of 23 October 1990, Series A, No.187.

65 *Hentrich v. France*, Judgement of 22 September 1994, Series A, No. 296-A.

66 Peukert, *op.cit.* 12.

67 *Greek Case*, Yearbook XII (1969), p.85.

68 *WASA Ömsesidigt and Others v. Sweden, (*App. No.13013/87), 14 December 1988, DR 58 (1988).

Protocol No. 1 (P1-1) is justified by the second paragraph before considering, if necessary, whether the requirements set out in the second sentence of the first paragraph are fulfilled'.[69]

It can be seen from this passage how the classification of interferences with property under P1-1 is fragile even in simple cases of taxation. What does the Commission really mean by saying that it will first examine whether the interference is justified by the second paragraph before considering whether the requirements of deprivation rule are fulfilled? Can an act of state – imposition of one-off tax – constitute both deprivation and control of the use of property? The difficulty here arises from the scheme of the interferences under P1-1. Indeed taxation is neither takings nor police power regulation but a different interference. So it should be considered as a distinct interference with property. The difficulty of Convention organs in classifying tax impositions can be seen in the following cases.

In the *Hentrich*[70] case the subject of complaint was exercise of the right of pre-emption by tax authorities. In that case the applicant had bought a piece of property. But the French tax law authorises the tax authorities to buy, within a certain time period, any property whose purchase price is too low in order to prevent tax evasion. After the expiry of that time period the regional authority exercised its right of pre-emption. The right of pre-emption is not intended to punish tax evasion, but is a measure to prevent non-payment of higher registration fees. The Court considered this measure as deprivation of property although it was a taxation measurement. But in the case of *Gasus Dosier*[71] the Court assessed the seizure of a third party's asset in the debtor's possession to recover the tax debts as control of the use of property. In that case the applicant (a foreign company) had sold a concrete-mixer and retained the title to it until the sale price was fully recovered. However, before that, the Dutch tax authorities seized the mixer for the tax debts of purchaser company. The Court treated the case as falling under the second paragraph of P1-1. Similarly in the *Building Societies* case, the Court ruled that retrospective annulment of restitution claims arising from exercise of an *ultra vires* tax law amounted to control of the use of property in the general interest 'to secure the payment of tax', which falls within the rule in the second paragraph of P1-1.[72] Although tax measures necessarily deprive the persons involved of their property, they are considered as control of the use of property. However, this approach makes the distinction between deprivation and control of the use of property unclear.

[69] *Ibid.*
[70] *Hentrich v. France*, Judgement of 22 September 1994, Series A, No. 296-A.
[71] *Gasus Dosier- und Födertechnik GmbH v. the Nedherlands*, Judgement of 23 February 1995, Series A no.306-B, § 59.
[72] The *National and Provincial Building Society, Leeds Permanent Building Society and Yorkshire Building Society v. UK*, Judgement of 23 October 1997, Reports 1997-VII, §79.

Similar considerations are also valid for confiscations and imposition of other contributions. The Court ruled in the *Handyside*[73] case that the destruction of books after a finding of obscenity had been made was justified under the second paragraph of P1-1. In this case the Court ruled that both provisional seizure of the books and punitive destruction of them constituted a control of the use of property. The Court reiterated this judgement in *Agosi*[74] and *Air Canada*[75] cases as well. The *Agosi* case concerned forfeiture, by court order, of smuggled gold coins belonging to a third party and subsequent refusal by the customs authorities to restore the goods. The gold coins belonging to the applicant were confiscated by UK customs after third parties had tried unlawfully to import them into the country. The Court examined the case under the second paragraph of P1-1. In *Air Canada* an aircraft belonging to the applicant company was seized by UK customs because a great amount of drugs was found in it. But on the same day the aircraft was released after the payment of some money (£50,000). The applicant complained that the seizure of its aircraft and the subsequent requirement to pay money for its return amounted to a deprivation of its property. However, the Court did not accept this argument and decided firstly, that the seizure of the aircraft amounted to a temporary restriction on its use and did not involve a transfer of ownership, and secondly, that the release of the aircraft subject to payment of a sum of money was a measure taken to prevent drug smuggling and constituted a control of the use of property.[76]

In a number of other cases the Court also applied the second paragraph of P1-1 where interference with property was realised as a part of criminal proceedings. For example in the *Vendittelli*[77] case the Italian government had sequestered the applicant's flat in conjunction with the institution of criminal proceedings against him for infringements of town planning regulations in order, both, to preserve the evidence of the offence and to prevent any aggravation of the offence. The Court ruled that the impugned measure was designed not to deprive the applicant of his property but only to prevent him from using it, so it amounted to control of the use of property. Similarly, in the *Raimondo*[78] case where the Italian government confiscated several plots of land, buildings, and automobiles belonging to the applicant since he was suspected of connections with the mafia, the Court examined the complaint under the second paragraph of P1-1. It ruled that the seizure constituted a provisional measure and did not purport to deprive the applicant of his possessions but only to prevent him from using them. It was therefore the second paragraph of P1-1 which was relevant.

Another area in which the interference with property is examined under the second paragraph of P1-1 is the execution of court judgements and the mediation role of the state in civil law obligations. However, the case-law is not

---

[73] *Handyside v. UK*, Judgement of 7 December 1976, Series A, No.24, §63.

[74] *Agosi v. UK*, Judgement of 24 October 1986, Series A, No108.

[75] *Air Canada v. UK*, Judgement of 5 May 1995, Series A, No.316-A.

[76] *Ibid.* §33-34.

[77] *Vendittelli v. Italy*, Judgement of 18 July 1994, Series A, No. 293-A.

[78] *Raimondo v. Italy*, Judgement of 22 February 1994, Series A, No. 281-A.

unambiguous in this area. In a number of cases the Commission ruled that P1-1 was not concerned with judgements and execution of judgements relating to civil claims or to obligations between private individuals.[79] The Commission found that the mere fact that a judicial authority provided a forum for the determination of such a private law dispute did not give rise to interference by the state with property rights under P1-1.[80] In an application the Commission ruled that the obligation to pay costs did, in particular, not deprive the applicant of any possession or concerned the use of property within the meaning of P1-1.[81] In another application it stated that P1-1 was, in essence, directed against arbitrary seizure of property and did not in principle affect the enforcement of judicial decisions on disputes between individuals.[82]

The reasoning in these decisions, obviously, is not acceptable, because inevitably one's property rights are affected by the execution of judicial decisions and they constitute interference with property rights. However, such interferences, in principle, do not violate property rights because they are under the regulation (police) power of a state. Nevertheless, being under police power does not leave such interferences outside the control of the Convention organs. The Court should review whether such interferences strike a fair balance. In a later decision, the Commission ruled, as an issue of fact, that 'the commission must nevertheless make sure that in determining the effects on property of legal relations between individuals the law does not create such inequality that one person could be arbitrarily and unjustly deprived of property in favour of another'.[83] So, the Court should examine whether enforcement of judicial decisions created an unjustified inequality between individuals and imposed a disproportionate burden on one of the parties to the relationship.[84]

7.2.3. Interference with the Substance of Property

Although the letter of P1-1 mentions only two types of interference, the Convention organs have developed another type of interference, interference with

---

[79] Admissibility Decision of the Commission App. Nos. 1420/ 62, 1477/62, 1478/62, Yearbook VI, 590; App. No. 8906/80, 7 Dec.1982 (unpublished).

[80] App. No. 10000/82, Decision. 4 July 1983, D.R. 33 p. 247; App. No. 11949/86, Decision 1 December 1986, *Ruiz Mateos v. UK*, App. No. 13021/87, 8 September 1988, 57 DR 268.

[81] App. No. 4573/70, 13 December 1971 (unpublished); App. No. 7822/77, 11 July 1977 (unpublished).

[82] App. No. 6874/75 and 6980/75, 4 March 1976 (unpublished).

[83] App. No. 12462/86, 13 July 1987 D&R 53 p.234; See also App. No. 11425/85, 5 October 1987 D&R 53 p.76.

[84] See Chapter 6 above. It can be argued, here, that Article 6 is the relevant provision with execution of judgements rather than P1-1. However, the protection of P1-1 is much wider than Article 6 since it only provides procedural guarantees. For example, it does not examine whether a valuation of property, which will be compulsorily sold to pay debts of the owner (to execute a court Judgement), is arbitrary. But P1-1 requires that all interferences with property should be proportional.

the substance of property. For the first time in the *Sporrong and Lönnroth* case, the Court decided that expropriation permits which remained in force for a long time (twenty-three and eight years) did not constitute deprivation because the applicants could continue to utilise their possessions and the possibility of selling subsisted (though became very difficult). Neither were they intended to limit or control use, because they were an initial step in a procedure leading to deprivation of possession. Rather they had to be examined under the first sentence of the first paragraph. The Court stated that all the effects complained of stemmed from the reduction of the possibility of disposing of the properties concerned. As a result of limitations the right in question lost some of its substance, but it did not disappear.[85]

By this judgement the Court invented a new type of interference with property. According to the Court if an interference does not transfer the property to public authorities, nor does it aim to limit or control the use of the property, then it constitutes interference with the substance of property. This judgement has created precedents and the Court repeated this opinion in many other cases.

The Court found, in a number of cases, that the provisional transfer of agricultural land in connection with a very long-term consolidation programme did not amount to deprivation, although provisional transfer of lands took a very long period (sixteen years) and meant that the applicants no longer enjoyed the benefits of ownership in practice, because the applicants retained the hope that they might one day recover their full property rights. It ruled that the situation fell within the ambit of the first sentence of P1-1.[86]

Similarly in some cases concerning planning regulations the Court ruled that restrictions such as construction prohibitions imposed over applicants' property and leaving the status of property uncertain for a long period of time without paying compensation constituted interference with the substance of property. In this regard the *Katte Klitsche de la Grance v. Italy,*[87] *Phocas v. France,*[88] *Iatridis v. Greece,*[89] and *Pialopoulos and Others v. Greece*[90] cases can be taken as examples. However, the criteria applied by the Court in these cases are questionable. For example construction prohibitions were considered as interference with the first sentence in *Katte Klitsche*, *Phocas* and *Pialopoulos* while they had amounted to control of the use in *Sporrong and Lönnroth*. Indeed in all these cases the public authorities exercised their police power. So they all constitute police power regulations. However, in some of these cases the public

[85] *Sporrong and Lönnroth v. Sweden,* Judgement of 23 September 1982, Series A, No. 52, § 63-65.

[86] *Poiss v. Austria*, Judgement of 23 April 1987, Series A, No. 117; *Erkner and Hofauer v. Austria*, Judgement of 23 April 1987, Series A, No. 117; *Prötsch v. Austria,* Judgement of 15 November 1996.

[87] *Katte Klitsche de la Grance v. Italy*, Judgement of 27 October 1994, Series A, No.293-B.

[88] *Phocas v. France,* Judgement of 23 April 1996, Reports 1996-II.

[89] *Iatridis v. Greece,* Judgement of 25 March 1999, Reports 1999-II.

[90] *Pialopoulos and Others v. Greece,* Judgement of 15 February 2001, (App. No. 37095/97).

authorities did not meet the requirements of the proportionality test, that is, they acted arbitrarily in exercise of their power.

In the *Greek Refineries*[91] case the Court interestingly ruled that retroactive annulment of arbitration awards by legislation amounted to neither an expropriation nor a measure to control the use of property rather it fell to be dealt with under the first sentence of the first paragraph.[92] However, it ruled later in *Pressos Compania Naviera*[93] that retrospective annulment of compensation claims arising from tort constituted deprivation of property. But there was no difference between the facts of the two cases. The decision in the former case was criticised vastly.[94] There was no reason not to find deprivation in that case.

As mentioned above, the Court, in two cases against Turkey,[95] decided that the fact that displaced persons in Northern Cyprus were forbidden access to their property and lost all control over them due to the division of the island, constituted continuing interference with property. However, this interference did not amount to a deprivation of property, rather interference with the general rule in the first sentence of the first paragraph of P1-1. However, even if the Court's argument concerning validity of TRNC legislation was accepted, the Court still should have found a *de facto* deprivation, had it applied the criteria it established in *Papamichalopoulos*.[96] It can be said here that, playing devil's advocate, the Court deliberately refrained finding *de facto* deprivation because otherwise these cases might have been out of the jurisdiction of the Court *ratione temporis*.[97]

The Court has also found that unreasonable delay in payment of compensation for expropriation amounted to interference with the general rule in the first sentence of P1-1.[98]

---

[91] *Stran Greek Refineries and Stratis Andreadis v. Greece*, Judgement of 9 December 1994, Series A, No.301-A.

[92] *Ibid.*

[93] *Pressos Compania Naviera S.A. and Others v. Belgium*, Judgement of 20 November 1995, Series A, No.332.

[94] Sermet, *op.cit.* 13 p. 29; Harris et al, p.524.

[95] *Loizidou v. Turkey*, Judgement of 18 December 1996, Reports. 1996-VI; *Cyprus v. Turkey*, Judgement of 10 May 2001 (App. No. 25781/94) § 187.

[96] *Papamichalopoulos and Others v. Greece,* Judgement of 24 June 1993, Series A, No.260-B.

[97] In *Papamichalopoulos* the Court did not discuss the competence of the Court *ratione temporis* properly since the respondent government did not contest in that issue. The Court decided that the applicant did not lose his title to his property, but found a *de facto* expropriation. Here, the problem of whether the owner loses his title to a property in cases of de facto expropriation, and if so when he loses remained undiscussed. In *Loizidou* a number of dissenting judges did not agree with the majority in terms of the Court's jurisdiction *ratione temporis*. Judge Petiti said that the applicant lost her title to her property at the time of the coup d'état even before a *de facto* expropriation in 1985 by the local authorities. See also separate dissenting opinions of Judges Baka and Jambrek.(*Loizidou v. Turkey*, Judgement of 18 December 1996, Reports. 1996-VI).

[98] *Matos e Silva, Lda., and Others v. Portugal*, Judgement of 27 August 1996, Reports 1996-IV; *Almeida Garrett, Mascarenhas Falcao and Others v. Portugal*, Judgement of 11 January 2000 (App. Nos. 29813/96 and 30229/96) § 48.

The Court is increasingly using the concept of interference with the substance of property when it has difficulty in classifying interferences. For example in the *Beyeler*[99] case the Court stated that 'having regard to the foregoing, the Court does not consider it necessary to rule on whether the second sentence of the first paragraph of Article 1 applies in this case. The complexity of the factual and legal situation prevents its being classified in a precise category...the Court therefore considers that it should examine the situation complained of in the light of general rule.'[100] However, after finding that the applicant had property interests in the painting, there was no reason not to find deprivation in exercise of right of pre-emption by the Italian Ministry of Cultural Heritage.

In the *Ambruosi*[101] case also the Court ruled that deprivation of right to the payment of fees, costs, and expenses of a lawyer against state (as the respondent of cases) arising from a no-win no-fee agreement between her and her clients amounted to interference with the applicant's right to peaceful enjoyment of possessions. The Court did not find a deprivation because the applicant's right to claim her legal fees and costs from her clients persists. However it is suggested that no one can be forced to dissolve his/her contract, therefore the Court, without considering that possibility, should have found deprivation.

To sum up, the invented form of interference with general right to peaceful enjoyment of possessions or the substance of property seems problematic. The Court's criteria are not clear and consistent. And since interference with the substance of property does not necessarily mean violation of the right to property, there is no difference between examining a case under the first sentence and the second sentence or the second paragraph of P1-1. In any case the Court should examine lawfulness and legitimacy of interference and whether a fair balance was struck between the individual and the general interests of the community. So it can be said that this invention is hardly helpful in determining whether an act of state violated property rights.

7.2.4. A Proposed Taxonomy of Types of Interference with Property

The above-mentioned classification of interferences with property rights by the Convention organs' can be criticised in three interrelated respects. Firstly, the classification is not clear about when compensation is required. Although the text of the Convention does not include a compensation requirement, without a compensation guarantee in cases of taking of property for public interest, a right of

---

99 *Beyeler v. Italy*, Judgement of 5 January 2000 (App. No.33202/96) para.98.

100 *Ibid.* §106. In this case the applicant bought a painting of Van Gogh, which was declared a part of the cultural heritage of Italy, through an intermediary in Italy in 1977. The end buyer's name (the applicant) was not revealed to public authorities until 1983. After several attempts to sell the painting to different public and private galleries the painting was finally sold in 1988 for USD 8, 500,000. Following this sale the public authorities, claiming that the 1977 contract was null, exercised their right of pre-emption for the 1977 sale in 1988.

101 *Ambruosi v. Italy*, Judgement of 19 October 2000 (App. No. 31227/96).

property would be meaningless. Thus, the Court established that compensation is an inherent feature of the right to property. However, the Convention organs' classification of the types of interference with property makes it more difficult to determine when compensation is required. The Court seems to adopt the rule that deprivation of property requires payment of compensation. Nevertheless, this solution hardly makes the question of compensation easier, rather, it makes it more complex because not every deprival of property requires compensation. Both taxation and the exercise of police power may result in deprival of property, but they do not entail that the owner be compensated. In order to avoid the compensation requirement in cases of taxation or police power regulation, the Convention organs define such deprivations as control of the use of property. However, this instigates a conceptual problem which is the second point of criticism. Although some interferences clearly deprive the owner of his property, the Court defines these interferences as control of the use of property. Then the question of which interferences constitute real deprivation arises.

Another problematic aspect of the Court's approach to the compensation issue is that the Court established that deprival of property requires payment of compensation on the grounds that deprival of property is a more serious interference than any other type of intervention. However, the correctness of this assumption is questionable, because the magnitude of economic loss resulting from use restrictions can be as serious as that of deprivation. For example, prevention of a high-tech plant from production for one or two years may cause more damage than expropriation of land on which it is built. Therefore, it is not always true that deprivation of property brings about more serious damage than use restrictions, and that it requires payment of compensation. On the other hand, even if deprivation causes more loss, there is no moral difference between partial and full deprivations of property interests. Both use and exchange values of property constitute opportunities for the owner to realise his plans and his autonomy. So every restriction on property rights reducing the owners' opportunities needs to be justified.

The third criticism of the Convention organs' classification of interferences with property is that the Court's criteria for each of the types seem to be becoming less and less clear. For example, although in all the following three cases the public authorities annulled the applicants' claims by retrospective laws, the Court found a different type of interference in each of them. In *Pressos Compania Naviera*[102] it ruled that retrospective annulment of compensation claims arising from tort constituted a deprivation of property. In the *Greek Refineries*[103] case the Court found that retroactive annulment of arbitration awards by legislation amounted to interference with the substance of property.[104] And lastly in the *Building Societies* case the Court decided that retrospective annulment of

[102] *Pressos Compania Naviera S.A. and Others v. Belgium*, Judgement of 20 November 1995, Series A, No.332.

[103] *Stran Greek Refineries and Stratis Andreadis v. Greece*, Judgement of 9 December 1994, Series A, No.301-A.

[104] *Ibid.*

restitution claims arising from exercise of an *ultra vires* tax law amounted to control of the use of property.[105] It is difficult to understand why similar actions constitute different kinds of interference. It can be argued that the last interference was constituted control of the use because it was concerning taxation. Then it can be asked why, in the *Hentrich*[106] case, the Court found deprivation of property although exercise of the right of pre-emption was a taxation measurement.

This ambiguity in the classification of interferences has led the Court to apply directly a balancing test without attributing too much importance to determining the type of interference. However, if the Court applies in every case only a balancing test without any other criterion, it may endanger the rule of law by creating tremendous uncertainty in the Convention system.[107] Since the only authority who decides whether an interference strikes a fair balance between individual and common interests is the judges of the European Court, the criteria will change according to the judges' own understanding.

In order to realise a greater justice, the aims of the interference with property and limits of the public authorities' power should be clear. Then, the proportionality test can be applied to determine whether the public authorities exercised their power in a justifiable way. Therefore, in this book a triple taxonomy of legitimate interferences, which depends upon the purpose of the state's action, will be suggested. This classification makes reference to a state's three different powers corresponding to three different types of interference. These are taking of property by the power of eminent domain for public interest purpose, taxation and controlling the use of property by police power regulations. Only the case of taking of property for public interest requires payment of compensation. In cases of taxation and police power regulation compensation does not need to be paid.

Although P1-1 left taxation intact, the moral basis of taxation can be examined here in order to determine the limits of it. Taxation can be justified on the grounds of equal sharing of public burdens. In order to justify unequal taxation, two different theoretical arguments can be posed, reciprocal benefit and redistributive justice considerations. If a tax burden is imposed as a return for a reciprocal benefit it cannot be argued that other people who do not utilise such benefit should also bear the burden of such public policies. But redistributive taxation is a matter of controversy. In this book Raz's autonomy-based freedom theory is suggested as a justificatory base of redistributive taxation.[108]

---

[105] The *National and Provincial Building Society, Leeds Permanent Building Society and Yorkshire Building Society v. UK*, Judgement of 23 October 1997, Reports 1997-VII, § 79.

[106] *Hentrich v. France*, Judgement of 22 September 1994, Series A, No. 296-A.

[107] Allen, T., "Limitations on Constitutional Property Rights" in Paul Jackson and David C. Wilde (eds.) *Property Law: Current Issues and Debates* (Ashgate: Dartmouth, 1999) p. 203.

[108] Indeed, the growth of the welfare state has threatened the rule of law principle to some extent. Firstly, it has enormously widened the discretionary power of public authorities over economic rights and liberties and left many actions of administrators out of judicial review. Secondly, when the modern welfare state creates the goods and it

The taking of private property for public use can also be justified by Raz's theory. However, a number of theories propose that the taking of private property for public use can be permissible only if the loss of the owner is compensated. The classical theory requiring payment of compensation is the principle of equal sharing of public burdens. This principle finds its roots in natural law theory.[109] There are also some utilitarian explanations for the question of why payment of compensation is required for the taking of private property for public interest. Utilitarian theories emphasise the importance of security and stability of property regimes in order to encourage private individuals for fruitful investments.[110] According to utilitarian theories, taking without compensation makes property unstable and discourages fruitful investments. Therefore, the loss of owners should be compensated in cases of taking private property.

Some American theorists such as Rubenfeld[111] propose an instrumentalisation theory. According to this theory, taking of property without compensation makes an individual the instrument of public policy that is contrary to autonomy of the individual. Autonomy of the individual requires that individuals should be treated as ends of the public policy not simply means of it. So public authorities should first make the private property their own by paying compensation and then they should use it. All these theories have some basis and strengthen the requirement of compensation.

The third kind of legitimate interference with the right to property is police power regulations that restrict the use of property. As indicated in Chapter 4, two different types of regulation can be distinguished regarding property rights. The first type of regulation defines the nature and acquisition of property. It defines how property can be acquired and which entitlements it includes. This kind of regulation is not the issue here. The power of a state in this regard is not limited. However, if a new regulation of this kind limits the existing entitlements it should take into account the legitimate expectations of individuals. The second kind of regulation restricts the use of existing rights and this kind of regulation is the main concern here.

---

distributes in the form of benefits, licences, and enforcement actions, the risk of arbitrary power often lies in wrongful withholding of advantages rather than wrongful invasion of private rights. P1-1 did not bring any real limitation on contracting states' power in this respect. The Court has adopted the principle of proportionality to P1-1 as the basis of limits of states' discretionary power. However, this protection can be broadened by adopting a theoretical basis and restricting the application of proportionality within this theoretical framework.

[109] For example Hugo Grotius writes '… But we must also observe this, that a King may two ways deprive his subjects of their right, either by way of punishment, or by virtue of his Sovereign Power. But if he do it the last way, it must be for some publick advantage, and then the subject ought to receive, if possible, a just satisfaction for the loss he suffers, out of the common stock…' *The Rights of War and Peace* (London, 1725) B. II Ch. XIV para. VII. (Translation of De *Jure Belli Ac Pacis*, 1625).

[110] Michelman, Franc I., "Property, Utility, and Fairness: Comments on the Ethical Foundations of 'Just Compensation' Law" (1967) 80 *Harvard Law Review* 1165-1258.

[111] Rubenfeld, J. "Usings" (1993) 102 *The Yale Law Journal* 1077.

Two different philosophical explanations for justification of such regulations were proposed in Chapter 4. Those are 'the harm principle' and Rawls' 'liberty principle'.[112] According to the harm principle, which was first defined by Mill[113] and used by Raz[114] in a more expanded meaning, the limit of liberty is others' liberty. One's liberty should be restricted if it violates others' rights. So, if use of property injures others' rights it is legitimate to limit such use of property. Rawls' liberty principle proposes that liberty can be restricted only for the sake of liberty.

However, in regulation of P1-1, Rousseau's political theory and his later follower Duguit's social function theory of property were very influential.[115] In brief these theories place individual possessive rights a rank lower than societal claims to promote public good in the hierarchy of values of political society. However, such an approach is inadmissible from the point of view of autonomy-based freedom theory. In this regard also, in this book, Raz's autonomy-based freedom principle and expanded harm principle will be suggested as a compromise between the social function theory of property and the liberal individualistic theory of property. So, public authorities may legitimately apply policies in order to promote an autonomy enhancing society. For example, they can apply urban planning or environmental protection programmes in order to raise quality of life. However, this right is not unlimited. They should observe the equality of individuals under public burdens and requirements of the principle of proportionality.

The suggested criteria to be applied in distinguishing between different types of interferences are to be examined now. The most important difference between takings and taxation is the singling out feature of takings. That is, while taxation imposes an equal burden on everybody in the same position, takings impose the burden of public policy on only a single individual or a small group of people. The most important restrictions over taxation are lawfulness and non-discrimination requirements. The discrimination question is especially important in cases of private taxes.

In order to distinguish takings from police power regulations a number of criteria can be proposed. If there is a formal expropriation or nationalisation, it is obvious that there is taking of property. But if there is not such a formal taking it is difficult to distinguish takings from police power regulations. The first criterion to be applied is whether there exists a physical invasion of private property by public authorities. If so, it can normally be said that that measure constitutes taking rather than police power regulation. However, there are some exceptions to this rule. If

---

112 Rawls, J., *A Theory of Justice* (Revised Edition) (OUP: Oxford, 1999) (First Published 1971).

113 Mill, J.S., *On Liberty* (Everyman: London, 1972) [First Published 1859] p.78.

114 Raz, J., "Autonomy, Toleration and the Harm Principle" in Ruth Gavison (ed.) *Issues in Contemporary Legal Philosophy* (Clarendon Press: Oxford, 1987).

115 Antinori, M. R., "Does Lochner Live in Luxembourg?: An Analysis of the Property Rights Jurisprudence of the European Court of Justice" (1995) 18 *Fordham International Law Journal* 1778.

there is a reciprocal benefit, or if physical invasion does not prevent the owner using his property as a whole, or if it is a requirement to open for commercial use, the measure in question constitutes police power regulations. The second criterion is that if a regulation forbids harmful use of property, it is not conceived as taking, rather a police power regulation. However, this criterion should not be applied strictly in cases where a use of property becomes harmful as a result of policy or technological chance. In such cases, legitimate expectations of owners should be respected. In every single case, it is necessary to look at whether an individual is subjected to bear an unequal public burden and if so, his loss should be compensated. If these criteria fail to determine whether a measure constitutes taking or police power regulation then a balancing test should be applied. The difference between this suggestion and the Court's current approach is that the Court directly applies a balancing test without applying other criteria suggested here. In the next section conditions of legitimate interference with property will be examined.

7.3. Grounds of Legitimate Interference with Property Rights under the ECHR

Having examined the types of interferences with property rights, the next question is under what conditions those interferences are to be considered as legitimate. P1-1 elaborates these conditions in the second sentence for deprivation and in the second paragraph for control of the use of property. Accordingly, a person can be deprived of his/her property only 'in public interest and subject to the conditions provided for by law and by the general principles of international law'. A state can control the use of property by law in accordance with the general interest. The grounds enunciated in the text of P1-1 can be summarised simply as legality and legitimacy of interference. The Convention organs have developed other conditions for an interference with property rights to be legitimate such as payment of compensation for taking of property and balancing the individual interests and general interest of community.

The Commission and the Court have made no distinction between the concepts of 'public interest' and 'general interest' and have treated them as having the same meaning.[116] Since the Convention organs have determined whether payment of compensation is required according to the effect of interference over property rights – that is, they have established that only in cases of deprivation is compensation required – they have not needed to make a distinction between the purposes of different kinds of interferences. However, the classification proposed above depends on the purpose of the state's action. Therefore, in order to determine whether an interference requires payment of compensation, it is necessary to distinguish different objectives aimed at by the public authorities while they are interfering with property rights. That is, while in the compensable

[116] Sermet, *op.cit.* 13 p. 35.

taking of property the aim is to advance the public good, in non-compensable regulatory interference the aim is to prevent the harmful use of property.

However, the regulatory power of a state is not limited to the police power regulations aiming to protect health and order in society. It also comprises power to regulate for promotion of public good. For example, it includes the regulating structure of a profession to improve the competences of those who carry out that profession. In such cases if a regulation interferes with property interests, it is necessary to examine whether such interests constitute property protected by the Convention. For example, to practise a profession in some circumstances may constitute property, especially its goodwill amount to property. However, such a right can be exercised only within the limits drawn by the regulation. So if the conditions laid down by the relevant regulation are not satisfied, it is under the power of public authorities to withdraw such a right without compensation. This power should also be considered as a police power in this context. So, in the question of legitimacy it may not be necessary to distinguish between public and general interest.

Nevertheless, in an examination of whether compensation is required it is inevitable to make a distinction between police power regulations and taking for public purpose. One important question in this context, considering the dynamic social dimension of the right to property, is when a use of property should be regarded as harmful. According to the changed technological, social, and environmental conditions, a use that was considered harmless two decades ago might become harmful today. Therefore, the meaning of the concept of 'general interest' may change from time to time or from one society to other. One question is who should decide what use is harmful, legislator or judiciary? In other words, whether national authorities should have the sole margin of appreciation or can international judges review the decisions of the national legislator?

7.3.1. Legality/Lawfulness of Interference

The legality requirement is a general condition for all measures limiting human rights. Any act of public authorities restricting the fundamental rights of individuals should have a legal basis that is objective and accessible for all the public. This requirement aims to protect individuals against the arbitrary actions of public authorities. The requirement of lawfulness of interference has no distinct features when property rights are in question. Therefore, the Court's jurisprudence in this regard will be examined briefly and much more concern will be attached to the interpretation of the phrase 'by the general principles of international law'. However, this provision has lost its practical meaning since the Court has interpreted it as valid only for the taking of non-nationals' property.

P1-1 subjects the deprivation of property to 'the conditions provided for by law and the general principles of international law'. Similarly the control of use should be based on 'such laws as it [state] deems necessary'. This legality requirement is intended as a protection against arbitrary interferences with property.[117] That is, interference with property is possible only if national law permits. The Court established that the first and most important requirement of P1-1 was that any interference by a public authority with the peaceful enjoyment of possessions should be lawful.[118] And it also made reference to the principle of the rule of law as an inherent feature of all the Articles of the Convention in order to support the lawfulness requirement.

National law comprises both written provisions (laws, decrees, regulations) and unwritten laws (precedent and customary law). So any interference with property should have a basis in domestic law. However, the Convention organs do not examine whether national law has been applied correctly.[119] They do not function as a 'fourth instance'.[120] In the admissibility decision of *O.N v. Bulgaria*[121] the Court reiterated that it was not its function to deal with errors of fact or law allegedly committed by a national court unless they had infringed rights and freedoms protected by the Convention.[122] The Court has also established that it is in the first place for the domestic authorities, notably the courts, to interpret and apply the domestic law and to decide on issues of constitutionality.[123] Therefore, the Court has a limited power to examine whether the impugned measures comply with domestic law.[124]

Nevertheless the 'law' in question must exhibit certain formal qualities. In this respect the European case-law is not restricted to property rights – it draws here on the concept of 'law' enshrined in Articles 8, 9, 10, and 11. However, the conception of legality articulated by the Court is procedural rather than substantive.[125] According to the established case-law the applicable provisions of domestic law should be sufficiently accessible, precise and foreseeable.[126] The relevant legal provisions should be accessible to citizens, and they should be

---

[117] Sermet, *op.cit.* 13 p.32.

[118] *Iatridis v. Greece,* Judgement of 25 March 1999, Reports 1999-II; *The Former King of Greece and Others v. Greece*, Judgement of 23 November 2000 (App. No. 25701/94) §79; *Carbonara and Ventura v. Italy*, Judgement of 30 May 2000 (App. No.24638/94) §56; *Belvedere Alberghiera v. Italy*, Judgement of 30 May 2000 (App. No. 31524/96) § 56.

[119] *Sporrong and Lönnroth v. Sweden,* Judgement of 23 September 1982 Series A no. 52 § 68.

[120] Van Dijk and Van Hoof, *op.cit.* 44 p.635.

[121] *O.N. v. Bulgaria*, Judgement of 6 April 2000 (App. No. 35221/97).

[122] See also *Garcia Ruiz v. Spain*, Judgement of 21 January 1999, Reports 1999-I.

[123] *The Former King of Greece and Others v. Greece*, Judgement of 23 November 2000 (App. No. 25701/94) para.82.

[124] *Alan Jacobsson v. Sweden*, Judgement of 25 October 1989, Series A no. 163 § 57; *Hakansson and Sturesson v. Sweden,* Judgement of 21 February 1990, Series A, No. 171-A § 47.

[125] McHarg, A., "Reconciling Human Rights and the Public Interest: Conceptual Problems and Doctrinal Uncertainty in the Jurisprudence of the European Court of Human Rights" (1999) 62 *The Modern Law Review* 671-96.

[126] *James and Others v UK* Judgement of 21 February 1986, Series A no. 98 § 67; *Lithgow and Others v. UK* Judgement of 8 July 1986, Series A no. 102 § 110; *Hentrich v. France*, Judgement of 22 September 1994, Series A no. 296-A § 42.

sufficiently precise to enable them reasonably to foresee the consequences which their actions may entail. And the law should provide adequate safeguards against arbitrary interference with the respective substantive right.[127] In the *Hentrich* case the Court found that French tax law, which gives tax authorities a right to take property by way of pre-emption, did not satisfy the standard of foreseeability and precision implied by the concept of law within the meaning of the Convention, and it was exercised by the tax authorities arbitrarily and selectively and in an unexplained way. The Court also stated that there were no procedural safeguards to prevent the unfair use of the power.[128]

The Court recently ruled in two different cases that the case-law on constructive expropriations in Italy evolved in a way that led to the rule being applied inconsistently, a factor which could result in unforeseeable or arbitrary outcomes and deprive litigants of effective protection of their rights and was, as a consequence, inconsistent with the requirement of lawfulness.[129] And it decided that unlawful occupation of the applicant's property by public authorities became irreversible by the decision of the domestic court and such a transfer of property was incompatible with P1-1 and, as a result, violated it. The Court found it unnecessary to examine whether a fair balance was struck since it found that the lawfulness requirement was not satisfied. Similarly in the *Iatridis*[130] case the Court ruled that the interference in question was manifestly in breach of domestic law, so incompatible with P1-1. So, if the lawfulness requirement has not been satisfied the Court finds directly violation of P1-1 without examining whether other requirements have been satisfied.

The Court in some cases examines directly the proportionality of the interference without examining the lawfulness, where it finds that the applicable rule is the first sentence of P1-1.[131] However, in *Beyeler*[132] the Court ruled that an essential condition for an interference to be deemed compatible with P1-1 was that it should be lawful.[133] And it examined the lawfulness of the interference as an element of the fair balance test. It found that a relevant Italian statute lacked clarity in certain respects, particularly in that it left open the time limit for the exercise of a right of pre-emption in the event of an incomplete declaration. Although it did not find that lack of clarity alone made the interference unforeseeable or arbitrary,

---

127 *Huvig v. France,* Judgement of 24 April 1990, Series A no. 176-B § 27; *Kruslin v. France,* Judgement of 24 April 1990, Series A no. 176-A § 36.

128 *Hentrich v. France*, Judgement of 22 September 1994, Series A no. 296-A § 42.

129 *Carbonara and Ventura v. Italy*, Judgement of 30 May 2000 (App. No.24638/94) § 56; *Belvedere Alberghiera v. Italy*, Judgement of 30 May 2000 (App. No. 31524/96) § 58.

130 *Iatridis v. Greece*, Judgement of 25 March 1999, Reports 1999-II, § 62.

131 *Sporrong and Lönnroth v. Sweden,* Judgement of 23 September 1982, Series A no.52 § 86 ff; *Matos e Silva, Lda., and Others v. Portugal*, Judgement of 27 August 1996, Reports 1996-IV; *Almeida Garrett, Mascarenhas Falcao and Others v. Portugal*, Judgement of 11 January 2000 (App. Nos. 29813/96 and 30229/96); *Ambruosi v. Italy*, Judgement of 19 October 2000 (App. No. 31227/96).

132 *Beyeler v. Italy*, Judgement of 5 January 2000 (App. No.33202/96).

133 See also *Iatridis v. Greece*, Judgement of 25 March 1999 Reports 1999-II, § 58.

therefore incompatible with the principle of lawfulness, the Court evaluated the uncertainty in the statute and the latitude it afforded the authorities as an element in determining whether the interference complained of struck a fair balance.[134]

In cases of *de facto* expropriation generally the interference is unlawful, so in such situations, without requiring any other examination, the Court may decide that there has been a violation of P1-1. In the *Vasilescu*[135] case the Court found violation of property rights by establishing that interference of public authorities with the applicant's property amounted to a *de facto* confiscation.

As for the reference to principles of international law, it is mentioned only in the second sentence of the first paragraph regarding deprivations. Inclusion of such a phrase into P1-1 finds its basis in the history of the drafting process. Since the drafters could not agree to include a general compensation rule in P1-1, they agreed to provide a compensation guarantee for the taking of alien property.[136] The Court also interpreted it as being applicable only to taking by a state of property of non-nationals, and not applicable to the expropriation by a state of property belonging to its own nationals.[137]

So what are the general principles of international law with regard to taking of alien property? General international law protects alien property against arbitrary expropriation and against nationalisation without compensation. Although the amount of compensation has been disputed widely and ideas are abundant, the international tribunals have generally agreed that in cases of unlawful expropriation the loss should be compensated fully, but in cases of lawful expropriation it is disputed whether full or appropriate compensation should be paid.[138]

In the past the Commission, by relying on the idea that principles of international law are applicable only for the taking of alien property, decided that in the case of expropriation in the public interest of property owned by the state's own subjects, the state was under no duty to pay damages if this is not provided for in domestic law.[139] The Court later indicated that the difference in treatment did not constitute discrimination since the differences in treatment had an objective and reasonable justification. In the Court's view non-nationals are more vulnerable to domestic legislation since, unlike nationals, they will generally have played no part in elections. Secondly, although the taking of property must always be effected in the public interest, different considerations may apply to nationals and non-nationals and there may well be legitimate reason for requiring nationals to bear a greater burden in the public interest than non-nationals.[140]

---

[134] *Beyeler v. Italy*, §110.
[135] *Vasilescu v. Romania*, Judgement of 22 May 1998, Reports 1998-III, § 53.
[136] See Chapter 5 p.155.
[137] *James and Others v UK* Judgement of 21 February 1986, Series A no. 98 § 66.
[138] Norton, P. M., " A Law of The Future or A Law of The Past? Modern Tribunals and the International Law of Expropriation" (1991) 85 *American Journal of International Law* 474.
[139] *Gudmundsson v. Iceland*, (App. No. 511/59) Yearbook III (1960) p. 394.
[140] Van Dijk, and Van Hoof, *op.cit.* 44 p.214.

However, the rationale of the Court is becoming more and more questionable since European integration is getting deeper and deeper under the EU framework. Considering that all members of EU are party to ECHR, it is inevitable that the interpretation of the Convention rights is affected by the developments within the EU. For example, although it is not binding at the moment, The Charter of Fundamental Rights of the European Union guarantees payment of fair compensation in cases of taking of property for public use in Article 17.[141]

This difference in treatment between nationals and non-nationals, however, has lost its importance since the case-law has established that taking of property without compensation is normally incompatible with P1-1.[142] Nevertheless, according to the case-law only reasonable compensation is necessary in cases of taking of nationals' property. This can make a difference between nationals and non-nationals if international law is interpreted as requiring full compensation. Nevertheless, the Convention organs did not treat alien property more favourably than nationals' property in cases where foreigners' property was involved. For example, in the *Gasus Dosier*[143] case, although a German company was deprived of its property by Dutch tax authorities, the Commission found this deprivation different to measures of confiscation, nationalisation or expropriation in which international law provides special protection to foreign citizens and companies. The Court did not examine the case in terms of nationality because it assessed the complained interference as a tax measure.

7.3.2. Legitimacy of Interference: Public Interest and General Interest

A state can interfere with property rights only for a public good. This requirement also aims to prevent abuse of sovereign power by way of arbitrary interferences. However, it is extremely problematic to decide when an interference is in the public interest. Can public interest be measured objectively or does it depend on preferences of individuals? And who should decide whether a measure is in the public interest? Should parliament's power be absolute in this respect or can its decisions be reviewed by courts?

In Chapter 4 the theoretical aspects of public interest were examined. It was indicated that whichever of the preponderance, unitary or common interest

---

[141] Article 17. Right to Property:

> 1. Everyone has the right to own, use, dispose of and bequeath his or her lawfully acquired possessions. No one may be deprived of his or her possessions except in the public interest and in the cases and under the conditions provided for by law, subject to fair compensation being paid in good time for their loss. The use of property may be regulated by law in so far as is necessary for the general interest.
> 2. Intellectual property shall be protected.

[142] *Lithgow and Others v. UK* Judgement of 8 July 1986, Series A no. 102.

[143] *Gasus Dosier- und Födertechnik GmbH v. the Nedherlands*, Judgement of 23 February 1995, Series A no.306-B, §59.

theories is accepted, the main determinant of the public interest will be the democratic government or legislator. The international judge's function in review of the legitimacy of the policies adopted by democratic parliaments, though it changes according to the accepted theory to some extent, will be limited. Respect for democracy, one of the aims of the Council of Europe, presses for such a limited review as well.

In Chapter 4 a two-step test has been suggested to decide whether a public policy interfering with private property rights is legitimate, that is, in the public interest. In the first step Raz's autonomy-based freedom theory, as a unitary overarching principle, can guide in deciding whether a proposed policy is serving the public interest. Accordingly, the judge should look at whether the aim of governmental policy is to serve to establish an autonomy-enhancing social and economic environment. In such an assessment the judge should look behind the expressed aim considering all conditions, especially if an alleged policy is benefiting some individuals or groups.

The Court's approach to the issue of public interest in the area of property rights seems as parallel to the common interest theory. Although the Court examines whether an alleged policy is in the public interest, it recognises a wide margin of appreciation to the states to determine what is in the public interest.[144] A public interest examination has been conducted in two steps. In the first step the Court examines whether the aim pursued by interference is a legitimate one. In the second step, it examines whether the means employed for achieving the legitimate aim pursued is proportional.[145]

The Court made clear its position in public interest examination in the *James*[146] judgement and reiterated that position in almost every property rights case. It has recognised that it is for the national authorities to make the initial assessment of the existence of a problem of public concern warranting interference with property rights. The Court will particularly respect a democratically elected legislature's judgement of what is in the public interest unless that judgement is manifestly without reasonable foundation. The Court based this approach on these considerations: firstly, because of their direct knowledge of their society and its needs, the national authorities are in principle better placed than the international judge to appreciate what is in the public interest. And secondly, the decision to enact laws interfering with property will commonly involve consideration of political, economic, and social issues on which opinions within a democratic society may reasonably differ widely.[147] So, definitions of public and general interest vary from country to country and over time. Therefore, the Court's supervision in this area is very limited.[148]

---

[144] Winisdoerffer, Y., "Margin of Appreciation and Article 1 of Protocol No.1" (1998) 19 (1) *Human Rights Law Journal* 18.

[145] *Ibid.*

[146] *James and Others v UK* Judgement of 21 February 1986, Series A No. 98.

[147] *Ibid.* § 46.

[148] See generally, Frowein, J. "The Protection of Property" in Macdonald, Matscher and Petzold (eds.) *The European System for The Protection of Human Rights* (Kluwer A P:

The Court made reference to some interesting points concerning the 'public interest' and 'general interest' in the *James* case, without making any fundamental distinction between them. Firstly, it ruled that a deprivation of property effected for no reason other than to confer a private benefit on a private party cannot be in the public interest. But it stated that the compulsory transfer of property from one individual to another might, depending on the circumstances, constitute a legitimate aim for promoting the public interest. So it found that the taking of property in pursuance of a policy calculated to enhance social justice within the community could properly be described as being in the public interest.[149]

Secondly, the Court held that the concept of public interest did not necessarily require that the transferred property should be put into use for the general public or that the community generally, or even a substantial proportion of it, should directly benefit from the taking. In particular, the fairness of a system of law governing the contractual or property rights of private parties is a matter of public concern and therefore legislative measures intended to bring about such fairness are capable of being in the public interest, even if they involve the compulsory transfer of property from one individual to another.[150] This approach of the Court seems much closer to a unitary theory of public interest rather than common interest theory.[151]

Thirdly, the Court ruled that a redistributive policy might be applied legitimately by exercising a power of eminent domain; it is not always necessary to exercise a direct power of taxation to apply redistributive policies.[152] However, it rejected that the measures complained of aimed at redistribution, rather they aimed to correct the injustice in a long-term leasehold system of tenure. 'The Act was designed to reform the existing law, said to be "inequitable to the leaseholder", and to give effect to what was described as the occupying tenant's "moral entitlement" to ownership of the house.'[153]

The Court in almost every property case has repeated that its supervision on legitimacy of aim pursued by interference is very limited.[154] The Court has

---

London, 1993); Gomien, D., Harris, D., and Zwaak, L., *Law and Practice of the European Convention on Human Rights and the European Social Charter*, (Strasbourg: Council of Europe Publishing, 1996); Sermet, Laurent, *The European Convention on Human Rights and Property Rights*, (Council of Europe Publishing: Strasbourg, 1998); Van Dijk and Van Hoof, *Theory and Practice of the European Convention on Human Rights* (Kluwer Law Int: London, 1998) (third edition); Harris, D., O'Boyle, M. and Warbrick, C., *Law of the European Convention on Human Rights* (Butterworths: London, 1995).

149 *James and Others*, § 40-41.

150 *Ibid* § 43; See also *Mellacher and Others v. Austria*, Judgement of 19 December 1989, Series A, No. 169 § 45.

151 See Chapter 4 for a detailed discussion of these theories.

152 *James and Others*, § 44.

153 *Ibid.* § 47.

154 See for some recent authorities, *Beyeler v. Italy*, Judgement of 5 January 2000 (App. No.33202/96) §112; *The Former King of Greece and Others v. Greece*, Judgement of 23

never, so far, ruled that the aim pursued by interference was not in the public interest. Although in some cases it was sceptical about the reasons raised by the respondent governments, it abstained from ruling that the aim pursued by interference was not in the public interest. For example in the case of *The Former King of Greece,* the Court rejected the government's argument that expropriation of lands belonging to the former royal family aimed to protect forest and archaeological sites. And it was also sceptical about the argument that expropriations aimed to preserve the constitutional status of the country as a republic, because the constitutional transition from monarchy to republic took place almost twenty years before the enactment of the contested law. Nevertheless, it found that that doubt could not suffice to deprive the overall objective of the expropriation of its legitimacy as being in the public interest.[155]

The Court found the following aims in the public interest: to secure greater social justice by correcting assumed unfairness in leasehold contracts,[156] to promote the rationalisation of agriculture,[157] to fight tax evasion,[158] to prevent misuse of agricultural and forestry land,[159] to terminate a contract which is considered to be prejudicial to the state's economic interests,[160] to protect a state's financial interests, to re-regulate tort liability and to bring the state's legislation into line with that of neighbouring countries,[161] to develop a major road,[162] to control the market in works of art for the purposes of protecting a country's cultural and artistic heritage,[163] and to preserve the constitutional status of the country as a republic.[164]

The Court also found that the following aims are in 'general interest': the protection of morals,[165] the regulation of the sale of alcoholic beverages within the framework of the state's social policy,[166] town and country planning,[167] protection

November 2000 (App. No. 25701/94) § 87; *Ambruosi v. Italy*, Judgement of 19 October 2000 (App. No. 31227/96).

155 *The Former King of Greece and Others v. Greece*, Judgement of 23 November 2000 (App. No. 25701/94) § 88.

156 *James and Others v UK* Judgement of 21 February 1986, Series A No. 98.

157 *Hakansson and Sturesson v. Sweden,* Judgement of 21 February 1990, Series A, No. 171-A.

158 *Hentrich v. France*, Judgement of 22 September 1994, Series A, No. 296-A.

159 *Holy Monasteries v. Greece* Judgement of 9 December 1994, Series A no. 301-A.

160 *Stran Greek Refineries and Stratis Andreadis v. Greece*, Judgement of 9 December 1994, Series A, No.301-A.

161 *Pressos Compania Naviera S.A. and Others v. Belgium*, Judgement of 20 November 1995, Series A, No.332.

162 *Katikaridis v Greece* and *Tsomtos and Others v Greece* Judgements of 15 November 1996, Reports 1996-V.

163 *Beyeler v. Italy*, Judgement of 5 January 2000 (App. No.33202/96) para.112.

164 *The Former King of Greece and Others v. Greece*, Judgement of 23 November 2000 (App. No. 25701/94) § 88.

165 *Handyside v. UK*, Judgement of 7 December 1976, Series A, No.24, para.63.

166 *Tre Traktörer Aktiebolag v. Sweden*, Judgement of 7 July 1989, Series A, No. 159.

167 *Alan Jacobsson v. Sweden*, Judgement of 25 October 1989, Series A no. 163 § 57; *Sporrong and Lönnroth v. Sweden,* Judgement of 23 September 1982 Series A no. 52.

of the environment,[168] housing policy,[169] the preservation of evidence of a criminal offence and the prevention of any aggravation of the offence,[170] to structure a profession in order to improve competence of those who carry on that profession,[171] and to fight against drug smuggling.[172]

As mentioned above the Convention organs have not made any distinction between public and general interest. They have treated all policy choices made by national authorities as legitimate aims. This approach is compatible with the common interest theory of public interest which argues that public interest is common interest of individuals as members of society. Since it is impossible always in a society to agree about aims of public policies, the policies determined by democratically elected majority will be treated *prima facie* as valid, unless they are clearly unreasonable. Determination of the aims of a political society is, to some extent, a subjective element of public interest. At the end, it is for the political society itself, through democratic process, to decide which goals it is going to pursue. However, this authority is not limitless. Human rights theories impose a universal morality that should be observed by any public decision maker. It was suggested in Chapter 4 that all public authorities' actions should aim to create and enhance an autonomy-enhancing society.

On the other hand, once the goals of political society are determined, it is, in principle, an objective question whether particular actions contribute towards public goals. Whenever public interest defences are invoked, then the role of the judge is limited to the technical task of checking that the actions complained of really do contribute to one of the objectives sanctioned by the rights document. The judge should consider how the rights of individuals are affected by governmental actions, rather than whether the decisions are, in principle, right. So the judges may engage in a rational balancing process, and hence give stronger protection to rights *via* the concept of proportionality.[173] Applying this test, the Court would ask not merely whether impugned acts serve legitimate collective goals, but whether it is necessary to encroach on rights to such a degree in order to achieve those goals. If not, the intervention is not proportionate and the defence fails.

The European case-law seems, in theory, to be following this approach. The Convention organs have never ruled that policy aims pursued by national

---

[168] *Pine Valley Developments Ltd. and Others v. Ireland*, Judgement of 29 November 1991, Series A, No 222; *Fredin v. Sweden*, Judgement of 18 February 1991, Series A no. 192.

[169] *Mellacher v. Austria*, Judgement of 19 December 1989, Series A, No. 169; *Scollo v. Italy*, Judgement of 28 September 1995, Series A, No.315-C; *Spadea and Scalabrino v. Italy*, Judgement of 28 September 1995, Series A, NO.315-B; *Immobiliare Saffi v. Italy*, Judgement of 28 July 1999; *A.O. v. Italy*, Judgement of 30 May 2000; *Edoardo Palumbo v. Italy*, Judgement of 30 November 2000, (App. no. 15919/89); *Velosa Barreto v. Portugal*, Judgement of 21 November 1995, Series A, No. 334.

[170] *Vendittelli v. Italy*, Judgement of 18 July 1994, Series A, No. 293-A.

[171] *Van Marle and Others v. Netherlands*, Judgement of 3 June 1986, Series A no. 101.

[172] *Air Canada v. UK*, Judgement of 5 May 1995, Series A, No.316-A.

[173] Alexy, R., "Individual Rights and Collective Goods" in C. Nino (ed.) *Rights* (Aldershot: Dartmouth, 1992).

authorities are not legitimate in principle. But they apply a proportionality test to determine whether applied policies are suitable and necessary to realise those aims, and they examine whether individuals have been forced to bear an excessive burden. However, this approach, as McHarg[174] indicated, gives greater weight to public interests than individual rights.

7.3.3. Proportionality of the Interference

As indicated above, the Convention organs leave a wide margin of appreciation to national authorities in determining the policy aims and means of realising those policies. The principle of proportionality has been developed by the Court as a corrective and limit to the margin of appreciation doctrine.[175] According to the Court the principle of proportionality is reached by a search, which is inherent in the whole of the Convention, for a fair balance between the demands of the general interest of the community and the protection of the individual's fundamental rights.[176] When a national authority is applying a restriction, allowed by the Convention, upon a right it should maintain a reasonable relationship of proportionality between the means employed and the aim sought to be realised.[177]

The origin of the concept of proportionality can be found in Continental administrative laws. The Federal Constitutional Court of Germany has applied it in the Constitutional Law.[178] Then it has been spread through the laws of Europe. Although the concept of proportionality is not specifically mentioned in the text of the European Convention or its Protocols, the Court established that the idea of proportionality is present in the provisions.

The principle of proportionality requires that a state interference with a fundamental right must satisfy three criteria: the interference must be appropriate to the achievement of its goal, and necessary to the achievement of its goal, and the harm to the right must not outweigh the contribution to the public good

---

[174] McHarg, A., "Reconciling Human Rights and the Public Interest: Conceptual Problems and Doctrinal Uncertainty in the Jurisprudence of the European Court of Human Rights" (1999) 62 *The Modern Law Review* 671-96.

[175] Matscher, F., "Methods of Interpretation of the Convention" in Macdonald, R., Matscher, F. and Petzold, H., (eds.) *The European System for the Protection of Human Rights* (London, 1993); p.79.

[176] *Soering v. UK*, Series A no.161 § 89 (1989).

[177] For a detailed discussion of proportionality in the case-law of ECHR see Eissen, M. A., "The Principle of Proportionality in the Case-law of the European Court of Human Rights" in Macdonald et al (eds.) *The European System for the Protection of Human Rights* (M. Nijhoff: Dordrecht, 1993); McBride, J., "Proportionality and the European Convention on Human Rights" in E. Ellis (ed.) *The Principle of Proportionality in the Laws of Europe* (Hart Publishing: Oxford, 1999).

[178] Kommers, D., *The Constitutional Jurisprudence of the Federal Republic of Germany* (second ed.)(Duke UP: Durham, 1997) p.46.

(proportionality in the narrower sense).[179] The first two requirements provide safeguards against arbitrary actions of public authorities when they choose the means of policy to achieve public goals. That is, if the chosen policy apparatus, which interferes with fundamental rights, is not appropriate to achieve the declared aim, there is an unnecessary and arbitrary interference with fundamental rights. Or, although it is possible to achieve the same goal by another means which interferes less with fundamental rights than the one preferred by public authorities, still there is an unnecessary and arbitrary interference with fundamental rights. For example, although it is possible to prevent damage to environment and health caused by harmful emissions of a factory by imposing the instalment of a filter, if public authorities decide to close the factory such a measure is disproportionate.

The third requirement (proportionality in the narrower sense) demands balancing between public and individual interests. This approach seems to be compatible with a model that reconciles rights and public interest. This model assumes rights as protected interests and the public interest as common interests. According to this model, whenever a conflict arises the rights and the public interest should be weighed against one another and whichever is the stronger should prevail.[180]

In the area of property rights, the principle of proportionality has been developed by the case-law gradually. The Court, in *Handyside*, stated that 'this paragraph (the second paragraph of P1-1) sets the contracting states up as sole judges of the necessity for an interference. Consequently, the Court must restrict itself to supervising the lawfulness and the purpose of the restriction in question'.[181] In this case the Court did not mention any requirement of proportionality between the aim pursued and the means employed to affect the aim. Similarly in the *Marckx*[182] case it said that the states are set up as the sole judges of the necessity for such a law. However, in *Sporrong* the majority of the Court decided that a fair balance must be struck between the demands of the general interests of community and the requirements of the protection of the individual's fundamental rights[183] and that this fair balance was not found if the person concerned had had to bear an excessive and individual burden.[184] The Court reformulated this requirement in the *James* case as follows: 'not only must a measure depriving a person of his property pursue, on the facts as well as in principle, a legitimate aim "in the public interest", but there must also be a reasonable relationship of proportionality between the means employed and the

---

[179] Neuman, G. L., "The U.S. Constitutional Conception of the Rule of Law and the *Rechtsstaatsprinzip* of the *Grundgesetz*", Columbia Law School Public Law and Legal Theory Working Paper (1999).
[180] McHarg, *op.cit.* 174 p.678.
[181] *Handyside v. UK*, Judgement of 7 December 1976, Series A, No.24, § 62.
[182] *Marckx v. Belgium*, Judgement of 13 June 1979, Series A no.31§ 64.
[183] *Sporrong and Lönnroth v. Sweden*, Judgement of 23 September 1982, Series A no. 52, § 69.
[184] *Ibid.* § 73.

aim sought to be realised'.[185] The Court added that 'a measure must be both appropriate for achieving its aim and not disproportionate thereto'.[186] Indeed the Court worded requirement of proportionality in its narrow sense in *Sporrong*, and wider proportionality in *James*. The Court stated that the proportionality test is applicable to the whole of the Article (P1-1).

The Commission, in the *Gillow*[187] case, noted that measure of proportionality differs in the application of deprivation and control of use rules since deprivation of property is inherently more serious than the control of its use. And it stated that proportionality must be assessed with reference to the severity of the restriction imposed. Sermet argues that two types of proportionality supervision are necessary: one applying to deprivation and another to the three other types of interference, because in deprivation of property, proportionality is respected if the dispossessed owner is awarded compensation. He claims that in other cases of interference with property, the supervision of proportionality varies in content, but is always defined in the same way.[188] His argument seems sound only if it is accepted that the compensation is a requirement derived by the principle of proportionality where national law does not clearly provide. However, the requirement of compensation can be inferred from the nature of right to property and the proportionality test can be applied to the whole of P1-1 similarly.

In application of the proportionality or balancing test the Convention organs have taken into account, whether legitimate expectations have been respected, whether procedural guarantees have been provided, whether the public authorities acted arbitrarily, and whether compensation has been provided. The Court has also taken into consideration the conduct of the applicant.

However, the Court does not apply a proportionality test in a rigorous fashion in property rights cases.[189] It hardly applies appropriateness and necessity tests in those cases. For example, in the *Tre Traktörer* case it stated that 'the burden placed on TTA (the applicant company) as a result of the contested decisions, though heavy, must be weighed against the general interest of the community. In this context, the states enjoy a wide margin of appreciation'. And ruled that even though the public authorities could have taken less severe measures under relevant law, having regard to the legitimate aim of Swedish social policy concerning the consumption of alcohol, the measure complained of did not fail to strike a fair balance.[190]

---

[185] *James and Others v UK* Judgement of 21 February 1986 Series A no. 98 § 50; *Lithgow and Others v. UK* Judgement of 8 July 1986, Series A no. 102 §120.

[186] *Ibid.* § 51.

[187] *Gillow v. UK*, Judgement of 24 November 1986, Series A no. 109 (Report of the Commission § 148-157).

[188] Sermet, *op.cit* 13 p.36.

[189] McBride, J., "Proportionality and the European Convention on Human Rights" in E. Ellis (ed.) *The Principle of Proportionality in the Laws of Europe* (Hart Publishing: Oxford, 1999).

[190] *Tre Traktörer Aktiebolag v. Sweden*, Judgement of 7 July 1989, Series A, No. 159 § 62.

In *Mellacher,*[191] similarly, the Court stated that the possible existence of alternative solutions did not in itself render the contested legislation unjustified. Provided that the legislature remained within the bounds of its margin of appreciation, it was not for the Court to say whether the legislation represented the best solution for dealing with the problem or whether the legislative discretion should have been exercised in another way. However, this approach is questionable because first, what is the limit of margin of appreciation if not the principle of proportionality? Second, if there are other solutions that require less interference with the fundamental right of property to achieve the same goal, how can restrictions without compensation on contractual rights be justified in a liberal free market society? Why should only house owners bear the burden of a housing shortage? Such a restriction can only be justified if landlords abuse such a situation and benefit from the hardship of the tenants.

Moreover, in most of the property cases the Court does not seek any evidence for the defence of the responded state. The Court takes the governments' claims regarding the relation between the restrictions on rights and the aims pursued as granted. For example, in the *Spadea and Scalabrino*[192] case an Italian legislation froze the enforcement of eviction orders. The Court found the legislation as justifiable because it had the aim of protecting the interests of tenants on low incomes and avoiding public disorder at a time when there was a housing shortage. In the Court's view this was seen as an emergency measure but this sort of measure had been in operation for over 40 years and there was no consideration of whether Italy had taken any other measure to redress the housing shortage. The Court seemed to acknowledge the existence of a housing shortage as a universal problem of modern society and the Italian approach is the only possible solution for such a problem.

The European Court's approach to necessity and appropriateness requirements is much looser than that of the German Constitutional Court. The German Constitutional Court also applies the necessity test flexibly as a requirement to meet the standard of rationality. It is less than 'strict scrutiny' and more than 'minimum rationality'.[193] For example, the Constitutional Court ruled that property may not be taken until efforts to buy it on the open market have failed.[194] It is suggested that the European Court should also apply a rational necessity test to determine whether a state interference with property complies with the requirement of proportionality.

The Court in *Van Marle*[195] considered whether legitimate expectations were respected and ruled that a fair balance between the means used and the

---

[191] *Mellacher v. Austria*, Judgement of 19 December 1989, Series A, No. 169 § 53.

[192] *Spadea and Scalabrino v. Italy*, Judgement of 28 September 1995, Series A, NO.315-B.

[193] Kommers, *op.cit.* 178 p.46.

[194] Currie, D., *The Constitution of the Federal Republic of Germany* (Chicago UP: Chicago, 1994) p.293.

[195] *Van Marle and Others v. Netherlands*, Judgement of 3 June 1986, Series A no. 101§ 43.

intended aim was at any rate ensured by transitional provisions enabling the former unqualified accountants to gain entry to the new profession on prescribed conditions.

In *Hentrich*[196] one of the main concerns of the Court's decision was whether procedural guarantees were provided. The Court ruled that, having regard to all factors, as a selected victim of the exercise of the right of pre-emption the applicant bore an individual and excessive burden that could have been rendered legitimate only if she had had the possibility – which was refused to her – of effectively challenging the measures taken against her. On the other hand, in the *Air Canada*[197] case the Court ruled that the scope of judicial review under English law was sufficient to satisfy the requirement of the second paragraph of P1-1. The Court similarly made reference to the procedural guarantees where it regarded that the interference amounted to control of use.[198] However, the sufficiency of this examination is still questionable, especially if the procedural requirements attaching to property rights are markedly less stringent than those which apply under Article 6.[199] How can the substance of a right (the right to property) be less important than its procedural guarantee (right to fair trial for civil rights)? The requirements of appropriateness and necessity should be strictly applied, especially in cases of control of use, taxation and confiscation, because there is no compensation guarantee.

In the assessment of the proportionality of the interference, one of the important factors taken into account by the Court is the conduct of public authorities. Particularly if there are unreasonably lengthy interferences, the Court has not hesitated to find the interference as disproportionate. First in *Sporrong* it found that unreasonably lengthy expropriation permits did not strike the fair balance between individual and common interests. Similarly in the *Pois*[200] and *Erkner and Hofauer*[201] cases, the Court found that the applicants who remained uncertain for a long time as to the final fate of their property had been made to bear a disproportionate burden. In the following similar cases concerning planning regulations also the Court ruled that restrictions such as construction prohibitions imposed over applicants' property and leaving the status of property uncertain for a long period of time without paying compensation did not strike the fair balance. In this regard the *Katte Klitsche de la Grance v. Italy,*[202] *Phocas v. France,*[203] *Iatridis*

---

[196] *Hentrich v. France*, Judgement of 22 September 1994, Series A, No. 296-A § 49.

[197] *Air Canada v. UK*, Judgement of 5 May 1995, Series A, No.316-A § 46.

[198] See for example, *Agosi v. UK*, Judgement of 24 October 1986, Series A, No108; *Gasus Dosier- und Födertechnik GmbH v. the Netherlands*, Judgement of 23 February 1995, Series A no.306-B.

[199] Sermet, *op.cit.* 13 p.37.

[200] *Poiss v. Austria*, Judgement of 23 April 1987, Series A, No. 117; See also *Prötsch v. Austria,* Judgement of 15 November 1996.

[201] *Erkner and Hofauer v. Austria*, Judgement of 23 April 1987, Series A, No. 117.

[202] *Katte Klitsche de la Grance v. Italy*, Judgement of 27 October 1994, Series A, No.293-B.

[203] *Phocas v. France,* Judgement of 23 April 1996, Reports 1996-II.

v. Greece,[204] and *Pialopoulos and Others v. Greece*[205] cases can be taken as examples. Unreasonable delays in the determination of compensation[206] or delaying the payment of compensation in an inflationary period and paying relatively less interest also breached the requirement of proportionality.[207] The Court ruled in a couple of cases that lack of police assistance for enforcement of orders for possession, coupled with what had already been a six-year wait because of the statutory suspension of the enforcement of such orders, imposed an excessive burden on the applicants and accordingly upset the balance that must be struck between the protection of the right of property and the requirements of the general interest. [208] In the *Vendittelli*[209] case the Court held that the delay of national judicial authorities to order the release of property sequestration placed a disproportionate burden on the applicant.

The Court, while assessing whether a fair balance has been struck between individual and common interests, takes into account the conduct of the applicant as well. For example, in *Beyeler,*[210] the applicant did not disclose to the vendor that the painting had been purchased on his behalf to be able to buy the painting for a lower price and he failed to declare to the authorities that he was the end purchaser for five years in order to avoid risk of a pre-emption order being made. The Court considered this conduct of the applicant when it was reaching a conclusion, but it also took the conduct of authorities into account and found that the fact that the authorities waited five years after they learned that the end purchaser was the applicant and exercised their right of pre-emption in 1988 for the sale made in 1977 did not strike a fair balance.

The Convention organs have treated the right of compensation as a requirement of balancing individual and public interest. However, this approach

---

[204] *Iatridis v. Greece,* Judgement of 25 March 1999 Reports 1999-II.

[205] *Pialopoulos and Others v. Greece,* Judgement of 15 February 2001, (App. No. 37095/97).

[206] *Matos e Silva, Lda., and Others v. Portugal*, Judgement of 27 August 1996, Reports 1996-IV; *Almeida Garrett, Mascarenhas Falcao and Others v. Portugal*, Judgement of 11 January 2000 (App. Nos. 29813/96 and 30229/96) §48.

[207] *Aka v. Turkey*, Judgement of 23 September 1998, Reports 1998-VI, § 43; *Gaganus and Others v. Turkey*, Judgement of 5 June 2001 (App. No. 39335/98); *Akkus v. Turkey*, Judgement of 9 July 1997, Reports 1997-IV; *Yasar and Others v. Turkey*, Judgement of 14 November 2000 (App. No.27697/95); *Hamdi Celebi v. Turkey*, Judgement of 30 January 2001(and 23 other decisions on the same date) (App. Nos. 19264- 19288/92); *Ismihan Ozel and Others v. Turkey*, Judgement of 27 February 2001 (App. No. 31963/96); *Ali Ozturk v. Turkey,* Judgement of 10 April 2001 (and 24 other decisions on the same date) (App. Nos. 19289- 19312/92); *Gulnahar Calkan v. Turkey*, Judgement of 5 June 2001(and 19 other decisions on the same date) (App. Nos.19661-19683/92).

[208] *Scollo v. Italy*, Judgement of 28 September 1995, Series A, No.315-C; *Spadea and Scalabrino v. Italy*, Judgement of 28 September 1995, Series A, NO.315-B; *Immobiliare Saffi v. Italy*, Judgement of 28 July 1999; *A.O. v. Italy*, Judgement of 30 May 2000; *Edoardo Palumbo v. Italy*, Judgement of 30 November 2000, (App. no. 15919/89); *Velosa Barreto v. Portugal*, Judgement of 21 November 1995 (App. No.18072/91).

[209] *Vendittelli v. Italy*, Judgement of 18 July 1994, Series A, No. 293-A § 40.

[210] *Beyeler v. Italy*, Judgement of 5 January 2000 (App. No.33202/96).

offers no guide to determine when compensation is required and how it should be calculated. The Court, therefore, examines on an *ad hoc* basis whether such a balancing requires payment of compensation. So, the compensation requirement will be examined next separately.

7.3.4. Compensation

In the context of property rights, it is necessary to distinguish between compensation that is required by P1-1 and damages which can be awarded as a form of just satisfaction in case of violation of P1-1 according to Article 41. Compensation is a requirement of P1-1 in cases of taking of property as a necessity of legitimate interference. If interference is legitimate then violation of property will not occur. But if the contracting parties fail to satisfy one of the conditions of legitimate interference, then P1-1 will be violated and the owner may ask for just satisfaction as a remedy for such violation depending on Article 41. Here only the compensation that is required by P1-1 in cases of taking of property will be examined. Article 41 will be examined in the next chapter.

The core of the right to property is a right to the thing itself not a right to the value of it. Therefore, compensation is not a replacement for property; it is only an indemnification for the losses of the private owner. So, the right to property cannot be regarded as merely a right to compensation and it cannot be said that a state has a power to take private property as long as it compensates the owner. Therefore, in order to take property by paying compensation there should be a strong public necessity.

In the past, the Commission decided that the state had no duty to pay compensation in the case of expropriation of property in the public interest, if this is not provided for in domestic law.[211] The case-law has gradually developed in this area. In the *James* case, the Court observed that under the legal systems of the contracting states, the taking of property in the public interest without payment of compensation was treated as justifiable only in exceptional circumstances. And it ruled that the protection of the right of property, in P1-1, would have been largely illusory and ineffective in the absence of any equivalent principle. The Court has assessed the compensation requirement in the context of a fair balance test. Accordingly, the taking of property without payment of an amount reasonably related to its value would normally constitute a disproportionate interference which could not be considered justifiable under P1-1. However, according to the Court, P1-1 does not guarantee a right to full compensation in all circumstances. Legitimate objectives of 'public interest', such as pursued in measures of economic reform or measures designed to achieve greater social justice, may call for less than reimbursement of the full market value. Furthermore, the Court's power of review is limited to ascertaining whether the choice of compensation terms falls outside the state's wide margin of appreciation in this domain.[212]

---

[211] *Gudmundsson v. Iceland*, (App. No. 511/59) Yearbook III (1960) p. 394.

[212] *James*, § 54.

The principles inferred from this judgement can be summarised as follows. Firstly, standard protection requires payment of a reasonable compensation. Secondly, the amount of compensation may be reduced if there is an economic reform or a social justice consideration. And lastly non-payment of compensation can be justified only in exceptional cases. This approach leaves a wide margin of appreciation to the states in both determining whether compensation is required and determining the valuation methods.

In *Lithgow* the Court held that the obligation to pay compensation derives from an implicit condition in the Article read as a whole rather than from the public interest requirement itself.[213] In that case, the Court repeated that the taking of property without payment of an amount reasonably related to its value would normally constitute a disproportionate interference. And it ruled that the states enjoy a wide margin of appreciation in adopting different valuation methods in the case of nationalisation than simple taking of property, because both the nature of property taken and the circumstances of taking in these two categories were different. Accordingly, it found that although the applicants suffered significant losses caused by application of different valuation methods, the applied valuation policies did not impose a disproportionate burden on the applicants. It is suggested that the Court should have examined whether those losses were justified.

Although the Court has theoretically accepted that in exceptional cases non-payment of compensation can be justified, it has not found such a situation yet. In a number of cases, although respondent governments contended that taking of property without compensation was justified, the Court did not accept such arguments. In *Holy Monasteries,*[214] while the Commission accepted that such an exceptional circumstance justified the absence of compensation, the Court did not agree. It ruled that measures expropriating a large portion of monastery agricultural property without compensation did not preserve a fair balance between the various interests in question.

In the *Pressos Compania Naviera*[215] case the Belgian government raised three reasons to justify retrospective extinguishing of tort claims resulting from piloting services against the state and relevant companies: the need to protect the state's financial interests, the need to harmonise the laws and the need to restore legal clarity in the field of tort. The Court did not accept those reasons as justifying retrospective annulment of compensation claims.

Similarly in the case of *The Former King of Greece*[216] the Greek government argued that most of the properties belonging to the former royal family were given to them as presents due to their position as head of state, and they were exempted from inheritance tax, therefore expropriation of those properties without

---

[213] *Lithgow*, §110.

[214] *Holy Monasteries v. Greece* Judgement of 9 December 1994, Series A no. 301-A § 74-75.

[215] *Pressos Compania Naviera S.A. and Others v. Belgium*, Judgement of 20 November 1995, Series A, No.332.

[216] *The Former King of Greece and Others v. Greece*, Judgement of 23 November 2000 (App. No. 25701/94) § 78.

paying any compensation was justified. The Court dismissed that argument and ruled that lack of any compensation for deprivation of the applicants' property upset the fair balance between the protection of property and requirements of public interest.

As for the valuation methods, the Court has recognised a wide margin of appreciation to the states. It respects the states' choice of methods unless it is manifestly without reasonable foundation.[217] The Court found in the *Katikaridis* and *Tsomtos*[218] cases that a system making the irrebuttable presumption that neighbouring property owners to a road derived real benefits from improvement of the road, leaving no chance to challenge, is unduly rigid. 'The compensation was in every case reduced by an amount equal to the value of an area fifteen metres wide, without the owners concerned being allowed to argue that in reality the effect of the works concerned either has been of no benefit or less benefit to them or has caused them to sustain varying degrees of loss.'[219] Therefore, the Greek law was manifestly without reasonable foundation.

The case-law suggests that a reasonable compensation should be paid in cases of expropriation. It does not require a full compensation or full market value. However, in a recent judgement, the Court found that lack of compensation for the loss of the applicant's source of income as a result of the expropriation of a part of a family farm and paying of only the value of the expropriated part did not bear a reasonable relation to the value of the expropriated property.[220] The Court noted that the expropriation complained of had made it financially unviable for the applicant to continue on the remaining portion of his land and has thus led to the loss of his source of income. Since the compensation paid by the government did not cover that loss, the Court found the violation of P1-1. Although this judgement constitutes an improvement in the Court's approach to the issue of compensation, there is still room for improvement in this regard. It is suggested that rather than an *ad hoc* case by case approach, the Court should make it clear that unless there are legitimate reasons to reduce the amount of compensation, government should pay full compensation for the taking of property.[221] The legitimate reasons that may justify less than full compensation can be correction of past injustices or reciprocal benefit.

The Court examined whether sufficient compensation was given only in cases of deprivation.[222] However, as indicated above, this approach is unfounded. It

---

[217] *Hakansson and Sturesson v. Sweden,* Judgement of 21 February 1990, Series A, No. 171-A.

[218] *Katikaridis v Greece* and *Tsomtos and Others v Greece* Judgements of 15 November 1996, Reports 1996-V.

[219] *Ibid.* § 49.

[220] *Lallement v. France*, Judgement of 11 April 2002, (App. No. 46044/99).

[221] For a contrary opinion see Allen, T., "Limitations on Constitutional Property Rights" in Paul Jackson and David C. Wilde (eds.) *Property Law: Current Issues and Debates* (Ashgate: Dartmouth, 1999); see also Allen, T., *The Right to Property in Commonwealth Constitutions* (CUP, Cambridge, 2000).

[222] Anderson, D., "Compensation for Interference With Property" (1999) *European Human Rights Law Review* 543.

causes both theoretical and practical difficulty. The fair balance test applied by the Convention organs results in *ad hoc* assessment of whether compensation is required. Nevertheless, such an assessment may lead to outweighing public interest because the judge will abstain from further weighing of the merits of competing claims in order to avoid conflicting with the decisions of democratically elected bodies. So, the margin of appreciation left to the states will always be wide. However, such an approach undermines the autonomy of the individual because individuals are always forced to give up their interest in favour of public interests.

Therefore, a different approach is needed to provide effective protection for individual rights and autonomy of the individual. It can be argued that the aim of the right to property is to protect autonomy of the individual by both serving to realise life plans and protecting the fruits of individual preferences. The scope of the protection for property rights is to prevent imposing the burden of public policies unequally and selectively on some individuals. So as a necessity of harm principle harmful use of property can be prohibited, but nobody can be imposed to bear an individual and unequal burden.

Although it is possible that a difficulty arises in determination of when a use is harmful, some general criteria can be offered. Such difficulty may arise especially in the areas of city and town planning and environmental protection. Firstly, the traditional nuisance rules are applied. Secondly, since the effects of use of property do not remain in property and it spreads over other properties and common resources such as air and water (spillover effect), such usage can also be limited or prohibited on an equitable basis. However, if a property is allocated for public use then compensation should be paid; for example, a factory can be forced to install a filter without compensation in order to reduce the harmful effects of emissions. But if private land is to be made into a natural preservation area, then the burden of such a policy should not be imposed on the owner only and should be shared by the public. Or if a demand for planning permission to build a ten-storey apartment block in an area where normally two-storey buildings are allowed is refused, no compensation is needed, because every neighbouring property has a right to a view and sunlight. But if a request of planning permission for conversion of a dwelling house containing seven self-contained flats to one large family house without making any external change is refused on the ground that it conflicts with the established policy objective of avoiding any reduction in the stock of low cost small accommodation, then compensation is required. There is no harmful usage, but an allocation of a private property for public use.

As indicated in Chapter 4, the definition of harmful use can change from time to time and place to place and it is for the democratically elected bodies to decide which use is harmful. But if a policy change makes a previously harmless use harmful, legitimate expectations of individuals should be respected. For example, if a factory, legally built 30 years ago, finds itself in the middle of a residential area as a result of city development, harm principle justifies the closure of the factory. But since the factory became harmful without the fault of the owner, legitimate expectations of him should be respected. For example, a partial compensation and allowing a transitional period can be a proportionate solution.

7.4. Conclusion

The right to property is not an absolute right and P1-1 allows the contracting parties to interfere with it for legitimate purposes. However to provide an effective guarantee for the right to property it is necessary to determine the limits of legitimate interference. The public authorities may interfere with property rights in many ways. So in order to be able to determine the limits of legitimate interference it is necessary, firstly, to categorise different types of interferences and then to determine the conditions of legitimate interference for each category separately.

The Convention organs define three kinds of interference with the right to property according to the effect of interference on property, namely deprivation of property, the control of the use of property and interference with the substance of property. However, this taxonomy is not functional and cannot guide when compensation should be paid. Therefore, the Court, without attributing any significance to this taxonomy, directly applies a fair balance test between private interests and public interests on an *ad hoc* basis. But such an approach makes the guarantee of property in P1-1 very ambiguous and unpredictable.

Therefore, in this book an alternative triple taxonomy of interference with property depending on the aims of the public authorities has been suggested. Accordingly, the interference with property can be examined in three categories; taxation, taking of property for public interest by eminent domain power, and limiting the property by police power regulations. The aim of public authorities in taxation is to enhance the public funds to finance public policies. Taxation imposes an equal burden for all individuals in the same position. The aim of takings is to advance the public interest by transferring a private property to public use. The aim of regulatory power is to prevent the harmful use of property. Only in the case of taking of property by eminent domain power should the public authorities pay compensation.

As for the conditions of legitimate interference, firstly any interference with property should depend on an accessible, precise, and foreseeable national law. If an action of public authorities lacks a legal basis, such an interference with property is not legitimate. Secondly, actions of public authorities interfering with property should pursue a legitimate aim. That is, it should be in the public interest. Public authorities enjoy a wide margin of appreciation to determine what is in the public interest. Therefore, the international judge has a very limited power to review whether the aim pursued by national authorities is in the public interest. In this book, Raz's autonomy principle has been suggested as the philosophical justificatory basis of the right to property and power of a state to interfere with it. Accordingly, every action of public authorities should aim to create and advance an autonomy-enhancing society.

Once it has been established that the aim pursued by national authorities is in the public interest, the next question is whether the applied policy apparatus is appropriate, necessary, and proportional to the aim pursued. This proportionality test suggests that the means used must be appropriate to the achievement of public end and it also must have the least restrictive effect on property rights. It also suggests that the burden on the owner must not be excessive relative to the benefits secured by the public authorities' aims. The European Court does not apply appropriateness and necessity tests, rather it applies only a proportionality test in its narrow sense; balancing private and public interests. It is suggested that the Court should apply a wider proportionality test.

The legality, public interest, and proportionality conditions are valid for all three types of interferences. The last condition of legitimate interference is compensation requirement. The Court treats compensation requirement as an element of the fair balance test, and it considers it is necessary to pay compensation only in cases of deprival of property. However, this approach is far from giving clear guidance in determining when compensation is required. The judge will decide in each case on an *ad hoc* basis whether compensation is required. This book suggests that a compensation requirement is valid only for taking of property by eminent domain power. The criterion distinguishing takings from taxation is its singling out feature. If an action of national authorities imposes the burden of a public policy on only one or some individuals unequally and selectively it constitutes taking of property and requires payment of compensation. The criterion distinguishing takings from police power regulations is the aim of police power regulations. If the aim of a state action is to prevent harmful use of property, it is a police power regulation and does not require payment of compensation. But if the aim of a state action is to advance public interest transferring private property to public use, it constitutes taking and requires payment of compensation. Nevertheless, social and technological changes may affect which use is harmful. Harmfulness of a usage may change from time to time and from one society to another. Therefore, it is for the democratically elected bodies to decide which use is harmful. Accordingly, if a legitimate use becomes harmful as a result of policy change, the legitimate expectations of the private owners should be respected.

The Court considers the amount of compensation also within the fair balance test. It requires payment of a 'reasonable compensation'. Since there is no clear criterion to decide what is 'reasonable', it is for the judge to decide, on an *ad hoc* basis, whether the compensation paid by national authorities is reasonable. But this approach also benefits the public interest because the judge abstains to find the compensation unreasonable unless there is obviously a clear injustice. It is suggested that unless there is a legitimate reason to reduce the amount of compensation, public authorities should pay full market value of the property. Legitimate reasons can be a correction of past injustices and reciprocal benefit.

The accession of former socialist states to the Convention has brought new challenges before the Court. One of the questions is whether the Court should loosen the standards for those countries who have not completed their transition from a centrally planned economy to a market-oriented economy in terms of P1-1. The Court, in a recent case, stated that:

> ... an important feature of the present case is the fact that it concerns legal regulation of economic activities in Bulgaria during a unique period of transition from a wholly state-owned and centrally planned economy to private property and market economy. The co-existence of legislation from such incompatible systems

> inevitably carried a measure of uncertainty as regards the outcome of a business dispute in an area as complex as that concerning the regulation of gas debt and in respect of transactions that had never before been tested in court. While legal uncertainty may not satisfy the Convention requirements of clarity and foreseeability and may contravene the prohibition of arbitrariness, in the assessment whether such a situation obtained in the present case and whether, consequently, there was an unjustified state interference contrary to P1-1, due account must be taken of the special transitional period in Bulgaria at the relevant time.[223]

The Court's approach to legality requirement, which is one of the basic tenets of the rule of law, in this case is worrying. And it certainly has loosened its standard of legality for Bulgaria in this case and found the application inadmissible. One possible explanation for this approach is that the Court is reluctant to rule judgements that will impose enormous economic burden on those countries whose economic system is still fragile. If that is the case, though such a pragmatic approach is understandable, it is questionable in terms of moral standards.

But in a number of cases, relating to those countries the Court found violation of P1-1 and did not mention about transitional period. However, it is still too early to reach a judgement in this respect. It can be expected that the more the economic systems of those countries become stabilised, the more the Court applies the balancing test in favour of individual interests.

[223] *Credit Bank and Others v. Bulgaria*, Admissibility Decision of 30 April 2002, (App. No. 40064/98)

Chapter 8

The Relations between P1-1 and Other Articles of the Convention

8.1. Introduction

In the last three chapters (Chapters 5, 6 and 7) the guarantee and protection of property rights provided by P1-1 was examined. This chapter looks at different external aspects of the right to property, mainly its relations with other articles of the Convention. P1-1 has relationships with a number of the articles of the Convention. Mainly Article 6 provides extra procedural guarantees for property rights. Article 8 protects some form of property (home and some chattels such as correspondence) in terms of the right to privacy. Article 14 protects property rights, *inter alia*, against discriminatory interference. Article 15 gives extra power to the contracting states to interfere with property rights during public emergencies. And Article 41 provides just satisfaction for violation of property rights by the contracting states. Here, first, the articles which provide extra substantive guarantees will be examined (Articles 8, 14 and 41) and then the procedural guarantee provided by Article 6 and, lastly, the extra limitation power provided by Article 15 will be scrutinised.

Article 41 (formerly Article 50) provides 'just satisfaction' for violations of P1-1. What kind of remedies can the Court award to the victim of such a violation? Article 41 is a general provision applicable to violations of all rights protected by the Convention and Protocols. Therefore, the general principles governing its application by the Court will be summarised briefly and greater consideration will be given to the Court's jurisprudence regarding just satisfaction in violation of P1-1. In particular, I will consider whether there is any distinctive feature of the concept of 'just satisfaction' in relation to violations of the right to property.

Article 8 protects a right to home and some chattels such as correspondence in terms of the right to privacy. But these things constitute possessions in the meaning of P1-1 as well. Therefore, it is important to examine relationships between P1-1 and Article 8 to determine when an interference with home and correspondence constitute interference with Article 8 and when an interference with P1-1.

Article 14 bans discrimination in enjoyment of the Convention rights on the grounds of sex, race, colour, language, religion, political or other opinion, national or social origin, association with a national minority, property or other status. This article provides an extra guarantee for property rights apart from P1-1.

Article 14 is significant especially for taxation because it provides the only limitation over the states' power of taxation, since P1-1 itself does not offer any kind of restriction over the taxation power of a state. It is necessary to examine what guarantees this article provides for property rights. When does a difference in treatment constitute discrimination in relation to property rights? The right to property is one of the most interfered rights of the Convention. All tax laws, economic, environmental and planning regulations interfere with property rights. Most of these regulations make a distinction between different social and economic groups and different industries, etc. One of the most difficult questions here is when such a difference constitutes discrimination on the grounds of property. For example, most progressive taxes are established on the grounds of difference in terms of property. The Court's case-law regarding the application of the prohibition of discrimination with relation to property rights will be examined.

There is a strong relation between P1-1 and Article 6 because while P1-1 guarantees the substance of the right to property, Article 6 provides judicial procedural guarantees for civil rights. The Court sometimes finds it unnecessary to examine claims under Article 6 and examines the case only under P1-1 and sometimes *vice versa*. In some cases it examines the complaints under both Article 6 and P1-1.

Article 15 gives the contracting states a power of derogation from their obligations under P1-1 in times of war or other public emergency. The accession of new states from Eastern Europe to the Convention may raise the application of Article 15 because some of the new members of the Convention such as Russia and the former Yugoslav Republic of Macedonia are experiencing active internal armed conflicts. Therefore, it is necessary to examine to what extent property rights guarantee under P1-1 can be derogated and what are the principles applicable to the derogation of property rights. What is the effect of the derogability on the place of the right to property within the hierarchy of rights?

8.2. Just Satisfaction For Violations Of P1-1

The European Convention on Human Rights provides in Article 41:

> If the Court finds that there has been a violation of the Convention or the protocols thereto, and the internal law of the High Contracting Party concerned allows only partial reparation to be made, the Court shall, if necessary, afford just satisfaction to the injured party.[1]

The European Court's practice of just satisfaction will be examined here only in terms of property rights cases.[2] There is nothing special about property rights cases

[1] Article 41 is a simplified version of former Article 50 by the Protocol 11.

[2] See generally Mowbray, A. R., "The European Court of Human Rights' Approach to Just Satisfaction"(1997) *Public Law* 647; Mowbray, A.R., *Cases and Materials on the European Convention on Human Rights* (Butterworths: London, 2000) ch.19; Harris, D., O'Boyle, M. and Warbrick, C., *Law of the European Convention on Human Rights*

in terms of procedural issues relating to just satisfaction claims, therefore general principles regarding the examination of a just satisfaction claim by the Court are also applicable for a case concerning just satisfaction claims in breach of property rights.

The Court does not afford just satisfaction without a claim from the applicant. If there is no claim for compensation, the Court does not consider *ex officio* whether the applicant has been harmed.[3] The claim for compensation should be presented by the 'injured party'. The Court interprets the term 'injured party' as synonymous with the term 'victim' as used in Article 34 to establish standing to file a case. That is, the person directly affected by the failure to observe the Convention can claim just satisfaction. However, under some circumstances an indirect victim can also apply to the Court.[4] The Court is also very strict about the limitation period for just satisfaction claims. According to Rule 60 of the Rules of Court, claims for just satisfaction should be set out in the written observations on the merits or if no such written observations are filed, in a special document filed within two months from the decision declaring the application admissible. In the past the Court rejected just satisfaction claims because they were not filed in time.[5] In addition, a claimant must supply itemised particulars of all claims made, together with relevant supporting documents or vouchers.

If the Court finds that the question of just satisfaction is not ready for decision, it may reserve the question and examine in a separate phase.[6] In the past, most of the just satisfaction claims were decided separately from the judgement in merits, which increased the length of the proceedings.[7] The Court retains this practice today only for complex cases. However, in most of the property rights cases where valuation is difficult, the rulings on just satisfaction are delivered separately.[8] One advantage of reserving a just satisfaction claim is that it gives the parties a chance to discuss the form of reparation and to reach a friendly settlement.[9]

(Butterworths: London, 1995) pp.682 ff; Van Dijk and Van Hoof, *Theory and Practice of the European Convention on Human Rights* (Kluwer Law Int: London, 1998) (third edition) pp.239 ff.

[3] *Ambruosi v. Italy*, Judgement of 19 October 2000 (App. No. 31227/96).

[4] *Colozza and Rubinat v. Italy*, Judgement of 12 February 1985, Series A, No. 89.

[5] See for example *Vendittelli v. Italy*, Judgement of 18 July 1994, Series A, No. 293-A.

[6] See Rule 75 of the Rules of Court.

[7] Shelton, D., *Remedies in International Human Rights Law* (OUP: Oxford, 1999) p.191.

[8] See *Sporrong and Lönnroth v. Sweden,* Judgement of 23 September 1982 Series A, No. 52; *Pine Valley Developments Ltd. and Others v. Ireland*, Judgement of 29 November 1991, Series A, No 222; *Papamichalopoulos and Others v. Greece,* Judgement of 24 June 1993, Series A, No.260-B; *Beyeler v. Italy*, Judgement of 5 January 2000 (App. No.33202/96; *The Former King of Greece and Others v. Greece*, Judgement of 23 November 2000 (App. No. 25701/94).

[9] See for example *Holy Monasteries v. Greece* Judgement of 01 September 1997, *Reports* 1997-V; *Katikaridis and Others v. Greece*, Judgement of 31 March 1998, *Reports* 1998-II; *Tsomtsos and Others v. Greece*, Judgement of 31 March 1998, *Reports* 1998-II.

8.2.1. Remedies for Violations of Property Rights

One of the traditional philosophical approaches to remedial law is Aristotle's famous theory of corrective (or remedial) justice. The theory of corrective justice requires that consequences of a wrongdoing should be restored by way of taking from the aggressor any gain he may have secured and to give it to the victim as a redress for his loss. In this way, equality between the wrongdoer and the victim is restored.[10] This theory is compatible with most of the theories justifying a right to property. For example, different forms of the labour theory of property claim that property is the fruit of the labour, so if someone acquires another's property by way of wrongdoing, such acquisition is not justified and it should be rectified. Therefore, the theory of corrective justice is not contrary to a labour theory of property. The same thing can be said for the autonomy-based freedom theory of property, which is adopted as basic justification of property in this book.

The economic theory of law provides a different theory for remedies. According to this theory, principles of the law should be derived from the effectiveness doctrine of economic analysis. That is, economic interests are the main driver of human behaviour and therefore, law should observe the realities of economic behaviour in order to be efficient. Accordingly, an activity that is profitable even after payment of all the costs it imposes on others is said to be efficient and economical. This approach is compatible with the utilitarian theories justifying property rights.

While corrective justice determines the consequences of a wrongful act, economic theory defines the substance of what constitutes the wrong.[11] The deterrence rationale seems inherent in the economic model and its cost benefit analysis. According to this theory, the remedies (or compensations) are justified as long as the cost to society of paying them will deter possible wrongdoers from imposing greater costs in the future. This approach may lead to losing the relationship between the compensation to be paid and the victim's loss and its magnitude, because the remedies are set at a level to deter the misconduct, a level that may be higher or lower than the actual losses of the victim.[12] Deterrence is a significant element when remedial law is the issue. However, it may give rise to complex questions such as what is deterrent and whether it changes from one person to another. For example, is a level of award that would serve to deter an individual enough when the state is the defendant?[13]

Economic theory, however, can hardly be used in human rights violations because human rights are based on moral theories rather than on an economic calculation.[14] Therefore, it seems reasonable to follow the aims of the corrective

---

[10] Aristotle, *The Ethics* (J.A.K. Thompson trans., 1955), p.148.
[11] Posner, R., "The Concept of Corrective Justice in Recent Theories of Tort Law" (1981) 10 *Journal of Legal Studies* 187.
[12] Shelton, D., *op.cit.*7 p. 41.
[13] *Ibid*, p.51.
[14] Dworkin, R., *Takings Rights Seriously* (Duckworth: London, 1977); see also Lyons, D., "Utility and Rights" in Waldron, J. (ed.) *Theories of Rights* (OUP: Oxford, 1984).

justice theory when remedies for violations of human rights are being determined. That is, the remedial award should aim to restore the effects of the wrongful act.

Under this approach, the nature of a redress for violation of human rights will depend on the nature of the wrongful act and its consequences. In the last chapter, the conditions of legitimate interference with property rights were examined. If the public authorities fail to meet those conditions, a violation of property rights occurs. In order to be able to redress such a violation, it is necessary to determine in what condition the public authorities have failed and in what position the applicant would have been had no violation occurred. It was suggested that if the public authorities fail to meet the lawfulness or public interest requirements, the remedy should be nullification of the act and the restitution of property because had the act met those requirements the act would not have been valid and limitation on property rights would not have existed. But if the failure is in the requirements of compensation or proportionality, the remedy should be compensation of material and immaterial losses. In any case, if there is a violations costs and expenses should be awarded because those expenses are directly linked to the wrongful act.

Here the European Court's practice of affording just satisfaction for violations of property rights will be examined. In the past the ambiguous language of the former Article 50 gave rise to controversy over the jurisdiction of the Court to award just satisfaction. The phrase '...if the internal law of the said Party allows only partial reparation' was interpreted as preventing the Court from awarding just satisfaction if there is a possibility of *restitutio in integrum* in domestic law. Indeed this passage is meaningful only in the context of international law of injury to aliens and represents the logic of treaty provisions on the enforcement of arbitral awards in inter-state proceedings from which the language of (former) Article 50 was derived.[15] However, it has no sound function in the European human rights system because one of the conditions of admissibility of an application is the exhaustion of domestic remedies. The Court ruled in the *Ringeisen* case that the necessity to apply (former) Article 50 exists once a responded government refuses the applicant reparation to which he considers he is entitled.[16]

8.2.1.1. Awards The term 'satisfaction' in the international law of state responsibility for injury to aliens comprises a number of remedies such as restitution, payment of pecuniary and non-pecuniary reparations, punishment of the guilty and assurances as to future conduct, and declaration of the wrong.[17] The European Court has awarded one or more of the following remedies so far: a declaration of violation, restitution,[18] pecuniary damages, non-pecuniary damages

---

[15] Article 50 was modelled after Article 32 of the 1928 General Act on Arbitration and Article 10 of the German-Swiss Treaty on Arbitration and Conciliation.

[16] *Ringeisen v. Austria*, Judgement of 22 June 1972 (Article 50), Series A No.15.

[17] Shelton, *op.cit.* 7 p.151.

[18] The Court ruled restitution only in two cases as an option for the responded state. See *Papamichalopoulos and Others v. Greece,* Judgement of 31 October 1995 (Article 50);

and costs and expenses. It ruled on various occasions that it has no jurisdiction to make 'consequential orders' such as directions requiring states to undertake specific actions or recommendations to the state to redress violations.[19]

8.2.1.1.1. Declaration of violation The Court did not demonstrate much enthusiasm for Article 41 from the beginning and interpreted its powers under Article 41 narrowly. In numerous cases it found that the judgement alone afforded just satisfaction for the injury. It can be said that a determination of violation of internationally guaranteed human rights by a state has great importance because governments generally do not want to be accounted in the international arena as a violator of human rights. Having a credible and authoritative finding of the facts and a legal determination that the state violated the applicant's human rights establishes the truth of the allegations and vindicates the victim. However, such a declaratory judgement generally has prospective effect only; as such it will rarely serve to redress the consequences of the harm already suffered.[20]

The European Court often denies non-pecuniary damages by finding that the ruling that the state has violated a right is, in itself, adequate to afford just satisfaction, even where the violation has already occurred and is ongoing.[21] The Court, thus, uses the declaratory judgements as a retrospective remedy, and not only a prospective measure to prevent future violations. The Court has never stated any basis other than 'equity' for distinguishing cases where non-pecuniary damages are necessary from those where they are not.

However only in exceptional property rights cases has the Court applied this doctrine. In the early *Marckx* case the Court found, among others, violation of Article 14 in conjunction with P1-1 in respect of limitations on the right of unmarried women to dispose of property. The Court ruled that the finding of a violation of the Convention rights constituted sufficient satisfaction.[22] In the

---

Brumerascu v. Romania, Judgement of 23 January 2001 (Just Satisfaction), (App. No. 28342/95).

[19] The authority of the European Court to order reparations under Article 41 is much narrower than that of its Inter-American counterpart. The corresponding provision of Inter-American Convention, Article 63, affords wider powers to the Inter-American Court in this respect. The American Convention provides in Article 63(1) that 'If the Court finds that there has been a violation of a right or freedom protected by this Convention, the Court shall rule that the injured party be ensured the enjoyment of his right or freedom that was violated. It shall also rule, if appropriate, that the consequences of the measure or situation that constituted the breach of such right or freedom be remedied and that fair compensation be paid to the injured party.' For a detailed examination of the Inter-American system on remedies see Pasqualucci, Jo M., "Victim Reparations in the Inter-American Human Rights System: A Critical Assessment of Current Practice and Procedure" (1996) 18 *Michigan Journal of International Law* 1.

[20] Shelton, *op.cit.* 7 p.200.

[21] A survey revealed that the Court found declaratory judgements as sufficient remedy in 42 of the 108 cases. See Harris, D., O'Boyle, M. and Warbrick, C., *Law of the European Convention on Human Rights* (Butterworths: London, 1995) p.685, fn.9.

[22] *Marckx v. Belgium*, Judgement of 13 June 1979, Series A no.31 para.68.

Pressos Compania Naviera case the Court examined the issue of just satisfaction for the twenty-fifth applicant. While the Court afforded financial awards for pecuniary damage, it held that declaration of violation affords just satisfaction for moral injuries.[23] Similarly in the *Ambruosi* case the Court did not afford any financial awards since the applicant did not file a claim for just satisfaction and the Court stated that the finding of a violation constituted in itself sufficient compensation for any non-pecuniary damage suffered by the applicant.[24] However, these cases are very exceptional in property rights violations. The Court generally affords financial awards for pecuniary and non-pecuniary damages if it found violation of property rights.

8.2.1.1.2. Restitutio in integrum Reparation under Article 41 is intended to place the applicant as far as possible in the position he would have been had the violation of his rights not taken place. The Court explained the objective of the European system on many occasions. Accordingly, a judgement in which the Court finds a breach imposes on the respondent state a legal obligation to put an end to the breach and make reparations for its consequences in such a way as to restore as far as possible the situation existing before the breach.[25] Therefore, the main objective of the reparation system of the European Convention is *restitutio in integrum*. As indicated in Chapter 7 the right to property protects the thing itself, not only the economic value of the thing. Therefore, the best remedy for violation of property rights is restitution of it. Monetary compensation is only a replacement for property if its restitution is impossible.

Nevertheless, the Court leaves to states to choose the means by which they will comply with a judgement in which the Court has found a breach. So if the nature of the breach allows for *restitutio in integrum,* it is for the respondent state to effect it because, according to the Court, it has neither the power nor the practical possibility of doing so itself.[26] Repeatedly the Court has declared that it lacks jurisdiction to direct the states to take certain measures such as the annulment or nullification of a legislative or other act or removal of a criminal record or abolishing a sentence, or issuing an order to release a prisoner, etc.[27] Although the Court's approach is compatible with the letter of Article 41 and the contracting states' intention revealed in *travaux préparatoires*[28] it is not the only possible interpretation of the article. One may interpret Article 41 under the teleological approach to the Convention. The Court interprets the Convention as a living

---

[23] *Pressos Compania Naviera S. A. and Others v. Belgium,* Judgement of 3 July 1997 (Article 50), *Reports* 1997-IV.

[24] *Ambruosi v. Italy*, Judgement of 19 October 2000 (App. No.31227/96).

[25] *Papamichalopoulos and Others v. Greece,* Judgement of 31 October 1995 (Article 50), Series A, No.330-B, § 34.

[26] *Ibid.* § 34.

[27] See for example *Corigliano v. Italy*, Judgement of 10 December 1982, Series A, No. 57; *Bozano v. Italy*, Judgement of 18 December 1986, Series A, No. 111.

[28] Council of Europe, *Collected Edition of the 'Travaux Préparatoires' of the European Convention on Human Rights* (Berlin, 1984) Vol. IV p.44.

instrument and an effective and real guarantee of the fundamental rights.[29] On the other hand, it interprets its powers under Article 41 so narrowly that it makes that aim practically impossible. In order to ensure that the protection of the Convention is effective, the remedies sanctioned by the Court should be capable of ending the violation. Otherwise national authorities may prefer paying the compensation and continuing to violate fundamental rights.

Although the Court is unwilling to change its approach in this respect, in other areas of the Convention, it has ruled in two property rights cases that restitution of the property would be the best remedy if it were possible, and held restitution as an optional type of just satisfaction. As indicated above in the violation of property rights, the restitution of property is necessary only in cases of failure of public authorities to meet requirements of lawfulness or public interest. If the national authorities failed to comply with the requirements of compensation or proportionality, the appropriate remedy would be compensating the pecuniary damage suffered or ordering the application of less restrictive measures. However, the latter seems unlikely to be ordered under the current approach of the Court.

The Court afforded the restitution of property as an optional just satisfaction in the *Papamichalopoulos*[30] and *Brumerascu*[31] cases in both of which the Court ruled in the judgements on merits that the interferences with property rights were unlawful. In the former, though the applicants' property was transferred to the Greek Navy during the dictatorial regime in 1967, they did not receive a form of redress for twenty-eight years and they were not allowed to use, dispose of or even access their property. The Court, in its judgement on merits,[32] found a *de facto* expropriation of property which is unlawful and contrary to the Convention. In the just satisfaction judgement the Court ruled, making reference to the decision of the Permanent Court of International Justice in the *Chorzow Factory Case* on 13 September 1928,[33] that the return of the land in issue would put the applicants as far as possible in a situation equivalent to the one in which they would have been had there not been a breach of P1-1. The Court also held that if the respondent state failed to make restitution within six months from the delivery of judgement, it should pay the applicants pecuniary damage for loss of enjoyment and the current value of the property.

Similarly in the *Brumerascu*[34] case the Court, finding a violation of P1-1 in the judgement on merits, considered that in the circumstances of the case the return of the property in question would put the applicant as far as possible in the situation equivalent to the one in which he would have been if there had not been a

---

[29] See above Chapter 5.

[30] *Papamichalopoulos and Others v. Greece*, Judgement of 31 October 1995 (Article 50), Series A, No.330-B, § 34.

[31] *Brumerascu v. Romania*, Judgement of 23 January 2001 (just satisfaction), (App. No. 28342/95).

[32] *Papamichalopoulos and Others v. Greece*, Judgement of 24 June 1993, Series A, No.260-B.

[33] Collection of Judgements of PCIJ, Series A no.17 p.47.

[34] *Brumerascu v. Romania*, Judgement of 28 October 1999 (App. No. 28342/95).

breach of P1-1. And it ruled that failing such restitution within six months from the delivery of judgement, the respondent state should pay the current value of the property to the applicant as a pecuniary damage (total 181,400 USD).

Although the Court found the interferences with property as unlawful in a number of other cases, it did not hold the respondent states liable to return to the applicants the properties in question. In the *Hentrich*[35] case, for example, although the Court found the deprivation of the applicant of his property unlawful, it did not rule for restitution of property in its just satisfaction judgement.[36] Similarly, in the *Vasilescu*[37] case the Court found that the deprivation of the applicant of her gold coins was unlawful and constituted a *de facto* confiscation; nevertheless it did not rule for the restitution of property but ruled for financial awards. However, in both these cases the reason why the Court did not require restitution is that the governments stated that restitution of the properties in question was impossible. The obstacle against restitution was, in the former, French law, and the authorities' failure to trace the property in question, in the latter. Therefore, there is no contradiction between these judgements and those mentioned above. Restitution of property is necessary only if it is possible. But it is questionable whether a domestic legal obstacle can be accepted as a real impossibility in international human rights law.

Since the Court has never found, so far, any government which has failed to meet the public interest requirement, there is no judgement in which the Court examines whether restitution is necessary. It can be said that there is no reason to refuse a restitution claim if the Court finds in a case that the interference with property is not in the public interest.

8.2.1.1.3. Pecuniary damages Compensation of losses suffered by the victim as a result of violation is the most common means of satisfaction if *restitutio in integrum* is not possible. The sum of money awarded as damages is designed to compensate the victims for harm they suffered, and it is intended to make the applicant as well off as he would have been had the violation never occurred. Corrective justice requires the payment of the full value of the injury to the victim.[38] Nevertheless, financial awards are sometimes incapable of restoring or replacing the rights that have been violated. Money sometimes cannot replace the thing lost by the violation of a human right. Another important issue is that valuation of loss is nearly always imperfect, though valuation of property losses is relatively easier than losses in violation of other human rights.

On the other hand, compensation is the best alternative when no restitution is possible and monetary awards restore the status quo to some extent. At least it is better than nothing. Considering the economic character of property

---

[35] *Hentrich v. France*, Judgement of 22 September 1994, Series A, No. 296-A.

[36] *Hentrich v. France*, Judgement of 03 March 1995 (Article 50), Series A No 320-A.

[37] *Vasilescu v. Romania*, Judgement of 22 May 1998 *Reports* 1998-III.

[38] Shelton, *op.cit.* 7 p.214.

rights, restorative capability of compensation is especially high in property rights cases. The biggest problem in this respect is the calculation of losses.

Now it is time to look at the European Court's jurisprudence on pecuniary damages in violation of property rights. Which losses do constitute material damages under the Court's jurisprudence? And how should the damages be calculated? The problems that will be raised here are not unique to property rights cases. Calculation of material damages when a human right is breached is not always easy and can be beyond the Court's knowledge. Therefore utilising expert opinion is a viable option for the Court though it has not developed a stable precedence in this regard.

In its first judgement regarding the just satisfaction for violation of property rights, the Court had to decide what losses the applicant had suffered because of long-term expropriation permits.[39] The applicants argued that a lifting of the expropriation permits and construction restrictions on the property could not be regarded as amounting to *restitutio in integrum* because of the economic losses which occurred during the years when use was restricted. So they claimed pecuniary damage under two headings: loss of net income, since the properties concerned had yielded only a very poor return during the periods in question, and diminution of the market value of the properties. They also claimed that they had not been able to invest in their properties, since the Stockholm City Council would never have given permission for a full-scale redevelopment, which would have been the only reasonable course in financial terms.

The applicants argued that the assessment of the damage should be based on the probable increase in value if there had been no expropriation permits and no prohibitions on construction. They requested the Court to award 13,284,540 Swedish crowns (SEK) to the Sporrong Estate and 10,912,303 SEK to Mrs. Lönnroth.

The Court's judgement in this case was far from being a clear guidance and included some contradiction. It agreed that compensation was necessary; however, it did not find the applicants' claims reasonable. The Court accepted neither that the return from the properties in question diminished nor the market value of the properties had fallen in real terms. It stated that a comparison between the beginning and the end of the periods of damage did not show that the applicants were prejudiced in financial terms. However, this did not mean that there was no loss; there were, in fact, other factors which should be considered. Firstly there were limitations on the utilisation of the properties. In addition, during the period in question the value of properties fell. Furthermore, there were difficulties in obtaining loans, secured by way of mortgage. The applicants were also left in prolonged uncertainty about the fate of their properties. As a result, without distinguishing between pecuniary and non-pecuniary damages, the Court awarded a total sum of 1,000,000 SEK.[40]

---

[39] *Sporrong and Lönnroth v. Sweden,* Judgement of 18 December 1984 (Article 50) Series A No. 88.

[40] *Ibid*.

The Court did not explain the basis of its valuation. Neither did it find acceptable the 'hypothetical redevelopment' method proposed by the applicants nor the 'actual use' method put forward by the government. It did not offer another method of calculation either. Therefore, it left the problem of calculating the pecuniary damage resulting from lost opportunities and diminution of value unsolved.

Later in the *Loizidou*[41] case the applicant claimed compensation for the loss of use of land and lost opportunity to develop or lease it based on a Valuation Report that estimated the loss at CYP (Cyprus Pounds) 621,900 from 1990 (the date Turkey accepted the compulsory jurisdiction of the Court). The Report's method of assessment presupposes that property prices would have risen consistently by 12 per cent each year from 1974 until 1997 and that the applicant would have actually sought to or have been able to rent her plots of land at 6 per cent of this enhanced value. The Court found the report speculative and presumed a consistent rise in the market value of land for twenty-three years questionable. Considering the uncertainties the Court awarded CYP 300,000 as a pecuniary damage on an equitable basis.

In cases of deprivation of property, the Court generally awards the current market value of the property.[42] However, it does not usually employ experts to assess property valuation. For example, in the *Hentrich*[43] case the applicant claimed FF (French Francs) 2,875,550 for unlawful loss of her land. The Court suggested that restitution of the land would be the best remedy – without making an order to that effect – and that failing restitution the calculation of pecuniary damage must be based on the current market value of the land. Consequently, the Court, without employing experts to value the land, awarded FF 800,000 on an equitable basis. Similarly in the *Vasilescu*[44] case the applicant claimed USD (US Dollars) 30,000 for loss of her gold coins; the government valued the items at USD 3,750. But the Court awarded FF 60,000 (USD 10,000) on an equitable basis. In the *Brumerascu*[45] case the applicant claimed USD 250,600 for loss of his land and a building on it relying on an expert report. The Court assessed the current market value of the properties in question at USD 215,000 using the prices on the Bucharest property market. One exception to this approach is the *Papamichalopoulos*[46] case where the Court employed expert reports as the basis of its awards.

---

[41] *Loizidou v. Turkey*, Judgement of 28 July 1998 (Article 50) *Reports* 1998-IV.

[42] *Papamichalopoulos and Others v. Greece*, Judgement of 31 October 1995 (Article 50); *Hentrich v. France*, Judgement of 03 March 1995 (Article 50), Series A No 320-A; *Brumerascu v. Romania*, Judgement of 23 January 2001 (just satisfaction), (App. No.28342/95); *Vasilescu v. Romania*, Judgement of 22 May 1998, Reports 1998-III.

[43] *Hentrich v. France*, Judgement of 03 March 1995 (Article 50), Series A No 320-A.

[44] *Vasilescu v. Romania*, Judgement of 22 May 1998, *Reports* 1998-III.

[45] *Brumerascu v. Romania*, Judgement of 23 January 2001 (just satisfaction), (App. No.28342/95.

[46] *Papamichalopoulos and Others v. Greece,* Judgement of 31 October 1995 (Article 50).

Difficult issues of property valuation arose in a number of Turkish cases regarding the burning of houses by the military forces in the southern part of the country, in which the Court found violations of Article 3, Article 8 and P1-1. The applicants in the *Selçuk and Asker*[47] case claimed pecuniary damages for loss of their houses, cultivated land, household property, livestock, and one applicant's mill, as well as the cost of alternative accommodation. But they did not substantiate their claims as to the quantity and value of their lost property with any documentary or other evidence. Neither the government nor the Commission provided any detailed findings or comments. Therefore, the Court determined the pecuniary awards, by necessity, on an equitable basis. In the similar case of *Mentes and Others*[48] the government proposed a valuation method and the Court agreed. The Court based its awards on the average rate per square metre proposed by the government and 50 per cent of the surface area claimed by the applicants. Although the applicants did not include a value for their personal property, agricultural machinery and tools, and livestock and feed, the Court awarded compensation for such losses as well on an equitable basis. In all these cases the Court did not require the applicants to prove their losses, accepting that the destruction of records and the security situation in the area created particular difficulties in adducing evidence.

In cases where the property interfered with in violation of P1-1 is a definite sum of money the Court awards interest-added total sums as just satisfaction. In the *Stran Greek Refineries*[49] case the Court found that retroactive annulment of an arbitral award by legislation constituted breach of P1-1 and awarded to the applicants the entire amount of the arbitral award and added interest from the date of judgement (total sum of USD 30,863,828.50).

However, if there is a dispute over the amount of money in question the Court determines the amount of just satisfaction on an equitable basis. In the *Pressos Compania Naviera*[50] case, the Court found that retrospective annulment of tort claims by legislation constituted a violation of property rights. Although the case was not ready for decision in terms of just satisfaction for other applicants, it was ready for the twenty-fifth applicant. There was no dispute over the damage but there was a dispute about fault of the government; therefore, the Court awarded half of the damage suffered as a just satisfaction instead of examining the degree of the fault of the responded state in the accident.

In a number of Turkish cases, the Court found violation of P1-1 because the government delayed the payment of additional compensation for expropriation and applied a statutory interest rate far less than the inflation rate. In those cases,

---

[47] *Selçuk and Asker v. Turkey,* Judgement of 24 April 1998, *Reports* 1998-II; see also *Akdivar and Others v. Turkey*, Judgement of 1 April 1998(Article 50) *Reports* 1998-II.

[48] *Mentes and Others v. Turkey*, Judgement of 24 April 1998, *Reports* 1998-II.

[49] *Stran Greek Refineries and Stratis Andreadis v. Greece,* Judgement of 9 December 1994, Series A, No. 301-B.

[50] *Pressos Compania Naviera S. A. and Others v. Belgium,* Judgement of 3 July 1997 (Article 50), *Reports* 1997-IV.

the Court awarded the difference between the inflation rate and the statutory interest rate as just satisfaction.[51]

To sum up, the Court awards the current value of the lost property, diminution of value and lost opportunities as pecuniary damages for violations of property rights. However, its practice regarding valuation is inconsistent. It rarely employs experts to determine the value of the losses suffered by the victim. Mostly the Court affords some monetary compensation on an equitable basis, but it does not explain how the amounts have been determined. It is suggested that the Court should employ experts to determine real damage as much as possible to restore the injury suffered by the victim. And sometimes, it awards a total sum without separating out pecuniary and non-pecuniary damages, and costs and expenses. This causes difficulty for applicants and governments because in some countries only non-pecuniary damages are exempted from tax.

8.2.1.1.4.Non-pecuniary damages Non-pecuniary damages comprise physical pain and suffering as well as mental anguish including anxiety, distress, and feelings of injustice, harassment, and humiliation.[52] In the cases of violation of property rights, the non-pecuniary injury is mostly psychological rather than physical. The European Court, in some cases, has presumed non-pecuniary injury. In other cases, though rarely in property rights cases, it has found that the judgement itself constitutes just satisfaction for non-pecuniary injury. While reaching such a conclusion, the Court generally considered the attitude and identity of the applicant. The Court denied affording monetary awards to terrorists,[53] convicted criminals, and homosexuals.[54] This approach of the Court has been criticised rightly by Wolcher.[55] She argues that the Court's law of remedies fails to distinguish in a principled fashion between legal and extra legal (ethical or political) grounds for decision.

The applicant is required to substantiate his allegations regarding moral damage and to show a link of causality with the breach found, but the Court has sensibly recognised that such matters as pain and distress cannot always be the

[51] *Aka v. Turkey*, Judgement of 23 September 1998, Reports 1998-VI, §43; *Gaganus and Others v. Turkey*, Judgement of 5 June 2001 (App. No. 39335/98); *Akkus v. Turkey*, Judgement of 9 July 1997, Reports 1997-IV; *Yasar and Others v. Turkey*, Judgement of 14 November 2000 (App. No.27697/95); *Hamdi Celebi v. Turkey*, Judgement of 30 January 2001(and 23 other decisions on the same date) (App. Nos. 19264-19288/92); *Ismihan Ozel and Others v. Turkey*, Judgement of 27 February 2001 (App. No. 31963/96); *Ali Ozturk v. Turkey,* Judgement of 10 April 2001 (and 24 other decisions on the same date) (App. Nos. 19289- 19312/92); *Gulnahar Calkan v. Turkey*, Judgement of 5 June 2001(and 19 other decisions on the same date) (App. Nos.19661-19683/92).

[52] Shelton, *op.cit.* 7 p.226.

[53] *McCann and Others v. UK*, Judgement of 27 September 1995, Series A no. 324.

[54] *Ibid.* p.205.

[55] Wolcher, Louis E., "The Paradox of Remedies: The Case of International Human Rights Law" (2000) 38 *Columbia Journal of Transnational Law* 515.

object of concrete proof and has concluded in some cases that such damage must have occurred.[56]

Although the Court takes account of the respondent government's conduct when determining the moral damage, it has refused to award added amounts in the nature of aggravated or punitive damages. In the above mentioned *Loizidou* case the applicant claimed CYP 621,900 in non-pecuniary damages for her distress, frustration, and feelings of hopelessness as well as for factors related to the considerations of public interest and public order of Europe. The applicant stated that a high award should be made to act as an inducement to the government to observe the legal standards set out in the Convention and should take into account the dilatory attitude of the government and its unfounded objections. The Court awarded CYP 20,000 for the applicant's anguish and feeling of helplessness and frustration, but expressly rejected consideration of the general situation.[57]

It is difficult to calculate non-pecuniary loss. There is no objective test to measure the severity of a victim's pain, though common human experience recognises the reality of physical and emotional suffering. Therefore, the inherently subjective reaction to claims of pain and suffering may lead judges to award widely varying amounts for similar injuries.[58] The European Court awarded monetary compensation for moral injury in almost all of the property cases where it found violation of P1-1 if the applicant claimed. However, it is difficult to find consistent criteria employed by the Court to determine the amount of the compensation. Still, some elements affecting the amount of compensation can be inferred from these judgements. The conduct of the parties and the duration of the violation seem to affect the amount of the compensation awarded by the Court. The Court occasionally awards the full amount claimed by the applicant. For example, in the *Scollo*[59] case the Court found the violation of P1-1 in respect of suspension of the enforcement of an eviction order for a long time and failure of the respondent state to provide police assistance. The applicant claimed ITL 30,000,000 in respect of non-pecuniary damage. The Court awarded the whole of this amount as a non-pecuniary loss.

However, generally the Court awards a small proportion of the claim. For example in the *Aka*[60] case the applicant claimed USD 20, 000 in respect of non-pecuniary damage which he and his family had suffered through the poverty and insecurity they had endured through not receiving sufficient compensation for the expropriation of their land, which had been their only means of subsistence and their only home. But the Court awarded USD 1,000 for non-pecuniary damage on an equitable basis. The Court awarded the same amount (USD 1,000) as non-

---

[56] Harris, D., O'Boyle, M. and Warbrick, C., *Law of the European Convention on Human Rights* (Butterworths: London, 1995) p. 687.

[57] *Loizidou v. Turkey,* Judgement of 28 July 1998 (Article 50) (App. No. 15318/89), *Reports* 1998-IV.

[58] Shelton, *op.cit.* 7 p.261.

[59] *Scollo v. Italy*, Judgement of 28 September 1995, (App. No. 19133/91) Series A, No.315-C.

[60] *Aka v. Turkey*, Judgement of 23 September 1998, Reports 1998-VI.

pecuniary damage in more than 100 similar (inflation) cases. But this does not make it easier for us to understand the Court's rationale in awarding non-pecuniary damage, because duration of the violation, amount of the pecuniary damage, personal conditions of the applicants were all different but, non-pecuniary injury was the same.

One question related to the non-pecuniary damage for violations of P1-1 is whether legal persons can suffer non-pecuniary injury. In the cases where the applicants were legal persons, the issue of moral injury was not discussed properly. In *Sporrong*[61] the Court did not make a distinction between pecuniary and non-pecuniary damages and awarded a total sum. In *Greek Refineries,*[62] the applicant did not claim non-pecuniary damage. In *Pressos Compania,*[63] the Court found the judgement itself sufficient satisfaction for non-pecuniary damages. But in *Immobiliare Saffi,*[64] the Court expressed its unwillingness to rule on whether a legal person can experience anxiety, which merits compensation, due to the infringement of its property rights. It held that 'as regards non-pecuniary damage, the Court considers that it is unnecessary to examine whether a commercial company may allege that it has sustained non-pecuniary damage through anxiety as, having regard to the facts of the case, it decides to make no award under this head'. It is suggested that the Court should express that legal persons cannot claim non-pecuniary damage by its nature.

To sum up the Court has not established clear criteria about when and to what extent non-pecuniary damages should be awarded. It has tended simply to recite that it has made the assessment on an equitable basis. It is suggested that to ensure that non-pecuniary injury awards are not just matters of *ad hoc* vague judgement, the Court should identify the criteria it utilises in determining the levels of awards in particular cases. For example, the duration and severity of violation and arbitrariness in public authorities' conduct can be elements of assessment.

8.2.2. Concluding Remarks

The violation of human rights constitutes a kind of constitutional tort and remedies for such violations should be capable of restoring the situation previous to violation. For an effective protection of human rights the Court should take the just satisfaction issue seriously and treat the violation of Convention rights as an autonomous European tort. The Court's approach to remedies seems to represent the corrective justice theory. The aim of the remedies, according to the Court, is to redress all the consequences of violation and to re-establish the situation that would have existed had the violation not taken place. The Court has never considered the

---

[61] *Sporrong and Lönnroth v. Sweden,* Judgement of 18 December 1984 (Article 50) Series A No. 88.

[62] *Stran Greek Refineries and Stratis Andreadis v. Greece*, Judgement of 9 December 1994, Series A, No. 301-B.

[63] *Pressos Compania Naviera S. A. and Others v. Belgium,* Judgement of 3 July 1997 (Article 50), *Reports* 1997-IV.

[64] *Immobiliare Saffi v. Italy*, Judgement of 28 July 1999, (App. No. 22774/93).

deterrence element when determining just satisfaction. However, it interprets its powers under Article 41 so narrowly that it makes questionable whether the Court's practice of just satisfaction satisfies requirements of corrective justice. The Court reiterates in almost all cases that the applicants do not have a right to just satisfaction, but the Court has discretion to award compensation. This approach of the Court leads it to award damages on an equitable basis rather than seeking objective criteria in order to determine the real value of the damages. It also consistently rejects the claims requesting it to make consequential orders in order to end violation. The Court leaves the state discretion to choose appropriate means to end and restore the violation.

All these elements make Article 41 a very weak safeguard of fundamental rights. The possibility of realising corrective justice is low. But the corrective justice indicates the minimum that must be done to restore the moral order. It is suggested, thus, that the Court should aim at least to realise corrective justice while determining the just satisfaction awards. The deterrence element can also be considered to prevent violations of human rights. The Court's attempts to rule restitution of property in the cases of unlawful deprivation should be welcomed as positive steps in this regard.

8.3. The Relationship Between the Right to Property and the Right to a Home and Correspondence

Article 8 guarantees respect for home. It provides that 'Everyone has the right to respect for... his home and his correspondence'.

Home and correspondence, as well as being a part of the assets of the owner, are possession within the meaning of P1-1. Therefore, they are under the protection of both Article 8 and P1-1. How can the scopes of these two articles be distinguished in a case concerning an interference with the applicant's house or correspondence?

The Convention organs had to decide what constituted 'home' within the meaning of Article 8 in the *Gillow*[65] case. The Commission and the Court decided that although the applicants had not lived for nineteen years in Guernsey, their evident intention to live in their house in Guernsey made that house their 'home' within the meaning of Article 8. In this case, the Court found violation of Article 8 on the grounds that housing authorities had not granted residence allowance to the applicants, imposing them to bear an excessive individual burden. Although the Commission found violation of P1-1 as well, the Court could not examine the case under P1-1 because the United Kingdom had not extended the application of Protocol No. 1 (P1) to Guernsey.

In the *Larkos*[66] case the issue was one of a difference of treatment between tenants of privately owned dwellings and that of state-owned dwellings in terms of benefiting from a law which protects from eviction on expiry of a lease.

[65] *Gillow v. UK*, Judgement of 24 November 1986, Series A, No.109.
[66] *Larkos v. Cyprus*, Judgement of 18 February 1999, *Reports*- 1999-I.

The applicant claimed breach of Article 14 in connection with the right to home and the right to property. The Court examined the case under Article 14 in conjunction with Article 8 and found a violation. But it refused to examine allegations under P1-1 separately. It can be inferred from this judgement that a tenant's right to live in a rented house constitutes a right to home rather than a right to property. However, such an approach can be seen as acceptable for simple practical reasons. Theoretically, as indicated in Chapter 2, whatever status of rent rights is accepted in domestic private law – property or contract – it constitutes property for the purposes of constitutional property.

The Court has established that entry into a house by the police for search or to prevent breach of peace amounted to interference with the right to home rather than interference with the right to property.[67] Although the applicant in the *McLeod* case claimed before the Commission that entry of the police into her home also constituted breach of her right to peaceful enjoyment of her possessions, she did not reiterate this claim before the Court, and therefore the Court did not examine the issue. The Commission had found no violation of both rights.[68]

According to established case-law the right to home life may give rise to positive obligations for a state to ensure respect for home and family and private life even in the sphere of interpersonal relations. However, the Court held, in the *Velosa Barreto*[69] case, that effective protection of respect for family and private life could not require the existence in national law of legal protection enabling each family to have a home for themselves alone. In this case, the applicant lived with his family and parents-in-law, and had inherited from his parents a house that had been let. He launched proceedings unsuccessfully to have the lease terminated on the grounds that he needed the house as his own home. Such a termination was possible in national law, but the national tribunals decided that there was no sufficient need. The Court ruled that the alleged interference pursued a legitimate aim and did not fail to strike a fair balance between the respective interests. The Court examined this case under P1-1 as well, concluding that the restriction on the applicant's right to terminate his tenant's lease constituted control of the use of property and pursued a legitimate social policy aim, and consequently did not violate the right to peaceful enjoyment of possessions.

Once it is established that premises are a home, then the first protection is of a right of access and occupation, and a right not to be expelled or evicted from them.[70] The Court ruled in a number of Turkish cases that burning of houses by security forces constituted grave violations of both Article 8 and P1-1.[71]

---

[67] *Chappell v. UK*, Judgement of 30 March 1989, Series A No.152-A; *Niemietz v. Germany*, Judgement of 16 December 1992, Series A no. 251-B; *Cremieux v. France*, Judgement of 25 February 1993, Series A No. 256-B; *McLeod v. UK,* Judgement of 23 September 1998, *Reports* 1998- VII.

[68] *McLeod v. UK*, Report of the Commission of 9 April 1997, *Reports* 1998-VII.

[69] *Velosa Barreto v. Portu*gal, Judgement of 21 November 1995, Series A no.334.

[70] Harris, D., O'Boyle, M. and Warbrick, C., *Law of the European Convention on Human Rights* (Butterworths: London, 1995), p.318.

[71] *Akdivar and Others v. Turkey*, Judgement of 16 September 1996, Reports 1996-IV; *Mentes and Others v. Turkey*, Judgement of 28 November 1997, Reports 1997-VIII;

Displacement of people from their homes and prevention of re-access to them also amount to violation of both articles.[72]

The interests protected by home also include the peaceful enjoyment of residence there. Environmental nuisance such as noise, smell, and fumes may constitute interference with the right to a home and private and family life. The Court ruled that excessive noise generated by air traffic amounted to interference with the right to a home[73] and a regulation that allows the increase of such noise during the night-time violated the right to a home.[74] In those cases, the Commission did not find the complaints under P1-1 admissible although it was possible that such noise also might reduce the value of houses. In the *Lopez Ostra*[75] case, the applicant complained about smells, noise, and pollution fumes caused by a plant for the treatment of liquid and solid waste sited a few metres away from her home. Although the Spanish authorities were not directly responsible for the toxic emissions, the Court found that Spain was nevertheless in violation of Article 8, since the local municipality had permitted the plant's construction on its land and subsidised its construction. In this case, the applicant did not raise a complaint under P1-1.

To sum up, it can be said that although the line is sometimes hard to draw, P1-1 protects ownership rights over a house but Article 8 protects the continuity of a peaceful residency in the house. But since residency in a house also constitutes a form of use of property, every interference with home also constitutes an interference with property. Nevertheless, the Court can avoid examining a complaint under P1-1 if it finds that the interference with home concerns only privacy and does not have any economic effect on the house. Such an approach is favourable for simple practical reasons – judicial economics – rather than a theoretical basis. The same approach can also be suggested for interference with correspondence. If an interference of public authorities with correspondence creates any economic effect, it should be considered as interference with both P1-1 and Article 8. But if the actions of public authorities affect only privacy of the individual, it should be considered as an interference with correspondence only.

Selcuk and Asker v. Turkey, Judgement of 24 April 1998, Reports 1998-II; *Aksoy v. Turkey*, Judgement of 18 December 1996, Reports 1996-VI; *Dulas v. Turkey*, Judgement of 30 January 2001, (App. No. 25801/94); *Bilgin v. Turkey*, Judgement of 26 November 2000, (App. No. 23819/94).

[72] *Loizidou v. Turkey*, Judgement of 18 December 1996, *Reports* 1996-VI; *Cyprus v. Turkey*, Judgement of 10 May 2001 (App. No. 25781/94).

[73] *Arrondelle v.UK*, Decision of the Comm. (App. No. 7889/77) DR 19 (1980); *Powell and Rayner v. UK*, Judgement of 21 February 1990, Series A No. 172.

[74] *Hatton and Others v. UK*, Judgement of 2 October 2001 (App. No. 36022/97).

[75] *Lopez Ostra v. Spain*, Judgement of 9 December 1994, Series A. no 303-C.

8.4. The Right not to be Discriminated Against in Respect of Property Rights

8.4.1. The Relationship Between P1-1 And Article 14

Article 14 of the Convention provides:

> The enjoyment of the rights and freedoms set forth in this Convention shall be secured without discrimination on any grounds such as sex, race, colour, language, religion, political or other opinion, national or social origin, association with a national minority, property, birth or other status.

This provision provides protection for individuals against discrimination in respect of the right to property like other rights set out in the Convention. Article 14 does not grant an independent right to non-discrimination, but a parasitic right which depends on other Convention rights[76] and reliance can only be placed upon it when another Convention article is engaged. That is, it does not prohibit every kind of discrimination, but only discrimination against enjoyment of the other Convention rights.[77] Therefore, in order to be able to invoke Article 14 an applicant should prove that there is a Convention right that has been interfered with discriminatively. In terms of the right to property, there should be a possession in the meaning of P1-1, but it is not necessary to establish that P1-1 has been violated.

That is even if the Court has not found violation of P1-1 separately, it can find violation of Article 14 in conjunction with P1-1. For example, in the *Inze*[78] case, the applicant did not allege the violation of P1-1, but he claimed that Austrian law which gave priority to legitimate heirs over illegitimate ones as to who should succeed to an entire farm had violated his rights under Article 14 in conjunction with P1-1. The Court stated that the test was not whether P1-1 had been violated but whether the applicant's claim fell within its ambit. The government disputed that the applicant had not possession within the meaning of P1-1, rather he was seeking a right to acquire possessions. The Court held that since the applicant's mother had died at the material time the applicant had automatically acquired hereditary rights over the estate and become co-owner of it, and he could properly bring the complaint.[79]

The concept of the ambit of the right to property deserves some attention here. Although the Court interprets the concept of possession widely comprising all pecuniary rights and legitimate expectations, in some cases the Court failed to distinguish different rights. For example in the *Van der Mussele*[80] case where the

---

[76]Harris, D., O'Boyle, M. and Warbrick, C., *Law of the European Convention on Human Rights* (Butterworths: London, 1995) p.463.

[77]A new Protocol 12 to ECHR has been opened to signatures that will create a freestanding anti-discrimination provision. See Moon, G., "The Draft Discrimination Protocol to the European Convention on Human Rights: A Progress Report" (2000) *European Human Rights Law Review* 49.

[78] *Inze v. Austria*, Judgement of 28 October 1987, Series A no.126.

[79] See also *Mazurek v. France*, Judgement of 1 February 2000 (App. No. 34406/97).

[80] *Van der Mussele v. Belgium*, Judgement of 23 November 1983 Series A no. 70.

complaint was relating to lack of remuneration for services provided by a trainee advocate and lack of reimbursement of expenses paid out of his own pocket, the Court found P1-1 inapplicable, neither separately nor in conjunction with Article 14, because no debt in favour of the applicant ever arose and the expenses incurred by the applicant were relatively small and resulted from the obligation to perform work compatible with Article 4. The court examined the case only in terms of Article 4. Similarly in the *Schmidt*[81] case the Court decided that the obligation to pay a financial contribution in lieu of service in the fire brigade fell within the scope of Article 4 rather than P1-1. Indeed the Court, taking into account the fact that no man was ever obliged to serve in a fire brigade because the fire service was never short of volunteers, stated that difference in treatment was in the payment of levy. That is, the obligation in practice was simply payment of a fire brigade tax. Therefore, it should have been handled under P1-1.

The second aspect of the relationship between Article 14 and P1-1 is whether it is necessary to examine a case in terms of Article 14 if the Court has already found violation of P1-1. The Court's approach in this regard is well established. Accordingly, it reiterated in many cases that 'where a substantive Article of the Convention has been invoked both on its own and together with Article 14 and a separate breach has been found of the substantive Article, it is not generally necessary for the Court to consider the case under Article 14 also, though the position is otherwise if a clear inequality of treatment in the enjoyment of the right in question is a fundamental aspect of the case'.[82] However, it is difficult to draw a line between the cases in which inequality of treatment is a fundamental aspect and those where it is not. The Court, only in the *Chassagnou*[83] case among property cases, found inequality of treatment – making a difference between small and large landowners in terms of the obligation to transfer hunting rights to local hunting associations – as a fundamental aspect of the case and it examined the case under both P1-1 taken on its own and Article 14 in conjunction with P1-1 and found violations of those articles separately. The Court is unwilling to examine whether Article 14 has been breached if it finds violation of P1-1. Only in the cases where the interference with property is clearly discriminatory does the Court find it necessary to examine P1-1 and Article 14 separately. However, since equality before the law is a significant aspect of the rule of law, it is important to determine whether this principle is respected. Thus, it is suggested that the Court should examine every genuine claim about discrimination properly.

The scope of the protection of Article 14 extends not only to those elements of a right that a state is obliged by the Convention to guarantee, but also those other elements of the right that it voluntarily guarantees.[84] For example, P1-1 does not oblige a state to pay a fixed amount of money as a pension to policy holders of a compulsory social insurance system. But if a government makes an

---

[81] *Schmidt v. Germany*, Judgement of 18 July 1994, Series A no. 291-B.

[82] *Chassagnou and Others v. France*, Judgement of 29 April 1999, Reports 1999/II § 89.

[83] *Ibid.*

[84] Tomlinson, H. and Clayton, R., *The Law of Human Rights* (OUP: Oxford, 2000) p.1235.

unjustified difference between different policy holders, it can constitute a breach of Article 14 in conjunction with P1-1. This was the case in *Gaygusuz v. Austria*[85] where the applicant was refused emergency assistance on the grounds that he did not have Austrian nationality. The applicant was resident in Austria in the material time and he met all the conditions necessary to get emergency assistance except Austrian nationality. The Court found this distinction of treatment on the grounds of nationality as unjustified and discriminatory.

8.4.2. The Meaning of Discrimination

Under Article 14, every difference in treatment will not be conceived as a prohibited discrimination. In the Court's view a difference in treatment is discriminatory if it has no 'objective and reasonable justification', that is, if it does not pursue a legitimate aim or if there is no reasonable relationship of proportionality between the means employed and the aim sought to be realised.[86]

It was argued that Article 14 does not guarantee only a formal equality – equal treatment of equal cases – but also a substantive equality, i.e. unequal treatment of unequal cases in proportion to their inequality.[87] In the area of property rights, this approach may justify a progressive income tax provided the progressive measure is proportional. But it is questionable to what extent this approach is compatible with the non-discrimination rule on the grounds of property. Nevertheless the problem becomes much more complicated when the Court's approach to reverse (or positive) discrimination is taken into consideration. According to the Court, promoting disadvantaged groups through affirmative action is not contrary to Article 14 because certain legal inequalities correct factual inequalities. For example, the Commission decided that a tax advantage to married women had objective and reasonable justification because it encouraged married women back to work.[88] It is another question how this differentiation on the grounds of sex is justifiable. In order to escape from such complex issues the Court leaves some margin of appreciation to states in justification of difference in treatment. But this margin is much narrower than the states' margin of appreciation in justifying interference with property. This will be discussed further below.

In order to establish a breach of Article 14 there should be a) a differential treatment of equal situations b) without a legitimate aim c) or in a disproportionate fashion.[89]

It is for the applicant to prove that there has been a differential treatment of equal situations. To do so the applicant should show (a) that he has been treated substantively different and less favourably than others and (b) that the basis of the distinction is a personal characteristic or status which he exhibits and (c) the others

---

85 *Gaygusuz v. Austria*, Judgement of 16 September 1996 *Reports* 1996-IV.
86 *Chassagnou and Others v. France,* § 91.
87 Van Dijk and Van Hoof, *op.cit.* 2 p.719.
88 *D G and D W Lindsay v. UK,* (Dec. of the Comm.)(1986) 49 DR 181.
89 Van Dijk and van Hoof, *op.cit.* 2 p. 719.

to whom he is comparing himself are in an analogous situation.[90] It is not difficult generally for an applicant to identify how he has been treated less favourably than others. Mostly the differentiation of treatment arises from an obvious rule or practice. For example in the *Marckx,*[91] *Inze,*[92] *and Mazurek*[93] cases Belgian, Austrian and French laws respectively made a distinction between legitimate and illegitimate children in terms of hereditary rights. Or in the *Chassagnou* case there was a differentiation between small and large landowners.

However, it is sometimes difficult for an applicant to establish that he and others are in a similar situation. In *Van der Mussele*[94] the applicant, a trainee advocate who was required to act in legal aid cases on a *pro bono* basis, claimed that he was discriminated against because other professionals analogous to his position such as medical doctors, dentists, and including other lawyers, were not obliged to offer free service. The Court rejected the claim on the grounds that there were fundamental differences between the Bar and other professions cited in terms of legal status, conditions for entry to profession, nature of the functions involved, manner of exercise of these functions, etc.

Thus, it is not sufficient for an applicant to show differential treatment, but he also needs to illustrate that his position is analogous to that of others to whom he compared himself.[95] For example, in *Pine Valley Developments*[96] two applicant property developers successfully claimed that remedial legislation, introduced to correct a misapplication of a planning law, had been drafted so as to exclude them from its benefit but not other holders of planning permission in the same category.

However, the Court does not require an applicant to show on what grounds he has been discriminated against because Article 14 does not limit the prohibited basis of differential treatment. The list of prohibited grounds enunciated in the Article is non-exhaustive and open-ended. It prohibits discrimination on 'any grounds such as sex, race, colour, language, religion, political or other opinion, national or social origin, association with national minority, property, birth or other status'. Therefore, the applicants can claim that they have been discriminated on any personal characteristic or status and the Court accepted a number of other states coming within the residual category such as sexual orientation, marital status, legitimacy, trade union status, military rank, professional status, etc.[97] The Court does not pay much attention to the basis of differential treatment separately but considers it as an element in the examination of whether national authorities

---

[90] Tomlinson and Clayton, *op.cit.*84 p.1238.

[91] *Marckx v. Belgium*, Judgement of 13 June 1979, Series A no.31.

[92] *Inze v. Austria*, Judgement of 28 October 1987, Series A no.126.

[93] *Mazurek v. France*, Judgement of 1 February 2000 (App. No. 34406/97).

[94] *Van der Mussele v. Belgium*, Judgement of 23 November 1983, Series A no.70; see also *Fredin v. Sweden*, Judgement of 18 February 1991, Series A no. 192.

[95] See also *Spadea and Scalabrino v. Italy*, Judgement of 28 September 1995, Series A, No. 315-B.

[96] *Pine Valley Developments Ltd and Others v. Ireland*, Judgement of 29 November 1991, Series A No. 222.

[97] Tomlinson and Clayton, *op.cit.* 84 p.1241.

have provided a reasonable and objective justification for the difference in treatment. Thus, it is better to examine the basis of differential treatment together with the justification for it.

Once the applicant proves that he has been treated differently from those in a similar position, it is for the state to prove that differentiation of treatment has a legitimate aim and that it is proportional.

8.4.3. Justification for Differential Treatment

As mentioned above, every difference in treatment does not constitute discrimination under Article 14; such a difference, according to the established case-law, is discriminatory only if it has no objective and reasonable justification. In the Court's approach, a distinction is not justified if it does not have a legitimate aim or there is no reasonable proportionality between the means employed and the aim sought to be realised. The contracting states should establish that the differential treatment in enjoyment of the right to property among the members of different groups in the same position has a legitimate aim in the general interest. Moreover, the means employed should be proportionate to the aims pursued. It is not difficult for a state to show a legitimate aim for its differential treatment. The more contentious issue is whether the differential treatment is proportionate to its aims.[98]

The contracting states enjoy a margin of appreciation in determining to what extent a differentiation is necessary for the general interest. The states' margin of appreciation in this respect, however, is much narrower than the margin of discretion allowed to them to interfere with property rights under P1-1.[99] Nevertheless, there have not been established clear criteria, by the Court, to determine the limits of the margin of appreciation left to the states under Article 14. The Court is less tolerant for some grounds of discrimination such as race, sex, illegitimacy, religion or nationality. The rationale behind this approach is that there is a strong consensus among the members of the Council of Europe and global international community to prevent discrimination on these grounds. Therefore, if there is a common European standard the margin of appreciation left to the states is very narrow or even does not exist.

If there is no common European standard, the Court will assess the proportionality by considering solely the national situation.[100] In the proportionality assessment the Court should consider the wider concept of proportionality. That is it should strictly apply necessity and appropriateness tests. Thus, the existence of an alternative and less restrictive means of achieving the same goal in the circumstances should be regarded as evidence of the disproportionality of the measures applied by the government.[101]

---

[98] *Ibid.* p.1243.
[99] Harris et al. *op.cit.* 2 p.467.
[100] *Ibid* p.482.
[101] Tomlinson and Clayton, *op.cit.* 84 p.1243.

The Court has never allowed making a distinction between legitimate and illegitimate children in terms of their civil rights, no matter what reason was raised by the government. The Court found a violation of Article 14 in conjunction with P1-1 in the *Marckx,*[102] *Inze,*[103] *and Mazurek*[104] cases where Belgian, Austrian and French laws respectively made a distinction between legitimate and illegitimate children in terms of inheritance rights.[105] In these cases the Court referred to the international treaties as evidence of the fact that there is a clear European consensus against discrimination of illegitimate children in terms of civil rights. And if there is a European consensus, the margin of appreciation left to the states is very narrow or does not exist.

Difference in treatment on the grounds of sex also, according to the Court, requires very weighty reasons to be regarded as compatible with the Convention. The Court, accordingly, found a violation of Article 14 in conjunction with P1-1 in the *Van Raalte*[106] case where national legislation made a distinction between unmarried men and women over the age of 45 in terms of obligation to pay contributions towards a child benefit scheme. In order for such a positive discrimination to be compatible with Article 14 there should be objective social reasons.

The margin of appreciation left to the states in discriminating on the grounds of nationality in terms of enjoyment of property rights is a wider one. A state can make differences in terms of taxation or other contributions or benefits between its own nationals and other nationalities or between different nationalities provided that those policies depend on objective and reasonable basis. For example, preferential treatment given to nationals of EU in terms of tax or customs obligations in comparison with nationals of a non-member state may be justified by objective reasons such as mutual treaties. However, if the difference on the basis of nationality lacks reasonable justification, it may constitute a breach of Article 14. In the *Gaygusuz*[107] case the applicant, a Turkish national resident in Austria, claimed that he had been discriminated against on the grounds of nationality because he was refused emergency assistance although he paid contributions to an unemployment insurance fund, by which the assistance was financed, on the same basis as Austrian employees and he met all other statutory conditions. The Court found that making a distinction between nationals and non-national residents as regards entitlement to emergency assistance had no reasonable justification and amounted to a breach of Article 14 in conjunction with P1-1.

The Court has not found discrimination in terms of property rights on the basis of religion so far. The applicant churches in *Holy Monasteries*[108] claimed

---

[102] *Marckx v. Belgium*, Judgement of 13 June 1979, Series A no.31.

[103] *Inze v. Austria*, Judgement of 28 October 1987, Series A no.126.

[104] *Mazurek v. France*, Judgement of 1 February 2000 (App. No. 34406/97.

[105] *Ibid.* § 51-55.

[106] *Van Raalte v. Netherlands*, Judgement of 21 February 1997, *Reports* 1997-I; see also *Schmidt v. Germany*, Judgement of 18 July 1994, Series A no. 291-B.

[107] *Gaygusuz v. Austria*, Judgement of 16 September 1996, Reports 1996-IV.

[108] *Holy Monasteries v. Greece*, Judgement of 9 December 1994, Series A, No.301-A.

discrimination on the grounds of religion but, having found a breach of P1-1, the Court was unwilling to examine a discrimination claim and simply stated that the differentiation between different churches was justified. However, it can be said that the margin of appreciation of national authorities in differentiating on the basis of religion is also a narrow one and needs very weighty reasons. The Court found a violation of Article 14 in conjunction with P1-1 on the grounds of residence in the *Darby*[109] case where national legislation made a distinction between resident and non-resident non-members of the church in terms of exemption from the church tax.

The most complicated category is discrimination on the grounds of property. This is especially true if the discriminated right is also the right to property. It may not be difficult to find discrimination in the enjoyment of other rights on the grounds of property. For example, if right to vote has been connected with financial status of the citizens, discrimination is obvious and unacceptable. However, in a capitalist society most of the regulations – concerning taxation, environment, planning, and social and economic order – affect different economic groups differently. When does such a difference constitute discrimination in the enjoyment of property rights? From the beginning, in many cases the issue of discrimination on the grounds of property have been raised before the Strasbourg organs. In *James and Others*[110] the applicants complained that leasehold reform legislation was discriminatory on the grounds of 'property' because it was a measure redistributing property which applies only to a restricted class of property, that is long leasehold houses occupied by the leaseholders. The Court did not agree in that the aim of the legislation in question was not simply a redistribution of property but to correct the imbalance between landlords and occupying tenants under the long leasehold system of tenure thus, it was inevitable that the contested legislation should affect landlords coming within that restricted category rather than all or other property owners. Accordingly taking no account of personal circumstances of the landlord and the tenant was justified by the aim pursued. As a result, the court found that the differentiation had a reasonable and objective justification.

The Court, in this case, made no distinction between the levels of the margin of appreciation left to the state under P1-1 and under Article 14. The Court repeatedly made reference to its findings under P1-1 review, during the examination of complaints under Article 14 without making any distinction between the levels of margin of appreciation. However, the Court should have examined the complaints under Article 14 with more scrutiny. But the problem here is that sometimes it is difficult to distinguish complaints under Article 14 on the grounds of property from those under P1-1. The applicant may repeat the same complaints from a different angle under Article 14. Therefore, in many cases the

---

[109] *Darby v. Sweden*, Judgement of 23 October 1990, Series A No.187.

[110] *James and Others v. UK*, Judgement of 21 February 1986, Series A no. 98.

Court found the differential treatment on the grounds of property having reasonable justification[111] or even not necessary to examine.[112]

As mentioned above, another problem regarding discrimination complaints on the grounds of property is the difficulty of distinguishing comparable positions. For example, are landlords of residential property in a similar position to landlords of non-residential property, or shareholders of two different companies, or house owners in two parallel streets? The Court interprets similarity in this regard very narrowly and finds the positions dissimilar if there is any legal, procedural, or factual difference. For example, launching a legal procedure can make a difference.[113]

The Court found differential treatment on the grounds of property as discriminatory in only two cases. In *Pine Valley*[114] the Court found the remedial legislation introduced to correct a misapplication of the planning law which was drafted in such a way as to exclude the applicants from the benefit of the law but not other holders of planning permission in the same category as discriminatory. Similarly, in the *Chassagnou*[115] case the applicants claimed, *inter alia*, that the French law making a distinction between small and large landowners in terms of obligation to transfer hunting rights over property to the local hunting association was discriminatory. The law obliged only owners of landholdings less than 20 hectares to transfer hunting rights over their property to local hunting associations without considering whether the owner is a hunter or not. The government argued that making a difference between small and large landowners was reasonable because it was necessary to pool small plots of land in order to promote the rational management of game stocks. The Court dismissed the government's argument on the grounds that it did not explain how the general interest could be served by the obligation for small landowners only to transfer hunting rights. Accordingly, it found that there was no reasonable justification for difference in treatment and it constituted discrimination on the grounds of property.

However, these decisions hardly help us to reach general conclusions about discrimination on the grounds of property. What is the distinctive character of these two cases? It can be raised that public authorities singled out the applicants in *Pine Valley* in application of the law. However, the situation was the same in the *Fredin*[116] case but the Court did not find violation there. Or it can be said that the

---

[111] See for example, *Lithgow and Others v. UK*, Judgement of 8 July 1986, Series A no.102; *Spadea and Scalabrino v. Italy*, Judgement of 28 September 1995, Series A, NO.315-B; *National and Provincial Building Society, Leeds Permanent Building Society and Yorkshire Building Society v. UK*, Judgement of 23 October 1997, Reports 1997-VII, §79.

[112] *Matos e Silva, Lda., and Others v. Portugal*, Judgement of 27 August 1996, Reports 1996-IV; *Beyeler v. Italy*, Judgement of 5 January 2000 (App. No.33202/96); *Mellacher and Others v. Austria*, Judgement of 19 December 1989, Series A, No. 169.

[113] *Building Societies* case, *op. cit.* 111.

[114] *Pine Valley Developments Ltd. and Others v. Ireland*, Judgement of 29 November 1991, Series A, No 222.

[115] *Chassagnou and Others v. France*, Judgement of 29 April 1999, Reports 1999/II.

[116] *Fredin v. Sweden*, Judgement of 18 February 1991, Series A no. 192.

French law made a clear distinction in terms of public burdens on the grounds of property in the *Chassagnou* case. Nevertheless, examination of the Commission's decision in the *WASA Ömsesidigt*[117] application reveals that the same situation was at issue but the Commission found the application inadmissible.

To sum up, if there is a suspect category of discrimination such as sex, race, nationality, or religion or there is a common European practice, the Court does not hesitate to find violation of right not to be discriminated. The margin of appreciation left to the states in this respect is very narrow. But if differentiation depends on property, the Court finds discrimination only in exceptional cases and it has not produced clear criteria in this regard. In terms of taxation also, suspected categories are viable reasons to find discrimination. The Court has not examined any allegation that taxation is discriminatory on the grounds of property so far. But the Commission's practice left a wide margin of appreciation to the states in this regard. It is suggested that since property is a human right, any interference with it should have a clear justification. If interference imposes an unequal burden on some property owners, the government should show how such unequal treatment was justified. For example, reciprocal benefit, or prevention of harm to others, or correction of a past injustice can be just excuses for such an unequal treatment. If the government fails to justify unequal burden, the Court should find violation of the Convention. That is, the burden of proof must be on the respondent (government) side.

8.4.4. Concluding Remarks

Article 14 provides extra protection for property rights in addition to the guarantees set out in P1-1. The right not to be discriminated against in Article 14 provides a guarantee for individuals to enjoy property rights equally. The scope of the guarantee provided by Article 14 is much wider than that of P1-1 in terms of equality. As indicated in Chapter 7, P1-1 provides a guarantee for individuals not to be burdened by public policies unequally. That is, if an individual's property is taken for public use, the loss arising from that taking should be compensated. Equality before the public burdens is the basis of compensation requirement for taking of property by eminent domain power. But the scope of Article 14 comprises all three kinds of interferences and it protects against any kind of discrimination in enjoyment of property. However, the Court's unwillingness to examine discrimination claims in the cases where it has already found violation of P1-1 weakens this protection. In the past, the Court was very reluctant to examine discrimination claims in the property cases making reference to the margin of appreciation of the states. In many cases, it dismissed the claims simply by saying that the material before it did not support the claim by any evidence. Nevertheless, the Court is less tolerant to a differential treatment on the grounds of one of the suspected categories such as sex, race, nationality, or religion. In those cases, the respondent governments' margin of appreciation is very narrow and they should show strong reasons justifying difference in treatment.

---

[117] *WASA Ömsesidigt and Others v. Sweden,* App. No.13013/87, 14 December 1988.

In order to invoke a discrimination claim the applicants must show that they have been treated differently and less favourably than others in the same position. In some cases, it may be difficult for an applicant to prove that his situation is analogous to those who have been treated better than him. This difficulty arises especially in the cases where the applicants claim discrimination on the grounds of property. Once an applicant has shown that he has been treated differently from others in analogous situations, it is for the government to prove that differential treatment has a reasonable justification. The margin of appreciation left to the states in this regard is very narrow if there is a common European standard. If there is no common European standard, the Court will examine the claims considering sole national conditions. The government should show that difference in treatment has a legitimate aim and that the means employed are proportionate to that aim. The Court's scrutiny is less tight if the basis of differentiation is property. It is suggested that the Court should apply, in such cases, a wider proportionality test; that is, the means employed should be both necessary and appropriate to realise the pursued aim. And the burden of proof should be on the government side especially in taxation cases given that P1-1 imposes no restriction on a government's power of levying taxes. That is, if some individuals are levied an unequal burden, the government should prove that they are in a different position to others.

Finally, it is worth examining what will be the implications of Protocol 12[118] on property rights if it comes into force. Protocol 12 will lift the requisite relation between the Convention rights and the prohibition of discrimination, but it is unlikely that lifting of requisite relation will have a negative effect on property rights. At least existing guarantee will survive because Protocol 12 bans any discrimination in enjoyment of legal rights. It even extends the scope of the discrimination ban over some economic rights which are not protected by P1-1 such as employment rights. Thus, implications of Protocol 12 over property rights will be positive.

8.5. Relations between P1-1 and Article 6

Article 6, paragraph 1 of the Convention protects the right to a fair hearing by a tribunal in the determination of civil rights and obligations. The relevant part of Article 6(1) provides that 'in the determination of his civil rights and obligations...

---

[118] Protocol 12 reads, in Article 1 titled 'General prohibition of discrimination', as follows:

1) The enjoyment of any right set forth by law shall be secured without discrimination on any ground such as sex, race, colour, language, religion, political or other opinion, national or social origin, association with a national minority, property, birth or other status.

2) No one shall be discriminated against by any public authority on any ground such as those mentioned in paragraph 1.

everyone is entitled to a fair and public hearing within a reasonable time by an independent and impartial tribunal established by law'.

The concept of 'civil right' under Article 6 comprises the right to property as well.[119] Both concepts of 'civil right' and 'possession' have autonomous meanings within the Convention irrespective of the meanings they have under national laws. The concept of civil rights is a wider one and possessions or property rights are inclusive in it. How then, can the scopes of P1-1 and Article 6 be distinguished in a case concerning the right to property?

P1-1 protects the substance of the right to property while Article 6 provides procedural guarantees for a dispute concerning property rights. P1-1 lays down the circumstances in which it is permissible for a state to interfere with property rights, but Article 6 guarantees access to the courts and a fair trial before them in determining whether any interference is lawful in terms of domestic law.[120] Therefore, in cases where P1-1 is at issue the review of the Court will concern the result of the relevant domestic proceedings, whereas in cases where Article 6 is invoked it will focus on the organisation and conduct of the proceedings.[121] It is obvious that procedural guarantees provided by Article 6 are not confined to disputes between public authorities and private persons but comprise any disputes between private persons as well. On the other hand, P1-1 can be invoked only in cases where there is responsibility of a state in a dispute between private persons.[122]

It is vital to the operation of P1-1 and Article 6 that there should exist a right that is interfered with. If the applicant has no possession, P1-1 cannot be applicable since P1-1 does not guarantee a right to acquire property. However, for Article 6(1) to apply, it is not necessary that the right which is subject of the dispute be established as belonging to the applicant, but the outcome of the dispute must be directly decisive for the right. For example, in the *Malhous*[123] case the Grand Chamber of the Court found the application regarding P1-1 inadmissible because the applicant did not have possession. In this case the applicant's father's property was expropriated in 1948 without compensation by the Communist regime in Poland and after the collapse of that regime, in 1991 a law was passed which enabled the old owners to claim the restitution of their properties provided that they had not been transferred to natural persons. The applicant entered into restitution agreements with two legal persons, but the national land authorities refused to approve these agreements on the grounds that some of the properties in

[119] *Sporrong and Lönnroth v. Sweden,* Judgement of 23 September 1982, Series A, No. 52.

[120] Van den Broek, P., "The Protection of Property Rights Under the European Convention On Human Rights" (1986) 1986/1 *Legal Issues of European Integration* 52.

[121] Strasser, W., "The Relationship Between Substantive Rights and Procedural Rights Guaranteed by the European Convention on Human Rights" in F. Matscher and H. Petzold (eds.) *Protecting Human Rights: The European Dimension* (Berlin, 1988).

[122] See Chapter 6 on horizontal applicability of P1-1.

[123] *Malhous v. Czech Republic*, Admissibility Decision of Grand Chamber on 13 December 2000 (App. No. 33071/96); see also *Prince Hans-Adam II of Liechtenstein v. Germany*, Judgement of 12 July 2001 (App. No. 42527/98).

question were transferred to natural persons. The applicant launched some judicial procedures against this refusal, unsuccessfully. The Court ruled that the applicant's father lost the ownership of the properties in 1948, examination of which is out of the Court's jurisdiction *ratione temporis*. And the 1991 law did not give ownership if properties were transferred to natural persons. Therefore, the applicant did not gain ownership of the properties in question. However, the Court found the complaints that domestic courts, in examination of his application against the national land authority's decision, did not hold a public hearing in breach of Article 6 were admissible. And later in the judgement on merits, it found a violation of Article 6.[124]

In order to apply Article 6 there should also be a dispute or contestation. In *Van Marle*,[125] for example, the Court ruled that the decisions of the Board of Admission and the Board of Appeal on whether the applicants were competent to register as accountants did not amount to a dispute within the meaning of Article 6 and, therefore, Article 6 was not applicable to the case. But the goodwill of a profession constituted possession within the meaning of P1-1.

The availability of access to a court and the opportunity to challenge the lawfulness of interferences with property rights is a significant element of the right to property under P1-1.[126] The right of access to a court is also conceived as a requirement inclusive in the right to fair trial. For example, the Court found, in *Stran Greek Refineries*,[127] that retroactive annulment of arbitration awards by legislation amounted to a violation of P1-1. And the Court ruled in the same case that such legislation, which was issued shortly before the hearing in the Court of Cassation in the case for recognition and enforcement of arbitration awards, was designed to influence the judicial determination of the dispute and prevented any meaningful examination of the case by a court in breach of Article 6(1). Nevertheless, the Court reached different results in some other similar cases. In *Pressos Compania Naviera* where the Belgian state annulled, by a legislation with retrospective effect, the tort claims against the state resulting from piloting services, the Court found it unnecessary to examine claims under Article 6 considering the finding of the violation of P1-1.[128] In the *Building Societies*[129] case, where restitution claims for alleged double taxation was deprived retrospectively, the Court examined the case under both P1-1 and Article 6 without finding violation of either. In the *Hentrich* case, the Court ruled that a selective and arbitrary application of the right of pre-emption in a low-price-sale by French tax authorities constituted violation of P1-1. In that case, the national tribunals refused

---

[124] *Malhous v. Czech Republic*, Judgement of 12 July 2001 (App. No 33071/96).

[125] *Van Marle and Others v. Netherlands*, Judgement of 3 June 1986, Series A no. 10.

[126] *Hentrich v. France*, Judgement of 22 September 1994, Series A, No. 296-A.

[127] *Stran Greek Refineries and Stratis Andreadis v. Greece*, Judgement of 9 December 1994, Series A, No.301-A.

[128] *Pressos Compania Naviera S.A. and Others v. Belgium*, Judgement of 20 November 1995, Series A, No.332.

[129] *National and Provincial Building Society, Leeds Permanent Building Society and Yorkshire Building Society v. UK*, Judgement of 23 October 1997, Reports 1997-VII.

the applicant the opportunity to challenge pre-emption through establishing that the price agreed between the parties corresponded to the real market value of the property by stating that legislation in force conferred a discretionary power on the national authorities. The Court held that the requirement of equality of arms was not met and consequently, there had been a violation of the right to a fair trial.[130]

However, the case-law regarding the relationship between P1-1 and Article 6 is not clear about when examination of one of the articles makes the examination of the other unnecessary and when the claims should be examined under both articles. In some cases, the Court examined both articles separately; in others, it examined the case only under P1-1 and found the examination under Article 6 unnecessary and in some others *vice versa*. The Court examines the case under both articles if national administrative and judicial proceedings take an unreasonably long time, leaving the status and final fate of the property uncertain. For example, in the *Sporrong,*[131] *Scollo,*[132] *Matos e Silva,*[133] *Pialopoulos,*[134] *Raimondo,*[135] *Sciortino,*[136] *and Zwierzyski*[137] cases administrative and judicial, or enforcement procedures took an unreasonably long time, leaving the status of the applicants' property uncertain and the Court found violations of both P1-1 and Article 6. Regarding the delay of procedures the Court examines the procedures and outcomes of them separately. That is, one set of actions or inactions of national authorities may amount to a breach of two different articles of the Convention.

Sometimes financial losses of the applicants may emerge merely as a result of delayed procedures. In these cases, those losses can be evaluated as pecuniary damage of the violation of Article 6. In such cases, however, judicial procedures follow mostly long administrative procedures that cannot be regarded within the scope of Article 6, and end financial losses are caused by the accumulative effect of those different procedures. Therefore, material injury caused by violation of Article 6 may not cover all real losses of the applicant. Thus, the Court's approach in this regard is in principle right. In some cases, the duration of judicial procedures can be reasonable within the limits of Article 6. However, if other circumstances affecting the value of the property such as inflation are disregarded, the final effect of the procedures can be regarded as violating P1-1 even if they do not amount to breach of Article 6.[138]

---

130 *Hentrich v. France*, Judgement of 22 September 1994, Series A, No. 296-A.

131 *Sporrong and Lönnroth v. Sweden,* Judgement of 23 September 1982, Series A no. 52.

132 *Scollo v. Italy*, Judgement of 28 September 1995, Series A, No.315-C.

133 *Matos e Silva, Lda., and Others v. Portugal*, Judgement of 27 August 1996, Reports 1996-IV.

134 *Pialopoulos and Others v. Greece,* Judgement of 15 February 2001 (App. No. 37095/97).

135 *Raimondo v. Italy*, Judgement of 22 February 1994, Series A, No. 281-A.

136 *Sciortino v. Italy,* Judgement of 18 October 2001 (App. No.30127/96).

137 *Zwierzyski v. Poland*, Judgement of 19 June 2001 (App. No.34049/96).

138 *Aka v. Turkey*, Judgement of 23 September 1998, Reports 1998-VI, §43; *Gaganus and Others v. Turkey*, Judgement of 5 June 2001 (App. No. 39335/98); *Akkus v. Turkey*, Judgement of 9 July 1997, Reports 1997-IV; *Yasar and Others v. Turkey*, Judgement of

In some cases, the Court examined the case under only one of the articles and it found the examination of the other article unnecessary. For example, in the *British-American Tobacco Company*[139] case, the applicant company claimed violations of its rights under P1-1 and Article 6 because Dutch authorities had refused their patent application and they did not have a fair hearing before an independent and impartial tribunal. The Court examined the claims under Article 6 without finding violation and decided that complaints regarding P1-1, namely the denial of judicial remedy, were in substance identical to those raised under Article 6 and no separate issue arose. Similarly, in the *Almeida Garrett*[140] case, the Court found it unnecessary to examine complaints under Article 6, after finding violation of P1-1. And finally, in some other cases, the Court examined the allegations under both articles and found no violation of them.[141]

To sum up, property rights can be the subject matter of investigations under both P1-1 and Article 6. The examination under Article 6 will focus on the organisation and the conduct of the proceedings in a dispute regarding property rights before the national judicial authorities. The focus of the examination under P1-1 will be the result of such proceedings. Therefore, if the complaints are merely related to the judicial procedural issues, the Court will examine the case only under Article 6. But if the complaints extend to the result of such procedures and regard the substance of the right to property, it will be better to examine a case under both articles. Procedural guarantees do not always guarantee a substantive fair result. So, compliance of an interference with property with Article 6 does not mean that it meets the requirements of P1-1and a separate examination under P1-1 could be necessary.

Article 6 functions as the American due process guarantee for property rights. But its scope is much narrower than due process clause because the guarantee of due process clause comprises both administrative and judicial procedures while Article 6 is applied for only judicial procedures. Therefore, administrative procedures can be complained of only under P1-1.

---

14 November 2000 (App. No.27697/95); *Hamdi Celebi v. Turkey*, Judgement of 30 January 2001(and 23 other decisions on the same date) (App. Nos. 19264- 19288/92); *Ismihan Ozel and Others v. Turkey*, Judgement of 27 February 2001 (App. No. 31963/96); *Ali Ozturk v. Turkey*, Judgement of 10 April 2001 (and 24 other decisions on the same date) (App. Nos. 19289- 19312/92); *Gulnahar Calkan v. Turkey*, Judgement of 5 June 2001(and 19 other decisions on the same date) (App. Nos.19661-19683/92.)

[139] *British-American Tobacco Company Ltd. v. the Netherlands*, Judgement of 20 November 1995, Series A No. 331.

[140] *Almeida Garrett, Mascarenhas Falcao and Others v. Portugal*, Judgement of 11 January 2000 (App. Nos. 29813/96 and 30229/96); see also *Pressos Compania Naviera S.A. and Others v. Belgium*, Judgement of 20 November 1995, Series A, No.332; and *Holy Monasteries v. Greece* Judgement of 9 December 1994, Series A no. 301-A.

[141] See for example, *Air Canada v. UK*, Judgement of 5 May 1995, Series A, No.316-A; *National and Provincial Building Society, Leeds Permanent Building Society and Yorkshire Building Society v. UK*, Judgement of 23 October 1997, Reports 1997-VII, §79.

8.6. Derogation from Property Rights in Times of War or Other Public Emergency

As indicated above the right to property is not an absolute right and contracting states are allowed to interfere with property for public interest under P1-1. Article 15 allows contracting states in times of war or other public emergency threatening the life of the nation to take measures derogating from their obligations under the Convention to the extent strictly required by the exigencies of the situation. Property rights are not exempted from this derogation power, so they can also be derogated if exigencies of the situation require. So far, no member of the Council of Europe has made any notification of derogation from property rights. The Court, therefore, has had no chance to produce jurisprudence in this respect. But a limited number of states have applied emergency rules for some time in some parts of their countries since the Convention came into force, and they made derogation notifications for such periods. In a number of cases, thus, the derogation issue was raised and some case-law has emerged in terms of application of Article 15. Although the case-law in this regard is still poor, the general approach of the Court to Article 15 can be extracted from this limited case-law.

Since Article 15 gives the contracting states extraordinary powers to interfere with fundamental rights during the time of public emergency, supervision of the Convention organs over procedural requirements has a great importance for effective protection of human rights. However, the scope of this section is to examine to what extent property rights can be derogated. Therefore, procedural requirements such as proclamation and notification will be disregarded here. The issue that will be examined here is mainly in what situations can derogation powers be applied to property rights and what is the limit of this derogation power?

8.6.1. The Causes of Emergency Rule

It is not difficult to interpret the term 'time of war' as a precondition of derogation powers. Such a situation does exist if a state declares 'war' or engages in an international armed conflict.[142] Whether civil war is also to be considered as war is irrelevant here since derogation powers are not confined to the time of war but extend to other public emergency situations. However, the notion of 'emergency' referred to in Article 15 needs to be scrutinised. The term emergency is, by its nature, an elastic concept. The circumstances that endanger the safety of nations are infinite. They comprise natural or environmental catastrophes such as earthquake, floods, or epidemics, economic crises and any exceptional situation that puts the security of the state in peril.[143] Therefore, the extent and variety of corresponding measures are necessarily open to various interpretations.

The first question here is when emergency measures can be used. That is, what should be the magnitude of threats to security and order of the society before

---

[142] Van Dijk and Van Hoof, *op.cit.* 2 p.735.

[143] Macdonald, R., "Derogations under Article 15 of the European Convention on Human Rights" (1997) 36 *Columbia Journal of Transnational Law* 225.

justifying the use of emergency powers? To what extent have contracting states a margin of appreciation in this respect and what should be the role of international supervision over it? The second question is what should be the quantum of corresponding measures aiming to ameliorate the emergency situation? What is the limit of contracting states' power in this respect?

As for the first question, the ambiguity over the meaning of the term emergency may endanger the protection of the Convention rights.[144] It is generally argued that the elements of temporariness and exceptional nature are common denominators that make the issue of emergency possible.[145] The Commission identified four characteristics of a public emergency under Article 15 in the *Greek* case. Accordingly, it must be actual or imminent; its effects must involve the whole nation; the continuance of the organised life of the community must be threatened; and the crisis or danger must be exceptional, in that the normal measures or restrictions, permitted by the Convention for the maintenance of public safety, health and order are plainly inadequate.[146] The Court has not attempted to refine or modify these formulations, and therefore, they are still in place.

In the history of the Convention, terrorism or violent internal unrest has been the only reason advanced by governments declaring a state of emergency. The Court has left some latitude to the contracting states in choosing and applying measures to confront terrorism and it found the conditions advanced by the respondent states sufficient to justify emergency rule.[147] In none of these notifications was the right to property included in the list of derogated rights. Terrorism or internal conflict may not require derogation from property rights, but some other causes of emergency rule such as economic crises or natural disasters or war may justify interference with property rights more harshly than allowed under P1-1. For example, existence of a war may justify, under certain circumstances, temporary takings of property for military purposes without compensation.

---

[144] The European Commission for Democracy through Law (Venice Commission), following an extensive survey in this respect, identified the danger posed by the lack of a clear definition of emergency in European laws and recommended Eastern European states to define emergency situations as 'exceptional threats' in their constitutions. See Ozbudun, E. and Turhan, M., "Emergency Powers" (1995) (Report of the European Commission for Democracy through Law).

[145] Gross, O., "'Once More Unto the Breach': The Systematic Failure of Applying the European Convention on Human Rights to Entrenched Emergencies" (1998) *Yale Journal of International Law* 437.

[146] *United Kingdom v. Greece,* (Report of the Commission on 5 November 1969) Yearbook XII (1969); see also *Lawless v. Ireland*, Commission Report (1960-1961) Series B.

[147] See *Lawless v. Ireland*, Judgement of 1 July 1961, Series A no. 3; *Ireland v. UK*, Judgement of 18 January 1978, Series A no. 25; *Brogan v. UK*, Judgement of 29 November 1988, Series A no.145-B; *Brannigan and McBride v. UK*, Judgement of 26 May 1993, Seies A no. 258-B; *Aksoy v. Turkey,* Judgement of 18 December 1996, Reports 1996-VI.

None of the contracting states has proclaimed emergency rule because of economic reasons thus far. In such a situation, one of the most affected rights will probably be the right to property. Whether economic hardships can justify derogations from human rights is a matter of controversy.[148] Such a broad interpretation of the concept of emergency carries certain dangers.[149] Nevertheless, sometimes the magnitude of the disruption caused by economic crisis can be sufficient to threaten the organised existence of a nation. In such cases, the mere economic character of the threat should not affect the states' right to take measures to ameliorate the situation. If the cause is economic, the Court may apply a higher standard of review in its scrutiny of the states' assessment of the situation and apply a narrow margin of appreciation in judging the question of necessity. The International Law Association recommended a heavy burden and strict limitation on a state restricting human rights in an economic emergency. A state should provide strong evidence of its justification to establish its *bona fide* and the democratic principles underlying its actions.[150]

Given the wide margin of appreciation left to national authorities to interfere with property rights under P1-1, granting more power to national authorities in this respect during emergency rule may make the property guarantee meaningless under the Convention. Therefore, if a state interferes with property rights severely depending on the emergency powers, it should prove that such interference was inevitable to protect the existence of the whole nation.

The Court has established that the geographic scope of the emergency does not necessarily have to comprise the entire country of the state. If the severity and magnitude of the threat exceeds the threshold, a state can make derogation notification for some geographic territory. If it does so, derogation notification is valid only for that territory, and the state cannot depend on such notification for measures taken outside that territory.[151] If the threat is not imminent, it cannot justify emergency rule.[152]

8.6.2. Limits of the Derogation Power

Article 15 allows emergency measures 'to the extent strictly required by the exigencies of the situation' and 'provided that such measures are not inconsistent with its other obligations under international law'. Thus, the main limitations over the derogation power of a state are the requirement of proportionality and that of

---

[148] A group of international law experts who convened in 1984 in Siracusa, Italy, formulated a list of principles concerning the limitation and derogation provisions in International Covenant on Civil and Political Rights. Principle 41 provides: Economic difficulties *per se* cannot justify derogation measures. See The Siracusa Principles on the Limitation and Derogation Provisions in the ICCPR. (1984).

[149] Macdonald, *op.cit.* 143 p.226.

[150] International Law Association, Report of the Fifty-Ninth Conference held at Belgrade 105-07 (1982).

[151] *Sakik And Others v. Turkey,* Judgement of 27 November 1997, *Reports* 1997-VII; *Simsek v. Turkey*, Report of the Commission on 1 March 1999 (App. No.28010/95).

[152] The *Greek* case 12 YB 1 (1969).

compliance with international law obligations. Other limitations set out in Article 15 such as non-derogable rights (§ 2) and notification obligations (§ 3) are not directly relevant to property rights. Therefore, only requirements of proportionality and compliance with other international law obligations will be examined here.

The text of Article 15 offers strict proportionality supervision over the emergency measures by the Convention organs[153] because it allows a state to take measures only 'strictly required by the exigencies of the situation'. In this respect, the severity, duration, and scope of threat are elements to be considered in assessment of proportionality.[154]

First, the Court should ask whether the measures are necessary. The state should show that measures allowed under P1-1 would not have been sufficient to cope with the threat. For example, if a state wishes to expropriate some individual property for military usage without compensation during a war, it should demonstrate that such expropriations are necessary to end the war and that the state of war makes it impossible to pay compensation. But, if, in such a situation, the state refuses restitution of property or payment of compensation after the war ends, the Court should not hesitate to find failure of the state in meeting the requirements of proportionality.

Second, the measures must be connected to the emergency in the sense that they must *prima facie* be suitable to reduce the crisis. For example, if as a result of a massive earthquake, most of the residential dwellings are damaged and a severe housing shortage occurs, the rents may increase rapidly. Limitations on rents in such a situation can be considered relevant to the crisis. However, if in such a situation national authorities choose to nationalise some industries by taking advantage of a disaster, there is no connection between the crisis and the measure taken.

Third, the Court should examine whether the severity of the threat is proportionate to the degree of the measure taken by national authorities. Existence of other less drastic alternative measures may lead to a finding of disproportionality. The Court may engage in weighing individual and common interests against each other. For example, if national authorities choose to prohibit access to agricultural and residential property in rural areas in order to prevent claimed terrorists getting food and money from the rural population, such a measure cannot be considered proportionate because the burden imposed on the rural population by such a prohibition may cause them severe hardship. Other alternative measures can be found to achieve same goals. In a number of Turkish cases concerning the allegations that Turkish security forces were involved in the burning and destruction of houses and their contents in the south-east part of the country where emergency rule was in force, the Court found grave violations of both Article 8 of the Convention and P1-1.[155] Indeed the Turkish notification of

---

153 Harris et al, *op.cit.* 2 p.498.

154 Macdonald, *op.cit.* 143 p.228.

155 See for example *Akdivar and Others v. Turkey*, Judgement of 16 September 1996, Reports 1996-IV; *Mentes and Others v. Turkey*, Judgement of 28 November 1997, Reports 1997-VIII; *Selcuk and Asker v. Turkey*, Judgement of 24 April 1998, Reports

derogation included neither the right to property nor the right to home. But even if it was so, there is no reason to expect that the result of the cases would be different, because the Court already considered all prevailing circumstances when reaching such a decision. Since the government denied the involvement of security forces, it did not claim any purpose for such actions. But considering the Court's conclusion about involvement of security forces, it can be guessed that the aim was to force applicants to move from distant rural areas to cities or towns. Nevertheless, even such an aim does not justify the burning of houses.

Finally, the derogating state should implement safeguards to avoid abuse of emergency powers. For example, independent judicial control should be available for emergency powers. The safeguards should also be real and effective.[156]

It is difficult to say that, so far, the Court has applied the proportionality test within these lines. The Court has left some margin of appreciation to the contracting states in determining the scope, severity, and duration of emergency measures. The Court did not undertake a strict view in determination of the necessity of measures. Nor has it substituted its assessment of the most appropriate policies to deal with the emergency. The doctrine of margin of appreciation lessens the Court's level of review over the derogation powers and consequently fails to minimise the potential for abuse.[157]

The derogation of rights under Article 15 should not be inconsistent with the other international law obligations of the contracting states. In this context, humanitarian law and other human rights documents are relevant. Neither The International Covenant on Civil and Political Rights, nor the Charter of Fundamental Rights of the European Union, however, provide a wider guarantee for property rights during emergency rule. Apart from these human rights documents, Geneva Red Cross Conventions and their protocols can be especially relevant. For example, Article 17 of the second additional protocol (Protocol II) relating to the Protection of Victims of Non-International Armed Conflicts,[158] 8 June 1977, prohibits displacement of the civilian population during internal conflicts. Such a displacement may also comprise limitations of access to property.

1998-II; *Aksoy v. Turkey*, Judgement of 18 December 1996, Reports 1996-VI; *Dulas v. Turkey*, Judgement of 30 January 2001 (App. No. 25801/94); *Bilgin v. Turkey*, Judgement of 26 November 2000 (App. No. 23819/94).

156 Macdonald, *op.cit.* 143 p.229 .

157 Van Dijk and van Hoof, *op.cit.* 2 pp. 743 ff; Harris et al, *op.cit.* 2 pp.496 ff.

158 Article 17. Prohibition of forced movement of civilians:

1. The displacement of the civilian population shall not be ordered for reasons related to the conflict unless the security of the civilians involved or imperative military reasons so demand. Should such displacements have to be carried out, all possible measures shall be taken in order that the civilian population may be received under satisfactory conditions of shelter, hygiene, health, safety, and nutrition.

2. Civilians shall not be compelled to leave their own territory for reasons connected with the conflict.

In such a case, the Court should review whether the requirements of this provision have been met. The Court's jurisprudence in this regard is still very poor.

8.6.3. Conclusion

Article 15 allows the contracting states to derogate from their obligations under P1-1 during times of war or other public emergency. The effective supervision, by the Court, of the application of Article 15 is of the utmost importance because of its far-reaching consequences. The Court should strictly examine both whether the actual conditions justify a proclamation of emergency rule and whether the exigencies of the situation strictly require the measures taken by the national authorities. The Court's scrutiny in proportionality examination for interferences exceeding the limits drawn by P1-1 should be stricter and the margin of discretion must be a very narrow one considering the wide margin of appreciation left to the states under P1-1 already. If a state wishes to interfere more harshly than is allowed under P1-1, it should demonstrate that such a severe interference is necessary to deal with the emergency situation. The onus on the state must be an especially heavy one if the cause of emergency is economic crisis. The current approach of the Court to supervision of the application of Article 15 is far from effective in reducing the possibility of abuse of emergency powers. Following the events of 11 September 2001, a number of harsh measures have been taken by some states to fight against terrorism, such as confiscation of bank accounts which are suspected of holding terrorist money. Such serious measures can easily undermine property rights of some vulnerable dissident groups, and therefore they should be strictly reviewed by the Court to prevent disproportional interferences with property.

If the rights contained in the Convention are grouped hierarchically according to their derogability, the right to property can be placed at the bottom of such a hierarchical schema because it is not among the non-derogable rights and the states enjoy a wide margin of appreciation to interfere with property rights.

Chapter 9

Conclusion

This book aimed to provide answers to the questions of whether the right to property is a human right and how far public authorities can interfere with property rights legitimately. It can be said that the theoretical part of the book has produced fairly clear answers to these questions. Regarding the first part of the question (is property a human right?) it suggests that if autonomy is part of an individual's human dignity and a moral value that should be respected by others, at least four sound arguments can be put forward to justify property rights as human rights. To be able to live an autonomous life, individuals should be free from coercion and manipulation and should have an adequate range of opportunities. Both use and exchange values of property constitute opportunities for individuals to plan and shape their lives (autonomy argument). A system of private property also promotes individuality and self-realisation (personality argument). Furthermore, respect for autonomy requires respect for the outcomes of peaceful autonomous conduct. Therefore, people should be entitled to the fruits of their own initiative (labour theory). And such a system of private property encourages fruitful initiative and increases the well-being of society (utility argument). All these arguments justify property rights as *prima facie* human rights.

As for the definition of property, the autonomy principle requires, for the purposes of constitutional and human rights law, an expansive definition of property to include all patrimonial rights and legitimate expectations arising from both public and private law relationships. Since both exchange and use values of property constitute opportunities for individuals for an autonomous life and since government's interference may affect all of these interests, the guarantee of constitutional or human rights law should also comprise all of those interests. Therefore, constitutional property should comprise open-ended use rights, control powers, and transmission powers with respect to things. Things, which can be objects of property, comprise all material and ideational values that can be separated from personhood permanently. But the guarantee of property should not be extended to comprise personality rights. Therefore, someone's kidney, for example, cannot be considered as property unless it is separated from the body completely. As long as the kidney is part of the body, it should be protected by a right to personality and bodily integrity but not by a right to property.

Although anything that is separable from personality can be an object of property, political society, taking account of the scarcity of things, can decide what things are to be allowed private appropriation. Democratically elected bodies enjoy a margin of appreciation in this regard.

Regarding the second part of the question (how far can government interfere with property rights legitimately?), the book suggests that, to create an autonomy-enhancing society, government can interfere with the right to property. The interference may occur in the form of taxation, taking, or regulation. Nevertheless, a government's power of interference is not unlimited.

Firstly, interference should pursue a legitimate aim. The aim of taxation and taking can be advancement of public interest. Taxation should be imposed on all people in the same position equally. Unequal taxation can be justified on the grounds of redistributive justice or reciprocal benefit. The difference between takings and taxation is that takings single out the owners of property taken by public authorities in terms of bearing the burden of public policy. Since takings impose the burden of public policy only on one person or some of society unequally, the cost of public policy should be diffused throughout society by compensation.

Two different types of regulation can be distinguished regarding property rights. The first type of regulation defines the nature and acquisition of property. It defines how property can be acquired and which entitlements it includes. Such regulation generally precedes ownership and defines the nature of ownership. Therefore, the application of such regulation does not constitute interference with property. For example, if a statute regulating copyright sets the duration of copyright over a published material as 50 years, extinction of copyright over a publication after 50 years does not constitute interference with property. But a change in this kind of regulation may affect the patrimonial rights of individuals and such regulations should respect the legitimate expectations of the individuals.

The second type of regulation aims to prevent harmful use of property and restricts the existing rights over things. Such regulation is called 'police power regulation'. The concept of police power regulation necessarily comprises a wide range of regulations from urban planning to environmental protection rules, from consumer protection laws to neighbourhood obligations. The harmful use is a dynamic concept; the meaning of it can change from one country to an other or from time to time. It is in political society's discretion to decide what use is harmful. This dynamic aspect of the harmful use principle may endanger the stability of property. Therefore, if a law makes a formerly legitimate use harmful, legitimate expectations of individuals should be respected. An important question is how can police power regulations be distinguished from takings, or in other words when does a regulation constitute taking of property? The significance of this question is that taking of property requires payment of compensation, whereas police power regulations do not. The thesis suggests that an answer to this question should be sought in the aim of interference. If the aim is prevention of harm, compensation is not necessary, but if the aim of interference is to prescribe a private property for public use, it constitutes taking and requires payment of compensation. The amount of the compensation should be full market value of the property taken by public authorities unless there is a legitimate reason justifying the reduction of compensation such as past injustice or reciprocal benefit.

Secondly, the interference should depend on accessible, precise, and foreseeable legal rules. Autonomy principle requires that individuals must be able to see the consequences of their actions. Uncertainty in the legal system prevents such foreseeability and public authorities may interfere with property rights arbitrarily. Therefore, legality of interference is a significant safeguard against arbitrary actions of public authorities.

Thirdly, the interference with property should be proportional. The means employed by public authorities should be both appropriate and necessary to pursue goals and there should be a fair balance between the harm inflicted on property rights by interference and its contribution to public good. The proportionality principle also aims to protect property rights against arbitrary interferences of public authorities.

Having established the moral standards of the interference with property rights as human rights in this way, the next question of the book is 'how far does the case-law of the Convention organs regarding P1-1 comply with those standards?' Firstly, the Convention recognises that property is a human right. Through including a property rights guarantee into the European Convention on Human Rights the contracting states proclaimed that the right to property is one of the fundamental human rights. Secondly, the case-law about the definition of property or 'possession' is compatible with the definition suggested in this book. The Convention organs have defined the concept of possession in P1-1 expansively to include all pecuniary interests and legitimate expectations arising from both public and private law relationships.

As for the powers of interference of public authorities with property rights, however, it is difficult to say that the case-law complies with the standards suggested in this book. The taxonomy of interferences with property adopted by the Convention organs is dysfunctional to analyse whether an alleged interference has breached the right to property. The case-law is not clear about the levels of interference allowed by the Convention to the states. It seems that the Convention offers no limitation to the power of taxation. Moreover, the Convention case-law does not guarantee a right to full compensation for takings clearly. The compensation issue is considered as an element of a balancing test. Furthermore, the case-law does not suggest any criteria to distinguish takings from police power regulations. Therefore, the Court applies directly a balancing test between individual interests and the public interest on an *ad hoc* basis. This balancing test is a narrow proportionality test. The Court does not apply a proper proportionality test. It does not review whether the public policy applied by public authorities is appropriate or necessary. It only looks at the effect of public policy on individual interests and weighs the harm inflicted on private interests against the contribution of it to public good. But such an approach favours the public interest rather than individual rights.

It is proposed that the Court should apply the taxonomy of interferences suggested in this book to determine when compensation is required. It is also suggested that the Court should apply a wider proportionality test rather than a narrow balancing test. Accordingly, it provides some extra apparatus for the Court to employ when examining whether an interference has violated the right protected by P1-1.

Development of the jurisprudence of the Convention organs depends on the historical realities of the progress of the protection system of the Convention. Until the late 1980s, many of the contracting states did not recognise the right of individual application to the Commission and jurisdiction of the Court. Therefore, the amount of the applications was not too much. Moreover, at that time the Commission was reluctant to find applications about P1-1 admissible, because it did not want to interfere with social and economic policies of the contracting states. But following the political changes that took place during the 1990s the amount of applications that reached the Court increased considerably. The number of member states recognising the right of individual application and jurisdiction of the Court increased as well as the number of member states party to the Convention. And following the entry into force of 11th Protocol in 1998 both individual application and jurisdiction of the Court became compulsory for all member states. Accordingly, both the magnitude and variety of the applications regarding P1-1 have escalated significantly and the number of the judgements rose consequently. But the amount of applications from former socialist countries has not increased as sharply as expected, at least up to now.

During this period the jurisprudence of the Court has also developed. However, it is difficult to follow a chronological change in the Court's approach to P1-1 because the Court has no precedent and does not fully explain the grounds of its judgements. In its judgements the Court generally uses general terms such as 'margin of appreciation', 'balancing interests', 'on equitable basis'. But the meaning of these terms differs according to the personal beliefs of the judges and this leads to an inconsistency among the judgements of different Chambers of the Court. However, a slight change can still be seen in jurisprudence relating to P1-1. Although the Court has not changed the criteria it employed for P1-1 cases, apart from creating a new category of interference (interference with the essence of property) in *Sporrong and Lönnroth*, it can be said that its approach to the balancing test has changed slightly in favour of individual interests recently. The Court is finding more and more violations of P1-1 in the last couple of years. It is not as reluctant as it was before to find violation. But it is still far from the standards suggested in this book.

One of the worries was that the accession of former socialist countries might force the Court to loosen its standards for these countries in terms of P1-1. The Court takes account of the transition conditions when deciding about the admissibility of cases from those countries. But in a number of judgements regarding former socialist countries, the Court found violation of P1-1, and did not mention the transitional period. There is no clear indication in those judgements that the Court has loosened its standards for former socialist states. But it is still too early to say something in this respect because there is not enough judgement yet.

The effects of the changes that took place during the 1990s has not been examined by the Court fully yet. For example, the Court has not examined whether human genetic material constitutes property in the meaning of P1-1. Neither have environmental regulations been challenged before the Court in detail. There is no established case-law in this regard. But both the magnitude and variety of the cases coming before the Court is increasing and the case-law regarding P1-1 is getting enriched consistently. It is expected that within a couple of years most of these issues will come before the Court and most of the ambiguities in the application of P1-1 will be cleared.

Bibliography

Ackerman, B. A., (1977), *Private Property and Constitution,* Yale University Press, New Haven.

Alexander, G. S., (1999), "Constitutionalising Property: Two Experiences, Two Dilemmas" in J. McLean (ed.) *Property and Constitution,* Hart Publishing, Oxford.

Alexy, R., (1992), "Individual Rights and Collective Goods" in C. Nino (ed.) *Rights,* Dartmouth, Aldershot.

Alkema, E. A., (1988), "The Third-Party Applicability or 'Drittwirkung' of the European Convention on Human Rights" in Matscher, F. and Petzold, H. (eds) *Protecting Human Rights: The European Dimension,* Heymanns, Koln.

Allen, T., (1999), "Limitations on Constitutional Property Rights" in Jackson, P. and Wilde, D. (eds.) *Property Law: Current Issues and Debates,* Ashgate, Aldershot.

Allen, T., (2000), *The Right to Property in Commonwealth Constitutions*, Cambridge University Press, Cambridge.

Anderson, D., (1999), " Compensation for Interference with Property" 6 *European Human Rights Law Review* 543.

Antinori, M. R., (1995), "Does Lochner Live in Luxembourg?: An Analysis of The Property Rights Jurisprudence of The European Court of Justice" 18 *Fordham International Law Journal* 1778.

Arechaga, J., (1978), "State Responsibility for the Nationalization of Foreign Owned Property" 11 *New York University Journal of International Law and Policy* 179.

Aristotle, (1941), *Politics*, in Richard McKeon, (ed.) *The Basic Works of Aristotle,* Random House, New York.

Aristotle, (1976), *The Ethics* (trans. by J.A.K. Thompson) Penguin, Harmondsworth.

Aronovitz, A.M., (1997), "Individual Patrimonial Rights Under the European Human Rights System: Some Reflections on the Concepts of Possession and Dispossession of Property" 25 *International Journal of Legal Information* 87-104.

Baker, C. E., (1999), "Disaggregating the Concept of Property in Constitutional Law" in Mercuro, N. and Samuels, W. J. (eds.) *Fundamental Interrelationships Between Government and Property,* Jai Press Inc, Stamford.

Barry, N., (1990), *Political Argument*, Harvester Wheatsheaf, London.

Barzel, Y., (1989), *Economic Analysis of Property Rights,* Cambridge University Press, Cambridge.

Becker, L.C., (1976), "Acquisition of Property by Labour" 73 *The Journal of Philosophy* 146.

Becker, L.C., (1977), *Property Rights: Philosophical Foundations,* Routledge and Kegan Paul, London

Becker, L.C., (1981), "The Moral Basis of Property Rights" in Pennock and Chapman, (eds) *Human Rights* (NOMOS XXIII), New York University Press, New York.

Bell, J., (1992), *French Constitutional Law,* Clarendon Press, Oxford.

Bell, J., (1993), "Public Interest: Policy or Principle?" in Roger Brownsword (ed.) *Law and The Public Interest,* Franz Steiner Verlag, Stuttgart.

Bentham, J., (1987), *The Theory of Legislation,* C. K. Odgen (ed.) Littleton, London.

Bentham, J., (1996), *An Introduction to the Principles of Morals and Legislation*, Oxford University Press, Oxford.

Berlin, I., (1969) "Two Concepts of Liberty" in *Four Essays on Liberty,* Oxford University Press, Oxford.

Bernhardt, R., (1988) "Thoughts on the Interpretation of Human Rights Treaties" in Matscher and Petzold (eds.) *Protecting Human Rights: The European Dimension,* Heymanns, Koln.

Beyleveld, D. and Brownsword, R., (1998), "Patenting Human Genes: Legality, Morality, and Human Rights" in Harris, J. W., (ed.) *Property Problems: From Genes to Funds,* Kluwer Law International, London.

Blackstone, W., (1966), *Commentaries on the Laws of England* (1766), Dawsons, London.

Boulier, W., (1995), "Sperm, Spleens, and Other Valuables: The Need to Recognise Property Rights in Human Body Parts" 23 *Hofstra Law Review* 693.

Boyle, J., (1999), *Shamans, Software, and Spleens: Law and The Construction of the Information Society,* Harvard University Press, London.

Buchanan, J. and Brennan, G., (1984), "Towards a Tax Constitution for Leviathan" in Buchanan J. and Tollison, R. (eds.) *The Theory of Public Choice II,* University of Michigan Press, Michigan.

Cain, A. S. P., (2000), "Property Rights in Human Biological Materials: Studies in Species Reproduction and Biomedical Technology" 17 *Arizona Journal of International and Comparative Law* 449.

Calabresi, G. and Mellamed, A. D., (1972), "Property Rules, Liability Rules, and Inalienability: One View of the Cathedral" 85 *Harvard Law Review* 1089.

Campbell, K., (1992), "On the General Nature of Property Rights" 3 *The King's College Law Journal* 79.

Clapham, A., (1993), "The 'Drittwirkung' of the Convention" in Macdonald at al (eds) *The European System for the Protection of Human Rights,* M. Nijhoff, Dordrecht.

Clapham, A., (1993), *Human Rights in Private Sphere,* Clarendon Press, Oxford.

Clark, L., (1978), "Privacy, Property, Freedom and the Family" in R. Bronaugh (ed.) *Philosophical Law,* Greenwood Press, London.

Cohen, G. A., (1977) "Robert Nozick and Wilt Chamberlain: How Patterns Preserve Liberty", *Erkenntis,* 11.

Cohen, G. A. (1979), " Capitalism, Freedom and The Proletariat" in A. Ryan, *The Idea of Freedom,* Oxford University Press, Oxford.

Collected Edition of the "*Travaux Préparatoires*" of the European Convention on Human Rights, (1985), M. Nijhoff, Dordrecht.

Corbett, K., (1996), "The Rise of Private Property Rights in The Broadcast Spectrum" 46 *Duke Law Journal* 611.

Cordes, M. W., (1998), "The Public/Private Balance in The Land Use Regulation" *Michigan Law Review* 1.

Cranston, M., (1967), "Human Rights: Real and Supposed" in D. Raphael (ed.), *Political Theory and Rights of Man,* Macmillan, London.

Currie, D., (1994), *The Constitution of the Federal Republic of Germany,* Chicago University Press, Chicago.

Curtis, Jerome J. Jr., (1989), "Comparison of Regulatory Takings Under the United States Constitution and the European Convention on Human Rights" 14 *European Law Review* 67.

Demsetz, H., (1967), "Toward A Theory of Property Rights" 57 *American Economic Review* 347.

Demsetz, H., (1973), "The Property Rights Paradigm" 33 *Journal of Economic History* 16

Devlin, P., (1965), *Enforcement of Morals,* Oxford University Press, Oxford.

Djajic, S., (2000), "The Right to Property and the Vasilescu v. Romania Case" 27 *Syracuse Journal of International Law and Commerce* 363.

Dolzer, R., (1981), "New Foundations of the Law of Expropriation of Alien Property" 75 *American Journal of International Law* 553.

Donahue, C., (1980), "The Future of the Concept of Property Predicted from Its Past" in J. R. Pennock, and J. W. Chapman (eds.) *NOMOS XXII: Property*, New York University Press, New York.

Douglas W. K., (1988), "The Original Understanding of the Taking Clause is Neither Weak nor Obtuse" 88 *Columbia Law Review* 362.

Douzinas, C., (2000) *The End of Human Rights: Critical Legal Thought at the Turn of the Century,* Hart Publishing, Oxford.

Drzemczewski, A., (1979), "The European Convention on Human Rights and Relations between Private Parties" 26 *Netherlands International Law Review* 163.

Duguit, L., (1917), "The Law and the State" 31 *Harvard Law Review* 1.

Dworkin, R., (1975), "The Original Position" in N. Daniels (ed.) *Reading Rawls,* Blackwell, Oxford.

Dworkin, R., (1977), *Taking Rights Seriously,* Duckworth, London.

Eissen, M.A., (1993), "The Principle of Proportionality in the Case-law of the European Court of Human Rights" in Macdonald at al (eds.) *The European System for the Protection of Human Rights,* M. Nijhoff, Dordrecht.

Eleftheriadis, P., (1996), "Analysis of Property Rights" 16 *Oxford Journal of Legal Studies* 31.

Ely, J., (1992), *The Guardian of Every Other Right: Constitutional History of Property Rights,* Oxford University Press, Oxford.

Epstein, R., (1985), *Takings: Private Property and The Power of Eminent Domain,* Harvard University Press, Cambridge.

Fischel, W.A., (1995), *Regulatory Takings: Law, Economics and Politics,* Harvard University Press, Cambridge.

Flew, A., (1997), "Social Justice isn't Any Kind of Justice" 2 *Liberal Dusunce* 55.

Frowein, J., (1993), "The Protection of Property" in Macdonald, Matscher and Petzold (eds.) *The European System for The Protection of Human Rights,* Kluwer Academic Publications, London.

Garner, J.F., (ed) (1975), "Compensation for the Compulsory Acquisition of Land" in *Compensation for Compulsory Purchase,* London.

Gewirth, A., (1981), "The Basis and Content of Human Rights" in Pennock and Chapman, (eds) *Human Rights* (NOMOS XXIII), NYUP, New York.

Gewirth, A., (1984), "Can Utilitarianism Justify any Moral Right" in *Human Rights: Essays on Justification and Application,* The University of Chicago Press, Chicago.

Gomien, D., Harris, D. and Zwaak, L., (1996), *Law and Practice of the European Convention on Human Rights and the European Social Charter,* Council of Europe Publishing, Strasbourg.

Gray, K., (1991), "Property in Thin Air" 50 *Cambridge Law Journal* 252.

Gray, K., (1994), "Equitable Property" 47 (2) *Current Legal Problems* 157.

Gray, K. and Gray, S., (1999), "Civil Rights, Civil Wrongs and Quasi-Public Space" *European Human Rights Law Review* 46.

Gross, O., (1998), " 'Once More Unto the Breach': The Systematic Failure of Applying the European Convention on Human Rights to Entrenched Emergencies" *Yale Journal of International Law* 437.

Grotius, H., (1725), *The Rights of War and Peace*, London (Translation of *De Jure Belli Ac Pacis*, 1625).

Harris, D., O'Boyle, M. and Warbrick, C., (1995), *Law of the European Convention on Human Rights,* Butterworths, London.
Harris, J. W., (1996), *Property and Justice,* Clarendon Press, Oxford.
Harris, J. W., (1997), *Legal Philosophies* (second edition) Butterworths, London.
Harris, J.W., (1999), "Is Property a Human Right?" in McLean, J. (ed.) *Property and Constitution*, Hart Publishing, Oxford.
Hart, H.L.A., (1963), *Law, Liberty and Morality,* Oxford University Press, London.
Hart, H.L.A., (1984), "Are There Any Natural Rights" in J. Waldron, *Theories of Rights,* Oxford University Press, Oxford.
Hart, H.L.A., (1989), "Rawls on Liberty and Its Priority" in Norman Daniels (ed.) *Reading Rawls,* Stanford University Press, Stanford.
Hayek, F.A., (1982), *Law, Legislation and Liberty* vol. 1 *Rules and Order,* Routledge & Paul Kegan, London.
Hegel, G. W. F., (1965), *The Philosophy of Right* (trans. by Knox) Clarendon Press, Oxford.
Held, D., (1970), *Public Interest And Individual Interests,* Basic Books, New York.
Helfer, L.R., (1999), "A Human Rights Analogy in Adjudicating Copyrights Claims under TRIPs" 21 *European Intellectual Property Review* 8.
Hervada, J., "The Principles of the Social Doctrine of the Church" at http://www.columbia.edu/cu/augustine/arch/social.html.
Hirş, E., (1944), "Eser Sahipliği: Fikri ve Sınai Hakların Mahiyeti Hakkında Yeni bir Görüş" 1 *Ankara Üniversitesi Hukuk Fakültesi Dergisi* 330.
Hohfeld, W.N., (1923), *Fundamental Legal Conceptions as Applied in Judicial Reasoning,* Yale University Press, New Haven.
Honoré, A. M., (1960), "Rights of Exclusion and Immunities Against Divesting" 24 *Tulune Law Review* 453.
Honoré, A. M., (1961), "Ownership" in A. G. Guest (ed.) *Oxford Essays in Jurisprudence,* Clarendon Press, Oxford.
Hunt, M., (1998), "The 'Horizontal Effect' of the Human Rights Act" *Public Law* 423.
Jacobs and White, (1996), *The European Convention on Human Rights*, Clarendon Press, Oxford.
Jones, P., (1994), *Rights,* Macmillan, London.
Juergensmeyer, J. C., (1996), "Florida's Private Property Rights Protection Act: Does it Inordinately Burden the Public Interest?" 48 *Florida Law Review* 695
Kant, I., (1945), *Grandwork of the Metaphysic of Morals*, in H. Paton (ed.) *The Moral Law,* Hutchinson, London.
Knowles, D., (1983), "Hegel on Property and Personality" 33 *The Philosophical Quarterly* 45.
Kocourek, A., (1928), *Jural Relations,* Bobbs-Merrill, Indianapolis.
Kommers, D.P., (1997), *The Constitutional Jurisprudence of the Federal Republic of Germany,* Duke University Press, London (Second Edition).
Kramer M. H., (1997), Book review of Harris' *Property and Justice* 56 *Cambridge Law Journal* 642.
Lametti, D., (1998), "Property and (Perhaps) Justice" 43 *McGill Law Journal* 633.
Lametti, D., (1998), *The Deon-Telos of Private Property: Ethical Aspects of the Theory of and Practice of Private Property,* unpublished D. Phil. Thesis, Oxford.
Leisner, W., (1996), *Eigentum Schriften zu Eigentumsrecht und Wirtschaftsverfassung* 1970-1996, Herausgegeben von Josef Isensee, Berlin.
Locke, J., (1988), *Two Treatise of Government*, Peter Laslett (ed.), Cambridge University Press, Cambridge.

Lyons, D., (1984) "Utility and Rights" in J. Waldron (ed.) *Theories of Rights,* Oxford University Press, Oxford.

Macdonald, R., (1993), "The Margin of Appreciation" in Macdonald et al (eds.) *The European System For The Protection of Human Rights,* M. Nijhoff, Dordrecht.

Macdonald, R., (1997), "Derogations under Article 15 of the European Convention on Human Rights" 36 *Columbia Journal of Transnational Law* 225.

MacPherson, C. B., (1978), *Property: Mainstream and Critical Positions*, Blackwell, Oxford.

Malloy, Robin P., (1992), "A Classical Liberal critique of Takings Law: A Struggle Between Individualist and Communitarian Norms" in Nicholas Mercuro (ed.) *Taking Property and Just Compensation,* Kluwer AP, London.

Massey, S. J., (1984), "Justice Rehnquist's Theory of Property" 93 *Yale Law Journal* 541.

Matscher, F., (1993), "Methods of Interpretation of the Convention" in Macdonald, Matscher and Petzold (eds.) *The European System for the Protection of Human Rights,* M. Nijhoff, London.

McBride, J., (1999), "Proportionality and the European Convention on Human Rights" in E. Ellis (ed.) *The Principle of Proportionality in the Laws of Europe,* Hart Publishing, Oxford.

McHarg, A., (1999), "Reconciling Human Rights and the Public Interest: Conceptual Problems and Doctrinal Uncertainty in the Jurisprudence of the European Court of Human Rights" 62 *The Modern Law Review* 671-96.

Mercuro, N., (ed.) (1992), *Taking Property and Just Compensation,* Kluwer Academic Publishers, London.

Merrills, J. G., (1995), *The Development of International Law by the European Court of Human Rights*, Manchester University Press, Manchester.

Michelman, F., (1975), "Constitutional Welfare Rights and A Theory of Justice" in Daniels, N. (ed.) *Reading Rawls,* Blackwell, Oxford.

Michelman, F., (1967), "Property, Utility and Fairness: Comments on the Ethical Foundations of 'Just Compensation' Law" 80 *Harvard Law Review* 1165.

Mill, J.S., (1965), *Principles of Political Economy: With Some of Their Applications to Social Policy,* in J. M. Robson (ed.) *Collected Works of John Stuart Mill,* Routledge and Kegan Paul, London.

Mill, J. S., (1974), *On Liberty,* Penguin Books, London.

Mincke, W., (1998), "Property: Assets or Power? Objects or Relations as Substrata of Property Rights" in J. W. Harris (ed.) *Property Problems: From Genes to Pension Funds,* Kluwer Law International, London.

Miranda, A., (1998), "The Legal Status of the Pre-Embryo: Some Comparative Considerations Prompted by *Davis v. Davis*" in Harris, J. W., (ed.) *Property Problems: From Genes to Funds,* Kluwer Law International, London.

Moon, G., (2000), "The Draft Discrimination Protocol to the European Convention on Human Rights: A Progress Report" *European Human Rights Law Review* 49.

Morrison, C.C., (1981), *The Dynamics of Development in the European Human Rights Convention System,* Martin Nijhoff, The Hague.

Mowbray, A.R., (1997) "The European Court of Human Rights' Approach to Just Satisfaction" *Public Law* 647.

Mowbray, A.R., (2000), *Cases and Materials on the European Convention on Human Rights,* Butterworths, London.

Munzer, S., (1990), *A Theory of Property,* Cambridge University Press, Cambridge.

Munzer, S., (1993), "Kant and Property Rights in Body Parts" 6 *Canadian Journal of Law and Jurisprudence* 319.

Munzer, S., (1994), "An Uneasy Case Against Property Rights in Body Parts" *Social Philosophy and Policy* 259.

Munzer, S., (1998), "Human Dignity and Property Rights in Human Body Parts" in Harris, J. W., (ed.) *Property Problems: From Genes to Funds,* Kluwer Law International, London.

Murphy, J. G., (1994), *Kant: The Philosophy of Right,* Mercer University Press, Georgia.

Neuman, G.L., (1999), "The U.S. Constitutional Conception of the Rule of Law and the Rechtsstaatsprinzip of the Grundgesetz" Columbia Law School Public Law and Legal Theory Working Paper.

Nigri, D. F., (1998), "Theft of Information and the Concept of Property in the Information Age" in Harris, J. W., (ed.) *Property Problems: From Genes to Funds,* Kluwer Law International, London.

Norton, P.M., (1991), "A Law of the Future or a Law of the Past? Modern Tribunals and The International Law of Expropriation" 85 *American Journal of International Law* 474.

Nozick, R. (1974), *Anarchy, State and Utopia,* Basic Books, New York.

O'Neill, O., (1982), "Nozick's Entitlements" in J. Paul (ed.) *Reading Nozick: Essays on Anarchy, State and Utopia*, Blackwell, Oxford.

Olivecrona, K., (1974), "Locke's Theory of Appropriation" 24 *Philosophical Quarterly* 231.

Örücü, E., (1986), "The Core of Human Rights and Freedoms: The Limit of Limits" in T. Campbell et al (eds.) *Human Rights,* Basil Blackwell, Oxford.

Ost, F., (1992), "The Original Canons of Interpretation of the European Court of Human Rights" in Delmas-Marthy (ed.) *The European Convention For The Protection of Human Rights: International Protection versus National Restriction,* M. Nijhoff, London.

Oswald, L.J., (2000), "Property Rights Legislation and Police Power" 37 *American Business Law Journal* 529.

Pasqualucci, Jo M., (1996), "Victim Reparations in the Inter-American Human Rights System: A Critical Assessment of Current Practice and Procedure" 18 *Michigan Journal of International Law* 1.

Penner, J., (1996), "Bundle of Rights Picture of Property" 43 *UCLA Law Review* 711.

Penner, J., (1997), *The Idea of Property in Law,* Oxford University Press, Oxford.

Penner, J., (1998), "Hohfeldian Use Rights in Property" in Harris, J. W. (ed.) *Property Problems: From Genes to Funds,* Kluwer Law International, London.

Pennock, J. R. and Chapman, J. W. (eds) (1981), *Human Rights* (NOMOS XXIII), New York University Press, New York.

Perry, M. J., (1998), *The Idea of Human Rights: Four Inquiries,* Oxford University Press, Oxford.

Petzold, H., (1993), "The Convention and the Principle of Subsidiarity" in Petzold et al (eds.) *The European System for the Protection of Human Rights,* M. Nijhoff, Dordrecht.

Peukert, W., (1981), "Protection of Ownership under Article 1 of the First Protocol to the European Convention on Human Rights" 2 *Human Rights Law Journal* 37-78.

Posner, R., (1981), "The Concept of Corrective Justice in Recent Theories of Tort Law" 10 *Journal of Legal Studies* 187.

Posner, R., (1998), *Economic Analysis of Law* (fifth edition) Aspen, New York.

Pottage, A., (1990), "Property: Re-appropriating Hegel" 33 *Modern Law Review* 259.

Proudhon, J., (1966), *What is Property?* Howard Fertig, New York.

Radin, J. M., (1983), "Property and Personhood" 33 *Stanford Law Review* 957.

Rainbolt, G., (2000), "Review of *Property and Justice*" 111 *Ethics* 173.

Rawls, J., (1993), *Political Liberalism,* Columbia University Press, New York.

Rawls, J., (1999), *A Theory of Justice* (Revised edition) Clarendon Press, Oxford.

Raz, J., (1986), *Morality of Freedom*, Clarendon Press, Oxford.

Raz, J., (1987), "Autonomy, Toleration and the Harm Principle" in Ruth Gavison (ed.) *Issues in Contemporary Legal Philosophy,* Clarendon Press, Oxford.

Reeve, A., (1986), *Property,* Macmillan, London.

Reich, C. A., (1964), "The New Property" 73 *Yale Law Journal* 733.

Robertson, A.H., (1965) "The Political Background and Historical Development of the European Convention on Human Rights" in *European Convention on Human Rights* published by The British Institute of International and Comparative Law, Supplementary Publication No. 11, Stevens and Sons Lim, London.

Robertson, A. H. and Merills, J.G., (1993), *Human Rights in Europe: A Study of the European Convention on Human Rights,* (Third Edition) Manchester University Press, Manchester.

Robertson, M., (1999), "Liberal, Democratic, and Socialist Approaches to the Public Dimensions of Private Property" in McLean, J., (ed.) *Property and Constitution,* Hart Publishing, Oxford.

Rosas, A., (1992), "Property Rights" in Alan Rosas et al (eds.) *The Strength of Diversity: Human Rights and Pluralist Democracy,* M.Nijhoff, The Hague.

Rose, C., (1994), *Property and Persuasion: Essays on the History, Theory and Rhetoric of Ownership,* Westview Press, Oxford.

Rose, C., (1996), "Property as the Keystone Right?" 71 *Notre Dame Law Review* 329.

Rose, C., (2000), "Property and Expropriation: Themes and Variations in American Law" *Utah Law Review* 1.

Rosen, A. D., (1993), *Kant's Theory of Justice,* Cornell University Press, London.

Rubenfeld, J., (1993), "Usings" 102 *The Yale Law Journal* 1077.

Rudden, B., (1998), "Things as Thing and Things as Wealth" in Harris, J. W., (ed.) *Property Problems: From Genes to Funds,* Kluwer Law International, London.

Ryan, A., (1984), *Property and Political Theory,* Blackwell, Oxford.

Ryan, A. (1986), *Property,* Open University Press, Milton Keynes.

Salter, M.G., (1998), "Hegel and Social Dynamics of Property Law" in Harris, J. W., (ed.) *Property Problems: From Genes to Funds,* Kluwer Law International, London.

Samuel, G., (1999), "Are Property Rights So Simple in Europe?" in P. Jackson and D. C. Wilde (eds.) *Property Law: Current Issues and Debates,* Ashgate Dartmouth, Aldershot.

Samuel, G., (1999), "The Many Dimensions of Property" in Janet McLean (ed.) *Property and Constitution,* Hart Publishing, Oxford.

Sandel, M., (1982), *Liberalism and the Limits of Justice,* Cambridge University Press, Cambridge.

Sax, J., (1964), "Takings and Police Power" 74 *Yale Law Journal* 36.

Sax, J., (1971), "Takings, Private Property and Public Rights" 81 *Yale Law Journal* 149.

Scanlon, T., (1975), "Rawls' Theory of Justice" in N. Daniels (ed.) *Reading Rawls,* Blackwell, Oxford.

Scanlon, T., (1982) "Nozick on Rights, Liberty and Property" in J. Paul (ed.) *Reading Nozick: Essays on Anarchy, State and Utopia*, Blackwell, Oxford.

Schachter, O., (1984), "Compensation for Expropriation" 78 *American Journal of International Law* 121.

Scheffler, S., (1976), "Natural Rights, Equality and the Minimal State" 6 *Canadian Journal of Philosophy* 59.

Schneiderman, D., (2000), "Constitutional Approaches to Privatisation: An Inquiry into the Magnitude of Neo-liberal Constitutionalism" 63 *Law and Contemporary Problems* 83.

Sermet, L., (1998), *The European Convention on Human Rights and Property Rights* (revised edition) Council of Europe Publishing, Strasbourg.

Shelton, D., (1999), *Remedies in International Human Rights Law,* Oxford University Press, Oxford.

Shestack, J., (1998), "The Philosophic Foundations of Human Rights" 20 *Human Rights Quarterly* 201.

Simmonds, N.E., (1996), *Central Issues in Jurisprudence: Justice, Law, Rights,* Sweet and Maxwell, London.

Snare, F., (1972), "The Concept of Property" 9 *American Philosophical Quarterly* 200.

Spiller, P.T. and Cardilli, C., (1999), "Towards A Property Rights Approach to Communications Spectrum" 16 *Yale Journal on Regulation* 53.

Stanley, J. A., (2001), "Keeping Big Brother out of Our Backyard: Regulatory Takings as Defined in International Law and Compared to American Fifth Amendment Jurisprudence" 15 *Emory International Law Review* 349.

Stillman, P. G., (1991), "Property, Contract and Ethical Life in Hegel's Philosophy of Right" in Cornell, Rosenfeld, Carlson (eds.) *Hegel and Legal Theory,* Routledge, London.

Strasser, W., (1988), "The Relationship Between Substantive Rights and Procedural Rights Guaranteed by the European Convention on Human Rights" in F. Matscher and H. Petzold (eds.) *Protecting Human Rights: The European Dimension,* Berlin.

Stücke, A., (1991), *Eigentum an Wirtschaftssubventionen,* Berlin.

Taylor, C., (1979), "What is Wrong with Negative Liberty" in A. Ryan, *The Idea of Freedom,* Oxford University Press, Oxford.

Tebbit, M., (2000), *Philosophy of Law: An Introduction,* Routledge, London.

Ten, C. L., (1987), "Comment on Autonomy, Toleration, The Harm Principle" in Ruth Gavison (ed.) *Issues In Contemporary Legal Philosophy,* Clarendon Press, Oxford.

Tilton, T., (1990), *The Political Theory of Swedish Social Democracy: Through the Welfare State to Socialism,* Clarendon Press, Oxford.

Timmons, D. and Womack, L., (2000), "Eminent Domain or Domination?" 24 *Real Estate Issues* 44.

Tomlinson, H. and Clayton, R., (2000), *The Law of Human Rights,* Oxford University Press, Oxford.

Trenor, W. M., (1985), "The Origins and Original Significance of the Just Compensation Clause of the Fifth Amendment" 94 *Yale Law Journal* 694.

Tully, J., (1980), *A Discourse on Property: John Locke and his Adversaries*, Cambridge University Press, Cambridge.

Vallentyne, P., (1999), "Review of *Property and Justice*" 108 *Mind* 581.

Van Den Broek, P., (1986), "The Protection of Property Rights under the European Convention on Human Rights" 1986-1 *Legal Issues of European Integration* 52.

Van Der Vyver, J. D., (1996), "Property In International Human Rights Law" in *Ius Commune* Book Series, No:18 International Colloquium 451.

Van Dijk and Van Hoof, (1998), *Theory and Practice of the European Convention on Human Rights,*(third edition) Kluwer Law International, London.

Waldron, J., (1988), *The Right to Private Property,* Clarendon Press, Oxford.

Weil, L. G., (1963), *The European Convention on Human Rights: Background, Development and Prospects,* A.W. Sythoff, Leyden.

Whale, S., (2002), "Pawnbrokers and Parishes: The Protection of Property under the Human Rights Act" *European Human Rights Law Review* 67.

White, L. J., (2000), "'Propertyzing' the Electromagnetic Spectrum: Why it's Important, and How to Begin" 9 *Media Law and Policy* 19.

Winisdoerffer, Y., (1998), "Margin of Appreciation and Article 1 of Protocol No.1" 19 (1) *Human Rights Law Journal* 18.

Wolcher, Louis E., (2000), "The Paradox of Remedies: The Case of International Human Rights Law" 38 *Columbia Journal of Transnational Law* 515.

Wolff, J., (1991), *Robert Nozick: Property, Justice and The Minimal State*, Stanford University Press, Stanford.

Wood, G., (1969), *The Creation of the American Republic 1776-1787,* University of North Carolina Press, New York.

Yıldız, M., (1998), *Avrupa İnsan Hakları Mahkemesi Yargısı,* Alfa, İstanbul.

Index